AMERICA IN TWO CENTURIES:
An Inventory

This is a volume in the Arno Press collection

AMERICA IN TWO CENTURIES:
An Inventory

Advisory Editor

DANIEL J. BOORSTIN

*See last pages of this volume
for a complete list of titles*

SOCIAL CONDITIONS IN AN AMERICAN CITY

A SUMMARY OF THE FINDINGS OF THE SPRINGFIELD SURVEY

SHELBY M. HARRISON

ARNO PRESS
A New York Times Company
1976

Editorial Supervision: ANDREA HICKS

Reprint Edition 1976 by Arno Press Inc.

Copyright © 1920, by The Russell Sage Foundation
Reprinted by permission of The Russell Sage Foundation

Reprinted from a copy in The Newark Public Library

AMERICA IN TWO CENTURIES: An Inventory
ISBN for complete set: 0-405-07666-5
See last pages of this volume for titles.

Manufactured in the United States of America

Library of Congress Cataloging in Publication Data

Harrison, Shelby Millard, 1881-
  Social conditions in an American city.

  (America in two centuries, an inventory)
  Reprint of the ed. published by the Russell Sage
Foundation, New York, which was issued as no. SE16 of the
Pamphlets of the Russell Sage Foundation, Dept. of
Surveys and Exhibits.
  1. Social surveys--Springfield, Ill. I. Title.
II. Series. III. Series: Russell Sage Foundation, New
York. Dept. of Surveys and Exhibits. Pamphlets ; SE16.
HN80.S7H37   1976   309.1'773'56   75-22821
ISBN 0-405-07693-2

SOCIAL CONDITIONS IN AN AMERICAN CITY

Shall the Capital City Lead?

For a hundred years state pride has expressed itself in big round domes and fluted pillars. Springfield and the Springfield survey raise a new question—Why not put the imagination and resources of the commonwealth into making the capital city of each state its standard municipality in health, housing, education, charity, corrections, recreation, industrial relations, and governmental efficiency? The meetings of the legislature, the annual state fairs, encampments of the militia, civil, trade, and professional conventions, and numerous visitors to the capital city are so many opportunities for extending such leadership.

SE16

SOCIAL CONDITIONS IN AN AMERICAN CITY

A SUMMARY OF THE FINDINGS OF THE SPRINGFIELD SURVEY

BY

SHELBY M. HARRISON

DIRECTOR, DEPARTMENT OF SURVEYS AND EXHIBITS
RUSSELL SAGE FOUNDATION

THE SPRINGFIELD SURVEY

Russell Sage Foundation
New York
1920

Copyright, 1920, by
The Russell Sage Foundation

WM · F. FELL CO · PRINTERS
PHILADELPHIA

THE SPRINGFIELD SURVEY
SPRINGFIELD, ILLINOIS

CONDUCTED UNDER THE DIRECTION OF THE

DEPARTMENT OF SURVEYS AND EXHIBITS
RUSSELL SAGE FOUNDATION

THE SURVEY COMMITTEE

SENATOR LOGAN HAY, Chairman

A. L. BOWEN, Secretary	J. H. HOLBROOK, Treasurer
VICTOR BENDER	SENATOR H. S. MAGILL, JR.
MRS. STUART BROWN	DUNCAN McDONALD
VINCENT Y. DALLMAN	LEWIS H. MINER
COL. HENRY DAVIS	GOVERNOR W. A. NORTHCOTT
HENRY DIRKSEN	DR. GEO. T. PALMER
REV. G. C. DUNLOP	GEORGE PASFIELD, JR.
E. A. HALL	FERD. C. SCHWEDTMAN
FRANK P. IDE	E. S. SCOTT
MRS. FRANK P. IDE	DR. L. C. TAYLOR
ROBERT C. LANPHIER	W. A. TOWNSEND

R. E. WOODMANSEE

PREFACE

It has often been remarked that Americans take business and family life seriously but not so politics and government. If that is an accurate observation, there is comfort in the signs of a change going on—in the indications of increasing popular interest in public affairs. One such sign has been the rapid spread of surveys aimed toward the improvement of community conditions, surveys having the backing of responsible groups of citizens in the different communities. There has been at the same time, and possibly as part of the same process, an increase in the demand for printed matter on survey methods and procedure.

Although the number of social surveys has increased by leaps and bounds, the survey can hardly be said to have gone very far beyond its experimental stage. Much remains to be learned as to the best methods to be employed in using it and as to the place it should take among the many kinds of effort to be called into play in working for better conditions of living. It is possible from an office desk to construct answers on the many points about which we still need instruction, but when done we would still have only theoretical answers. The discoveries of greater value will come through what each survey can add to the practical experience already accumulated.

The Springfield survey was one of these ventures, and brought in its quota of practical experience. It had the good fortune to be carried on under very favorable circumstances, particularly with reference to the co-operation given within and without the city. There seemed therefore to be special reason for writing out the record of it as fully as possible.

In addition to the number furnished for circulation in Springfield, several thousand copies of each of the nine separate reports were printed. These have been taken by study groups in social, civic, and religious organizations, college libraries for reference use in teaching, and by others interested in standards in work for

PREFACE

community welfare. For the convenience of those who might find a briefer statement of the survey findings more suited to their purposes, and particularly now since the supply of the full pamphlet reports is nearly exhausted, the present summary has been prepared. It has seemed worth while in doing this to include a short statement of the purpose, sequence, and methods of the survey and a description of the Exhibition, which also was a part of the survey method. These are in addition to references to methods made throughout the chapters which contain the findings.

On the other hand it hardly needs to be said that in cutting the reports to a fifth or a fourth of their original size, it has been impossible to include a great deal of detail concerning either facts found or measures recommended. All the important findings are presented, but often the minor qualifications applying to the facts and conclusions, and also the numerous items in procedures recommended, such, for example, as the fourteen rules laid down in the report on the correctional system for the conduct of juvenile probation work, had to be omitted. Readers interested in the precise details will find it desirable to consult the full reports.

SHELBY M. HARRISON.

TABLE OF CONTENTS

	PAGE
SURVEY COMMITTEE	v
PREFACE	vii

PART ONE
INTRODUCTION

I. General Purpose, Sequence, and Methods of the Survey	1
II. General Facts Regarding Springfield	21

PART TWO
THE SPRINGFIELD FACTS SUMMARIZED

III. The Public Schools	35
IV. Care of Mental Defectives, the Insane, and Alcoholics	74
V. Recreation in Springfield	90
VI. Housing in Springfield	113
VII. The Charities of Springfield	124
VIII. Industrial Conditions	164
IX. Public Health	211
X. The Correctional System	254
XI. City and County Administration	304

PART THREE
PUTTING THE FACTS TO WORK

XII. The Exhibition of Survey Findings	353

APPENDICES

A. Results of the Survey	399
B. Springfield Survey Blanks	422

LIST OF ILLUSTRATIONS

	PAGE
Frontispiece	ii
Springfield as Manufacturing Center	5
Springfield as Mining Center	7
A View Down One of the Exhibit Aisles	13
The Springfield Flag	15
Lincoln's Springfield Law Office	18
Sangamon County Court House	22
Distribution of Population in Springfield	23
Ward Map of the City	24
Springfield as Trade Center	26
Topography of Springfield and Vicinity	29
Abraham Lincoln Homestead in Springfield	30
At a Central Point	31
The Twenty-one Public School Buildings	37
Organization of Public Schools	39
School Room Lighting	44
High Blackboards and Non-adjustable Desks	47
Poor Material and Workmanship in School Buildings	49
Vocational Education	69
Insane Persons in County Jail Annex	82
Inadequate Treatment for Alcoholics	87
Children's Corner in Washington Park	103
The Single-family House a Civic Asset	114
Housing Among the Colored Population	118
Wise Economy in Street Making	120
Size and Extent of the Charities Problem	142
The Playhouse at the Exhibition	147
Cells at the Sangamon County Poor Farm	153
The Smoke Nuisance	166
Wages in Five-and-Ten-Cent Stores	182
Pneumonia in Springfield	212
Births in Springfield, 1913	214
Deaths of Infants Under One Year, Springfield, 1908–1913	216
Deaths of Infants Under Two from Diarrhea and Enteritis, Springfield, 1908–1913	218
Cases of Diphtheria Reported to the Health Department, Springfield, 1909–1913	220
Deaths from Tuberculosis, Springfield, 1908–1913	223
Drainage Area of the Sangamon River above Springfield	234

LIST OF ILLUSTRATIONS

	PAGE
Comparison of the Number of Wells and Privies Found in 1910 and 1914	237
Private Wells in Springfield, 1914	238
Privies in Springfield, 1914	239
Sanitary Conditions in Springfield Wards	241
Manure Accumulations in Springfield, 1914	245
Smallpox in Springfield	248
Preventable Mortality in Springfield Wards	251
Social Statistics of Springfield Wards	253
Ineffectiveness of Fines	260
Springfield Police Headquarters	264
Inside the "Bull Pen," City Prison, Springfield	266
The County Jail, Springfield	267
Cost of Feeding Prisoners in Springfield	270
Murders and Suicides	273
Indeterminate Sentences	278
Sangamon County Jail Annex, Springfield	285
Juvenile Offenders in the Springfield Press	290
Unbusinesslike Methods in Payment of Claims Against City and County	313
Fire Department Equipment	317
Along a Well-Paved Avenue	327
A Railroad and Street Crossing	329
Ruts in a City Dirt Road	331
Deaths at Grade Crossings, Springfield, 1908–1913	332
Section of Land Value Map in County Clerk's Office in Springfield	337
Section of One of the Land Value Maps Used by City Assessors in New York City in 1917	340
The Long Ballot	347
The "One Way" Route	355
First Regiment Armory as Exhibition Hall	356
"Information" at the Exhibition	357
How They Rank in Arithmetic	360
Grades of Boys and Girls Thirteen Years Old	361
The School Playground Demonstration	362
A Booth in the Recreation Exhibit	364
Why Not Light Up the Schools and Churches?	366
Family Homes for Family Life	368
Birth Registration	371
The Tenth Baby	373
A Scene from "Two Birthdays"	375
Which will Better Protect the Community?	378
A Problem in Mathematics and Morals	380
City Housekeeping	383
Industrial Springfield in Miniature	385
Seasonal Employment Among the Miners	386
The "Last Word" Section	387

PART ONE
INTRODUCTION

I

GENERAL PURPOSE, SEQUENCE, AND METHODS OF THE SURVEY

The survey of Springfield had its more immediate beginning in a group of Springfield citizens who had given thought to social conditions in their city, had become dissatisfied, and had decided that the time had arrived to get out of their maze of conflicting opinions and beliefs and, if possible, on to a basis of certitude in working for community advance.

There were some citizens, for example, who believed Springfield's public schools the equal of any in the state; others believed they needed to be readjusted to the changed conditions under which the oncoming generation must live and work. Some boasted of the city as the "healthiest place in Illinois"; others believed the number of deaths from preventable causes was too high, and public health appropriations too meager. Some believed that local strikes were due to union agitators who merely wanted to kick up a disturbance; others, that they indicated something wrong with wages, employment opportunities, and general working conditions.

Again, there were those who believed law breakers got what they deserved, but others were of opinion that ill treatment of offenders provoked crime. Some believed the welfare of the insane to be relatively unimportant as a public matter; others that there must be a better way than to treat them like criminals. A few thought that playgrounds, sports, and other recreation activities were among the frivolities; but others that they could be constructive and reconstructive social forces. Some thought the material relief being given out to persons asking for aid was meeting the situation sufficiently; others that something more thoroughly helpful could be done. And so on; the opinions and beliefs were as conflicting and various as they are in every live, growing, American city. This group of interested citizens thought the best method of making headway was to give them the test of fact.

INFLUENCE OF A PREVIOUS SURVEY

A number of considerations entered into the decision to apply scientific method to these and other local problems. Important among them was the very evident usefulness of a survey of certain phases of housing and sanitary conditions conducted several years before by Dr. George Thomas Palmer. In connection with his duties as health officer of the city, a house-to-house canvass was made and a large map was prepared representing in different colors the various conditions found. The map with the other publicity which accompanied it was the first statement of ascertained fact regarding general sanitary conditions prevailing throughout the city that had ever been put before the citizens.

The immediate result was a sufficient awakening of public interest to enable an ordinance to be passed setting certain higher standards for the regulation of sanitary and housing conditions. A further result, and one which had a special bearing upon the later movement for the general survey, was the disturbing of a certain feeling of complacency about local matters and a raising of doubts as to whether conditions generally in the community were all that, in the absence of recent and significant information, they were assumed to be.

The activities of a survey committee of the Illinois State Conference of Charities and Correction also furthered the growing feeling that an essential first aid to progress was real knowledge of the affairs of the town and gave this Springfield group a sense that more than the improvement of local conditions might hang on their enterprise.

THE SURVEY COMMITTEE AND GENERAL PLANNING

Following a preliminary study and report of conditions in the city made by the Department of Surveys and Exhibits of the Russell Sage Foundation at the request of a few especially interested Springfield citizens, the decision was reached to go ahead; and a survey committee of twenty-four was organized.

The chairman was Logan Hay, a state senator and a leading lawyer of the city, and among the other members were a former lieutenant-governor of Illinois, a state commissioner, the city superintendent of schools, other public officials, business men, labor leaders, clergymen, doctors, women's club leaders, editors, teachers, and social workers.[1] The secretary of the committee was A. L. Bowen, head of one of the state departments; the treasurer, J. H. Holbrook, a prominent business man.

Planning and direction were put into the hands of the Department of Surveys and Exhibits of the Russell Sage Foundation; and, using its preliminary report as a basis, nine main lines of inquiry were determined upon as follows:

PUBLIC SCHOOLS.
CARE OF MENTAL DEFECTIVES, THE INSANE, AND ALCOHOLICS.
RECREATION.
HOUSING.
CHARITIES.
INDUSTRIAL CONDITIONS.
PUBLIC HEALTH.
THE CORRECTIONAL SYSTEM.
CITY AND COUNTY ADMINISTRATION.

Had time and funds permitted, other subjects would have been added, such as city planning; taxation, in greater detail; the religious forces of the city, etc. All of these, however, were dealt with in some degree as parts of the nine main divisions; in the case of city planning, moreover, there already was a movement on foot which promised to handle the question reasonably soon.

INVESTIGATING THE FACTS

Building on the experience of previous surveys, four main steps beyond the organizing of the survey staff and of the local forces in Springfield were planned: first, investigating the facts of the local problems; second, the analysis and interpretation of the facts gathered; third, the formulating of constructive recommen-

[1] The full personnel of the general survey committee will be found on page v.

dations; and fourth, the educational use of the facts and recommendations.

Fact gathering is the ABC of surveys. This is merely another way of saying that the survey is an attempt in the field of civic and social reform to do what the civil engineer does before he starts to lay out a railroad; what the sanitarian does before he starts a campaign against malaria; what the scientific physician does before he treats a case; what the modern financier does before he develops a mine. It is, in short, an attempt to substitute tested information for supposition, belief or conjecture.

Analysis and Interpretation

The next step was analysis and interpretation. Once facts are in hand, what do they mean? Do they show satisfactory conditions or conditions calling for change? If it is found, for example, that 25 per cent of the elementary school pupils of a city are over age, that is, two or more years behind the grade in which children of their ages would ordinarily be found, does it mean that they are badly taught, or that the city has a defective educational system? Or should other facts be related to this one before any conclusion can be drawn with safety? Unfavorable home and family conditions, ill health, ill adapted courses of study, foreign birth and recent immigration, or badly enforced school attendance enter into the backwardness of this over-age group.

Obviously, the facts gathered, if they are to be of real use, must be organized and basic principles and general truths drawn from them.

Constructive Recommendations

Third came the working out of recommendations for improvement. The survey aims at results. It is diagnosis to the end that prescription may be written. Where conditions are notoriously bad, results may follow by merely turning the light on them. But in general the process is not so simple. Conclusions as to what the facts mean should be accompanied by recommendations as to first and later steps to be taken.

The survey having gone deeply into the city's problems, the community will expect and want its best judgment as to their

PURPOSE, SEQUENCE, AND METHODS

solution, but the community will also, and should, reserve the right to accept or reject the measures suggested, according as the majority of its people are impressed and convinced of their necessity and effectiveness.

Educational Use of Survey Conclusions

Fourth came the work of presenting the facts and recommendations to the public. Above all, the survey is an educational measure, spreading its information in the untechnical phrases of everyday speech. It is a means to better democracy by informing the community upon community matters and thereby providing a basis for intelligent public opinion.

To this end the various publicity media—daily press, graphic exhibit, illustrated periodical, public address, and entertainment, as well as printed pamphlet and book report—should be utilized; and the plans of the survey as they were developed placed much emphasis upon this part of the project.

SPRINGFIELD AS MANUFACTURING CENTER

The city's manufactures are near the average for places of Springfield's size and are diverse, ranging from agricultural implements to watches, building brick to shoes, grist mill products to asphalt paving, and on through a long list.

The picture shows the plant of the Illinois Watch Factory, the largest Springfield factory, which was employing nearly 1,000 workers at the time of the survey.

Co-operating Organizations and Individuals

To carry forward the investigations in all nine fields effectively, the Department of Surveys and Exhibits succeeded in enlisting six other departments of the Russell Sage Foundation and five other national organizations to co-operate with the five Illinois state organizations, the local social agencies and the thousand volunteer workers who took part in the nine main divisions of the field investigations or the exhibit which followed. The six departments of the Foundation enlisted were:

CHARITY ORGANIZATION DEPARTMENT.
DEPARTMENT OF EDUCATION.
DEPARTMENT OF CHILD-HELPING.
DEPARTMENT OF INDUSTRIAL STUDIES.
DEPARTMENT OF RECREATION.
DIVISION OF STATISTICS.

The five other national organizations which co-operated were:

AMERICAN ASSOCIATION FOR ORGANIZING FAMILY SOCIAL WORK (at that time the American Association of Societies for Organizing Charity).
NATIONAL TUBERCULOSIS ASSOCIATION (at that time the National Association for the Study and Prevention of Tuberculosis).
NATIONAL COMMITTEE FOR MENTAL HYGIENE.
NATIONAL HOUSING ASSOCIATION.
UNITED STATES PUBLIC HEALTH SERVICE.

Five state organizations also co-operated, as follows:

ILLINOIS CONFERENCE OF CHARITIES AND CORRECTION.
ILLINOIS STATE BOARD OF HEALTH.
ILLINOIS STATE DEPARTMENT OF FACTORY INSPECTION.
ILLINOIS STATE FOOD COMMISSION.
ILLINOIS STATE WATER SURVEY.

This large outside co-operation—particularly that of the national organizations—was contributed, in part, because of the representative character of the city, and the consequent belief that what was done here might prove useful elsewhere. It will be recalled that in 1910 there were 200 cities of the United States ranging from 25,000 to 150,000 in population. Springfield, with roughly 58,000, falls sufficiently within these limits to be fairly typical of the others. It is located in the heart of a rich agricultural region, is the center of important mining, manufacturing, and trade enterprises, and is one of 48 state capitals. These basic activities increase the ties of common interest between it and other American communities, whether built on four or three or two or one of these major enterprises of the Springfield district. It also shares with other cities many kindred problems relating to social and living conditions and to questions of public policy in dealing with them.

SPRINGFIELD AS MINING CENTER

A bed of soft coal averaging over five feet thick and furnishing power for the factories above, underlies the city and a wide surrounding territory. Numerous mine tipples stand near the city, and 2,500 or more Springfield residents are employed in the industry.

SURVEY STAFF

Each of the main lines of investigation was carried on under the direction of one or more persons of extended investigating experience in the subjects of their particular survey division and of practical administrative experience in the same fields. Thus the school survey was directed by Dr. Leonard P. Ayres, and associated with him were R. R. Lutz, A. H. Richardson, and Edna C. Bryner, all of the regular staff of the Department of Education, Russell Sage Foundation.

Through the courtesy of Surgeon General Rupert Blue of the United States Public Health Service, it was possible for the National Committee for Mental Hygiene to secure the services of Dr. Walter L. Treadway, a commissioned medical officer of the corps, to make the study of the care of mental defectives, the insane, and alcoholics. Dr. Treadway brought to his task a personal familiarity with local conditions, as before entering government service he had been a member of the medical staff of the Jacksonville State Hospital for the Insane, which receives patients from Springfield. Dr. Thomas D. Salmon, Director of Special Studies, National Committee for Mental Hygiene, acted in an advisory capacity.

The study of recreation conditions and needs was made by Lee F. Hanmer, Director, and Clarence Arthur Perry, Associate Director of the Department of Recreation of the Russell Sage Foundation.

Through the co-operation of the National Housing Association, the study of housing was made by John Ihlder, the field secretary of that association.

The charities division of the survey was made under the direction of Francis H. McLean, General Secretary of the American Association for Organizing Family Social Work. Assisting him were Florence L. Lattimore, Associate Director of the Department of Child Helping, Russell Sage Foundation, who made the study of the children's institutions of the city; Caroline Bedford, assistant to the director of the Charity Organization Department, Russell Sage Foundation; and Margaret Bergen, Associate Secretary of the American Association of Societies for Organizing Family Social Work.

The survey of industrial conditions was made by Zenas L. Potter, of the Department of Surveys and Exhibits, and Louise C. Odencrantz, of the Department of Industrial Studies, Russell Sage Foundation, with Mary Van Kleeck, director of the latter department acting in an advisory capacity throughout.

The public health survey was made under the direction of Franz Schneider, Jr., sanitarian on the staff of the Department of Surveys and Exhibits. Assisting him were Dixon Van Blarcom, field investigator of the National Tuberculosis Association, who made the study of the tuberculosis situation in Springfield, and Annie B. Murray, also of the Department of Surveys and Exhibits.

The division which surveyed the correctional system of Springfield was under the direction of Zenas L. Potter, of the Department of Surveys and Exhibits, who had the benefit of the advisory assistance at important points of Dr. Hastings H. Hart, Director of the Department of Child-Helping, Russell Sage Foundation.

City and county administration were studied by D. O. Decker, civic commissioner of the Commerce Club, St. Joseph, Missouri, and former member of the staff of the New York Bureau of Municipal Research; and Shelby M. Harrison, Director of the Department of Surveys and Exhibits, Russell Sage Foundation.

The assistance of Earle Clark of the Division of Statistics, Russell Sage Foundation, was had by all divisions of the survey, particularly in preparing the statistical matter included in the different reports.

As already suggested, something over one hundred Springfield volunteer workers assisted in the investigations. These were in addition to the volunteers who worked on the Exhibition.

The general publicity plans, including the exhibition of survey findings and the circulation of the findings through the newspaper and periodical press, were prepared and carried out under the direction of E. G. Routzahn, Associate Director of the Department of Surveys and Exhibits. Mary Swain Routzahn, also of the staff of the Department of Surveys and Exhibits, was the director in immediate charge of the Exhibition; and Walter Storey was Director of Design and Construction for the Exhibition.

Time and Method of the Investigations

The first of this group of surveyors reached Springfield in early March 1914, and the investigating was begun at once. All sections of the survey were under way by early May, and all the field investigating was completed by the first part of July. Thus, except where otherwise specifically stated, the facts presented apply to conditions found in the spring and summer of 1914.

In very general terms the method of investigation comprised study of the records, published and unpublished, compiled and uncompiled, of organizations and institutions in the community

THE SPRINGFIELD SURVEY

and of outside agencies which had data on Springfield; personal visits to and observation of Springfield organizations and institutions in operation; the gathering of facts through intensive studies or tests planned for certain sections of the city, or of the population; special studies of the activities of a particular agency or group of agencies and interviews with officers in charge; firsthand observation of conditions throughout the city; written inquiries and personal interviews with individuals in possession of experience or information pertaining to the problems in hand; and studies of legislation relating to local conditions and procedures.

Publication of the Springfield Findings

The preparation of the reports was begun immediately upon the close of the investigations; the report of the school section, the first to finish in the field, was completed and made public by the time the last work of investigating was being done.

The plan followed in publishing the survey findings was to print the report of each of the nine sections in separate paper bound volumes, liberally illustrated with maps, diagrams, and photographs. Before these reports were issued, however, the findings were fully summarized in the local Springfield press, the newspapers of the city handling from twelve to thirty-two full column stories on each. The press material was prepared for both morning and evening papers by the survey staff and delivered under release dates. Practically the full text of each report was thus reproduced and given wide circulation through this very serviceable co-operation of the daily press. Editorial discussion of the reports as well as letters to the editors commenting on controversial points centered further attention and thought upon the information and proposals being brought out.

Throughout Illinois the survey's data were made use of also. Since many situations in the city required state action before relief could be secured, advance newspaper summaries were supplied to practically all of the daily papers of the state and to many of the weeklies. Through the interest and help of the Springfield correspondents to Illinois papers and the local editors, much that the survey had to say was thus put before citizens and legislators in many parts of the commonwealth.

PURPOSE, SEQUENCE, AND METHODS

Then there were the facts brought to light having general application and educational value; and the project itself was believed to have significance as another venture in methods of improving community conditions. Press stories summarizing the more salient points of each report were therefore sent at different times to a large number of daily papers, weeklies, magazines, trade papers, and other periodicals throughout the country. A large amount of the material sent out was used; and a number of papers stated also that the articles, when not used in news columns, were useful to editors and editorial writers.

It is not possible in the space to go into greater detail regarding what was done to get the survey data widely known and used. Suffice it to say that in addition to what has already been described, material was supplied which was thought to be of interest to newspapers and periodicals of specialized constituencies, such as health journals, religious weeklies, educational magazines, labor papers, and the like; and the full reports were supplied to special writers and editors who reviewed them in the technical and popular monthly magazines. The Department of Surveys and Exhibits also issued several brief pamphlet interpretations of the survey project and of the material brought out in the investigations.

Following publication of the advance articles in the Springfield papers, from 500 to 1,000 copies of the printed reports of each survey division were supplied to the Springfield committee. Detailed suggestions for their local distribution were also put in the hands of the committee.

An additional edition was printed for distribution by the Russell Sage Foundation; and these have gone to libraries, college teachers, students, and others interested in surveys in different parts of the United States and in a number of foreign countries.

SURVEY EXHIBITION

In the November immediately following the field work the Exhibition of Survey Findings and Recommendations was held in the state armory. It was open for ten days and attracted thousands of visitors, including many from distant parts of the state.

THE SPRINGFIELD SURVEY

Several reasons prompted the Exhibition. It would afford an opportunity to present the major findings of the survey in such simple, graphic, and entertaining ways as to gain the attention of and be understood by the great body of people of the city—particularly many who are not habitual readers of periodicals or printed reports. It would create an additional event in the community which would give news value to the survey's facts and recommendations; it would turn the survey conclusions into something that could be seen today and again tomorrow and the next day, something that would afford a center where, as in a church or a civic society, people could consider an important subject *together*. It would give opportunity for further participation in the survey project by the people of the city; and finally it would help citizens to visualize the survey as a whole.

For two months preceding, a special campaign of publicity and promotion was carried on which kept the survey before people. Those familiar with publicity work will recognize the value of such things as the invitations sent out by a hospitality committee to mayors throughout the state; exhibit models and devices displayed from time to time in public places; unexplained cartoons posted in the windows at exhibition headquarters; the street railway company's offer to transport school children free to the Exhibition; prizes offered for the five best grammar school essays on "What I Saw at the Springfield Survey Exhibition"; special days assigned to societies and organizations; a daily department in one of the newspapers under "The Survey Question Box"; a proclamation by the mayor making the last day of the exhibit Springfield Exhibition Day, and urging "all loyal citizens of Springfield to take this last opportunity to inspect and study the many interesting and instructive things there to be found."[1]

CO-OPERATION IN PREPARING EXHIBITS

A large part of the work of preparing exhibits and conducting the publicity campaign was done through local volunteer committees—including an advisory committee, a general executive com-

[1] For a detailed description of the Survey Exhibition and the campaign of which it was the center, see Chapter XII in Part Three, Putting the Facts to Work.

A View Down One of the Exhibition Aisles

mittee under the chairmanship of R. C. Lanphier, committees on automobiles, decoration, drayage, lettering, lighting, photographs, printed matter, speakers, special days, ushers, and many others. As the campaign grew, more and more people lent their help until more than 900 were at work, not only because their committee leaders were energetic and enthusiastic and the spirit of the campaign contagious, but because the things they had to do were interesting. They made models and mechanical devices, tried their hands at art work, wrote special stories for the newspapers, handled office matter, snapped photographs, and made public addresses before churches, lodges, labor unions, school clubs, and other organizations and societies. They helped stage and take part in the short plays written to bring out some of the important lessons of the survey.[1]

Survey Costs

The survey committee in Springfield raised $6,000 for the survey, $1,000 of this coming from the board of education, and another large contribution coming from the municipality. Later the committee added $3,500, subscribed popularly, toward the cost of the Exhibition. Additional expenditures by the Russell Sage Foundation and the co-operating national, state, and local organizations brought the total outlay up to approximately $25,000.

Survey Results

The survey, as the writer has pointed out on numerous other occasions, shows conditions and needs and furnishes a program of improvements; but after all, the program must be carried out very largely by other agencies than that making the investigation, and they should be credited with much, perhaps with most, of what may be regarded as results. In 1916, two years after the survey findings were presented in the Exhibition, I tried to list developments which pretty clearly had their beginning in survey recommendations—or at any rate, the advances made in the community *since* the survey, which had been specifically recommended

[1] See Chapter XII in Part Three, Putting the Facts to Work, for a more detailed description of the work done on the exhibits by volunteers and the method of organizing this co-operation.

PURPOSE, SEQUENCE, AND METHODS

by the survey, no matter what other agencies had also helped. The list included over forty major items, and a more recent checking up has added others. Instead of printing the original or a revised list, however, it seems better at this time to confine the discussion to the testimony of citizens of Springfield—particularly since several have expressed themselves publicly on the subject. Their statements became known to us only after reference had been made to them in the public prints. They are

THE SPRINGFIELD FLAG

The municipal flag was chosen from some 41 designs submitted in a public contest held in 1917. It consists of 20 white stars on a blue field, arranged in a circle to symbolize the 20 states admitted to the union before Illinois. The large star in the center represents Illinois; the middle of this white star being a red star to stand for the capital city. The design is by Salem T. Wallace of Springfield.

reproduced in full in Appendix A, Results of the Survey, beginning on page 399.

In considering developments, it is only fair to say that some of the changes would doubtless have come about had there been no survey; for Springfield, as was pointed out in 1917 by Dr. Palmer, had been making rapid strides in improving local conditions in the last eight or ten years before the survey. After making full allowance, however, for the influence of the gradual awakening of the city to its civic needs which was taking place in the years before the survey, Dr. Palmer makes this significant statement:

"If the entire expenditure for the Springfield survey had been charged to schools and charities, the results would have proven the investment exceedingly profitable."[1]

But, aside from specific developments, there is another way of looking at the question of results. There is the point of view taken by A. L. Bowen, Secretary of the State Charities Commission, as it was then called, in an address a year after the survey exhibition, as follows:

"In any campaign such as the survey has been and still is, we must always look for two classes of results. We must ferret out the intangible or abstract results. We must find the tangible or concrete results. Very often the intangible results of a great public welfare movement are by far the most important and far-reaching. I think this is true in the matter in hand. The intangible results of the Springfield survey are worth more to our community than those which we can actually see with our eyes or touch with our hands. I would say a new community conscience, or perhaps more truthfully, an aroused and stimulated community conscience, is the most noteworthy effect of the survey. Our attitude of a community toward all questions affecting its well-being has radically changed. We see new meanings in them and react to them in a different manner. Our sense of duty in many cases where it formerly would have been dormant now asserts itself and prompts us to action. There is a new spirit in our work."[2]

Similarly, Vachel Lindsay, a resident of Springfield and an observer and writer of distinction, ended a magazine article descriptive of the survey exhibition with this paragraph:

"I at least feel that the picture of this survey exhibit will re-

[1] From Some Outcomes of the Springfield Survey, a paper by Dr. George Thomas Palmer read at the Second Annual Better Community Conference held in Urbana, Illinois, in April, 1917, reprinted in Appendix A, the paper beginning on page 411.

[2] The full text of Mr. Bowen's address will be found in Appendix A, beginning on page 399.

main in the minds of the citizens as the general concept toward which they are all going. The spirit of that final dinner, with its new leaders springing up and its sober resolution, will probably abide. We have the serious expectation that henceforth Springfield's graver rank and file and leading citizens of whatever party are enlisted for steady lifetime tasks, each in his chosen place."

On a recent visit to Springfield I was told by one citizen that there was a great deal of feeling abroad that "the only way to get anything in Springfield now is to go to the people for it. In the old days there were other ways." If this be an accurate judgment, it means a most significant and democratic stride ahead, and the survey, by "going to the people," helped at least to the new conviction.

Follow-up Work

The survey as originally planned did not provide machinery for organized follow-up work. Something along this line was later done by the survey committee however. The committee organized itself into sub-committees which were charged with carrying out the recommendations in each of the main fields covered. In addition, the Council of Social Agencies, formed as a result of the charities survey, afforded an opportunity for discussion and conference; and existing social agencies have modified their activities in many cases to conform to the recommendations. In this connection much credit is due to Margaret Bergen, the new secretary at that time of the Associated Charities; H. S. Magill, superintendent of the public schools; and Sheriff J. A. Wheeler, Mrs. Frank P. Ide, and to ministers in a number of the churches.

A still later development was the decision of the survey committee in December following the field work, to appoint a committee to consider the form of organization which could best carry forward the general purposes of the survey. Under the chairmanship of Frank P. Ide this committee made a report recommending the organization of a city club to follow up the survey and to promote other civic enterprises. The entrance of the United States into the World War, however, made it necessary to lay aside some of these activities. The great bulk of the follow-up work in the meantime was and is being carried out through the organizations whose work were touched in the findings and recommendations.

Springfield's Contribution to Other Cities

So much for local developments. There is another side to the enterprise and that is the contribution which Springfield citizens may have made outside of their city to the general movement for better community conditions. It is a movement which might very well have taken its inspiration from a memorable appeal made by a citizen of this same Springfield, Sangamon County, Illinois, some fifty-odd years before and since become so widely known and quoted as to form the golden text of our political Holy Writ. It ran: "that we here highly resolve that the nation shall, under God, have *a new birth of freedom;* and that the government of the people, by the people, and for the people shall not perish from the earth." These words were pronounced when the states were at grips over a national social question. The appeal was for a rehallowing of government

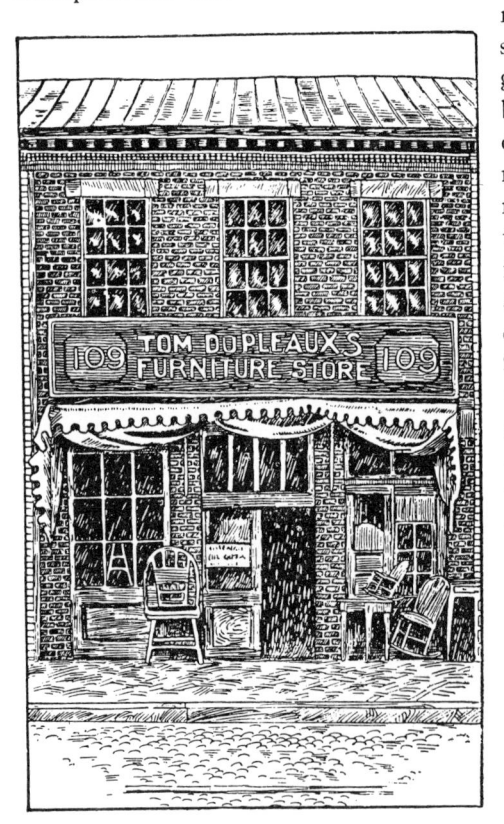

LINCOLN'S SPRINGFIELD LAW OFFICE
From 1837 to 1860 the law office of Abraham Lincoln, of Lincoln and Stuart, was housed in the second floor of this building.

18

to the task of serving the men and women who are the government.

Democracy is subject—sometimes profitably, sometimes not—to the dominating forces of any period whether political, ecclesiastical, economic, or other. Its forces ebb and flow with them, and must be refreshed whenever substantial rights have been invaded, or, indeed, whenever there are new gains to the common weal to be won. That is why, is it not, that each oncoming thirty years or so has its job to do and a farther peg to climb to?

Something that is fundamental in the fabric of our public affairs has been inweaving in the last dozen years or more—something that also bears the marks of high resolve and carries the infection of life and youth and renaissance. It is a process of peaceful civic renewal, through the scrutinizing of conditions surrounding our daily living, with a view not only to correcting those that are unwholesome but to quickening any that show promise.

Back of this scrutinizing and this resolve is the recognition that times have changed; that new circumstances to the harm of some folks have arisen; that simultaneously new forces have been gathering to cope with just such difficulties; and that these forces, in the form of new knowledge and experience and more effective methods, must be made to count at once.

So has come the insistence that changed conditions shall not leave people with less independence, less opportunity, and less comfort than before; rather that more shall be wrung out of life for them.

The successful working of this leaven of civic renewal depends upon the correcting power of facts, which must be gathered carefully and faithfully as the truth-loving scientist in any field gathers them—plus such a telling of the facts as will make them common knowledge. American experience is piling up the conviction that communities will act upon facts when they have them.

One of the forms of this new type of social exploration and reporting has been the community survey. Since 1907 in Pittsburgh the survey idea has spread enormously. Distinctive and vital as its formula is in itself, it is essentially synthetic and has drawn method and momentum from the collateral movements and agencies, nation, state, city, public and private, which make ascertained fact the rock bottom on which to base social policies and proposals.

The Springfield survey, seven years later, began with a group of Springfield citizens who took to heart the human prosperity of that capital city, set in the Illinois prairies, where Abraham Lincoln lived and voted; practised law and legislated; above all, made common cause with his neighbors, and discussed with them the how and wherefore of town affairs, state affairs, national affairs, until the most deep-seated social problem of his time became the subject of his scrutiny and his resolve.

From this small group the contagion of civic interest spread until a thousand Springfield citizens became part and parcel of the survey through personal contributions of time and through participation in some of its many activities. And though the dominating motive with them was to make things better at home, they always had a second hope that the contagion might spread beyond their own borders and thereby mean a contribution, even if modest, to the welfare of other cities than their own. So, large or small, they pray that their endeavor may be of some worth in advancing orderly, disinterested, thorough scrutiny as a basis for constructive state and municipal action—in the name of the well-being of the plain folks whose numbers are legion, and for whom the fellow-townsman and precursor of this Springfield committee spoke so forcefully two generations ago.

II
GENERAL FACTS REGARDING SPRINGFIELD

Springfield is built where four currents quick with energy and possibilities for community building come together—manufacturing, mining, agriculture, and commerce. Indeed, a fifth, the business of public service, might be added since the offices of state, county, and city governments bring in a thousand and more workers and their families.

These main currents together with many lesser interests and activities by 1910 had brought to the city a population of about 52,000, and to Sangamon County, exclusive of Springfield, about 39,000—a population for both county and city of 91,000. From 1910 to 1914, the year of the survey field work, the city's total increased to approximately 58,000.

The Population by Groups

In the composition of its population, Springfield was seen to be an unusually American city. Of each 100 inhabitants 81 were native whites and six were Negroes, who in the vast majority of cases were also American born. The remaining 13 were foreign-born whites. The native-born white male population of voting age in the city represented 73 per cent of all males of voting age, a rather high proportion when it is remembered that the proportion of male adults in the foreign-born population was relatively high. Six per cent of the total number of males of voting age were Negroes.

Since 1910, however, when the last census figures were compiled, women have become voters in Illinois. This has obviously increased the number of voters, but the inclusion of women in the figures would probably not greatly change the proportions between the native-born whites, foreign-born whites, and Negroes of voting age, on the one hand, and the whole number of persons of voting age on the other.

Of course not all the foreign-born males old enough to vote were necessarily voters. As a matter of fact, only 58 per cent in Springfield in 1910 had become naturalized, and only 7 per cent more had taken out first papers. The proportion of foreign-born males of voting age who had been naturalized or had taken out first papers in the same year was about the same for Sangamon County as a whole as it was for Springfield, but the proportion for the city and county was much higher than for all Illinois cities of 25,000 or more taken together. The largest foreign-born groups in the

SANGAMON COUNTY COURT HOUSE
A center of civic and historical interest. The building in an earlier day was used as the state capitol.
With the head offices of state, county, and city governments and their thousand or so of workers, the business of public service is an important economic factor in the community.

city, over 70 per cent of the 7,000 born outside the United States, were natives of Germany, the British Isles, Russia, and Finland.

About 5 per cent of Springfield's population ten years of age and over were illiterate, the larger numbers being among the foreign-born and the Negroes.

The growth of the city in number of inhabitants for the last sixty years had been relatively normal, following the same general trend as that of the state of Illinois. The number of foreign

GENERAL FACTS REGARDING SPRINGFIELD

born had increased but slightly, while their proportion had undergone an uninterrupted decrease. Similarly the number of Negroes had remained comparatively small and their proportion in the last twenty years had shown a decline.

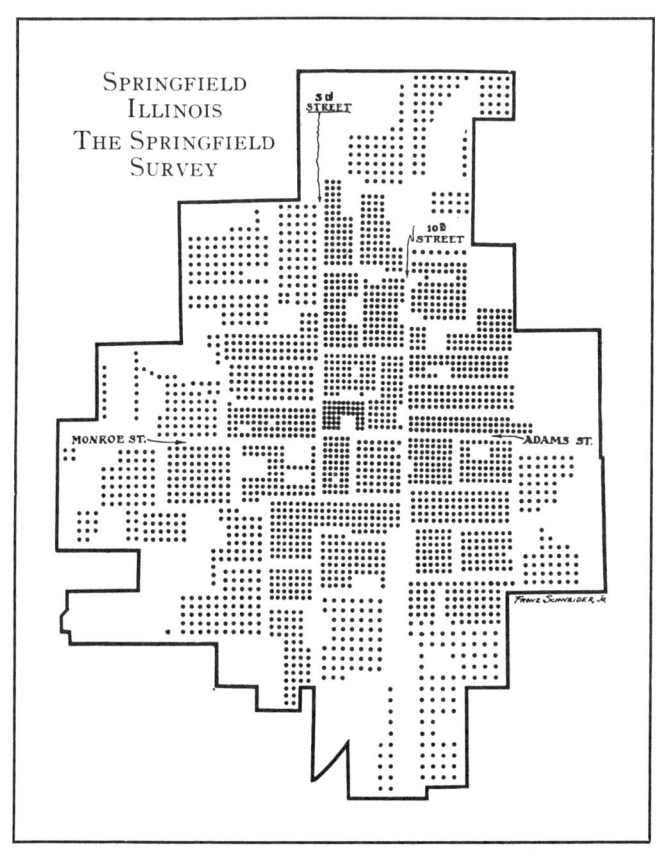

DISTRIBUTION OF POPULATION IN SPRINGFIELD
According to the United States Census of 1910. Each dot represents 20 persons. The actual distribution is very closely approximated here, as parks, railroad yards, and blocks not built up for habitation are excluded.

DISTRIBUTION OF POPULATION

The population at the time of the survey was rather evenly distributed, the density being greatest near the center of the city where there were a number of lodging houses and apartments. The range of variation in the 42 enumeration districts used in the federal census was from 3.6 to 26.4 persons an acre of gross area,

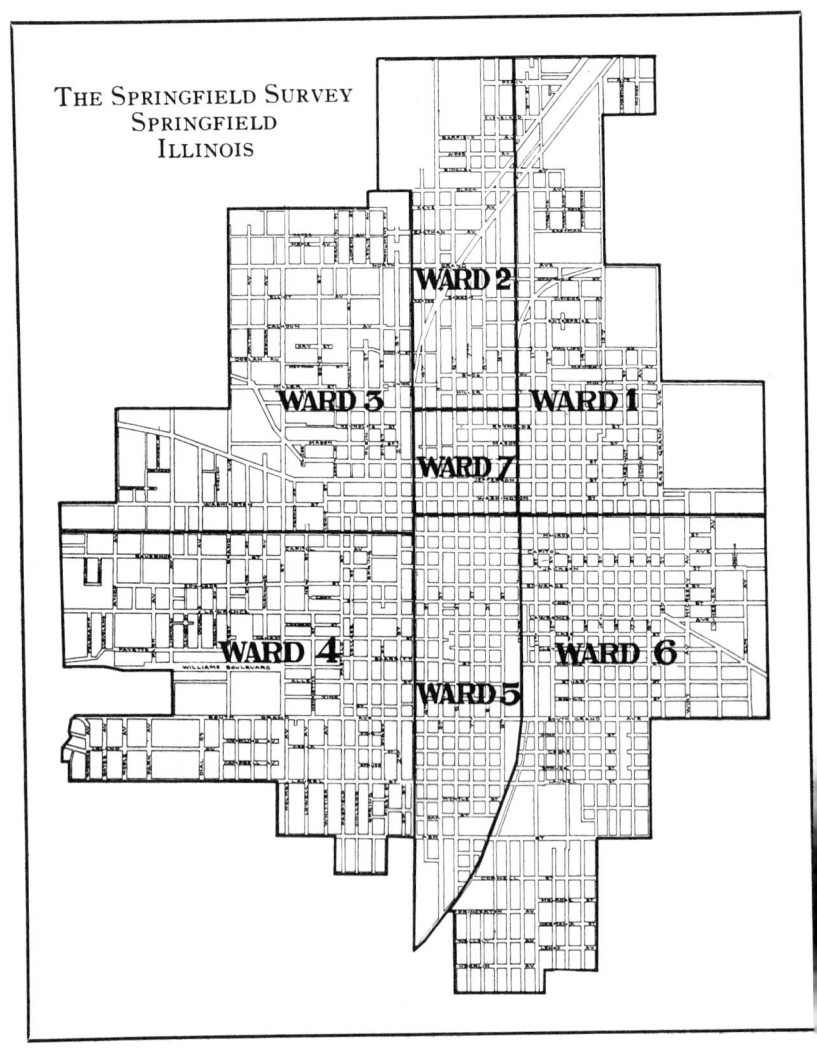

WARD MAP OF THE CITY
For a general description of the ward populations see page 25.

and from 6.4 to 28.9 persons an acre of net or built-up area. In considering these figures it should be remembered that densities in the great cities run up into the hundreds.

The different character of the population in different parts of the city is a matter of considerable social significance. Thus while Negroes and foreign-born whites did not form a large proportion of Springfield's total population, 19.1 per cent in 1910, these two components together made up 36 per cent of the population in ward one, and 24 per cent of that in ward six. The comparable figures for wards four and five were, on the other hand, 11 and 10 per cent respectively. Similarly the percentages of illiterates in wards one and six were 11.2 and 7.4, as against 1.8 and 1.3 in the fourth and fifth wards.

Such differences in the composition of the population tend to make the public health, public schools, recreation, and other problems increasingly difficult in certain districts and demand special activity on the part of the public authorities and others in such districts. The first and sixth wards, or the east side, had, in addition to a large percentage of Negroes and foreign-born whites, the larger proportions of children of school age; and the evidence also indicated that the birth rate was higher in these sections. The eastern and northern parts of the city contained, in short, the younger, poorer, and more foreign parts of the population and most of the Negroes, while the southwestern section was more purely native white, was older, and its people were more comfortably situated. Ward seven, embracing the district in the center of the city and around the court house, was somewhat peculiar, having an excess of males, a markedly lower proportion of infants and children of school age, and rather more than the average of foreign born and illiterates.

The People by Occupations

That work and work conditions are important factors of human welfare would be obvious from the mere number of persons directly affected, if for no other reasons; and in this regard Springfield was no exception. The 1910 census gave Springfield a population of 42,269 persons ten years of age and over. These represented 20,759 males and 21,510 females. Of the males, 17,014, or 82 per cent, were employed in gainful occupations; and the number of women and girls so occupied was 5,201, or 24 per cent of all females in this age grouping. Taking the numbers in both sexes, 22,215 persons, i.e., 53 per cent of all individuals ten years old or older, or 43 per cent of all people in the city were engaged in work commonly classed as gainful.

The occupation groups giving employment to the largest number of males were manufacturing and mechanical pursuits, trade, mining, and transportation. Those giving employment to the largest number of women and girls were domestic and personal service, manufacturing and mechanical industries, and profes-

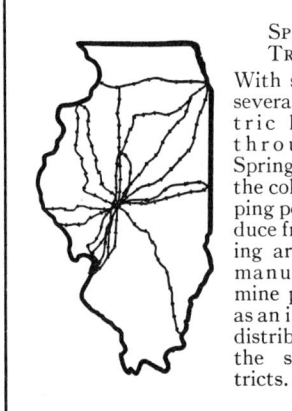

SPRINGFIELD AS TRADE CENTER

With six railroads and several interurban electric lines passing through the city, Springfield has become the collecting and shipping point for farm produce from a large farming area, and also for manufactured and mine products, as well as an important inward distribution point to the surrounding districts.

sional and clerical service. Including persons of both sexes, more than twice as many were engaged in manufacturing and mechanical pursuits as were employed in' any other occupation group.

Since Springfield's manufactures were about the average for places of its size, the city could hardly be regarded as pre-eminently a manufacturing center. Fourth city in the state in population, it ranked eleventh in the number of factory wage-earners and fourteenth in the value of its products. But when its commercial, mining, and transportation activities were added to its manufactures, the city took a relatively high place among cities of its size as a business and industrial center. And as a factory city Springfield had recently been gaining ground. While the increase in population from 1900 to 1910 was 51 per cent, the number of wage-earners in industry from 1899 to 1909 increased 66 per cent, and the value of manufactured products advanced 145 per cent. In 1909 the United States census reported 4,355 persons engaged in manufacturing, and in 1910 the number was 6,821—a few new groups not counted in 1909 having been included in 1910.

Springfield's manufactures are diverse, the most important industries of the city at the time of the survey, judged by the value of their output and listed in the order of their importance, being the making of grist mill products, shoes, zinc products, watches, agricultural implements, and electrical supplies. Judged by the number of persons given employment, a test more important for our purposes, the list in the order of the number employed was: watches, shoes, electrical supplies, agricultural implements, asphalt paving, and zinc. The Elevator Milling Company, which topped the list of the Springfield factories in value of output with an annual product worth $2,250,000, employed but 40 men, while the Illinois Watch Company, with an annual output valued at about $1,100,000, employed 940 persons —by far the largest number to be found in any factory in the city.

The surface of Sangamon County in which Springfield is located, and of adjoining counties, is covered by a stratum of the same fertile soil found in other parts of the corn belt. The soil extends over low hills, well adapted to farming, and the territory is well populated. The district is underlaid with a bed of soft coal averaging over five feet in thickness, and village settlements have sprung up around the mine tipples. With no large centers nearer than 30 miles, Springfield is the collecting and shipping point for farm products from a large area, as well as for its own manufactured and mine products. It is thus the trade center of a thriving territory, and the third largest occupation group—second among the men alone—is composed of those engaged in trade.

A number of coal mines located in or near the city, besides supplying industries with cheap motive power, furnish employment to approximately 2,500 male residents. These form about 10 per cent of all Springfield males ten years of age and over, and since, with the exception of managers and supervising officials, they are all members of labor unions, their numbers and purchasing power have done much to give strength locally to the organized labor movement.

Persons employed on the steam railroads and electric lines, with those engaged in meeting local transportation needs, numbered over 2,000.

Geographical Characteristics of the City

The city proper occupies about eight and one-half square miles on the level prairie about four miles to the south of a meander in the Sangamon River. Its surface is very flat, the difference in elevation between the highest and lowest points of land within the city limits being only about 70 feet, and for about four-fifths of the city's area the difference is less than 20 feet.

The north-south diameter of Springfield is a little more than four miles, and its east-west dimension about three miles. The streets run either north-south or east-west, the few exceptions being some of those which follow railway or trolley lines. In width the streets range from 40 to 80 feet and practically all blocks are bisected by alleys.

Six railroads, exclusive of the Interurban Electric Line, enter Springfield. Although these roads pierce the city limits at 13 points, only three lines of track actually cut through the city. The railroads are of social importance in influencing living conditions along their routes and in establishing lines of division between parts of the community.

Aside from the central part where the stores, offices, and public buildings are crowded together there are no large sections, except on the outskirts, wholly devoid of dwelling houses. The railway lines have their stations and freight houses in separate districts, and the various factories are surrounded by residential districts. The multiple dwelling had just begun to appear but tenements were not yet numerous. Outside of the downtown district most families enjoy a yard. Few house sites even in this more crowded section are smaller than 40 by 150 feet and most of them are larger. It is in general a city of single family homes.

In addition to those who make the city their home and center of livelihood, many visitors from other cities are entertained in

TOPOGRAPHY OF SPRINGFIELD AND VICINITY

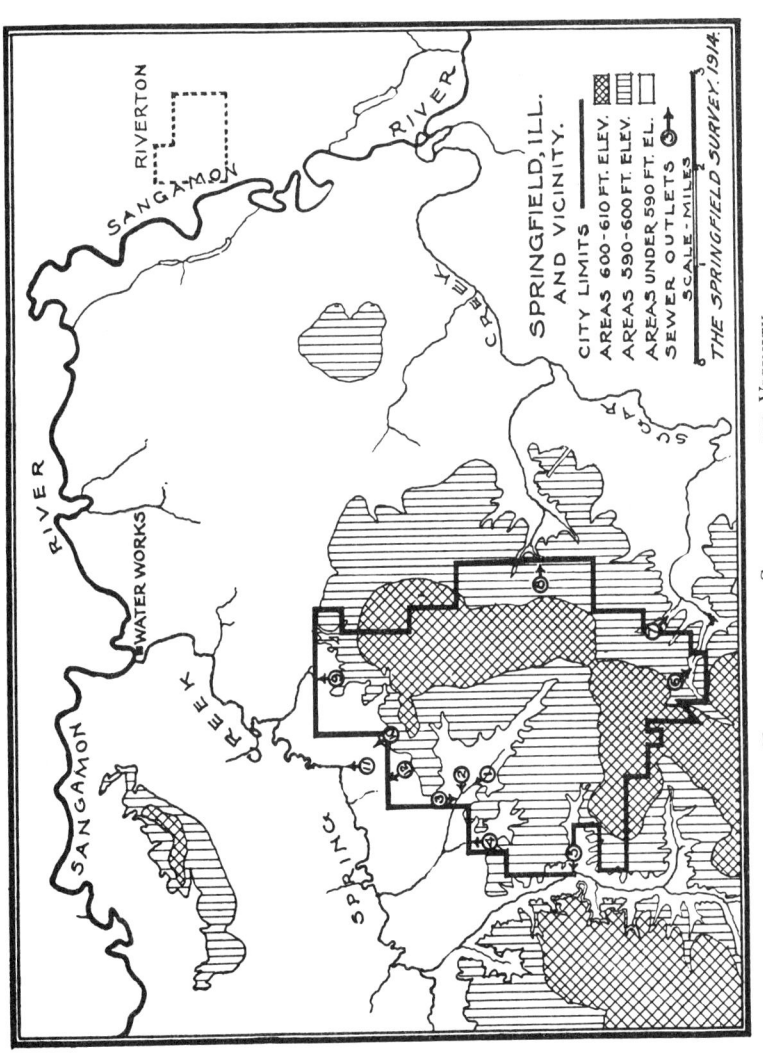

For about four-fifths of the city the variation in elevation is not over 20 feet between the highest slope and deepest ravine. The darker shading indicates the higher points of land.

connection with the meetings of the legislature, the annual state fair, the annual encampment of the state militia, and sessions of many civic, trade, and other conventions. The number of visitors to the old Lincoln homestead located in Springfield runs about 30,000 a year, many of them visitors from other states and from foreign countries.

Thus Springfield may hardly be regarded as a city of many extremes; it is rather a city of many averages. Located about midway between the northern and southern states and near the center of population of the country, it has shared in the cross-

ABRAHAM LINCOLN HOMESTEAD IN SPRINGFIELD
The Homestead is maintained as it was at the time it was occupied by the Lincoln family, and is open daily to the public. The number of visitors, many of them from foreign countries and from other states, approximates 30,000 a year.

currents of political, social, and economic forces of the East and the West, the North and the South. It is not congested. Its increase in population has been at a comparatively regular yearly rate. Like most other American cities it had grown without the guidance of a city plan and the usual rectangular block prevails. Commission government was adopted at about the time it was being adopted in many other places.

GENERAL FACTS REGARDING SPRINGFIELD

Also like other cities its social and civic life had many weak spots, but set over against them was a liberal allotment of social, civic, and economic strength. Its four-ply business structure—manufacturing, mining, agricultural, and trade—not to mention its enterprising local leadership and traditions of public spirit, were to be reckoned among the latter. But economic strength can hardly be regarded as an end in itself. Springfield's workshops, mine pits, farm and trade resources should furnish the

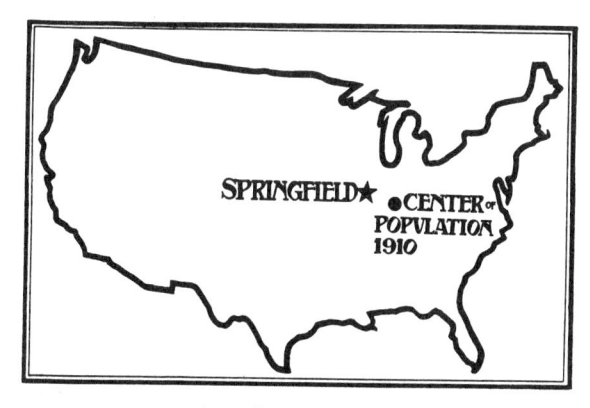

AT A CENTRAL POINT
Located about midway between the northern and southern states and near the center of population, Springfield has shared in the cross-currents of political, social, and economic forces of the East and the West, the North and the South.

groundwork for a structure of social well-being, the output of which should mount far above factory output, coal tonnage, farm products, and trade values. Even without special economic advantages the community's responsibility for promoting the welfare of its people must be acknowledged, but with these advantages the responsibility is much increased.

PART TWO
THE SPRINGFIELD FACTS SUMMARIZED

III

THE PUBLIC SCHOOLS[1]

If one had been able to take an instantaneous census of the occupations of all the people in Springfield on a day at the beginning of the survey, he would have found about 10,500 people, or almost one-fifth of all the people in the city, engaged in attending school. Of every hundred of these young persons 67 would have been found in the public schools, 26 in the parochial and private schools, and seven in the business colleges. To house these pupils it would have been found that there were 21 public school buildings, eight parochial schools, two private schools, and two business colleges conducted in business blocks, making a total of 33 buildings. The average attendance of those in the public day schools was 7,082.

The public schools of the city were being administered under what was known as Springfield School District No. 186, which included the city of Springfield and considerable adjacent territory in addition. Although the district was a state and not a municipal organization, including as it did more than twice as much territory as the municipality, more than nine-tenths of the inhabitants of the district were living within the city's borders.

In 1854 the state legislature granted the city of Springfield a common school charter, which vested in the city council the functions which were exercised at the time of the survey by the board of education. An amendment to this charter in 1869 created a school board of nine members appointed by the city council. In 1903 a state law was enacted to apply to cities having a population of over 35,000 by the Federal Census. This law fixed the number of members of boards of education at seven and provided for their election by the legal voters of the school

[1] Summary of report on The Public Schools of Springfield, Illinois, by Leonard P. Ayres, Ph.D.

district. The members were to serve for two years, and two or three members were to be elected each year. It was not until after the census of 1910 that the provisions of this law were applied to Springfield, the reorganization being effected in April, 1911. Under the provisions of this legislation the schools were being administered.

The new law conferred upon the board of education all the powers granted by the state law on boards of education in school districts, trustees of schools in townships, and boards of directors. It elected its own treasurer, determined the amount of money needed for educational and building purposes, and certified the same directly to the county clerk. Almost the only restriction of its power was that propositions to purchase school sites and to erect school buildings, as well as the issuance of bonds for such purposes, must be submitted to a vote of the people of the school district.

There were 20 schools, including the high school, the Teachers Training School, 17 graded elementary schools, and one ungraded one-room school. All of these except the one-room school were within the boundaries of the city. They were administered by a superintendent elected by the school board, 18 principals, and four general supervisors of special subjects—drawing, music, household arts, and health.

Nine employes of the board were attached to the central office—a secretary, assistant secretary, the superintendent's private secretary, treasurer, attorney, architect, who was also superintendent of buildings, bookkeeper, truant officer, and stenographer. Each building except the one-room school had a custodian or janitor with additional assistants.

There were 224 teachers, five of special subjects—domestic science, drawing, and music—and two of manual training.

The Board of Education

The school board was holding regular meetings twice a month, and these were supplemented by adjourned, called, and special meetings, so that it was in session for several hours almost every week. In addition the board was divided into six committees, and each member belonged to at least three of them. In the

The Twenty-one Public School Buildings

aggregate, the board and its several committees transacted a great amount of detailed administrative business.

Members of the Springfield board of education were unsparingly generous in the time and attention they devoted to the hundreds of petty details of school administration. But the truth is that much, if not most of the business transacted, would much better have been left to its employed administrative officers. The altruistic interest and personal self-sacrifice of the members were splendid assets to the city, but their effectiveness could have been greatly enhanced if the board had devoted itself in far larger measure to broader questions of policy and delegated to its officers the details of administration.

The superintendent and the principals of Springfield were paid on the basis of specialists and they should be given much responsibility. It is a waste of money to purchase high-grade experience and ability and then not permit that ability and experience to be used. The principles underlying efficient management of a system of education are in salient respects similar to those underlying the effective organization of a corporation. The directors of a corporation delegate to managers and superintendents the responsibility of executive detail, confining their activities to supplying funds, supervising expenditures, and determining what additions or reorganizations of the business are to be undertaken. The same functions may well constitute the bulk of the work of an efficient board of education.

The suggested change in policy was illustrated by reference to the organization of the board's committees. There were committees on teachers, textbooks, course of study and rules, school houses and furniture, high school, finance and supplies, manual training, and domestic science. It is almost certain that the affairs of the board would have been more efficiently administered by having only three sub-committees—one on educational affairs, one on buildings, and one on finance. This, however, could be accomplished only through the delegation of responsibility. Matters pertaining to the construction of school houses, the selection of textbooks, the formulation of courses of study, the selection, assignment, transfer, and dismissal of teachers and janitors require expert knowledge and should be delegated to

ORGANIZATION OF PUBLIC SCHOOLS

BOARD OF EDUCATION
7 MEMBERS

SUPERINTENDENT OF SCHOOLS

| SECRETARY | TREASURER | ARCHITECT | TRUANT OFFICER |
| ASSISTANT SECRETARY | BOOKKEEPER | ATTORNEY | STENOGRAPHER |

SECRETARY TO SUPERINTENDENT

SUPERVISORS — **SPECIAL TEACHERS**

| HOUSEHOLD ARTS | MUSIC | DOMESTIC SCIENCE | MUSIC |
| DRAWING | HEALTH | DRAWING | MANUAL TRAINING |

HIGH SCHOOL
PRINCIPAL
37 TEACHERS
883 PUPILS

DUBOIS
PRINCIPAL
12 TEACHERS
438 PUPILS

ENOS
PRINCIPAL
14 TEACHERS
424 PUPILS

LAWRENCE
PRINCIPAL
13 TEACHERS
417 PUPILS

STUART
PRINCIPAL
13 TEACHERS
417 PUPILS

ILES
PRINCIPAL
12 TEACHERS
415 PUPILS

RIDGELY
PRINCIPAL
11 TEACHERS
412 PUPILS

BUNN
PRINCIPAL
11 TEACHERS
378 PUPILS

DOUGLAS
PRINCIPAL
12 TEACHERS
372 PUPILS

LINCOLN
PRINCIPAL
11 TEACHERS
364 PUPILS

FEITSHANS
PRINCIPAL
11 TEACHERS
359 PUPILS

PALMER
PRINCIPAL
10 TEACHERS
353 PUPILS

CONVERSE
PRINCIPAL
9 TEACHERS
346 PUPILS

HAY
PRINCIPAL
8 TEACHERS
313 PUPILS

McCLERNAND
PRINCIPAL
8 TEACHERS
282 PUPILS

EDWARDS
PRINCIPAL
8 TEACHERS
273 PUPILS

MATHENY
PRINCIPAL
8 TEACHERS
238 PUPILS

TRAINING
PRINCIPAL 6 TEACHERS
15 PUPIL TEACHERS
227 PUPILS

HARVARD PARK
PRINCIPAL
4 TEACHERS
156 PUPILS

PRYOR
1 TEACHER
24 PUPILS

employed officers of the board who are or should be professional experts.

The best efforts of the most competent men and women of the city are needed for the solution of such important school problems as finance, the selection and purchase of sites, the approval of plans for new buildings, the final decision as to extensions or reorganizations of the educational system, the promotion of needed municipal or state legislation, and the presentation of the needs and policies of the school system to the people of the city. These problems can never be adequately met while the board is spending most of its time considering minor details relating to the purchase of supplies, the equipment of specific rooms, the cleaning of floors, the making of repairs, and the thousand-and-one little matters involved in carrying on so great a business as the Springfield school system.

Offices of the Board

The offices of the board of education were exceptionally satisfactory, and the office employes were for the most part efficient. An important economy was possible by dispensing with the services of the attorney and the bookkeeper of the board. Both of these employes appeared to be able and conscientious men, but the business of the school system was not of a nature to require the employment of such officers. Few cities, even of the largest size, employ an attorney as a regular member of the staff; and the work of the bookkeeper, who was employed during the day in a bank and did his work for the board in the evening, could be assigned to the secretary and clerk and a modern system of bookkeeping installed. The filing and record systems were thoroughly and carefully administered, but they were more complex than was necessary and should be simplified. This held true in general of the work of the entire office.

Purchase of Supplies

Although Springfield was spending more money per pupil than most cities, the schools were not furnished with either an unusual amount or an especially high quality of class room supplies. The reason was that the purchase of supplies was handled by a committee of the board through local dealers. A considerable sum of money could be saved, board members relieved of a large amount of detailed work, and supplies secured at the lowest wholesale rate if a bureau of supplies were organized as a division of the office organization of the board.

The Administration of Compulsory Education

For the enforcement of the compulsory school attendance law, effective for children from seven to fourteen years of age, the city employed one officer. Since there was no complete official record of the children of school age, no one could know how many were evading the law. The method used for locating absentees was to ask school children whether they knew of any who were not in school. The principals of the schools then reported such truancy cases as were brought to light and the attendance officer investigated each case, leaving, where necessary, a printed admonition from the board. If this was not sufficient to secure the attendance of the children the case was reported to the juvenile court, which might or might not issue a warrant for the arrest of the parent.

Records showed that there was little inclination on the part of the judge of the juvenile court to co-operate with the attendance officer; warrants for parents were seldom issued, and when they were brought to court the judge almost invariably discharged the case or at most imposed a fine and then suspended sentence. Thus school attendance in the city was no more than mildly compulsory.

Age and School Certification

According to state law no child between the ages of fourteen and sixteen might leave school to go to work without securing an age and school certificate. These certificates were issued by the superintendent of schools on the request of the parent and on receipt of a certificate from the school principal showing that the child was at least fourteen years of age and could read and write.

School records indicated that approximately 600 children left the public and private schools of Springfield each year between the ages of fourteen and sixteen. As only about 200 received age and school certificates, it is evident that the great majority of the children were evading the law. This was largely explained by the fact that if the child left school but worked at home instead of securing employment, no attempt was made to enforce the attendance law or to require the child to obtain an age and school certificate. Probably most of the girls and a considerable number of the boys who dropped out of school at fourteen or fifteen years of age did not secure regular employment and so did not take out age and school certificates.

The fact that school attendance in Springfield was only mildly compulsory went far toward explaining why Springfield had a greater proportion of illiteracy in its native white population than any other city of over 30,000 in Illinois, and why the proportion was increasing instead of decreasing. The entire situation with respect to enforcement of the attendance law was in an unsatisfactory condition. This did not seem to be due so much to lack of energy on the part of the attendance officer as to a general indifference on the part of the entire community—an indifference which, as already indicated, was a factor in Springfield's bad showing in the matter of illiteracy.

In order to remedy conditions, at least two competent attendance officers should be employed; this would facilitate reorganizing the administration of compulsory attendance and the issuance of age and school certificates. The taking of the school census needed to be completely reformed so as to show the names and addresses of the children who ought to be in school; and the co-operation of the judge of the juvenile court should be secured.[1]

The School Plant

Springfield has been most generous in providing for the education of its children; school sites were found to be ample in size

[1] In the period since the survey, improvements have been made in the school census, as well as at many other points where different divisions of the survey made recommendations. As pointed out elsewhere, no enumeration of these changes is here attempted, as this summary aims to present only the findings and recommendations of the earlier and fuller reports. Some references, however, to changes which have taken place in Springfield since the survey are made in a discussion of results which will be found in Appendix A, page 399.

THE PUBLIC SCHOOLS

and well located, buildings were of brick and in good repair, rooms were large, and there was a seat for every child. The buildings were extraordinarily uniform in plan and construction, however, and the newest buildings were a quarter of a century behind the times in design. The reason for this uniformity in both older and newer types of building was that the board of education had employed the same architect for the past thirty-two years. It would be well for Springfield to profit by the experience of other cities, and instead of putting up more buildings according to the plans now in use, secure new plans embodying the most modern practice.

If every foot of space in a school building is not most advantageously utilized, expense piles up with no accompanying increase in accommodations. In the newer buildings in Springfield space was unwisely lavished on rooms that were too large and too high, corridors that were too wide, and cloak rooms that were too large.

In all three dimensions, length, width, and height, the rooms were larger than is sanctioned by the best practice of modern school architecture. Each room was planned to accommodate 50 children, although the prevailing size of a class was 36, and the school authorities did not plan and should not expect to have 50 children in any class. An undue amount of fuel is required to keep the rooms warm and an unreasonable amount of work to keep them clean. Light will not carry well across rooms that are so wide, and children in the rear of them have difficulty in seeing what is written on the front blackboards. It is also hard for them to hear and for the teacher to keep their interest. Moreover, the size of the rooms offers constant temptation to increase the size of classes to a point where efficient work is impossible.

Corridors were even more prodigal of space than class rooms. There was almost enough corridor space on a floor with six class rooms to accommodate five additional ones of the standard size in New York or Boston.

As a result of this wasteful use of space Springfield school buildings were exceedingly expensive. A comparison with the better buildings of the same size in other cities showed that Springfield schools were 50 per cent larger in size for the accommodation of the same number of children than were corresponding buildings in other places.

In future, class rooms should be smaller and with lower ceilings; coat rooms should be somewhat narrower, and the width of corridors reduced from 25 feet to about half that width.

Lighting

According to the best school architects, in a well-constructed class room window area should be equal to one-fifth of the floor area. The problem of adequate lighting is rendered difficult in Springfield by the prevalent coal smoke in the air which rapidly deposits a bluish film on the surface of the window glass and

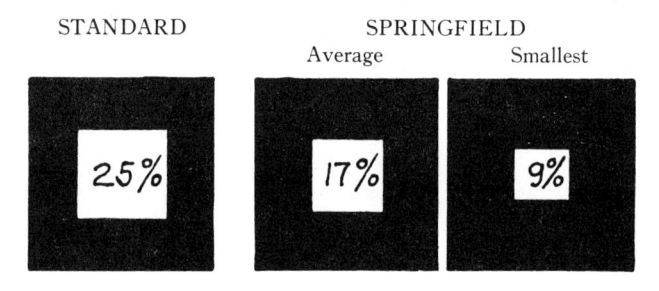

STANDARD SPRINGFIELD
             Average   Smallest

25%   17%   9%

SCHOOL ROOM LIGHTING

Window area should equal 25 per cent of floor area as indicated in the first square. In the Springfield schools the window area averaged 17 per cent and ran as low as 9 per cent in some rooms.

seriously reduces its transparency. For this reason the standard provision should be for one-fourth of the floor area.

In none of the class rooms was the window area equal to one-fourth of the floor area, and in less than one in three of them was it equal to one-fifth. Two-thirds of the school rooms would not meet even a low standard requirement, and in some conditions were so serious that the window area was equal to only one-twelfth of the floor area.

Proper location of windows is just as necessary as adequacy in size. Every class room should get light from but one side and this should be from the left of the children. Of every 10 class rooms in the city, seven had windows at the left and rear, one had them at the right and rear, while only two had them at the left only. Indeed there were four class rooms in the city in which the windows were at the left and front. The result of this situation was that in the great majority of rooms the teacher standing at the front of the room looked directly into brightly lighted windows.

In order to relieve the strain in their eyes, teachers would draw the shades over the rear windows. This in turn resulted in cutting off so great an amount of light that the rooms were seriously underlighted. Moreover, as the shades were difficult to adjust, they were frequently left drawn on cloudy days, which resulted in still darker rooms for the children to work in.

A series of careful tests of the illumination in school rooms with a Sharp-Miller photometer demonstrated by actual measurement that on cloudy days a large proportion of the school rooms were seriously underlighted. Many in the high school were so badly lighted that they were unfit to be used without artificial light.

Throughout almost the entire school system windows were wrongly located and lighting was inadequate. This condition was due largely to the design of the school buildings which in future should be planned with lighting from the left only. Conditions may in some part be remedied by installing a more satisfactory type of shade than those then in use, and rigidly insisting that principals and teachers give careful attention to their adjustment.

The practice with respect to the cleaning of windows varied greatly. In some buildings windows were washed twice a year while in others they were washed twice a month, or 20 times a year. This matter is so important that standard rules for cleaning windows should be adopted and officials should insist upon their observance. If the eyesight of the children is to be properly safeguarded, a more modern form of building design must be used in the future.

Temperature

The maximum temperature allowed in class rooms should be about 68 degrees. Records showed a temperature range from

58 to 86 degrees, with more than half the rooms registering over 70 degrees. Part of the fault may be attributed to the cheap and unreliable thermometers furnished to the schools. These needed to be replaced by reliable ones having conspicuous markers at 68 degrees.

Just as the air in the class rooms was as a rule overheated, so in general it was too dry. Humidity tests showed a range in Springfield class rooms from 19 to 46 degrees, while the proper humidity is about 50 per cent, with a range from 40 to 60.

Ventilation

Most of the schools in Springfield were ventilated by the gravity system, which in general is unreliable. In some buildings it was working well, in others moderately, and working little, if at all, in the rest. In the high and Edwards schools, systems of mechanical ventilation with fans had been introduced. If these systems are properly installed, as was the case in the Edwards School, they are more satisfactory than gravity systems. New buildings should be equipped with the best type of mechanical ventilation, and defects in the existing systems should be repaired.

Drinking Water

Bubbling fountains, a distinct advance over the dangerous and unhygienic common drinking cup, had been introduced throughout the schools. Unfortunately, however, many of them had been installed in the toilet rooms. Their installation in the corridors involves little additional expense and should be insisted upon in future buildings.

Janitor Work

Most of the Springfield school buildings were neat and clean, free from defacing marks, with yards and basements in good order. In general the floors of the schools were well cared for, being oiled once or twice a year and swept daily with a dust-absorbing compound.

It would be well for the superintendent of buildings to organize a school for janitors in which they may learn the best and most efficient methods of carrying on their very important part of the school work.

Furniture and Blackboards

Throughout the city non-adjustable seats and desks were in use. These would be satisfactory if care were always taken to place some seats and desks of varying sizes in each room. In each building some rooms should be equipped with the new movable combined seats and desks.

HIGH BLACKBOARDS AND NON-ADJUSTABLE DESKS
The two boys were sitting in school seats of the same size. The blackboards were too high for the smaller children. The schools are for the children; they should be adapted to their use.

All the newer buildings were equipped with slate blackboards of a good quality. Unfortunately, however, practically all the boards were installed as though they were to be used by high school children, even when the rooms have been designed for the use of primary grades. Blackboards in class rooms and hooks in coat rooms should be arranged with reference to the size of the children who are to use them.

Toilets

Throughout the schools the toilet facilities were seriously deficient. Only four schools in the city met the standard requirements, that in elementary schools there shall be one seat for each 15 girls and one seat and one urinal for each 25 boys. In nearly all the buildings toilet stalls had no doors. This is a thoroughly bad practice and should be remedied by providing for each toilet stall a short door placed well above the floor and set with spring hinges. All toilets in use were of the same size, whether for primary children or for the high schools. This should be corrected by supplying two sizes of seats in all new buildings.

Fire Protection

Conditions with regard to fire protection in the Springfield schools made possible the duplication of the Collinwood, Ohio, fire of March, 1908, in which 173 children and two teachers were burned to death within sight and in some cases within touch of their friends and parents. Buildings were of brick with wooden floors and partitions, neither fireproof nor fire-resisting; they were not provided with good fire-escapes, and coat rooms opened directly into corridors. The most seriously important factor in the situation was the bolted outside doors.

The first step to be taken in remedying this condition was to replace the bolts on all outside doors with panic bolts by which doors could be instantly opened from the inside by a slight pressure on any part of the bar. Fastening an outer door in any other way should be peremptorily forbidden. The fire drills need to be reorganized and all running forbidden. In old buildings winding stairways should be straightened or replaced by fireproof stairs.

New Auditorium for Old Building

Stimulated by the recently aroused interest in the wider use of the school plant, there was at the time an active campaign throughout the city for the addition of an auditorium to each building not possessing one. The plan of erecting expensive auditoriums in the yards, connected with school buildings by covered passageways, was both costly and short-sighted. Since most of the buildings should be replaced within twenty-five years and some in less time, all auditoriums built as annexes of old buildings should be planned as integral parts of the new buildings to be erected in the future. Where this is impossible they should not be built, but arrangements made to use the very wide corridor or upper grade rooms for public meetings by installing folding chairs and movable furniture.

POOR MATERIAL AND WORKMANSHIP IN SCHOOL BUILDINGS
The illustrations show patched, cracked, and defective lumber which, contrary to specifications, was being used as sheathing in the new Lincoln School under construction at the time of the survey. The lumber was second-hand, full of nail holes, and included many broken pieces and decayed spots.

QUALITY OF CONSTRUCTION

In quality of material and workmanship there was the widest variation among buildings of the city. Some represented a thoroughly high grade of construction, while in others there was evidence of poor material and deficient workmanship. A case in point was the new Lincoln School, then under construction, where the floor sheathing consisted of second-hand, decayed, and broken lumber. On such a foundation smooth floors cannot be laid, and there will be heavy bills for repairs before they have been long in use. This condition existed because specifications were of a generation long past, loose in the extreme, and lacking in nearly all the points of a proper specification. For future buildings new sets of specifications should be secured and the system of inspection reorganized so that they will be followed.

The Child in the School System

The Springfield school census of 1912 gave the number of children of school age as 15,387; that is, persons of from six to twenty-one years old. In the absence of later data these figures were taken as the basis for computation in the spring of 1914. The census did not, however, give the important facts of the number of children of each age in public schools, the number in private or parochial schools, and the number not in any school. For this reason the school census needed to be reformed so as to tell how many children there are of school age in the city, who they are, where they live, and where they attend school.

A majority of the children begin school at the age of six, and so the first grades are largely made up of six-year-old children. If a child enters at the age of eight or nine, or if he enters earlier but remains two or three years in the first grade, he is nearly certain to become a misfit in his class. He needs a different kind of teaching and a different sort of treatment from the other children, and his presence renders the teacher's work harder and its results poorer. Such a child is termed an over-age child and one eight or nine years old in the first grade, nine or over in the second, and so on in the other grades is classified as over-age.

In the elementary schools of Springfield there were 1,469 such over-age children—24 per cent of the average attendance. Of these 1,469 over-age children there were 235 more boys than girls. Only 21 per cent of the girls were in this group as against 27 per cent of the boys. As both boys and girls were entering at the same ages, this indicated that the boys made slower progress.

The theory on which the school grades are organized is that the children shall complete one grade each year, and so finish the eight elementary grades in eight years. If a pupil has taken three years to complete two grades or seven years to finish five grades, we may classify him as making slow progress. On this basis there were 1,502 pupils in the Springfield schools who had made slow progress. As in the case of the over-age pupils, this was 24 per cent of all. The number of slow boys was 266 more than the number of slow girls. As in the former comparison, we found that the percentage of boys making slow progress was greater than that among the girls. For the boys it was 28 while among the girls only 21.

Although when contrasted with the 29 other cities for which similar data were available, Springfield made a good showing in the relatively small proportion of children who were over-age for their grades or were making slow progress, nevertheless the numbers were of such size as to call for special treatment.

Out of these totals there were 1,000 children in the elementary schools who were both over-age and slow—617 boys and only 383 girls. The proportion of such children varied from 5 per cent to 27 per cent in the different schools. These children need individual teaching, and provision for giving it should be made.

There were 101 cases of extreme retardation, 63 being boys and only 38 girls. Special classes should be provided for children who are so seriously retarded that it is evident they cannot profit by the ordinary instruction in regular classes. In some cases, when the children are exceptional types, they should not be in the public schools at all, but in institutions.

When and Where Children Drop Out

Careful computations have been made as to the age at which children drop out of school. In general terms the results show that practically all of them remain until they are thirteen years old. By the time they are fourteen, one-fourth of them leave. Half leave before they are fifteen, two-thirds before they are sixteen, three-fourths before they are seventeen, and nine-tenths before they are eighteen.

Boys drop out in far larger numbers at the earlier ages of fourteen, fifteen, and sixteen, leaving a larger percentage of the girls to remain for several years more of schooling. Study of the dropping out of boys and girls by grades showed in the Springfield schools that they began to drop out in the fifth grade where one-tenth of them left and nine-tenths remained. By the time the sixth grade was reached a quarter had left. Less than half finished the eighth grade, one-third entered the high school, and one-fifth completed the high school. About one child in 35 went to college. Again, it is noteworthy that with each stage of progress a larger proportion of girls than boys remained in school.

Comparison between the progress made by boys and girls disclosed a seriously important condition. Both were entering the primary grades in about equal numbers. The girls went forward more rapidly than the boys; they stayed in school longer and a greater proportion of them graduated. There were more repeaters among the boys; a greater proportion were over-age for their grades; more of them made slow progress; they dropped out at lower grades and earlier ages; and fewer remained to graduate. These conditions were not due to any conscious discrimination or neglect in the school system. They had grown up without the school authorities being aware of them, and exist in greater or less degree in a large proportion of our cities, but not in all. Quite unconsciously the schools of this city, like those of many other cities, had developed a course of study, a system of examinations and promotions, and methods of teaching—in short, an entire school system—better fitted for the needs and requirements of girls than of boys.

These conditions can be remedied, and their alteration is one of the most important tasks which confront the schools. If the school work is artificial, formal, and abstract, if it is not interesting and vital both boys and girls drop out, but the boy goes first. The experience of other cities shows that when boys leave school in large numbers at early ages and in the lower grades it is not because the opportunities for securing employment are especially attractive, but because the schools are not offering them work which holds their interest and impresses them or their parents as worth while. Other cities also have remedied this situation and in a later section of this summary the problem with reference to Springfield will be discussed.

In general the promotion rates were well up, ranging from 85 to 90 per cent. This means that at the end of each term from 85 to 90 among every hundred children were promoted to the next higher grade. The promotion rate for the entire city at the end of June, 1913, was 90 per cent, while at the end of January, 1914, it was 87 per cent. This rate is high but not too high.

Springfield was fortunate in having few overcrowded classes. Classes ranged in size from 17 to 53, with an average of 36. Twenty-three rooms had less than 30 pupils, while 33 had more than 40. Wherever possible, children needed to be redistributed so as to have fewer overcrowded classes. Their welfare is vastly more important than the strict maintenance of school district boundaries.

The Teaching Force

The regular teaching force consisted of 238 teachers and principals. Of these 199 were in the elementary schools and 39 in the high school. In age they ranged from nineteen to seventy-one years, with an average of about thirty years. The teaching force was relatively stable, length of service in the schools being seven years. No definite policy existed in the matter of tenure of office, but in practice a teacher who gave satisfaction was retained indefinitely.

In the elementary schools teachers began at $450 and in the sixth year reached $800, the maximum salary for regular teaching positions. Principals received salaries of from $900 to $1,800. Salaries of high school teachers ranged from $800 to $1,400. Salaries were relatively high at the time, Springfield being fourth from the top in comparison with average salaries of elementary teachers in 16 cities.

As a body the teachers of Springfield were conscientious, well-bred, intelligent, and faithful. The only important criticism that could be brought against them, and educationally it is an important one, was that in training, methods, and ideals they were far too uniform.

The teaching force was recruited almost exclusively from the local school system. Of each 10 teachers in the elementary schools seven were graduates of the Springfield High School and six of the Teachers Training School. For many years past the principals of the Training School and the critic teachers had themselves been graduates of the Springfield Training School. Moreover, one-third of the teachers of the high school were graduates of the Springfield High School. Most of the teachers had supplemented their educational preparation by work taken in higher institutions of learning during the summer school sessions.

From time to time teachers had been appointed who were not graduates of the Training School, and some had entered the service from other cities. In general, however, the process of appointment may be characterized as an inbreeding one. Young women who had passed through the local elementary, high, and training schools and entered the service of the city were in the main of thoroughly good ability, but they had been shaped in the same mold and had emerged exceedingly uniform in methods and ideals.

The Teachers Training School

The local training school had been in existence for thirty-two years. During this period the ideals of the institution were good and its work well conducted. But the city needed only about 16 new teachers each year, and for their training it could not maintain a first-class normal school. The weakness of a small system that trains its own teachers is that since these teachers have all learned to do the same things in the same way, they do not profit through contact with one another. They have little to discuss in a professional way and slight opportunity for contact with new methods and different ideals, or the interchange of varied experience. The Springfield schools were suffering from just these results of the policy of excluding outside ideas and experience and recruiting from within.

The remedy for this condition was to suspend the training school and to attract to the service of the city the best teachers from other localities, near and far. There is probably no other way in which the efficiency of the system could be more rapidly increased. The training school building could be utilized at the same time to exceptional advantage as an intermediate school.

The schools of Springfield in the past had been almost independent district schools with but little co-ordination of work. Something of this tradition having been transmitted to the individual teacher, there had grown up a system in which the local schools and local principals were relatively independent of the superintendent, and within each school the class room teachers were more than usually independent of the principal. The schools lacked expert, constructive supervision. An assistant superintendent of high professional education and successful experience should be employed to study the educational problems of the city, to assist in class room supervision, check up the quality of the work of the teachers, and especially give them constructive advice looking toward the betterment of their work.

The Quality of Class Room Instruction

Members of the survey staff made 684 class room visits of which 273 were for the purpose of observing teaching methods; the remainder for noting details as to the equipment and condition of the school plant. In general the best teaching was found in the primary grades, and it tended to decrease in excellence in the upper grades.

The strongest feature of the work lay in the friendly and intimate relationship existing in the great majority of the class rooms between pupils and teachers. The least commendable general feature was that throughout the system there was far too little real teaching and too much hearing of recitations in which teachers questioned pupils to discover how well they had mastered the lessons assigned them.

This type of class room work is prevalent in many cities, but it is not the best sort of teaching and its general level of quality can be greatly improved. The real object of education is to teach children to think, and the work of the teacher is to make pupils think by interesting them in problems and stimulating them to solve them by thinking them through. This is not accomplished by hearing textbook recitations or asking leading questions to which the child contributes the expected answer. An even more serious condition arose from the inadequate professional, educational, and cultural preparation of some of the teachers.

Throughout the elementary schools the discipline was good. In nearly 700 class room visits no member of the survey witnessed one serious act of disorder. These conditions were due to the high level of personality among the teachers, the generally good home training of the pupils, and to the prevailing aim to secure order through interest rather than through coercion.

Tests of Spelling, Handwriting, and Arithmetic

Standard spelling tests in all grades from the second through the eighth indicated that in the general, children could spell as well as children in other city school systems. Measurement of the quality of handwriting of pupils in the four upper grades showed that it was in general as good as that of children in the same grades in other cities. In arithmetic, however, Springfield children did work in fundamental operations more rapidly but less accurately than average children in other cities. This was determined by the Stone tests given in the advanced divisions of the sixth grade to determine the ability of sixth-grade children in addition, subtraction, multiplication, and division. The test in reasoning was given to determine the ability of the pupils to reason in connection with problems of practical arithmetic. These tests indicated that in reasoning their work was less rapid and less accurate than the average work in other cities.

The Course of Study

The course of study was the product of a number of partial revisions of a course in use many years before. In some parts it was rigid and behind the times, while in others, where it had been reshaped, it was modern and progressive. At the time another revision was being made with the co-operation of supervisors, principals, and teachers. It was not enough, however, that the best experience within the system was being consulted. The results of the best thinking, the widest experience, and the most mature judgment of other cities, as crystallized in their courses of study and the published reports concerning them, should also be carefully considered with the object of producing the best possible course of study for Springfield.

The course in use prescribed 15 subjects of which 12 were assigned for all grades from the first to eighth inclusive. These were reading, history, language, phonetics, spelling, arithmetic, penmanship, physiology and hygiene, physical culture, drawing, singing, and manual training. Literature and nature study were assigned for the first four grades and geography was taught in the six upper grades. As a matter of fact, the course was only partially followed and what the printed course called for was not actually taught in all the class rooms.

There was no official time allotment for the city, and the teachers in each school determined for themselves the amount of time to be devoted in the daily program to each subject. This resulted in the widest variation in the amount of emphasis placed on different parts of the curriculum, and these variations were not the product of careful planning and serious thought but existed precisely because neither thought nor planning had been devoted to securing the best allotment of time.

The teachers, principals, and superintendent of the city were urged to make a careful study of time allotments in the best systems elsewhere, and then decide how much time they would devote to each subject in each of the grades in Springfield. This time allotment should then be used as a standard rather than as a requirement. Teachers should be permitted to depart from it whenever they could put forward a good reason for so doing, but such departures should be based on carefully thought-out reasons and not on chance or caprice.

Time Wasted on Useless Material

Tests of the existing course showed that it included much material that was so artificial and unrelated to the needs of real life that it should be abandoned and more useful matter substituted. When children work together in the solving of a problem or the making of a map their work is social and co-operative. When they are committing to memory the spelling of such words as "weigelia," "trichinae," and "paradigm," taken from the seventh-grade lists, they are individual and exclusive; when making something material or abstract because they need it in their business, they are active and alert; when listening to recitations concerning the distance in degrees from Portugal to the Ural Mountains, they are mostly passive and inert. When they are learning or making something real that has an object behind and a result to come, they are energetic; when they listen to or watch or read something unrelated to the work of the world outside, they are apathetic.

No small part of the responsibility for the subject matter taught was attributable to the unsatisfactory textbooks used. Yet it is always difficult to get new textbooks adopted, for while the cost is but a small part of the total cost of education, it falls directly on the parents and seems an extraordinary burden. Parents usually fight the move. Textbooks have been furnished free by Philadelphia for almost a century and by many cities for almost half a century. At the time of the survey they were provided for by compulsory law throughout 12 states and were supplied in portions of 15 other states. Springfield should adopt the policy of free textbooks—a policy which promotes educational efficiency, facilitates uniformity, and reduces expense to the community.

Financial Administration

Springfield was spending on its public schools each year about one-third of a million dollars. Of every dollar received, approximately 91 cents came from local taxes and the remaining nine cents from the state. The board of education was empowered to decide each year how large the tax rate for school support should be, and had full power in determining the extent of the levy so long as it did not take for each $100 of assessed valuation more than $1.50 for educational purposes, or more than $1.50 for building purposes. It could spend the money so secured as it saw fit, except that it could not acquire new sites or build new buildings until it had been authorized by a referendum vote of the people.

The assessed valuation of property in Springfield at that time was one-third of the real valuation. This meant that in actual fact the board of education could take each year from each $100 worth of property $1.00 for the support of the public schools. Of this $1.00 it might spend 50 cents for educational purposes and the remaining 50 cents for building purposes.

In point of fact the board was each year taking the full 50 cents for educational purposes and found it scarcely enough to pay salaries and meet the running expenses of the schools. But instead of asking for the 50 cents allowed by law, it actually took only 15 cents for building purposes and the payment of bonds. As compared with other cities of similar size, Springfield ranked a little above the average in expenditures for education.

Costs in High and Elementary Schools

The annual cost of educating one pupil in the high school is often more than twice as great as that of educating one pupil in the elementary school. Elementary education in Springfield, however, was relatively more expensive than the education given in the high school, and still the city's expenditure for each high school pupil was as much as that of the average city of similar size. The high figures were caused by the small classes and relatively generous salaries in the local schools.

A computation was made for Springfield and the other ten cities of similar size of the amount spent annually for each child in average attendance in day schools, for purposes other than instruction. The results showed that the per capita cost in Springfield was greater than the average for salaries of principals, maintenance of buildings, purchase of stationery and supplies, salaries of supervisors, and the purchase of water and light. In the salaries of janitors and the purchase of fuel it was less than the average for the 11 cities.

The system of collection and disbursement of funds was efficient in that it provided every reasonable safeguard and secured an accurate accounting. It was deficient in that there was undue delay between the collection of tax money and its delivery to the board of education by the county treasurer. The sums turned over, moreover, were nearly always considerably less than the total amount of school taxes that he had on hand. This and the delay resulted in the board's losing the interest on part of its funds for considerable periods of time. School moneys collected during the month should be delivered in full to the treasurer of the board at the end of each month.

Up to within two years ago the school district was practically free from debt, and the expense of constructing new schools was met from the building fund. In order to reduce the tax rate for buildings, however, the board of education decided to borrow the money to build the new Palmer and Lincoln schools instead of paying for them out of current taxes. Twenty-year bonds were issued at 4 per cent interest, with the result that the erection of a school such as the new Palmer or new Lincoln which cost $75,000 if paid for at once, cost $106,000 when paid for by such bond issue. Bonding is justifiable when it cannot be avoided, but in Springfield the current income from taxes, if rightly administered, was ample for the purpose. There were indeed reasons why the usual arguments for paying for public improvements through bond issues did not hold. It was strongly recommended by the survey that in the future erection of new buildings, Springfield abandon the unnecessary practice of issuing bonds; also that the present ones be amortized without the city becoming more deeply involved, and former tax rate for building purposes be restored.

It was also recommended that when the board should take this matter under consideration it also should consider submitting to a vote of the people a moderate advance in the tax rate for educational purposes. At the time the money gathered into the educational fund was no more than sufficient to meet current salaries and other expenses. Several of the most needed improvements in the work of the schools contemplated the employment of additional people, and these changes could not readily be effected unless the amount of assessed valuation in the city be increased or the tax rate for the educational fund be made larger.

Medical Inspection

Medical inspection was being carried on in the schools by one nurse, who was employed by the board of education and given the title of Supervisor of Health. Her work in the schools consisted of inspecting the children in each room for symptoms of contagious disease, and during the same visit making partial physical examinations for the detection of removable defects that might handicap the children either physically or mentally. She was entirely competent and devoted to her work, but it was impossible for one person to do thoroughly the amount of work that she was attempting. Springfield, with nearly 7,000 children in its public schools, should have the full-time services of at least two and preferably three nurses, and in addition the half-time service of a physician.

Probably the most satisfactory way to secure the services of a competent physician would be to have the board of education co-operate with the board of health in employing a municipal physician. Half of his time could be devoted to his duties as school physician and half of his salary paid by the board of education. Such an arrangement would make possible the employment of a first-class man and materially raise the level of hygiene and sanitation throughout the city.

Vaccination had been neglected in Springfield, with the result that three-fourths of the children were not vaccinated and the proportion was growing year by year. This condition constituted a danger which could be avoided by making vaccination a prerequisite to enrollment in the public schools.

A school dental clinic, then in its third year, was maintained in connection with the offices of the board of education and was thoroughly successful. Arrangements were being made with oculists of the city for an eye clinic similar in principle to the dental clinic. There was every indication that these efforts will be successful and prove of great benefit to the children.

Classes for Exceptional Children

There were at least three types of exceptional children for whom provision should be made. The first type consisted of children below normal in growth and nutrition for whom open-air classes were needed. Such classes were in successful operation in many American cities and have repeatedly demonstrated their ability to take weak, anemic, and sickly children and convert them within a comparatively short time into strong, healthy, and normal children. Many in the local schools were of the type promptly benefited by open-air classes.

The second sort of exceptional child is the one below par mentally. Probably not less than 1.5 per cent of the pupils in the city schools are so backward in their work that they cannot properly be cared for in regular classes. For these, special ungraded classes taught by exceptionally well-qualified teachers should be established. Included in this number of backward children there was a smaller number of feeble-minded pupils who should not be in the public schools at all but should be cared for in state institutions.

The third type of exceptional children for whom special classes are needed is made up of those having speech defects. These children seemed to be unusually numerous in Springfield and probably numbered from 150 to 200. Most were stutterers, more than three-fourths of whom could be cured by a few months of special teaching. They do not need to be taught entirely in separate classes, but should receive special instruction each day from a well-qualified teacher who has been trained in this work.

The High School

The high school had nearly 900 pupils in average attendance of whom about 50 came from outside the city. It was growing at the rate of about 50 pupils a year, and there was indication that it will continue to grow even more rapidly.

There were six girls in the high school for every five boys, 100 fewer boys in the entire school than girls. The highest class was composed of less than half as many pupils as the entering class, showing that the Springfield High School, like most other high schools, was losing a large proportion of its children during the first year and another large proportion during the second. Those who survive the first two years are apt to stay to the end and graduate.

The work of the school was nevertheless planned as though all the children who entered remained for the entire four-year course. The procedure was not economical. If most of the work of the high school is to be devoted to teaching children who remain only one or two years, it should be planned with that end in view; and on the other hand if all the work is to be planned as part of a four-year course, every effort should be made to retain the children for the four years.

The High School Building

The student body had outgrown the high school building which was overcrowded so seriously that no further expansion was possible. Eight rooms in the third story and eight more in the basement were in use as class rooms, laboratories, or shops. These rooms were never intended to be occupied by classes, and every consideration of hygiene and educational policy demanded that their use be abandoned. Extensive additions needed to be built at once, or a new high school constructed, or some reorganization effected whereby a number of the pupils might be moved to other buildings.

Teaching Force

The teaching force of the high school consisted of 39 men and women, including 25 college graduates, seven high school and six normal school graduates, and one teacher not a graduate of any school. Nearly one-third were graduates of the Springfield High School, which was causing the same inbreeding process that so seriously handicapped the efficiency of the teaching force in the elementary schools. Salaries ranged from $800 to $1,400 a year with an average of $1,065. These were sufficiently generous at the time for the city to be able to demand of the faculty at least a college education, and of most of the teachers specialization in their subjects.

As might be expected, the teaching methods of this corps of instructors ranged from excellent to distinctly poor. There was a great deal of the sort of teaching that consists of assigning home lessons to be learned from books and questioning the children to find out how much they have retained of what they studied the night before. It seemed to members of the survey that in general the quality of teaching in the high school was on a lower level than that in the elementary schools, when both were compared with the work ordinarily observed in other cities.

Courses of Study

The high school was offering four courses—academic or college, English and scientific, business, and normal. Each was four years in length, although there was a provision that certain pupils might arrange for the two-year business course. In practice there was no distinction between the four courses. Four recitations in four different subjects each day, led in four years to the 16 credits required for graduation. Seven of these credits were prescribed and nine were elective. The subjects fell into 10 main groups—English, mathematics, science, history, Latin, manual training, domestic science, commercial subjects, German, and French. More than half of all the teaching done in the schools was devoted to 13 subjects of English, mathematics, and science.

The emphasis placed on the different subjects had been largely dictated by the demands of college entrance examinations. Since only one in 16 of the pupils entering the high school went to college, these requirements should not be permitted to influence the work of the school in more than slight degree.

More Co-operation Needed

The greatest need of the high school was a better spirit of cooperation within its own ranks. Pupils were being given little advice and guidance in the matter of electing studies. Teachers were competing with one another to get pupils to elect their courses, with the result that they did not co-operate with the pupils, they did not co-operate with one another, and they did not co-operate with the principal. Several teachers showed members of the survey staff plans for their own departments in the contemplated additions to the building. In each case each teacher had drawn plans for his or her own department without in any way taking into consideration the needs of any other.

There were no adequate records in the principal's office to show in any unified or convenient way the significant fact about the institution as a whole or the individual children and their school records. Program making was of the most elementary sort, and while most of the work was arranged on the five-day basis and no attempt at a spiral program had been made, still the central office had no records whereby it could tell at any hour of the day in what rooms the different teachers could be found or what classes they were teaching. Similarly the records of the individual pupils were kept mostly by the class room teachers, and there was no way in which the central office could tell without making a special inquiry, such facts about each child as age, courses taken, standing in each subject, credits earned to date, intentions with respect to college, and so forth. The clerk in the central office attributed this lack of adequate records in part to reluctance on the part of the individual teachers to furnish information about the children in their rooms when requested to do so.

Something of this same spirit of lack of co-operation was reflected in the way in which the pupils changed from one room to another at the end of each recitation. These transfers were accompanied by considerable disturbance from running, much loud talking, and a great deal of unnecessary delay.

While it was true that the school needed a new building and better equipment, more adequate shops and laboratories, a gymnasium, and an athletic field, these changes would not of themselves have converted the high school into a truly efficient institution. Before it could become as effective as it ought to be, it needed to be better administered, students, teachers, and principals needed to be imbued with a more thorough spirit of co-operation, and the quality of class room teaching improved.

The Organization of Intermediate Schools or Junior High Schools

As the members of the survey studied the educational problems of the city, they became convinced that the interests of the schools could be most effectively forwarded by the organization of intermediate schools or junior high schools. The schools were organized, as are those of most cities, in eight elementary grades and four high school grades. Under the proposed reorganization the elementary schools would consist of the first six grades, three or four intermediate or junior high schools would be established to care for the seventh, eighth, and ninth grades, and the three highest grades would be cared for in the senior high school. Because of this division the proposed plan is sometimes referred to as the six-three-three plan. It was in successful operation at the time in a considerable number of other cities and in accord with the most progressive educational thought and practice.

Under this plan three or four of the school buildings would be converted into intermediate schools or junior high schools and would take care of all the seventh, eighth, and ninth grade pupils in the city. This would immediately relieve the overcrowded condition in the high school. Each of the new schools would be in the center of a group of elementary schools, and as the pupils of the seventh and eighth grades of these other buildings were transferred to the new school, those pupils at present in the first six grades of the converted school would be transferred out to take their places.

Then when the new high school should be erected the old building would serve admirably for an intermediate or junior high school. Thus the new plan provided temporary relief for the overcrowded conditions, and also offered effective use of the old high school building after the new one was erected.

The new plan was recommended as educationally superior because it provided a special type of schooling for boys and girls during the period of adolescence, when they most urgently needed an educational transition for the intermediate period between childhood and maturity. Schools so organized were in successful operation in other countries and in many cities of this country.

Under the intermediate school plan fewer pupils drop out in the sixth, seventh, and eighth grades. They enter and are well on the way toward graduation before they reach the completion of the compulsory attendance period. They are associated with children of their own ages and their school work is adapted to their needs and abilities. Under these improved conditions a far larger proportion of them complete the course and graduate. Moreover, these schools render less difficult the problem of vocational education. By bringing children together in schools designed and organized for them, there is greater opportunity to give them insight into the problems and processes of industry through contact and participation, also to let them experiment with varied forms of manual as well as mental activity.

Should the schools be reorganized as recommended, some opposition from teachers, principals, and parents must be expected. Such opposition is inevitable and is true of every innovation. In this case, however, it would not be either serious or of long duration. It should disappear as soon as the new schools are in operation and the pride of each neighborhood in its new acquisition overcomes the opposition of those who were at first inconvenienced by the change.

Vocational Education

Throughout all the grades from the first to the eighth inclusive work was being given in manual training and domestic science, and in the high school these courses were continued on a more advanced and comprehensive basis. Nevertheless, although these courses included work in sewing, cooking, carpentry, and machine shop processes, their main purpose was not direct preparation for money-earning occupations, and so they were not, strictly speaking, vocational courses. In recent years interest in vocational education in Springfield had been rapidly and steadily growing, and the sentiment in favor of the establishment of such courses in the public school system had become increasingly insistent. The school survey devoted a considerable portion of its time and effort to study of conditions in Springfield, with the object of determining what course the city might most wisely pursue in respect to the growing demands for vocational education.

As part of the investigation, facts were gathered concerning all the thirteen-year-old children in the public schools and their families. Boys and girls of this age were chosen because it was the last year of compulsory school attendance, after which they drop out in large numbers to go to work.

In order to discover what sort of occupation young people in the city actually enter, a study of the occupations of the older brothers and sisters was made. Similarly, information concerning the fathers was compiled to discover in what groups of occupations they were engaged and also what kinds of work the city needed to have done. In all, there were data concerning 373 thirteen-year-old boys, 358 girls of the same age, 233 older brothers less than twenty-one years of age who were at work, 183 older sisters of the same age at work, and 655 fathers. These cases were not selected; they include all the thirteen-year-old children in the public schools for whom the facts could be secured.

The first data secured showed that boys and girls, upon reaching the limit of the compulsory attendance period, were scattered throughout the grades of the elementary and high schools. Nearly one-half were in the sixth grade or below, which indicated that in Springfield, as in many other cities, the problem of securing a reasonably complete elementary schooling for all the children must be solved if any successful system of vocational education is to be instituted.

Occupations of Fathers, Brothers, and Sisters

Among the fathers of the children only one in six was born in this city and only one-half the children were born here. These facts were significant because it is often urged that the schools should develop courses in vocational education that will directly prepare children to enter local industries. If present conditions continue, however, and the majority of adults do not work in the same communities in which they receive their schooling, the problem of vocational education will not be solved by narrow specialization in local industries. The aim should be rather the development of that kind of general knowledge, adaptability, and resourcefulness which will be of greatest practical use in money-earning occupations.

Analysis of the figures giving the occupations chosen by the boys and girls and those in which their brothers, sisters, and fathers were actually engaged, showed that the aspirations of the young people were for types of life work far in advance of those to which their brothers, sisters, and fathers had succeeded in attaining. The same condition maintained with respect to the kind and amount of education that the boys and girls hoped to secure as compared with that which young people in Springfield actually were securing. Fifteen of the boys wished to be civil engineers, whereas only one father was a civil engineer. Twenty-six wished to become electricians or electrical engineers, but there were only two fathers so engaged. Seventy-six of the girls wished to become teachers, while only five of their older sisters had entered that profession. Seventy-one had chosen stenography, but only 14 of their sisters had entered the occupation. Ninety-one per cent of the boys and girls stated that they intended to enter high school, but we had reason to believe that probably less than 45 per cent would do so. Twenty-four per cent intended to go to college, but it was probable that not more than 3 per cent, or one-eighth as many, would succeed in getting there.

If the school system is to assist young people to prepare themselves for money-earning occupations, it must carefully consider the kinds of occupations that these young people wish to enter. While steadfastly bearing in mind that thirteen-year-old boys and girls are not generally competent to foresee the life work they will eventually wish to pursue, we must remember that these choices are our best guides in determining the objectives of our courses, and that the boys are quite likely to choose the sorts of occupations in which fathers and brothers are actually engaged.

VOCATIONAL EDUCATION

A panel illustrating the recommendation that the city establish courses of preparatory industrial training in its junior and senior high schools. The recommendation included utilizing for educational purposes the work that is incidental to the maintenance of the school buildings and equipment.

The boys' agreement of choice with father's or brother's was very close indeed if we group the occupations chosen into broad industrial classifications, and a fair amount of agreement was found when we made the classifications by individual occupations. Our next step then was to analyze the specific occupations which the boys and girls said they wished to enter, and decide what was the wisest course that the schools could follow in the attempt to help each boy and girl make the best use of his or her abilities, aptitudes, and aspirations.

The choices showed that the great majority of young people desired to prepare themselves for a relatively small number of occupations. These could be classified with fair accuracy under three heads depending on whether the training required was professional, commercial or industrial in nature. The college preparatory courses of the high school already opened the gates of opportunity to those who desired to secure a professional education, while the business courses offered training for those who preferred to enter commercial activities. Again, the existing courses in the high school offered in large measure preparation for girls in the particular kinds of industrial work which most of them had chosen. This left as our largest problem that of providing vocational education for substantially half of the boys.

There were 12 occupations which we had specified as requiring industrial preparation, and in that group were included some which hardly belonged there, such as farmers and perhaps bakers. It was evident that the city could not then undertake to establish 12 separate kinds of new courses or schools to train boys for these occupations. The complexity of the undertaking and the expense which would be entailed rendered it impossible. The question then was whether or not some general industrial education could be devised which would be of real practical value.

It was the opinion of the survey that such a form of education was both possible and practical, and that it did not consist of a mere extension of the manual training work being done in the wood-working shops in the elementary schools and the carpenter shop and machine shop in the high school. The main defect of these was that their work was not real. It was made up largely of problems conceived or invented to fit into a scheme of development that existed rather in the mind of the person arranging the course than in the interests of youth or the requirements of real life.

MAKING INDUSTRIAL EDUCATION REAL

In former years young people gained their most useful education through doing the chores of the home and the farm. Here they were brought into contact with a wide range of industrial operations and they developed a most adaptable sort of skill and knowledge in the handling of materials. Today a more highly organized and specialized civilization is taking away most of these chores and with them much that is best in the training of youth.

But Springfield had chores to do within its public school system. It had buildings to be altered, painted, and repaired; systems of heating and ventilating to be installed or changed; and electric wiring for lights and bells to be put in and kept in order. The community had chores to do and these chores were of precisely the sort to make them educationally valuable. They were diversified and real, dealing with many kinds of materials and involving the application of the simpler processes of the machine and building trades. Since the community had chores to do and had boys and girls who needed to do chores, why not bring them together, why not abandon the formal teaching of series of exercises in school shops and substitute instead the doing of short pieces of real work on the school buildings and grounds under the direction of skilled journeymen artisans permanently employed by the department of education to make repairs and alterations? Indeed this plan was exactly the recommendation of the survey.

The work done should be the regular work required for the maintenance and repair of the school plant. Classes should be small—from three to five boys for each mechanic—and all attempt to fit the work into any preconceived series of exercises should be abandoned. As a practical feature of the work each portion undertaken would carry its own cost accounting sheet, and financial records of all the work done would constitute a large part of the work of the commercial courses.

The work proposed would be centered in the intermediate

schools and the senior high school. In the intermediate schools it would be required of all boys, but in the senior high school it would probably be made elective, at least in the two upper classes. As it would take the place of manual training, the budget for salaries and supplies in this subject could be applied to the new work and the balance be defrayed from the building fund without any increase of appropriations.

The plan outlined was neither complete nor exclusive, and possible extensions and variations were numerous. It might be carried on with other forms of vocational education then offered in the evening schools, and it would in no way interfere with the establishment of continuation classes for young people already at work or part-time classes for high school pupils. Some of the simpler portions of the work of the city's hospitals and children's institutions might well be undertaken by the older girls. Another form of activity might well be furnished by the making and erection of playground apparatus for school playgrounds. Other possibilities could readily be foreseen, and it is certain that still more would shortly present themselves after the plan had been put into operation.

Educational Extension

The school plant of this city represented an investment of more than $1,000,000. It was in use less than one-eighth of the time. There was little doubt that the community could profitably secure more service from these costly buildings and extensive grounds and for a greater proportion of time than they then did.

By utilizing her school buildings for lectures, club meetings, entertainments, first-aid classes, and neighborhood and parents' meetings, Springfield had already made a distinctly creditable record. There was opportunity, however, for even wider use of the school plant. The evening school work could be developed more intensively, vacation schools could be organized, and the school yards be used as playgrounds. If the city is to secure full value from her ample school grounds they should be replanned so as to devote part of their areas to grass and flowers and other parts to playgrounds and play equipment. In addition there should be one centrally located athletic field for use by high school students and for the inter-school games of the entire city.

Little was being done in the way of teaching games to the children or developing athletics for the older boys and girls. The board of education should employ a director of physical training, thoroughly versed in school athletics and playground work. He could give the teachers practical instruction in the teaching of suitable games, organize a grammar school athletic league, and have charge of summer playgrounds in school yards and park places. Furthermore, some arrangement should be made whereby well-qualified teachers could be assigned to supervise after-school play and athletics in the school grounds. For this work they should receive extra compensation on a part-time basis.

The existing co-operation between the schools and the public library needed also to be extended and more branch libraries organized in the schools. Already Springfield was in line with some 30 cities which were using their school buildings for election purposes, having used four of hers for registration and polling places. In this extended utilization of school plants the educational and civic gains are even more important than the economic one, which, however, is also a factor to be considered by the city.

In letting school buildings to outside organizations, three arrangements are increasingly recommending themselves in this regard as embodying the best policy for a board to pursue.

1. Free use of school accommodations may well be given to all educational and non-exclusive recreational and social activities under the auspices of organizations allied with the educational system.

2. The use of accommodations at cost should be afforded to private organizations actively promoting community welfare and individual culture.

3. Privileges should be let at a profit to organizations of a religious, political or industrial character under regulations which prevent damage to the property.

Regulations drawn up by the board of education covering the use of school buildings provided in effect for use under the first two classes. They might well be extended so as to include the third, both from the standpoint of the income which would result from such use and the benefits to the community which would accrue from the offering of such privileges.

IV

CARE OF MENTAL DEFECTIVES, THE INSANE, AND ALCOHOLICS[1]

An inquiry was made in Springfield into facilities for detecting mental deficiency in children of school age, and into the methods employed in dealing with those persons of subnormal mentality in the schools, courts, and community at large. Although the relation of mental deficiency to delinquency, dependence, and immorality is more serious in adult life than in childhood, the phases of the problems which present themselves during the school age are more readily manageable, and the school population constitutes practically the only group to which we have access for satisfactory investigation.

In reading this chapter a few general facts should be borne in mind. Mental deficiency, or feeble-mindedness, is lack of normal mental capacity due to defective development of the brain. Though usually the result of conditions existing at birth, it is also caused by arrest or retardation of mental development through illness or injury during early childhood.

Feeble-mindedness ranges in degree from an almost entire absence of intelligence, to that in which the defect appears only in the most exacting mental activity and which is not incompatible with ability to acquire much information. Idiots—the term for the severest types of mental defectives—are rare.

Classification of degree of defect depends upon the investigator's point of view. Educators usually prefer one based on a comparison of the "actual age" of the child with his "mental age"; that is, a comparison between the actual age of the child and the age of a "normal" child who has about the same degree of intelligence. Average mental development of normal children at different ages has been determined largely by various psycho-

[1] Summary of report on Care of Mental Defectives, the Insane, and Alcoholics in Springfield, Illinois, by Walter L. Treadway, M.D.

logical tests, the most widely used being the Binet-Simon tests. Classification based on these is as follows: Idiots, those whose mental age is not over three years; imbeciles, those whose mental age is from three to seven years; morons, those whose mental age is from eight to twelve years. Actual age is not considered. The chief faults of this classification are that it is founded upon a rather unsatisfactory conception of the normal mental development of children, and disregards the very unequal development in different mental fields of normal persons; its wide use, however, makes it valuable for purposes of comparison.

In the usual handling of children in school, allowance is made for the shortcomings of pupils of low mentality; but in later life the combination of a childish mind with adult years brings the possessor into conflict with the law and custom, also with the rules of conduct devised for persons whose minds as well as bodies are those of adults. Mental defectives are often objects of charity because of their inability to care for their present and future needs; they are delinquent because of inability to understand laws, or from lack of self-control; sexually immoral because they cannot repulse the advances of others or maintain community standards. They are thus often a menace to the peace and safety of others.

The large number of mental defectives—estimated at from 20 in each 1,000 school children to two in 1,000 of the general population—makes proper care of them especially difficult. Many others not demonstrably defective are also so affected that their progress through school is unsatisfactory and success in later life problematical. The lowest estimate of mental defectives in this country is approximately 200,000. According to the United States Census Bureau on January 1, 1910, only 20,000 of these were in institutions especially provided for them. Careful investigation at that time showed in addition that at least one-third—a total of not under 40,000—of all inmates of prisons, penitentiaries, jails, workhouses, and institutions for juvenile delinquents were mentally defective.

Since only 26 states have public institutions for mental defectives, the severer types are usually placed in state hospitals for the insane, but county almshouses in all states contain them also.

Added to the number cared for in institutions, suitable or unsuitable, probably at least 130,000 are in none, and therefore often suffer abuse themselves or prey upon others. Their presence in the community constitutes a problem which requires knowledge not only of remedial but of preventive measures for its solution.

Inherited mental deficiency—by far the most common type—is preventable in only three ways: by physically incapacitating for reproduction those capable of transmitting the condition; by segregating them for life in special institutions; or by creating a conscience in this matter which will not permit a person with such heredity to marry. The first two methods can be applied only to mental defectives; the third is, apparently, the only one which will ever be applicable to normal persons capable of transmitting a mentally defective strain.

Investigation of the methods of dealing with mental deficiency in Springfield brought about studies of the following specific problems: (1) the proportion of mental defectives in schools; (2) what procedure, if any, was in use in schools for detecting abnormal mental conditions; (3) what special training was given children incapable of using facilities designed for those of average mentality; (4) what care was given mental defectives in the community; (5) what practical plans can be adopted for securing adequate care for mental defectives in the schools and communities.

The Proportion of Mental Defectives in the School Population

The average public school attendance in Springfield during the year of the survey was 7,082—883 in the high school and 6,199 in elementary schools. In view of the impossibility in the time available to make the large number of examinations required to determine the number of mentally defective children in the public schools, only children in those groups in which nearly all mental defectives in the schools are to be found were examined in this investigation. At the time of the inquiry there were just 1,000 children whose progress through the schools had been slower than normal. This was chosen as the best group for our study, for, although irregular attendance from many causes may account for retarded progress, in most schools careful examination shows that of the children who are over-age and slow in the first eight grades, about one-eighth are mentally defective. Ordinary methods of instruction are inadequate for them.

All the pupils who were both over-age and slow in the Training, McClernand, and Iles schools, these three being regarded as typical schools, were examined. Of those in attendance in March, 1914, 3.8 per cent were mental defectives. The percentage of mental defectives in the entire school population is, however, probably less than 3.8 per cent, for the pupils in the high school were not taken into account in making the calculation. Almost invariably, the higher the grade the lower is the proportion of mentally defective pupils, because of elimination of the worst cases, accumulation in the lower grades of those who early in life reach their limit in the acquisition of knowledge, and relatively the higher death rate among older members of this group. The inference is, therefore, that inclusion of the high school pupils in the calculation would lower the total percentage.

The number of children in the three schools examined for whom instruction in special classes would have been desirable was about 7 per cent of their entire enrollment, for, in addition to the mental defectives, others were sufficiently retarded to make their placement in special classes desirable.

The findings of the school nurse who made observations in the Enos, Hay, and Edwards schools were about the same as those of the Training, McClernand, and Iles schools.

An intensive study of each mentally defective child and his home surroundings was not possible in this survey. The few data which were gathered, however, showed the presence of cases of chronic alcoholism, mental deficiency, convulsions, tuberculosis, chorea (St. Vitus' dance), and the like, in the immediate families of some of these children, and are suggestive of the relations existing between mental deficiency and social and economic problems. It was significant, however, that although some of these conditions in children are serious and not infrequently forerunners of insanity, no treatment had been provided.

Examinations made in the Home for the Friendless (maintained by private philanthropy for children under ten years) and in the Redemption Home, an institution for women, bore out the evidence obtained in the public schools.

Measures to Detect Abnormal Mental Conditions in the Schools

Up to the time of the survey, practically nothing had been done in Springfield to ascertain the prevalence of mental deficiency among the school population and its relation to retarded progress through the schools. Many Springfield teachers were familiar with the work for backward children in other cities and stood ready to welcome the establishment of special classes.

Measures for the Special Training of Children Who Were Unable to Make Use of the Facilities Designed for Those of Average Mentality

The result of our inquiry into these measures was the same as in the preceding inquiry; up to the time of the survey, practically nothing along this line had been done in the Springfield schools.

What is Being Done for the Mentally Defective in the Community?

As already indicated, the most serious problems of mental deficiency lie outside the school, for, though defectives interfere with its work, they themselves are often safer and happier in it and of less danger to the community than they will be in later life. Because compulsory attendance was poorly enforced in Illinois and the school census was unsatisfactory, it was very probable that children whose mental defects were so marked as to be recognized by their parents, were never sent to school. From 10 to 15 were withdrawn by their parents during the last school year. Nothing whatever was being done for the education, supervision, or training of these children who were deprived of the benefits and restraints of the school system.

A number of these children were among the 150 to 200 coming into the juvenile court each year charged with delinquency. In 14 cases in 1913, mental deficiency was so noticeable that the condition was mentioned in the records, but nevertheless not all these children were sent to the Lincoln State School and Colony. The fact was that neither the judge nor the probation officer either possessed the training to enable them to detect mental deficiency nor did they secure the necessary information upon which to draw sound conclusions regarding the mental condition of these children. Moreover, the court seldom had a medical examination made.

Since but a small proportion of Springfield's mentally defective children could be accommodated in the institutions specially provided for them in the state of Illinois, the others were necessarily in their homes or in unsuitable institutions. Only a small percentage of the total number were confined in institutions of any sort; and thus it is seen that a large proportion were inadequately cared for.

Plans for Securing Adequate Care for Mental Defectives in Schools and Community

The crying need of Springfield was for special-class instruction, in order that the regular classes might be relieved of the dragging pupils and that the mental defectives themselves might have the benefit of environment and instruction best suited to their particular requirements. The first step in this direction should be the employment, as supervisor of special classes, of a competent, well-trained psychologist. Each child who appears to need special instruction should be examined and classified by her, and at the same time each should undergo a careful physical examination for correctible ailments.

In general, the supervisor of special classes should be allowed to effect an organization in accordance with her own knowledge of local needs and difficulties. Some educators believe that each class for subnormals should be regarded as a diagnosis station as well as a place for special training, though others contend that a general central class should be established for diagnosis and classification, and that only after a period of observation in this class and when a fairly accurate estimate has been made of their degree of mental defect and capacity for training should children be admitted to special classes in the schools most convenient to their homes.

The former plan, with its constant inflow and outflow, prevents a hopeless attitude on the part of the pupil and gives more experience to teachers. Ordinarily, half the subnormal-class pupils return to regular classes after the correction of some physical defect or faulty mental habit. Those who return are naturally not the true defectives, for mental deficiency is not curable and the special class cannot make these defectives normal; it can only make them happier and more useful.

It is suggested that the first class of this description, containing not more than 15 pupils, be established at the Training School, if that school is continued, and that it be used both as a diagnosis and classification station for children and a special-training class for teachers. After teachers are properly developed and trained (and every effort should be made to encourage them to increase their information and experience), new classes should be formed and the supervisor then devote herself entirely to their supervision.

The following out of such a program will mean not only better instruction for the normal children and the correction of those with faulty habits of work, but it enables mentally defective children to be placed in an environment in which they are not misfits and in which they can be trained to the limits of their capacity. In some cases they will be trained for happier and more useful life in the community; in others they will be fitted for the institutional life which the state must soon provide for those children who, however long they live, can never take up the tasks and responsibilities of adult life.

An adequate school census is essential to a solution of the mental deficiency problem. It is indispensable as a basis for the enumeration of the mentally defective and to determine the relation of mental deficiency to truancy and other forms of juvenile delinquency.

The Community

The place where the greatest need was found for expert work in the diagnosis of mental deficiency was in the juvenile court. It was therefore recommended that an examination by a competent psychologist be made of all children brought before the court. If the employment of a psychologist for this specific work is impossible, the court might contribute to the salary of such a person who should supervise the work of the special classes and examine cases from the juvenile court. When we remember to what extent conduct depends upon the concepts, the control, and the intelligence of the individual, it seems incredible that many thousands of children should pass through the juvenile courts of American cities every year and receive judgment affecting their entire after life without any serious attempt being made to determine their mental condition and its bearing upon the conduct which brought them into conflict with their environment.

The supervisor and all other special-class teachers should improve every opportunity to inform themselves and others on every aspect of the problem of mental deficiency by taking part in local civic and social activities in which the problem of mental deficiency plays an important part; also by observation in state institutions and by summer school study in order to secure adequate care for the mentally defective and stimulate the state to undertake preventive work.

No other factor can do so much to prevent the feeble-minded from becoming a burden and danger to others, and also help them make whatever contribution they can to the common welfare as the establishment of special classes in the public schools.

THE INSANE

It is difficult to measure the efficiency of diagnosis and treatment of mental diseases because of two factors peculiar to this class of ailments: (1) the law may have to be invoked because the patient is unaware of his needs and resists treatment; and (2) the slowly dying belief that mental diseases are essentially different from all others. The commitment laws of a community, facilities for care pending commitment and for emergency treatment, institutional provisions for committed cases, for parole, discharge, and after-care must therefore be studied in this connection.

LEGAL PROCEDURE IN COMMITMENT

A study of the Illinois commitment law showed it to be one of the least useful in the United States and not in accord with modern ideas regarding the nature of mental diseases and the needs of the insane. Commitments were being made after inquests before juries or commissions—survivals of the harsh practices of an earlier period—and no safeguards were provided for the welfare of the patients during the period of examination of mental condition or during transfer to institutions for the insane.

In 110 of the 113 cases before the Sangamon County court from January 1, 1913, to March 1, 1914, a commission sat as a board of inquest; one of the 113 was a jury case, and two were voluntary commitments. The county judge softened the rigors of the Illinois law as much as possible by making use of the commission plan of inquest and by conducting hearings in private instead of through a jury trial. He also tried to arrange the time for the hearings in such a way as to avoid the necessity of temporary detention of these patients in the county jail. In spite of his best efforts, however, during 1913, 78 persons were held in

> **THE INSANE ARE SICK**
>
> **MANY CAN BE RESTORED TO MENTAL HEALTH**
>
> **BUT**
> Springfield does not treat them
>
> **IT JAILS THEM**
>
> Insane Persons in County Jail Annex 1913
>
> | PERSONS | DAYS HELD |
> |---------|-----------|
> | 7 | 1 |
> | 27 | 2 |
> | 12 | 3 |
> | 6 | 4 |
> | 16 | 5 to 7 |
> | 6 | 8 to 11 |
> | 1 | 12 |
> | 3 | Over 20 |
>
> Many depressed persons having delusions of unworthiness confirm them when detained in jail

INSANE PERSONS IN COUNTY JAIL ANNEX
A panel showing that 78 persons in 1913 were held for a total of three hundred and fifty days or for an average of four and one-half days each. The jail was a most unsuitable place for the care of any sick persons.

the county jail annex for a total of three hundred and fifty days, or an average of four and a half days each. It is possible, at the discretion of the county physician, to keep a patient a number of weeks in this distinctly harmful environment. The practice, whether persons were held either before or after commitment, was most unfortunate, but with the erroneous views held by most people as to the nature of mental disease it was not surprising that it was being permitted.

Of course, no one can assert that the confinement of a person with mental disease in a jail is "treatment" in any sense of the word. The jail annex is a two-story building containing six cells. It is cold, dirty, and a most unsuitable place for the care of any sick persons. It is only ignorance on the part of the public of the simplest facts about mental disease that makes such a practice possible. If it were generally known, for instance, that depressed persons who have delusions of unworthiness and self-condemnation acquire confirmation of their false ideas by such a procedure it is likely that a substitute would speedily be found.

Treatment of Early Cases of Mental Disease and Those Awaiting Commitment in General Hospitals

The problem of mental disease should be attacked from the standpoint of preventive medicine. Patients still in the early stages should be treated in psychopathic hospitals or psychopathic wards of general hospitals, in order that they may not be prevented, by the humiliating and disabling legal preliminaries incident to treatment in hospitals for the insane, from seeking aid before it is too late.

At the time of the survey the general hospitals of Springfield not only were failing to make special provision for this class of sick persons but they withheld treatment if the condition was known at the time application was made. The Springfield Hospital had refused all mental cases, and St. John's Hospital would take a person suffering from mental disease only if the physician in charge of the case would employ a special nurse and assume all responsibility. Alcoholic cases were admitted under exceptional conditions. Nevertheless there were not a few patients in the yearly admissions to each of these hospitals who might have been treated with advantage in a psychopathic ward if one were provided. St. John's Hospital, with a capacity of 250 beds, had 3,800 admissions during the previous year and among these patients were 200 with some form of nervous disease. It was planned to increase the capacity of this hospital by the addition of a wing containing eight beds.

It was recommended that a small ward for each sex be set aside in the new wing of St. John's Hospital, and that no further use for this purpose be made of the county jail annex. Alcoholics and patients delirious from any cause could be cared for advantageously here. Recovery from mental disorder depends often upon a patient's being treated in a proper environment.

Institutional Provisions: Sangamon County Farm

Almshouses are manifestly unfit places for the insane; yet, in 1913, there were 19 cases in the Sangamon County Poor Farm, or 6.4 per cent of all cases of insanity in almshouses in the state, although the total population of this county is only 1.5 per cent of that of the whole state. On March 1, 1914, the number was 18, and in addition there were five others who were mentally defective. The insane patients were locked in cells at night, but during the day they were allowed the liberty of the grounds and most of them assisted in some of the work.

The facilities for the care of the insane in this county almshouse were no better or worse than those of the average institution of this type. This is equal to saying, however, that those who had the insane patients in their charge were without adequate personal training, that skilled medical supervision was lacking, and the physical condition of the almshouse was below reasonable requirements for the treatment of patients suffering from such complex disorders. While there are still a number of states which permit this condition of affairs to continue, in others, though there is no statutory prohibition, public sentiment will not tolerate such neglect, and many states have laws distinctly forbidding the care of the insane in almshouses.

To lessen the number of its insane in the county poor farm, Springfield should make determined efforts for the admittance of a fair proportion into the state hospitals. The city should at the same time strive for the enactment of laws which will require accommodation in the state hospitals of all the insane of Illinois, and ultimately for a statute absolutely prohibiting almshouse care for these patients. The installation of 20 additional beds in the Jacksonville State Hospital, estimated at the time to cost not more than $10,000, would give 20 patients the proper treatment which they have previously lacked, and would permit the demolishment of the cells being used in the basement of the Sangamon Almshouse.

THE STATE HOSPITALS

The law requires that the persons who take female patients to a state hospital must be of the same sex, exceptions being made only in the case of a husband, brother, father, or son, but it does not authorize the state hospital to send nurses for cases. The latter practice is extremely desirable, but in Illinois and in too many other states the atmosphere of trial and conviction must be carried to the very doors of the hospital in order that the ancient and mistaken conception of insanity as crime and not a disease may be adhered to. There is not the slightest necessity for a sheriff or a police officer to perform this duty, and positive harm not infrequently results.

Ordinary common-sense would tell a father not to call upon the police for aid in taking an unwilling child to a hospital. It is quite apparent that such a course would be the one best calculated to make a child resist treatment. But in the case of those whose judgment and perception are already distorted by mental disease and whose hope of recovery sometimes depends most of all upon their co-operation with the doctors and nurses in the hospital, we make use of just this measure. In several states it is expressly provided by law that nurses from the hospitals shall be sent for all cases to be transferred. Among the advantages of this practice is the fact that such nurses are often able to make valuable observations regarding the social and economic conditions of patients and their heredity.

State legislation requiring the accompaniment of patients to the Jacksonville State Hospital by nurses should be secured.

In the absence of such statute the county court or a philanthropic agency might employ nurses for this purpose.

Parole, Discharge, and After-Care

Before formal discharge, patients from state hospitals are ordinarily paroled for three months. If the patient is to be returned after that a new order of commitment is usually necessary though the judge may issue such an order upon the old verdict if he is satisfied that the patient is still insane. A discharged patient is given suitable clothing and traveling expenses not exceeding $20. Upon notice of his discharge, the county judge must enter an order restoring him to all his rights of citizenship and remove the conservator of his estate, if one has been appointed.

Any time before or after discharge or parole, the superintendent of a hospital may send a suitable person to confer with the family of a patient as to care and occupation most favorable for his continued improvement. The state provides no funds for the employment of physicians or nurses for this duty or for an effective system of after-care that could be based upon this power given the superintendent.

On March 1, 1914, there were 14 patients on parole in Springfield. The number of patients who returned to Springfield every year from the Jacksonville State Hospital was approximately 70. About 20 of these patients were considered by the hospital authorities to have recovered; about 40 had not recovered but had improved sufficiently to enable them to return to their homes; and the remaining 10 were removed by their relatives for one cause or another without any improvement having occurred. Most of these patients would be greatly benefited by some kind of well-directed help in their attempts to regain or preserve their health and to re-establish themselves in the community.

Systematic after-care work is urged. Any practical plan for undertaking after-care work in Springfield would require co-operation between the physicians of the Jacksonville State Hospital and a committee organized especially for social service in this field. A few persons willing to interest themselves in this work could very informally unite in a committee for mental hygiene and become affiliated with the Illinois Society for Mental Hygiene.[1] Such a committee should constitute the rallying point for all those who are dealing with one phase or another of mental diseases and mental deficiency in the community. It should include in its membership representatives of important agencies in Springfield, also physicians, clergymen, business men, teachers, and others who would welcome an opportunity for service in an important humanitarian field which thus far has been practically neglected. It would be especially desirable to have the county judge and the judge of the juvenile court upon the committee. A social service nurse who has had experience in an institution for the insane should be employed at once

INADEQUATE TREATMENT FOR ALCOHOLICS
Panel showing that 88 persons in 1913 were held in the jail annex for a total of four hundred and fifty days, or an average of five and one-tenth days each.

---

[1] Those interested in the subjects discussed in this chapter may secure additional information, pamphlets, etc., by writing to the National Committee for Mental Hygiene, 50 Union Square, New York City.

in order that systematic after-care work could be undertaken as the first step.

As a rule, no sooner is work of this sort begun than the urgent need is felt for a clinic to which mental cases may be referred for diagnosis or advice and to which paroled cases can be brought for examination. This need has been met in a number of places by arrangements whereby the nearest state hospital can furnish a member of the medical staff to hold such a clinic at stated intervals in a room provided for this purpose by the local general hospital or even by a school or a charitable society. In some states these clinics are held regularly in a number of towns in the vicinity of the state hospital.

This committee should not limit itself to after-care work, but should seek to be of practical service in every phase of the social and civic life of Springfield into which the problems of insanity and mental deficiency enter. Harsh features of administration of the commitment laws of Illinois could be nearly eliminated, and juvenile court and special-class work should be supported by such a committee.

Alcoholics

The institutional treatment of the alcoholic habit is an undertaking which a city the size of Springfield could hardly be expected to assume. There are in this country very few public institutions for the treatment of inebriety, and most of these, like hospitals for the insane, are conducted by the state. Illinois had not yet undertaken to provide state care for alcoholics and other inebriates. The provision of one or more state farm colonies for the treatment of inebriety had been proposed, but there was no evidence that this project was to be taken up in a practical way by the legislature. The most that a city like Springfield could do was to provide for efficient treatment of those suffering from acute alcoholic diseases.

The exact number of arrests in 1913 in which drunkenness was the direct contributing cause was not known. The records showed 726 arrests for drunkenness, 126 for drunkenness and disorderly conduct, one each for "drunkenness and fighting" and "drunkenness and threats," and two in which the charge was "drunk and demented." In all there were 856 arrests in which drunkenness was specifically charged. In addition to these there were 842 arrests for disorderly conduct, 84 for vagrancy, and 73 for begging in many of which cases drunkenness was probably the direct contributory cause.

Among so large a number of intoxicated persons there are certain to be many who are in need of immediate treatment. There was a rule that the city physician must always be called when an intoxicated person was unconscious when placed in a cell. This sound practice, complied with in many places, was imperative because of the many distressing results which followed placing unconscious persons in cells without very careful medical examination.

When the arrested person was not unconscious he was treated according to some general direction left by the city physician. Cases of delirium tremens and other forms of alcoholic delirium were sent to the county jail annex. It was reported that 88 persons arrested for alcoholism developed delirium tremens during 1913 and were treated in the annex. They were detained there a total of four hundred and fifty days, or for an average of about five days each. Three died. The recovery of the others could not be attributed very largely to the treatment received, for no nursing was provided and whether patients were up or in bed depended upon their own inclination.

The practice of confining persons with delirium tremens or with grave alcoholic diseases in the annex of the county jail is a method not in accord with the humanity and civilization of such a city as Springfield and should be abandoned. There was but one place in which the public treatment of such diseases could be carried out successfully and that was in the wards of a general hospital. The provision of a psychopathic ward in St. John's Hospital, as suggested in the part of this report relating to the insane, would make it possible to care for cases of alcoholism in accordance with the best modern methods.[1]

[1] These recommendations were made before national prohibition was adopted.

V

RECREATION IN SPRINGFIELD[1]

The Basis of Public Concern in Recreation

Cities which show the greatest development of public recreational facilities are mainly those in which the excessive delinquency of children in certain well-defined districts has called public attention to the external causes of viciousness. In these sections it had been found that the congestion of population had squeezed out the spaces and opportunities for a normal play life and steps were consequently taken to supply the deficiencies. The movement for playgrounds, thus originated, became finally a movement for all sorts of recreation facilities under public auspices. But in Springfield, up to the time of the survey, the conditions that hampered play were not conspicuously present and, as a consequence, its public conscience when these investigations were made had not been greatly burdened with recreation matters.

Nevertheless, in this city just as in other communities, there was occurring each year a great and preventable wreckage of human careers. The more spectacular tragedies—drunkenness, suicide, murder, or rape—were reported in the local press because they reached the courts. But they constituted only a fraction of the moral disasters which happen practically unnoticed in a year's time in a city like Springfield.

An immoral episode, growing out of an acquaintanceship begun at a dance hall, may not immediately plunge a young woman into public shame, yet it may be just as truly the principal cause of an irreparable breakdown in her subsequent family life. Boyish pilfering from a freight car may not result in quick arrest and yet be in reality the commencement of a career of thievery. The arrest of a mechanic for drunkenness may result in no violence to

[1] Summary of report on Recreation in Springfield, Illinois, by Lee F. Hanmer and Clarence Arthur Perry.

another's person or property, yet it may mark the end of a useful career, the beginning of a life of loafing.

The Effect of Environment

Who is to blame for the moral accidents in a community? Men and women are free moral agents, are they not? These are questions that can best be answered by reference to concrete cases. Drunkenness plays a leading rôle in most tragedies. A study of one very common set of circumstances under which intemperate habits are contracted may be illuminating.

Billiards is an extraordinarily attractive game. Scientific, unusually free from the factor of chance, it offers the player unlimited opportunities for the improvement of his ability to judge spaces, co-ordinate the muscles, and exercise persistence of endeavor. Being played indoors, by day or artificial light, the recreation afforded by billiards and pool is at all times independent of the weather, and it is an especial boon to the worker during the long winter evenings when outside sports are not so regularly available. Furthermore, these are eminently social games, drawing together persons of similar ages and tastes and allowing all the delights of jest and witticism to animate the spirits while the play is going on.

In Springfield, just as is the case in most other cities, the opportunity to play billiards was almost everywhere linked with powerful temptations to use alcoholic beverages. Of the 60 holders of billiard and pool licenses 36 also held licenses enabling them to have saloons on the same premises. Young men who frequented these pool rooms could not escape the odors from the bar room, the contagion of custom, or the compulsion of a hospitality that was none the less powerful because it took the form of alcoholic refreshment.

Obviously in the cases of young men who first enter pool and billiard rooms for the purpose of play and who gradually form habits of intemperance, there are two factors—a sad failure of will power and the influence of environment.

Springfield was working energetically through home, school, and church to inform and strengthen the wills of young people. These traditional instrumentalities which influence individual character will always be necessary to human development, and society must not only cherish them and keep them keen and effective but must increase their power in every possible way. And one such way is presented in a well-balanced scheme of public recreation.

The properly administered gymnasium, recreation center, and athletic field develop in youth the ability to meet high standards, moral and physical. Few fields of action in times of peace afford such relentless trials of a youth's soul as does the field of sport. It is here that he gains a self-control, a character bulwark that will support him in all the stresses of life.

In the case of the billiard room habitué, the pulling power of the saloon was also a factor in his downfall. So that after society has done everything possible to strengthen moral stamina only half its task is done. It still has obligations concerning the surroundings in which human beings work and play. "Safety First" is the motto in every up-to-date factory. If corporations have found it profitable to safeguard their employes in all possible ways, how much clearer is the obligation resting upon society to safeguard its members from the more masked and less immediate perils lurking in the surroundings of otherwise wholesome amusements.

Intemperance Not the Only Evil

The temptation to intemperance is not the only evil in the surroundings of the average commercially managed billiard room. Often gambling operations hover in the proximity, and sometimes the brothel is not far away.

To thousands of Springfield's young people dancing was a perfectly normal mode of social life, and the only feasible opportunity they had for enjoying it was surrounded by moral pitfalls of the most dangerous and insidious character. Take, for instance, the local public dance where pass-out checks were given to patrons, enabling them to visit neighboring saloons during the progress of the evening's program as often as they desired. The young women in attendance here might not only dance with partners who had been drinking, but, since introductions were not customarily required, the young women at any time might receive invitations from persons regarding whose irresponsible character and vicious habits they were absolutely ignorant.

RECREATION

Municipal Amusements

The only way whereby a municipality can escape blame for many of the catastrophes which have their beginnings in moral pitfalls of such dangerous character is to offer adequate opportunities for the pursuit of proper pleasures in surroundings free from contaminating influences. Milwaukee, for example, at the time of the survey had placed 25 of the finest type of pool and billiard tables in its public school buildings. Social dancing for young and old was also taking place in over two hundred school houses scattered throughout the country. Today this number has greatly increased.

Someone may say, "If billiard playing and social dancing contribute to the downfall of young people, why afford opportunities for them in public school houses? Why permit them to exist at all?"

Those who have given careful thought to these matters, however, are not at all convinced that they should be banished, even if it were possible to do so. The feeling is rather that it is wrong and unfair to the young people to allow so many of the intrinsically fine enjoyments of life to be associated with evil. Why not provide them so abundantly in irreproachable settings that they will automatically lose all their usefulness to the selfish and malign agencies now employing them as mere enticements?

A Dangerous Defect in City Life

The corrupt amusement resort, however, is only one of many environmental sources of evil found in the uncongested city. Back yards may be ever so ample, the parks easily accessible and equipped for play, and the woods not far off, and yet the scheme of life of the city be utterly devoid of one of the main necessities of a healthy boy's existence.

Records of the juvenile court show how a boy's natural love of adventure finds expression in wild deeds and dangerous exploits if undirected and misunderstood. Are attempts to wreck a train, hold-ups by knickerbocker bandits, petty thieving, and arson merely examples of juvenile depravity, or are they often blind imitations of the exploits of heroes in paper-covered thrillers and motion pictures?

Often such deeds display, on the part of the boy, physical courage, initiative, and ability to follow boldly and directly a course of action. They are the qualities of the huntsman, the trapper, the explorer, the pioneer, all reinforced and covered by the irrepressible urge to hasten the process of growing up by anticipating the acts of the grown-ups. A boy without these qualities would be as backward as a race whose early members had shown no disposition to rove, to extend their hunting territory, or settle new lands.

A study of the free, everyday acts of boys shows that their fondness of the incidents of primitive life is not confined to their addiction to dime novels and Wild West shows. During the course of this survey some 1,100 boys, ranging mainly from nine to fifteen years of age, wrote school essays upon "All the Things I Did Last Week," the week in question being one of vacation. Boys to the number of 134 reported such activities as these: made tents, shacks, log huts, or tree houses; camped out all night; cooked over outdoor fire; made and sailed rafts; played cowboys and Indians, civil war and "Robinson Crusoe"; imitated the field telephone men and played "Boy Scouts." How many more wanted to do similar things but were prevented by home tasks belonging to the house-cleaning period, can only be conjectured.

How to Meet It

Fortunately for the future of American boyhood an organization has been formed whose activities afford to an unhoped-for degree a full, as well as wholesome, outlet for these early instincts. In the hike, the woodcraft, wig-wagging and wireless telegraphy, first care of wounded, and the many other ways of matching wits against nature involved in frontier life, the Boy Scout finds the kind of expression that his primitive soul craves. The code of courtesy changes him from a brigand into a knight-errant without loss of zest. While the sanitary campaigns, street duty on parade, and other civic exercises all combine to prepare him for responsible, co-operative citizenship, at the same time they satisfy his impetuous desire to do the kinds of things adults do.

The Camp Fire Girls organization plays a similar rôle in the girl's life. Until this institution was developed people had forgotten that during the long ages while man roamed the hills in search of game, woman kept the fire burning in the hut, and her muscles and nervous system still respond emotionally to those primeval activities just as his do. They did not appreciate the necessity of having, in the midst of our changing home life, rites and ceremonies which would somehow preserve the romance and satisfaction of woman's age-long activities, and transplant them, not too precipitously, to the work of her new and larger place in the community scheme.

Recreation and Self-Realization

In every community there are individuals who possess latent abilities of a special order which, through lack of opportunity, they are prevented from exercising. There are young men with talents for drawing, for invention, for mimicry, for organization, who need only the privileges of a studio, a laboratory, a stage society, or a civic club to achieve distinction for themselves and their locality. There are girls with undiscovered voices, hidden social abilities, leanings toward letters, or a special taste for interior decoration which will be revealed to themselves and to their friends by the stimulus of a chorus, the management of a reception, a dramatic competition, or the dressing of a stage for amateur theatricals. Indeed, there are few individuals without some special qualification whose employment means personal success, whose denial spells lifelong failure. Since exercising special abilities is ordinarily play for their possessor, it frequently happens that enabling an adult to play is enabling him to keep on growing.

The extension of such cultural opportunities to the public in general constitutes one of the most important phases of the recreation movement. Modern school buildings—and to a lesser degree, park field houses—contain meeting rooms, auditoriums, stages, pianos, shops, laboratories, drawing rooms, and gymnasiums, wherein a wide range of cultural activities can be carried on. School houses can be made available for all the purposes mentioned above by employing special staffs to come on after the academic force has retired for the day. To establish social centers means to inaugurate a line of municipal action that tends not only to remove the waste of crime but to give that enrichment to community life which comes only through the complete self-realization of its individual members.

Community Art and Recreation

Proof of the close relationship between public recreation and community art is already remarkably abundant. Through playground work, folk and esthetic dancing have been given a permanent place in American life; while the annual play festival has developed an increasing demand for fantastic, picturesque, and historical representations in parades and outdoor scenes. In several cities beautiful, immense, epoch-making pageants have been presented, which grew obviously out of the advanced forms of play life that have been promoted by the municipality. In a less conspicuous but more widely extended way a vast amount of stimulation to musicians, dramatic clubs, artists, and art groups of all sorts has been given by the opening of public school buildings after class hours for diverting, cultural, and social occasions. Any city which wishes to lay the foundations for a broad community art development will achieve the greatest progress by first establishing a generous, far-reaching system of public recreation.

The Homes

Springfield, when we visited it, was, and still is, a city of homes. Its population is not only well distributed but the number of people per acre is comparatively low. People live for the most part in detached houses with yards and, in some cases, gardens. This means for the majority, at least, opportunity for home recreations ranging all the way from children's games, both indoor and outdoor, to social functions in the home and lawn parties, tennis, and croquet.

The great need was resources—a knowledge of things to do. Here appeared a serious gap in Springfield's recreation equipment. The essays previously mentioned, written by 2,275 grammar school children of the fifth, sixth, seventh, and eighth grades on "All the Things I Did Last Week" (Easter vacation), gave striking evidence of the dearth of proper resources for play.

The only activity that engaged the attention of any considerable number of boys was baseball (71 per cent). The only activities reported by over 20 per cent of the boys were baseball, motion-picture shows, reading, and kite flying; while the old standard games that American boys have been brought up on, such as prisoners' base, leapfrog, blind man's buff, bull in the ring, hare and hound, and duck on the rock, were reported as played by less than half of 1 per cent of the grammar school boys. Most of these standard games were mentioned by only one-tenth of 1 per cent, or about one boy in a thousand.

In the case of the girls, motion-picture shows, jumping the rope, roller skating, and hide and seek were the four most popular forms of recreation. The standard games that should bring girls together in safe, happy, co-operative play, such as I spy, London bridge, fox and geese, button button, and blind man's buff, were at the bottom of the list, indicating that they were played by comparatively few girls.

While the survey was in progress the children were observed during the play periods on the school grounds. With the exception of baseball and tag they seemed in most cases to be sadly lacking in knowledge of what to do. The boys ran about, tripping, pulling, and pommeling one another, and the girls amused themselves by standing about in small groups or playing an improvised tag game which consisted chiefly of chasing one another and screaming.

A remedy for this would of course be the teaching of games to children during the play period and of selecting these games in such a way that they might be used both on the school grounds and in the home yards. A few of the schools were already doing this in a limited way, but it needed to be extended to all the schools, for no child should be long in the public schools without knowing a good number of the standard playground games.

The responsibility does not, however, rest solely with the schools. Parents must give careful thought to plans for making their homes attractive to the children by providing opportunities and facilities for play and social life. It may not be conducive to comfort and quiet to have the neighbors' children playing in your back yard and to have your house used for neighborhood parties of various sorts; but young people are bound to come together somewhere, and if the home or the school or the church does not afford this opportunity the public amusement resorts will certainly have their patronage.

The Schools as Social Centers

During the months of February, March, and April of 1914, 26 evening entertainments, lectures, or social gatherings were reported to have occurred in the public school houses of Springfield. Only 11 out of its 20 school edifices, however, were used during this period for these purposes. Spread out among all the buildings this would make an average rate of about four occasions per building for the whole school year. Once every nine or ten weeks, then, the school house here played a part in the recreational life of its neighborhood.

How did Springfield, in this respect, compare with other cities? What amount of use for leisure time purposes constituted the prevailing standard? The truth is no one can answer these questions because school officials generally have not yet begun to record systematically the evening entertainments or meetings held in the edifices under their charge. In over two hundred American cities, however, outcroppings of the social center idea were then manifesting themselves in various sorts of evening activities.

At the same time nearly one-tenth of New York City's public schools were being used as recreation centers six evenings a week from October to April, while many others were used one or two nights a week for public lectures, night classes, and various other purposes. Chicago, nearby, was utilizing 24 schools two nights a week as social centers, while in others there were evening classes, political meetings, and miscellaneous activities.

Allentown, Pennsylvania, a city of the same size as Springfield, had two school centers, open three nights a week through the winter, which were managed by the local playground association with some support also from the school board. Duluth, Minnesota; Superior, Wisconsin; Youngstown, Ohio; and the New Jersey cities of Bayonne, Elizabeth, Hoboken, and Passaic—places ranging from 40,000 to 80,000 in population—were other municipalities which had social centers in certain of their schools.

Springfield, not having any schools which were actually known as live social centers, could not claim a position among these leaders.

A first step feasible in Springfield and recommended by the survey, was that of opening every school house two nights a week. It could be achieved simply by following the policy the board of education had already wisely initiated; the policy, that is, of encouraging the formation of voluntary associations to work in co-operation with the schools. There could and should be a mothers' club, or some other form of parent-teacher organization, as well as a neighborhood improvement association connected with each of the elementary schools of the city. At the time, only about a dozen schools had the help of such bodies, and in many of these the work was done mainly by the principals and teachers. Neighborhood organizations of this kind can easily foster such activities as popular choruses, basket-ball tournaments, folk dancing and indoor athletic activities, maintain reading and quiet game rooms, promote young people's clubs of all sorts—dramatic, debating, literary, social, civic and handicrafts—and hold motion-picture shows and social dances.

The administration of social center activities should be directed, stimulated, and supervised from the superintendent's office, working directly through the principals, and in certain matters, through the physical training department. Principals should regard the development of neighborhood organizations as part of their duties, but their aim should be to get the neighborhood increasingly to assume the load in the social center work, their function being to steer the activities rather than to do the actual work of carrying them on.

Social Center Equipment

The survey pointed out that the board of education could do a great deal to facilitate social center work by making a few inexpensive alterations in various rooms and adding the proper equipment. Practically all the schools had basement rooms that were suitable for games, reading, club meetings, or some other recreative purpose. Several class rooms in each building could be made available for evening social purposes by taking out the fixed desks and seats and installing movable furniture. Every school should be provided with an assembly room as soon as possible. Besides the regular school purposes such rooms serve for indoor baseball and basketball, dancing, motion-picture and dramatic performances, and all sorts of evening occasions. Any city that wants to do so can provide these accommodations for the use of its citizens.

The High School

On April 6, 1914, at the request of the survey, the students of the Springfield High School furnished detailed information regarding their outside amusements. The total number of cards filled out by the boys was 398; by the girls 459. The results may be summarized as follows:

1. Practically all the high school students attended the movies.
2. Of the boys, 86 per cent, and of the girls, 84 per cent, attended the theater. The boys who attended averaged about once a week and the girls went almost as frequently.
3. The majority of the visits to the theater were not made, in the case of either sex, with any other member of the family.
4. Social dancing was indulged in by 40 per cent of the boys and 48 per cent of the girls. A large number of the dances they attended were held in hotels.
5. In 61 per cent of the boys' homes and in 48 per cent of the girls' homes, parties for young people were seldom held.

Because the high school authorities had discouraged dancing in the high schools, the young people were holding many of their parties in hotels. The parents of Springfield may well ask themselves whether it is a desirable thing for any large number of young people to be forming the habit of dancing in places where open bars were not far distant and where the environment permitted unusual freedom. In view of the general tendency to hold social affairs outside the home is it not incumbent upon the high school authorities to formulate and carry out a positive and constructive policy regarding the social and recreational life of the high school students?

School Yards

Few cities have school yards that can compare in area with those of Springfield. The average size per school, exclusive of

Pryor, was 101,519 square feet, or 2.33 acres. The gross area for the 19 schools was 1,928,868 square feet, or 44.3 acres. The total free space for these schools, 1,727,146 square feet, or 231 square feet per pupil for the entire city. The school with the largest amount of open space was Enos, with 259,470 square feet, or 541 square feet per pupil. The smallest was the Teachers' Training School, with 23,199 square feet, or 100 square feet per pupil. This was ample to give space for a great variety of school-yard games and still allow certain areas to be set aside for flowers, shrubs, grass, and trees.

The surfacing in most of the school yards was very poor; few had good sod covering, and the play areas in practically all of them were muddy in bad weather and dusty in dry times. In order to utilize the school-yard space adequately, steps needed to be taken to develop good sods and to resurface certain spaces that were being used intensively for play.

Provision should be made at each school for the free use of these grounds by placing a teacher or some competent person in charge after school hours and on Saturday afternoons throughout the entire school year. When storms prevent outdoor activities, the playrooms in the basement could be used. Here were facilities that would have largely met the recreation needs of the children of grammar school age, if only a small amount of supervision and leadership had been provided. Only nine of the 20 public schools in the city had any playground equipment, and this in every case was limited. Although with good play leadership it is possible to carry on play activities without extensive equipment, it is highly desirable that a few good pieces, such as seesaws, swings, slides, giant strides, volley ball outfits, and goals for basketball and soccer football be provided. This equipment should be so constructed that it may be taken down and stored or locked as it stands when the play leader is not on the grounds.

Athletics in the high school were exceptionally well managed by an athletic association which had a governing board of faculty members and students. But the school labored under a great handicap in having no athletic field or gymnasium. There should be at least one large school athletic field centrally located where the high school students could practise and where inter-school tournaments and meets of all kinds could be held. Athletics for grammar school boys were practically unorganized. Springfield needs a director of physical training and play who will take the lead in organizing a grammar school athletic league and give such help as is needed in the high school athletics.

There were practically no athletics for the girls either in the high or elementary schools, except that the school board had an arrangement with the Young Women's Christian Association for taking groups of high school girls at stated times for gymnastics and games. Athletic activities properly selected to meet their needs should be made possible for the girls as well as for the boys. This should be a part of the task assigned to the director of physical training.

The Parks

Few cities have more beautiful parks than Springfield, and the park board had still higher standards toward which it was working. The total area of the nine parks was 446.5 acres, or one acre of public park for every 131 inhabitants.

Unusually fine field houses, open during the entire year, had been provided in Lincoln and Washington parks, which served not only for the accommodation of picnic parties but for evening social occasions of various kinds. A new park site had been secured in the eastern part of the city and was to be developed as a model playground for children.

In many ways the park board was improving and extending its facilities. It was looking to the school authorities, however, to provide play leadership on its equipped play spaces and athletic fields, for this work is regarded primarily as educational. Here was a splendid opportunity for team work between the park board and the school board; one providing the space and equipment, the other promoting the use of the parks by the public, organizing play leadership, and supervising recreational activities.

The Streets as Play Places

With its ample school grounds, park spaces, and home grounds, Springfield was not facing the necessity of the use of its streets for recreation. Since, however, the school grounds were closed after school hours and school buildings practically unused for recreational and social purposes, young people were forced to resort to the streets and commercial amusement places for their afternoon and evening recreations.

On a perfectly normal evening, two investigators standing at

CHILDREN'S CORNER IN WASHINGTON PARK

Few American cities had more beautiful parks or more acres of park space per inhabitant than Springfield, and the park board had still higher standards toward which it was working.

the corner of Fifth and Monroe streets for a space of thirty minutes (7:45 to 8:15 o'clock) counted 462 girls and 813 boys, a total of 1,275 young people passing that point in the few minutes indicated. No city can afford to have its young people spending their evenings in this manner. The provision of adequate recreational facilities will not only lessen the dangers of the downtown streets but will be a positive aid to culture and right living.

The Library

The Lincoln Library is centrally located, and from the standpoint of the traditional hours open to the public was apparently rendering a satisfactory service. It was conducting important extension work in connection with the schools and with several industrial plants, and was making a special effort to offer immigrants books in their own language. It had a children's room and special attention was given to their needs, although a trained story teller would have been a desirable addition to the library staff.

The fact that no records had been kept of the use of the children's department and the meeting rooms in the basement, made it difficult to analyze the full service rendered. Undoubtedly, closing the library at nine o'clock mitigated the wider use of its accommodations. It was recommended that the board of directors consider the advisability of a later closing hour, especially on club meeting nights.

The Museum

Springfield had an unusual resource for recreation education in the State Museum of Natural History. Although inadequately housed and further handicapped by insufficient funds, the museum under its able curator, Dr. A. R. Crook, offered to the people of Springfield facilities for most enjoyable and profitable use of free time.

Semi-Public Institutions

Of all the elements of a city's recreation, that afforded by private organizations, church societies, clubs, and social groups offers the least occasion for community concern. The coming together of individuals for social meetings, entertainments, card parties, dances, or amateur theatricals should be facilitated as part of every recreational program.

There is danger, however, that certain members of the community will abuse the privileges of free social intercourse. Instances in point were the so-called "athletic shows" and "dances," which in reality were prize fights, given mainly for profit and forbidden by law in Illinois. While it is to be expected that the police will prevent such violations of the law, individuals may do their part by refusing to participate in unwholesome kinds of entertainment and by providing for the community wholesome amusements and athletics.

Young Men's and Young Women's Christian Association

At the time of the recreation survey the Young Men's Christian Association was not in a satisfactory condition. Owing to a series of unfortunate circumstances, the support of the work had fallen off and public interest was at a low ebb. It is a source of satisfaction to report that the entire work was later reorganized, the building made attractive, and a competent staff of workers employed.

The Young Women's Christian Association was doing excellent community work and deserved substantial support. It was well housed and maintained an effective program. Camp Fire Girls had been organized under its auspices, and classes of high school girls were using the association building for physical training and games. Mixed social entertainments were frequently held in the building, and young women were permitted to meet their escorts in the parlors of the association.

The Churches

In many communities the churches have done pioneer work in establishing recreational opportunities for young people. Springfield churches, however, have not been especially active in this branch of social service. Aside from the traditional social and society meetings the churches were making little effort to provide for the social and recreational life of boys and girls.

When some of the recreation survey findings with reference to the conditions surrounding the young people of the city in their search for evening amusement were brought to the attention of certain of the leading pastors, steps were at once taken to deal in a preventive way, at least, with the situation. One result was the stimulating of a public inquiry into the conduct of one of the local amusement places with the result that measures for its regulation and control were put into operation. Another outcome was action that led to the removal of the red lights and the names on the doors in the "red light" district—the section that had been a conspicuously glaring insult to the decency of Springfield's citizenship for some time.

For these and other efforts to suppress evil the churches of the city should be given credit, but regulation and prohibition will be effective only if accompanied, as already pointed out, by positive action in providing right facilities for recreation. The churches of Springfield have a great opportunity to take the leadership in bringing public opinion to the point where it will demand that adequate provision be made for properly equipped and supervised playgrounds, athletic fields, and recreation centers for the youth of the city.

Commercial Amusements: Motion Pictures

In March, 1914, when the recreation survey was made, 10 motion-picture theaters, with a total of 3,232 seats, were in operation. Since the daily patronage was estimated at about twice the seating capacity, it will be seen that large numbers of people were enjoying this form of amusement. The character of the motion-picture entertainments was of average wholesomeness, and general conditions of ventilation, cleanliness, and safety were fairly satisfactory. It would be well, however, if some legal provision were made with a view to determining whether or not the moral and sanitary conditions required before licensing are afterward maintained. Some co-operation between the city authorities and the National Board of Censorship (now the National Board of Review of Motion Pictures) was also recommended.

Theaters

There were four theaters in Springfield, known as the Majestic, Gaiety, Empire, and Chatterton. Two of these were offering vaudeville performances three times daily; the third, burlesque nightly, while the fourth offered a varied program, including drama, comedy, vaudeville, musical comedy, burlesque, wrestling matches, and motion pictures. The combined seating capacity of these theaters was about three thousand. A conservative estimate would place their combined weekly receipts at about $4,000 during the regular season. The citizens of Springfield were thus spending about $6,000 a week upon motion pictures and theater performances.

In Springfield's least pretentious theater the visitor could pay either 10 cents or 25 cents for admission. The higher price admitted him to the gallery where were scores of boxes provided with tables and chairs. Women of questionable character offered to drink with visitors and received commissions on the liquors sold. The performances often exceeded the limits of decency and propriety. Thus night after night, men were surrounded by the temptation to excessive drinking and immorality, and thousands of country youths were being led into such an environment by an innocent desire to see the "shows" of the city.

While the bulk of the theatrical performances attended by Springfield citizens were fairly clean and wholesome, and any attempt at smuttiness or rawness on the stage was generally hissed by the audience, the theatrical life of the city was not a thing of which to be proud. A constructive effort like that of the Women's Club in bringing the Irish Players to Springfield is a step in the right direction. It might well be followed by systematic organization of patronage for high-grade dramatic offerings in accordance with the plan of the National Drama League. At the same time endeavors should be made to develop amateur theatricals at school social centers and other educational institutions, with a view to stimulating among young people generally such an appreciation of good drama that they will not be satisfied with performances of low and unrefined quality.

Dancing

There was, in Springfield, a large amount of uncontrolled and unsupervised dancing, and much of it carried on under conditions which might easily have been abused. Although there were only two licensed dance halls when the survey was made, dancing academies, public balls, hotel and club dances gave ample opportunity for this form of recreation. In many cases dance halls were near saloons, and pass-out checks afforded ample opportunity for drinking.

The city had no ordinances or police regulations on the subject of dance halls. It has been a police custom to oblige dance hall licensees to have a uniformed policeman in attendance so that very young girls and prostitutes might be kept out, but this did not apply to balls and parties given in the other halls.

A definite policy concerning public dancing should be formulated and put into effect. This should provide opportunities for young people to dance under proper conditions. A city ordinance should also be passed prohibiting the giving of pass-out checks or the holding of dances in halls connected with a bar (whatever the probabilities as to effective national prohibition may be), specifying the ages of those who may be admitted, and otherwise providing for the maintenance of order and decency at the public dances.

BILLIARDS, POOL ROOMS, AND SALOONS

According to the records in the city clerk's office, billiard and pool licenses were issued for 1914 to 60 persons. The total amount they paid into the city treasury was $1,293.65, and the number of tables covered by these licenses was 140. According to the record of the saloon licenses in force during the first half of 1914, 42 of these pool-room licensees also ran saloons on the same premises. More than half of the pool rooms were inside the saloon district, a district in the center of the city six blocks wide by nine blocks long. Accordingly the young men in the outskirts of the city who wished to play pool had usually to go downtown for their evening games where all of the attractions of Springfield's night life were in full swing. The temptations which surround the young man who wishes to play billiards or pool have been described on a previous page. The recommendation made by the survey was that the public-spirited people of Springfield might well begin to think of ways and means of placing this attractive and excellent game in surroundings where it can be enjoyed without exposure to moral hazards.

There were at the time of the recreational investigation,

220 licensed saloons in Springfield. Of these 111 were outside the saloon district in the center of the city. In 1908 an ordinance was passed providing that no further licenses outside the saloon district be given. For the fiscal year, beginning July, 1914, it was reported that there were 198 saloons in the city, 22 less than the preceding year. The referendum on the saloon question in the spring election of 1914 showed two things; first, the tenacity of the institution, and second, the fact that a large element in the population was seriously questioning the wisdom of allowing the saloon to exist. This thinking about the saloon question was a hopeful sign, but the solution of the problem, it was pointed out, is not to be found in a merely negative and sudden denial of the right to sell alcoholic beverages. Constructive as well as prohibitive plans must be worked out. If the institution is to be permanently undermined, and what is more important, if the citizens of Springfield, young and old, are to be given the opportunity to enjoy a social life that is character-building and that meets deep-rooted human needs, another institution, which will perform any useful function that may have been found in the saloon and at the same time be free from its objectionable features, must be set up in the community.

Athletics, Festivals, Pageants, and Public Celebrations

With its extensive park spaces and state fair grounds available for all forms of outdoor athletics, Springfield has an opportunity to do great things for its youth. No investment would yield the city greater returns than that of getting every young man actively interested in some branch of athletics.

There should be a great municipal athletic league, promoted and guided by public-spirited citizens. An unusual number of Springfield's industrial establishments had already organized baseball teams that operated through an informal federation. This might serve as a nucleus around which to build. Track and field athletics deserve even greater attention than team games, however, since they afford greater opportunity for extensive participation. A great municipal athletic field with dressing rooms, showers, and a large indoor swimming pool is an objective toward which the city might well work.

The play festival of the Teachers' Training School in May of the year of the survey was a good illustration of what might be done to enrich the play life of the city by festivals and outdoor celebrations. A pageant in which hundreds of people could participate, picturing dramatically the history and development of Springfield, would be a great means of inspiring and quickening public spirit toward substantial forward movements. Springfield might also consider plans for more extensive celebrations of public holidays.

A Recreation Program for the Future

"Work, play, love, and worship" are set down as the chief essentials in a human being's existence, by Dr. Richard C. Cabot in his recent book, What Men Live By. That the country at large is awakening to a realization of this vital importance of play is evidenced by the fact that since 1907 the American cities that provided, equipped, and supervised play and recreation centers had increased, up to the time of the survey, from 40 to 342. Play leaders and supervisors employed in these cities totaled 6,318,—2,462 men and 3,856 women. Springfield was not in that list.

A city-wide recreation program ought to take into consideration:

1. Home recreation and its supplementary aids.
2. School playgrounds for recess, after school, and summer use.
3. Athletic fields for school children, both as part of the school yards and as separate grounds.
4. Playgrounds for small children located in sections that are from one-third to one-half mile distant from school playgrounds.
5. School buildings, field houses, and public halls that may be used as evening recreation and social centers.
6. Parks, with large informally developed areas, as well as spaces for golf, tennis, baseball, track and field athletics, children's play, bathing, wading, and skating.
7. Semi-public institutions, such as a Young Men's Christian Association, church houses, clubs, and the like, that may serve special groups and on occasion be for public use.

8. Commercial amusements such as amusement parks, dance halls, skating rinks, bowling alleys, motion-picture shows, and theaters, that may well serve some of the community's recreation needs if properly regulated and controlled.

With the local conditions in mind, those described in full in the report of which this is a summary, the following plan of procedure was recommended:

1. Equip and use school yards and some park spaces for play.
2. Provide for a centrally located athletic field for the schools.
3. Place the administration of all playground and school athletic activities in charge of the director of physical training and play.
4. Teach games for playground and home yard use at play periods on school yards and other public playgrounds.
5. Remodel and equip school buildings for social center uses.
6. Provide for administration of social centers through additions to the staff of the superintendent of schools.
7. Encourage the co-operation of neighborhood organizations in the direction and support of the school house centers.
8. Organize school athletic leagues for both boys and girls, thus insuring proper supervision of such activities and adaptation of exercises to the needs of the different age and sex groups.
9. Have a standing city committee on holiday celebrations.
10. Organize a municipal athletic league for the young men of the city.
11. Provide for the extension of Boy Scouts and Camp Fire Girls.
12. See that there is proper inspection and control of the commercial amusements of the city.
13. Have a representative city committee on recreation to be responsible for a progressive and balanced development of all parts of the city-wide recreation program.
14. Do not attempt to do it all the first year. Make a beginning and work steadily toward the ultimate plan.

It would, to repeat, be impracticable to attempt to put into effect at once all the recommendations here made. The thought is rather that the recreation program here suggested (and presented in more detail in the full report), be considered as an ideal toward which to work. Few cities seemed to the survey members to have a better prospect of attaining such an ideal than has Springfield.

VI
HOUSING IN SPRINGFIELD[1]

The problem of good housing in Springfield, as it presented itself to the survey, was largely one of maintaining the general conditions prevailing at the time of our investigations—that is, the keeping of the single family house surrounded by good yards and lawns; preventing the increase of the multiple dwelling and the tenement-converted house which were appearing in several parts of town; and the enactment of an adequate housing code with the means to enforce it.

Unhampered by natural barriers, such as rivers or hills, or by traditions of crowding into close quarters inherited from the Old World, as is the case in some of the eastern cities, single family houses with ample yards were found to be the rule in Springfield—an advantage that once thrown away can practically never be regained. The city is surrounded on every side by the broad prairies of Illinois, and if it ever becomes overbuilt and insanitary, the inefficiency and indifference of its own people must bear the blame. Moreover, Springfield has not only these natural advantages and the experience of other cities from which to develop an intelligent, up-to-date policy for future building, but its city charter gave the municipal government fairly wide powers.

THE MULTIPLE DWELLING

Although the single family house was the rule, the modern tendency for a number of families to congregate in multiple dwellings—apartment houses, flats, or tenements—had already led here and there to the erection of new apartment houses or to the conversion to this use of houses formerly occupied by one family.

---

[1] Summary of report on Housing in Springfield, Illinois, by John Ihlder.
Because of limited time the study of housing confined itself to two main phases of the question: general housing tendencies in the city and how far the community had gone in endeavoring to control housing conditions through legislation.

While Springfield needed a few such houses for the convenience of couples without children, and of single men and women who prefer their own home, however small, to a furnished room or boarding house, the experience of other cities has shown that, unless measures are taken to check them, multiple dwellings, when once introduced into a neighborhood, eventually drive out the single family house. These dwellings may somewhat reduce housekeeping expenses and care, but in terms of home life they offer so much less than even the small cottage, that their unlimited erection should be systematically discouraged by the city authorities. It is the single family house that forms the basis of a good home and a wholesome, normal family life which presupposes children. The multiple dwelling is not built for children. A barracks becomes a mere temporary shelter; its tenants live their real life outside; they can never have the feeling for these places that people who live in a cottage have for their homes, and at best they are only poor substitutes for the individual family house with its own yard.

THE SINGLE-FAMILY HOUSE A CIVIC ASSET

It is such houses as these that form the basis of good homes and of wholesome, normal family life. Though the single-family house with a good-sized lawn was the rule in Springfield, the multiple dwelling had begun to appear.

These multiple dwellings too may become a menace to public health as well as to wholesome family life. For although the converted house usually has a yard which is shared by the various tenants, it often suffers, from a sanitary point of view, in the remodeling process. In cutting up rooms there is danger that some will be left with insufficient light and no ventilation, and that toilet and water facilities will be put in dark, inside closets and be made semi-public.

Even the new apartment houses frequently have some dark rooms. This is occasionally due to unskilful planning, occasionally to the desire of an owner to utilize every foot of land. When permitted, he is likely to build very close or up to his boundary line, trusting to his neighbor not to do likewise. Experience has proved the folly of such an assumption, for the depreciation of his property, caused by the erection of a multiple dwelling, often induces the neighbor to sell his, and then another apartment house is built, so close to the first as to shut out light and air from both houses and to increase their fire hazard.

One house was found in Springfield which came so near to the boundary of the lot that the builder had no space for an outside stairway in the rear. On one side was a vacant lot on which the accommodating owner permitted the tenants to place their garbage cans. A direct, but none too accurate throw, was the generally accepted method of emptying garbage, as the untidy appearance of these cans and the ground around them testified. On the other side this tenement house was darkened by the proximity of the next building.

A house visited on North Seventh Street was the worst example found of fire hazard, having also dark rooms and inadequate sanitary provisions. The living quarters consisted of two two-room, and five three-room apartments. While the latter were so arranged that the two front rooms of each had windows opening on the street, the third room in the rear was, until within a short time before our investigation, entirely without light or air, except for what came through the doorways leading into it from the front rooms or from the main hall. When Dr. George Thomas Palmer was health officer of the city he required the cutting in of skylights over the division walls between each rear room and the hall. No fire-escapes of any kind were provided, the only way out to the street being a staircase at one end of the hall, which was nearly a hundred feet in length and only four in width. The rear section of the building on this same floor was used as a storeroom, and was filled with furniture still in its paper wrappings. On the storeroom side of the hallway enough space had been taken to provide a small closet for each apartment. At the time of our visit one of these closets had a *pile of ashes dumped on the wooden floor*, and the others were filled with a miscellaneous collection of rubbish. In order that nothing might be lacking to increase the fire risk the ground floor was occupied by a garage. The only sanitary conveniences afforded the eight apartments were two water closets and two sinks at the rear of the two short branch halls, at either end of the long hall, the darkness of which lent them their only privacy. Such a dwelling should be looked upon as discreditable to any progressive community. The city, moreover, should forbid the construction of any multiple dwelling on streets not having these dwellings at present.

WATER SUPPLY AND SEWERAGE

Springfield, however, must do more than prevent the extension of existing evils if it is to retain its reputation as a city of homes. Every enlightened community now demands that an abundant supply of pure water shall be available for its citizens, and that convenient, sanitary water closets shall be inside the houses. Progress toward this ideal in Springfield was made while Dr. Palmer was health officer. But investigations of the public health division of the survey showed that 7,530 surface wells and 7,431 privy vaults still existed in the city.[1] Moreover, these were not situated merely on the streets having no water main or sewers, but in many instances families were using well water with the water main a few feet from their doors.

Water mains and sewers should be extended as fast as buildings are put up on new streets; and within a reasonable time after their installation—say one year—the owners of all buildings on these streets should be required to connect their houses.

GARBAGE

Springfield should take another step to guard the health of its people by establishing a system of municipal garbage and refuse collecting, gauged on the needs of the whole city. Uncollected garbage is a public nuisance and becomes a factor in the city's health problem. The prime motive of the private collector is to make money. Under such a system the very districts of the city which most need attention, but are least able to pay for it, are likely to be neglected. The systematic collection of garbage and waste of all kinds must be made if a city is to be clean and wholesome. As pointed out in the government efficiency section of the survey, collections can best be made by the city authorities.[2] The

[1] Schneider, Franz, Jr.: Public Health in Springfield, Illinois, pp. 87–95. (The Springfield Survey.)

[2] Decker, D. O., and Harrison, Shelby M.: City and County Government in Springfield, Illinois, pp. 86–87. (The Springfield Survey.)

present limitation in the tax rate is the chief difficulty preventing the immediate adoption of such a plan in Springfield, but this will have to be overcome in the near future and more efficient means employed for caring for the city's refuse.

Evils in Certain Districts

As stated earlier, Springfield dwellings usually are surrounded by large open spaces. Already, however, there were a number of instances of land overcrowding. In the downtown district, naturally, were some of the worst, chiefly on those streets into which the commercial interests of the city were gradually penetrating. It is hardly practicable to limit new business blocks to one story, or to require owners to keep the upper stories of buildings vacant until they are needed for business purposes. If they are to be used as apartments, however, they should be so arranged as to afford the occupants plenty of light and air, toilet and water facilities for each family, and a safe means of egress in case of fire. The downtown section of Springfield at the time of the survey, for instance Washington Street between Seventh and Eighth streets, did not fulfil these minimum requirements for health and safety. It consisted of a solid row of buildings of two and three stories, the first floors of which were being used for shops and in many cases the upper ones for dwellings. The middle rooms of these apartments were lighted either by a skylight, as in the case of those next the roof, or by a shaft extending from the second story to the roof. Neither afforded good ventilation, as the skylights were difficult if not impossible to open, and the shafts often covered. The light coming through them was little better. One apartment, occupied by three Negroes, had its only water faucet, the underneath waste pipe of which was untrapped, in the room of a Negro girl, while two Negro men occupied the dark middle room, separated from the girl's only by a screen. Not only are such conditions a menace to health but to morals. It is the duty of the city to learn whether there are other houses with similar conditions and then to set standards which will make their continuation impossible anywhere within its borders.

Housing conditions were especially bad in the Negro district, where the buildings were more dilapidated and the water supply and sanitary provisions inadequate. For these poor accommodations the landlords were charging exorbitant rents, even more than they would charge white tenants. The Negro, limited by custom if not by law to this part of the city, was obliged to pay these rents, and could not, if he would, live decently.

Contrary to the opinion often expressed that the wretched conditions in the Negro sections of our cities are due to the char-

HOUSING AMONG THE COLORED POPULATION
Many of the houses had ample yards, but cases were numerous where landlords had not provided houses meeting even minimum recognized standards.

acter and habits of the Negroes themselves, those who have made a study of Negro housing maintain that the majority would like better homes than they can get, and that many Negro homes are cleaner and better kept than are those of several nationalities of our more recent immigration. The fact that these bad conditions prevail in other cities is no excuse for Springfield. Disease and immorality in any part of the city affect its whole life, and Springfield must force the landlords in its Negro district to conform to the minimum standards set for the whole city.

Ridgely, a settlement of miners, is an example of one of the most puzzling phases of housing work—how to exercise proper control over suburban districts that lie just outside city boundaries, but which are already a part of the city's problem and as the district grows will inevitably come under the city's jurisdiction. One of the proposals made is that certain city officials be given jurisdiction over an area extending some three or four miles beyond the city limits, in order to prevent the development there of bad conditions which must be remedied later when these areas are annexed.

The miners' rows that are set down by themselves in the open country—such as that near the smelter—were in a somewhat different category from the Ridgely houses. Mine houses, because they are often regarded as temporary and are comparatively isolated, cannot always be subjected to city regulations. They should none the less be warm and sanitary, and more attractive in appearance than were the existing bare structures.

City Planning

Springfield has apparently been created by adding one real estate development to another, without much regard as to what the result would be. The rectangular street system, which is easiest for the real estate dealer, has been followed and so planned as to get the greatest number of building lots possible out of a given tract of land, the only radials of consequence being formed by the railroads which cut up every quarter of the city except the southwest. Moreover, the unrelieved checkerboard system has not prevented the creation of a number of dead-end streets, and of numerous jogs in others, some of them important. Many residential streets also have been laid out uneconomically—with such a broad roadway as to be wasteful of land and to entail unnecessary expense for upkeep. As streets vary in their functions, so they should vary in width and arrangement.

Definite recommendations as to width and arrangements of strects, block and lot sizes, the relations of the home to parks and playgrounds, as well as to factories and the business district, and other phases of city planning that directly affect housing conditions could not be made in so brief a report as this. The facts are cited here to show the need and urge the importance of a careful study of the local situation aimed at the adoption ultimately of a city plan which will insure economic and orderly growth of a more socially efficient city.

WISE ECONOMY IN STREET MAKING

This roadway on a street in the residence section of Springfield very wisely was made narrower than that usually found in the business districts and in other sections where the traffic was heavy. The room here provided for vehicles is ample, and a saving through a lower original expense for paving and through smaller later costs for upkeep is effected.

RECOMMENDATIONS

Experience has shown that no city can expect to get or keep good housing conditions unless it has and enforces a city ordinance or a state law that sets definite minimum standards below which *no* dwelling may fall. Springfield needed first of all a good housing code,[1] for which, fortunately, it already had the basis. The responsibility for its enforcement falls upon the health department and the building inspector. The inspector must examine the plans for all new houses to see that they fulfil

[1] A publication which has served as the basis for a number of codes enacted during the last few years, and which would offer suggestions here is A Model Housing Law, by Lawrence Veiller. Russell Sage Foundation Publication, New York.

the requirements of the law, and must inspect them while in course of construction to make sure that no changes which were not authorized by him have been made.

The health department should also keep a record of the number of one-, two-, and three- or more family houses that are in the city, and how many of each are built during each year. By this means Springfield can know what its building tendencies are and whether or not it is becoming a tenement-house city.

The health department, too, should pass upon the plans at least so far as light, ventilation, and sanitation are concerned. It must then see that the buildings are maintained in a sanitary condition. This means that it must have enough inspectors to make an original inspection of nearly all the dwellings in the city at least once a year. At the time, inspections were being made in Springfield chiefly on complaint. This was neither adequate nor fair, as it will sometimes happen that a very insanitary building has no complaints made against it while a much better building, perhaps next door, is frequently complained of. Such procedure not only leads to ill feeling and charges of favoritism, if not of actual corruption, but it fails to accomplish the purpose aimed at, to effectively improve the health conditions of the community.[1]

The regular inspections should include not only privy vaults and wells—inspection of which we hope will some day cease because they no longer exist—but of water-closets and water fixtures, their locations, ventilation, adequacy, cleanliness, and construction; size, lighting, and arrangement of rooms; sizes, number, and location of windows; drainage; and in multiple

[1] In the public health section of the survey, Mr. Schneider favors concentrating the supervision of housing conditions as far as possible under the building department, since the latter must pass on all buildings when first erected and is the department most familiar with the various details of the housing law. The disagreement with Mr. Ihlder's recommendation on this point has to do only with the exclusiveness of the supervision by the building department; he would have the health department also share in the responsibility for enforcing housing regulations. In view of the strong considerations to be taken into account on both sides of the question, it would seem best to base the decision upon matters of practical expediency in each given case. In Springfield, at the time of the survey field work, the immediate considerations of expediency appeared to point toward concentration in the building department.

dwellings, size, lighting, and arrangement of public halls and the means of egress in case of fire. All these are necessary if people are to be assured of dwellings that are safe and wholesome and that provide adequately for decency and privacy.

The city government was in possession of powers of which it had not taken full advantage. Some of these were:

Section 61. To prescribe the thickness, strength, and manner of constructing brick and other buildings and constructing fire-escapes thereon.

Section 62. To set fire limits.

Section 63. To prevent dangerous construction and condition of chimneys, fireplaces, etc.; to regulate and prevent the carrying on of manufactories dangerous in causing and promoting fires.

Section 75. To declare what shall be a nuisance and to abate the same; and to impose fines upon parties who may create, continue, or suffer nuisances to exist.

Section 76. To appoint a board of health and prescribe its powers and duties.

Section 78. To do all acts, and make all regulations which may be expedient for the promotion of health or the suppression of disease.

Section 81. To direct the location and regulate the management and construction of packing houses, renderies, tallow chandleries, bone factories, soap factories, and tanneries within the limits of the city or village and within the distance of one mile without the city or village limits.

Section 82. To direct the location and regulate the use and construction of breweries, distilleries, livery stables, blacksmith shops, and foundries within the limits of the city or village.

Section 83. To prohibit any offensive or unwholesome business or establishment within, or within one mile of the limits of, the corporation.

Section 84. To compel the owner of any grocery, cellar, soap or tallow chandlery, tannery, stable, pigsty, privy, sewer, or other unwholesome or nauseous house or place to cleanse, abate, or remove the same, and to regulate the location thereof.

Sections 61, 63, 75, 76, and 78 seemed to give powers necessary for the enactment of a fairly good housing code, pending such time as the legislature may increase them or may enact a housing law for all the cities of the state. Sections 81, 82, 83, and 84 gave power sufficient to make a beginning at least on a protected residence district ordinance such as Toronto and a number of American cities have enacted, and which should form part of the housing ordinance.

Such steps as Springfield must take to bring its housing conditions up to a standard of health and safety should be easy of accomplishment. The citizens particularly interested do not need to conduct a long campaign to educate public opinion.

The housing ideals of the majority of the people of Springfield were already far above the requirements of any law, as the homes of its citizens show. This was a heartening fact and one full of promise for the future. It remained only for the community to guard itself against a few who through greed, or ignorance, or indifference, were ready to sacrifice the general well-being for a temporary personal profit. To so guard itself definite minimum housing standards needed to be set.

VII

THE CHARITIES OF SPRINGFIELD[1]

INSTITUTIONS FOR CHILDREN

Dependent children, unlike delinquents, become subjects of charity because of difficulties primarily due not to personal handicaps, but to unfortunate situations in which their parents have in some way or other become involved. They are products of ill-adjusted social and industrial conditions which, unless changed, will continue to take their toll and reduce families and children to unfortunate and abnormal dependency.

In 1863, during the Civil War, the first dependent children for whom Springfield made organized provision came straggling over from Arkansas, ragged and tired, led by a few women refugees. To meet their needs the Home for the Friendless sprang into being, and has continued ever since as the chief child-caring agency for boys and girls from babyhood up to fourteen years or more. In 1881 there was organized the Orphanage of the Holy Child, an Episcopal institution receiving needy girls between the ages of three and nine and keeping them until they became eighteen. In 1898 a colored woman started the Lincoln Colored Home, which at the time of the survey took Negro boys and girls from two to six years of age and discharged them according to opportunity. The Springfield Redemption Home, organized in 1911, took dependent children and erring girls, keeping them as long as they needed the institution. With the exception of the delinquents held temporarily in the Detention Home or the annex of the county jail, and a few scattering placements in foster homes by the Humane Society and by priests who were sending children to the Roman Catholic Orphanage at Alton, these four agencies cared for practically all the dependent children in Sangamon County.

[1] Summary of report on the Charities of Springfield, Illinois, by Francis H. McLean; assisted by Miss Florence L. Lattimore, who prepared the part dealing with institutions for children.

That child dependency was a live issue in Springfield was shown by the fact that one out of approximately every 380 inhabitants was in one or other of these institutions. In 1913, the year before the survey, there were 318 inmates and an average daily population of 140. Those in charge stated that most of these children came from Springfield itself or from the district immediately adjacent.

Information and Record Keeping

Data which were essential to a full understanding of conditions surrounding child dependency in Springfield were not only not in print but for the most part were lacking. Two of these institutions were publishing reports which stated their financial operations, the movement of population through them, and miscellaneous items concerning events during the year. The Department of Visitation of Children Placed in Family Homes of the State Board of Administration printed very valuable reports covering all the child-caring agencies in the state, with standardized tables on finances and on the movement of population classified by age and sex. It also gave classified comments on the condition and administration of the institution plants, but none of this material revealed anything concerning the problems of child dependency or the way these institutions were functioning in relation to them.

A tabulation of the financial statements of the four institutions showed that the cost of operating Springfield's institutions for one year (1913) was nearly $15,000 ($14,721). The average per capita current expenses for the year ranged from $90 to $110. The per capita expenses of standard children's institutions elsewhere ranged from $150 to $200 and over, indicating that these Springfield institutions were administered with economy—indeed, with such economy as made the highest standards of work impossible.

Some very good forms of record cards had been adopted, but the requisite information had been only meagerly filled in. The entries were so fragmentary and unsystematic as to be almost useless. Not only was this true for children coming directly to the institutions, but for some of the children placed under the permanent guardianship of these agencies by the juvenile court the institutions had no information at all, although investigations had been made by the probation officers. Sometimes an institution received a child without any knowledge of his antecedents; and without finding out his history or the changes that may have taken place in his own family during the period while the child was in the institution, the managers proceeded to place him in a foster home.

Thus the records did not reveal how many of the children were orphaned, half-orphaned, or had both parents living. It took a special search through the records for 1913 of the Home for the Friendless, made at the instance of the survey, to show that of 173 children cared for, 65, or 38 per cent, had both parents living; that 47, or 27 per cent, had mothers living; and only 16, or 9 per cent, were whole orphans. There was, however, no way of finding out why these children were dependent, what manner of children they were, how they developed under the care of the institution, or what became of them after they were discharged. Obviously, there was needed greater emphasis upon gathering adequate information on each child's case, recording it, and using the record in a program of prevention of future child dependency.

Functions of the Institutions

Although the chief function of children's institutions is the physical care of their wards, other obligations are more or less bound up with this responsibility. After searching inquiry they should limit their work strictly to those who cannot be better cared for in their own homes or in foster homes; provide those who need the institution with the specific care which the condition of the individual child calls for; and see that institutional care is not given beyond the time when the child actually requires it, but that normal life is provided, under supervision, at the earliest possible moment. Even when children go back to their own homes it is the duty of the institutions to make sure that all is well with them and that future dependency is prevented.

Admission and Discharge

Each institution had rules of its own with regard to admission and discharge. The Lincoln Colored Home took any colored child in need, whether dependent, delinquent, or defective, provided he was old enough to require no special attendance. No board money was received for these children, but the county paid the institution a lump sum for services.

While in the home those who were old enough were sent to the Lincoln School. The superintendent was discharging these children as soon as possible by returning them to their homes, by placing them in foster homes in Springfield, or by allowing them to go to work.

The Orphanage of the Holy Child received only normal dependent girls who were presumably whole orphans. It required full surrender of them by relatives and kept the girls until they were eighteen years of age. Children of divorced parents were never admitted. All children were taken free, and whatever was paid in by relatives was regarded as a contribution to the work and not as board money. This was the only one of the four institutions which did not receive public funds. The children attended public school.

The Springfield Home for the Friendless gave temporary care to dependents and sometimes took high-grade defectives from the court. Relinquishment by the parents was not required, although if the investigation showed that the parents were unfit a legal guardianship was secured. Children were often boarded in this institution by relatives or friends for $1.00 a week or $5.00 a month, or by the county at 25 cents a day. They were sent out to the Stuart School while living in the institution, but it was the policy of the managers to discharge them as soon as possible by returning them to their own homes or by placing them out; and great care was taken to avoid keeping children in the institution if other arrangements could be made.

The Springfield Redemption Home was taking only rescue cases and dependent children who would not be received elsewhere. They came voluntarily or through the courts. A charge of $50 was made for each maternity case, and if the girl had not this amount she was permitted to stay in the institution and render service as payment. Many girls were discharged through marriages arranged by the superintendent and placed as domestics in private families where they went to work with their babies.

Applicants for the Home for the Friendless were visited by two managers who gave a verbal report to the executive committee. The question was then decided by vote. In the three other institutions the investigation and decision were made by the chief executive.

For some cases a great deal of vital information was gathered by the institution authorities, and again one would find a child received on the face value of a story told at the institution by the applicant. Obviously this work was very uneven.

Although the rules covering admission and discharge differ in each institution, the same principles of investigation and treatment apply to them all. Every application for institutional care of a child necessarily involves important policies not only with regard to the child in question but also with regard to his entire family. The institution must see that even those children who are not found to be eligible and are rejected are provided for by some other means.

Dependents in the Detention Home

The Springfield Detention Home was established for delinquent children; nevertheless 42 of the children held there in the period from June, 1912 to April, 1914, practically the last two years before the survey was begun, were classed as dependents. Seven boys and four girls were held more than fifty days each; five boys were held one hundred days each. This method of housing dependent and delinquent children in the same institution, pending disposition by the court, is to be thoroughly condemned—especially when it is impossible, as was the case in the detention home, to take care of them separately. Under circumstances then prevailing, the best solution was to make arrangements for holding them temporarily in the Home for the Friendless. The rule of this institution, requiring physical examination before admission, could be met by providing special isolation rooms in which children might be kept away from the regular group until they had had this necessary examination. In this way the rule of the home requiring physical examination before admission would not be infringed upon, nor the health of children put in danger. This service would be quite within the regular functions of the home, and would relieve the unfortunate situation in which delinquent and dependent children were being held without classification in the same detention place, and the still more serious practice of detaining poor children in the county jail annex.

Finding Homes for Children

The placing-out method had always been strongly approved in Springfield, and it would have been used far more than it was if there had been a specialized local agency to develop it. Although all the institutions except the Home for the Friendless lacked facilities for placing-out work, they preferred to place the children themselves.

Of great present value and of far greater potential value was the protection given to placed-out children by the State Department of Visitation, which was organized to correct abuses reported in foster homes. The state agent said that he was sending trained workers to foster homes reported to the department at least once a year and sometimes oftener. Copies of the visitors' reports were being sent to agencies responsible for placement, and if conditions were not approved by the department the child's removal might be demanded.

Strangely enough, children returned to parents and relatives did not share the protection given to children who were placed in foster homes. Over the former the State Department of Visitation had no power. Neither did the institutions usually consider it their obligation or their right to reinvestigate families even at the time when discharge was being considered, or to supervise a child after he had returned to his own home. In discharging their full responsibilities for establishing children in wholesome family life, whether in their own homes or in those of foster parents, Springfield institutions had considerable progress yet to make.

Value of Organized Effort

Aside from the possibilities and limitations of the institutional provision for these children, even though the personal service and individual work had been of much higher standard than it was, the investigation showed time and again the importance of organized co-operation on the part of several or many social agencies in the community. In this connection a number of cases were studied in some detail. One of them showed a complex situation in which the institution tossed back into the community a source of contamination which it would not itself treat. The main details were as follows:

A certain mother put her one-year-old baby to board in the institution at $5.00 a month because, so the record ran, she "had been deserted by the father" and had no one to care for the child. Although the examining physician at the institution had thought the child all right, it was found to be diseased and was returned the day after its admission with the recommendation that it be sent to a hospital. Nothing more was known of this case at the institution.

The writer's inquiry revealed the fact that this mother was a young woman who had married a much older man living in a nearby town. They did not get on well and the wife took the baby and left for Springfield, where she hoped to get work. But nobody wanted a baby around and the young mother put the child in the institution at the rate of $1.00 a week. The next day she obtained work in a shoe factory at $5.00 a week. When she reached home that night she found that the baby had been returned by the institution because it was distressingly ill with syphilis. She appealed to the city doctor who prescribed for the baby, but it could not be received at a hospital. She tried to care for it and do her work at the same time, but this was impossible. She gave up her position at the factory and appealed to the Redemption Home, which finally took her in because the baby was badly undernourished and the mother could not nurse it and work at the same time. After an inquiry into the situation, the manager brought about a reconciliation between the husband and wife and according to latest reports all was going well, although the baby was still in a critical condition.

This case fairly bristles with opportunities for both individual and community service. The critical situation in the young woman's home, her need of advice and direction with regard to her course, the institution's acceptance of the child without definite information about the needs and possibilities of the family or a thorough physical examination of the baby, the fact that the baby was being breast fed at the time of application, that the mother was obliged to wean it in order to go to work, her acceptance of less than a living wage, the fact that there was no place in Springfield where a syphilitic baby could receive hospital treatment; all of these combated her grit and perseverance in trying to keep her child.

The case is illustrative of many others, which taken together indicated that the institutions were offering at best but a partial and often haphazard treatment for the troubles which led to application for their care of children; they showed opportunities not yet grasped—the more urgent because often exclusively theirs—which could be worked out through organized co-operation and a definite community program of child welfare.

Dependent Children Outside the Institutions

But a child welfare program should not limit itself to those children who have come to the attention of the institutions. Equal protection should be extended to others. For instance, there was conspicuous social leakage in the work of the county courts in all parts of the state which allowed children to be given out for adoption without special investigation of the motives or character of those who give and those who take. An extreme instance illustrates the point: The county court of Sangamon County gave for adoption a very young baby to a woman who belonged to a notoriously immoral family. The woman herself was in an advanced stage of tuberculosis and under treatment at the tuberculosis dispensary at the time.

Regulation of maternity homes and accurate registration of births, both of which are discussed in more detail in the chapter dealing with public health, are also matters to be included in a child welfare program.

The obvious conclusion to be drawn in this connection is that the work of the Springfield institutions, except in the Redemption Home, though it should have been more was chiefly custodial until some turn in affairs or some applicant from a would-be foster home led to a child's discharge.

Institutions as Educational Forces: The Staffs

The actual work of bringing these children who are somewhat below par in health and very much below par in education and general training up to standard is chiefly in the hands of the institution workers. Yet none of the chief executives of Springfield institutions had had such training as would enable her to handle to best advantage the difficult tasks encountered. Neither were the workers adequate in numbers, sufficiently paid, nor had they a chance to qualify for the social aspects of their duties. The Lincoln Colored Home had a colored superintendent who was receiving her living and incidental expenses but no salary; also a practical cook who was on small wages. At the Orphanage of the Holy Child the only employe was the superintendent, whose salary was nominal. The Springfield Home for the Friendless, which had the most complex administrative problem of all, employed a superintendent whose salary was entirely inadequate for such a position, three "nurses" who were in reality mere housemaids, a seamstress, mender, cook, laundress, and a man for general work.

Although the work at the Rescue Home, combining maternity and nursery care, called for highly trained workers, the staff consisted of the manager, who was the founder, an assistant, matron, kindergartner, and a non-resident man superintendent, the husband of the manager. No one of these workers was regularly salaried. Those living at the home were receiving maintenance and "pin money."

Regardless of the qualifications of these workers, the highest standards of child protection and care were quite impossible because of certain crippling defects in the buildings themselves. The Orphanage of the Holy Child, a new building, was the only one of the four institutions in which there was not undue daily risk of loss of life by fire. The danger in the Lincoln Colored Home, also new, was due not only to the arrangement of the stairway but to the fact that the institution was overcrowded. The Home for the Friendless was relying entirely upon exterior fire-escapes which, from the second to the first floor, were vertical ladders with rungs so far apart and the stop so short of the ground that little children could not safely use them. The fire dangers at the Redemption Home were due to the overcrowding of the house to such an extent that an attic, reached by a narrow stairway, had been pressed into service as a dormitory.

HEALTH PROTECTION

All the institutions, except the Redemption Home, were insisting that the children be in good health at entrance. Yet health conditions were by no means what they should have been. Certificates of examining physicians were in reality mere passports for a child's entrance and were not regarded as serious records of his physical condition or needs. Although medical service was available, children were not re-examined unless they showed signs of illness. There were no routine examinations, mental or physical, to find out how the child was developing or to catch defects in the incipient stages, and no records of conditions found. There is also obvious need of more dental work.

Standards of personal hygiene swung from the excellent equipment and careful training at the Orphanage of the Holy Child, where each girl had a bed to herself and such other facilities and supervision as are found in a well-ordered family home, to the Redemption Home, where adverse conditions of plant and overcrowding checkmated even the most determined administrative efforts made to achieve high standards; to the Lincoln Colored Home, where modern equipment was rendered inadequate and proper standards were impossible because of its overcrowding with boys and girls of such wide range in age; and to the Home for the Friendless, where defects of plant and administration combined in creating a generally unsatisfactory situation. Likewise in the question of diet and the service of food, which are such important elements in health, great extremes of standards were discovered. And all of these matters are important from an educational as well as a health point of view.

EDUCATIONAL WORK

In no respect had these institutions made educational forces of themselves. No domestic science, manual arts, or craft work had been developed. Moreover, although it was clear that many of the children were backward, and some probably defective, no reliable information on their condition, of a kind that would assist in deciding upon the special attention needed, was available.

Recreation Needs

Neither outdoor nor indoor recreational facilities were sufficiently developed in these institutions for children. Playrooms were scantily equipped and dreary; yards were small and gave no opportunity for directed play. The only exception was the Home for the Friendless, which had equipped part of its yard with swings and turning poles and had provided upstairs playrooms for its girls; but even these provisions left much to be desired before recreation facilities would measure up to what was needed.

In general, the conclusion was unescapable that the care given in these institutions was chiefly a matter of material relief rather than special work in child nurture.

Next Steps in Children's Work

The essentials in a child welfare program in any community include:

1. A properly run juvenile court with efficient probation service.
2. Provision for the temporary care of children awaiting the action of the court. Such provision may be given either in a detention home for dependent and neglected children, in one of the existing orphanages, or preferably by boarding them out with selected private families under careful supervision of a children's aid society, as in Boston.
3. A well-organized child-caring society which shall handle:
    a. Case studies.
    b. Protective work.
    c. Temporary aid for children whose parents are in temporary distress.
    d. Placing-out work with efficient supervision of children in private families.
4. A receiving home for the temporary care of children awaiting placement.
5. Hospital provision for sick children.
6. Special provision for orthopedic cases through connection

with a state orthopedic hospital or with a private institution with skilled orthopedic service.

7. Provision for the deaf and blind in state schools especially for this purpose.

8. Provision for training backward children in one or more public schools.

9. Provision in state institutions for delinquents for whom the probation system is not suitable.

The state of Illinois had already made provision for the blind, deaf, feeble-minded, and delinquents, although some of this provision was inadequate for the numbers of children needing it. The care of the sick, crippled, dependent, and neglected children was left entirely to private persons and private organizations, except when dependents were cared for by the juvenile court.

Some of the juvenile court children were, however, boarded with the private institutions. If there were a thorough classification of the children in these asylums many would be found who would be designated as preventive cases, medical cases, cases of mental deficiency, orthopedic cases, and so forth, which the Springfield institutions for children had not equipped themselves to treat.

If, following a thorough classification of these children, a redistribution were made on a basis of actual child need, it would have been discovered that much further development should be made by the state as an administrative unit. Very properly there should be state protective work for neglected children, state placing-out work, and state care in reception homes. But it will be necessary for some time to come for private agencies to initiate and to carry on the work of demonstrating and standardizing methods in child-care.

A County Child Welfare Organization Needed

The county is an exceedingly advantageous administrative unit, and the present Springfield agencies should take Sangamon County into their activities and develop themselves on a county-wide scope. There is great need of vigilance to prevent neglect of children in rural districts. Springfield of course should be the headquarters of the county.

A well-rounded county-wide organization for child welfare which would stand firmly for comprehensive and sympathetic case work and for preventive and remedial measures in community betterment was urgently needed. Such an organization should be prepared not only to do constructive work in its county but to make a thorough social, medical, and mental diagnosis of each application, and it should stand ready to supply treatment either through provision of its own or by co-operation with the resources of other existing agencies. It should initiate an up-to-date placing-out service with a department for mothers with babies—both white and colored—and a strong protective department prepared to prosecute whenever necessary. The work of this organization, however, should be closely connected with the Illinois Children's Home and Aid Society, having headquarters in Chicago, so that the county might thus co-ordinate its work with a state program and avail itself of the resources of that society in this placing-out and supervisory work.

Future Scope of Institutions

When the work for children in Sangamon County has been reorganized and adjusted, it will be discovered that the need for such an institution as the Springfield Redemption Home has fundamentally changed. Dependent children who were being cared for in that institution, without their mothers, would be placed in family homes for temporary or permanent care as the case may be; confinement work would be given over to hospitals, and after discharge, mothers with their babies would be placed out in families by the department for mothers and babies of the central organization on child welfare. It was not altogether clear that the Redemption Home could be adapted to the much needed educational work for young expectant mothers.

There was not, in a discriminating program, any social justification for an institution like the Orphanage of the Holy Child, admirably managed as that institution was. It took the kind of girls who were suited to normal homes and kept them for long years of artificial life without being in any sense an educational institution. It did not give them anything which a family home could not give, and it could not give them that essential in which a good family home excels—experience in normal human relationships.

The limited institutional activity which may still find a place in an enlightened program of child welfare, to be of best use, should be carefully worked out as to plant, equipment, and administration. The plants of the Orphanage of the Holy Child and the Lincoln Colored Home were of about the best size. They would have been much richer in opportunity if they had had sufficient grounds about them, such as surrounded the unwieldy congregate plant of the Home for the Friendless.

In developing or planning children's institutions for Springfield, homelike points should be emphasized, and barracks furniture, dark playrooms, and insanitary features must go. Each institution should provide only for those children who may not, for the time being, be better cared for in a family home. It should be kept small and be brought up to the highest efficiency in diagnostic work with sufficient and well-equipped staffs of workers, with well-planned sanitary cottages, provision for isolation of incoming and sick children, provision for medical and psychological examinations, and for efficient training of the children. Improvements should be made in the investigation work and record keeping, as well as in the interpretation of data collected so that the institutions may become not only better educational forces for such children as, after study, are found to need the care of an institution, but that they shall make themselves into educational forces aimed at removing the causes of future child dependency.

Chief executives should be chosen not only for their practical ability but for their social vision and co-operative spirit, and they should be given opportunity to experiment with new methods. Except in cases of children requiring custodial care all their lives, the institutions should regard themselves as means to an end, the end being the re-establishment of children in family life. A very important next-step toward that end is the establishment of a central organization for child welfare.

CARE OF THE SICK OUTSIDE THEIR HOMES

Among the 1,764 Springfield families which in 1913 were known to have received some kind of charitable aid outside their homes from public or semi-public agencies, there were 1,238 in which sickness was a factor in the reduced condition of the family. If we add the 11 families in which mental deficiency was a factor, and the 39 in which intemperance played a part—both of which in their treatment are to be regarded in the nature of diseases—the total reached 1,288. The importance of provision for these needs is apparent.

The City Physician

Except for the dispensary maintained by the Springfield Tuberculosis Association there was no free medical dispensary in Springfield. In lieu of this there was a city physician appointed by the county board of supervisors. His district covered the city of Springfield, and his work included also medical supervision of the county and city jails. This official, by requirement a practicing physician, was paid $100 a month. He was required to treat all sick poor who applied and was obliged to meet from his own salary the cost of all prescriptions filled.

A more unsatisfactory system could hardly be imagined. The salary was not alluring as a source of income nor did it permit the provision of the accessories needed in a well-ordered dispensary. The doctor who was city physician at the time of the survey had no classified records, no medical histories, nor even an index of cases. The list of patients treated for about seven months numbered 358. This meant too great a demand on the time and strength of one doctor and could result only in a wholesale service, with hurried examinations and admission to a hospital when it was obviously necessary.

The city should establish under its health department a free medical dispensary, which would include certain home visiting, to take over the general medical service being performed by the city physician. This dispensary should sooner or later provide for those suffering from tuberculosis. Under this plan there could be a more equitable distribution of calls for free service between members of the medical profession. The natural point at which to start a movement for this change seemed to be the Sangamon County Medical Society.

Hospital Care

Except in the children's ward of the Springfield Hospital there were no free beds in the city hospitals. Persons were received into St. John's as county charges upon the authorization of the city physician, the county paying a weekly rate of $4.00 which did not cover cost. Patients admitted as county charges became patients of the city physician regardless of what physicians had been treating them in their homes. In 1913 the city physician, without official assistance, was responsible for 557 patients—a burden altogether impossible for one man to carry to the satisfaction either of himself or those in need of help.

This system, with neither dispensary nor free beds, with too many and too varied calls for medical service coming to an official appointed annually by a political board and inadequately paid, offered no guarantee that sickness in poorer families would be handled with proper skill, though in these weaker families the need of the greater skill is especially urgent. Moreover, for a growing progressive city the system was too inadequate to last much longer. If instead of the office of the physician who happened to be city physician, a dispensary organized under the city department of health, with its regular staff, its established procedures, its continuous records, and its continuous clinics, were the point where cases were first considered, the selection of the right physician for each case could be properly made.

Tuberculosis Dispensary and Sanatorium

In addition to maintaining one visiting nurse the Springfield Tuberculosis Association was operating a free dispensary. Dr. George T. Palmer, who had charge, contributed his time. This was perhaps too great a service to expect from one person, and sooner or later the cost of this dispensary service should be assumed by the city or county.

The Tuberculosis Association and the county have also cared for a number of indigent cases at the Open Air Colony, a private sanatorium. In addition to the weekly payment of $4.00 made by the county, the cost to the association of the 18 patients helped was $8.40 a week.

The county board of supervisors should be urged to establish a new basis of weekly payments, more nearly representing the cost for care of county patients admitted to St. John's Hospital and the Open Air Colony. Ultimately, and the time should not be distant, the city and county should provide hospital facilities of their own; but in the meantime an increase to at least $6.00 a week for service in either of these local hospitals was recommended by the survey.

Care of Mental Defectives

There are many degrees of mental deficiency, and only persons suffering from certain forms may need custodial care. Insanity, when once determined, generally points to hospital care, and children suffering milder forms of mental deficiency require institutional treatment. From January 1, 1913, to March 1, 1914, 113 persons were committed by the Sangamon County Court to the Jacksonville State Hospital for the insane.

Unfortunately there was no place in Springfield for the detention of persons suffering from mental illness; they were held in the county jail annex until the court could appoint a commission and hold a hearing. The general hospitals would not admit patients of this class, and St. John's Hospital took such patients only when a special nurse could be provided, which eliminated most indigent cases. The result was that a considerable number of the insane were kept at the Sangamon County Poor Farm. An inspector of the Illinois State Charities Commission found 24 insane inmates there in 1914.

Almshouses are entirely unfitted for the treatment of mental diseases. The remedy lies in reducing the number cared for in these places as rapidly as possible; in demanding that a fair proportion of the patients of the county be received at the state hospitals, and that accommodations at the state hospitals be increased until they provide for all the insane of Illinois now confined in almshouses.

Neither should the indigent insane be detained in the county jail annex; they should be cared for in hospital wards pending transfer to the state hospital.

The situation with regard to the care of persons among the

poor suffering from acute alcoholic diseases was very like that of the insane; they were sent to the county jail annex. It was required that the city physician be called when an intoxicated person who was unconscious was placed in a cell. This commendable practice should be made to apply to others who are in serious condition; but until the state of Illinois provides for alcoholics, confinement in the county jail annex should be discontinued and arrangements made for treatment in one of the hospitals.

In addition to these specific measures having to do with the institutional care of the sick poor, their welfare would be promoted still further by broadening the general preventive health work of the city and of the Springfield Tuberculosis Association. Later hospital social service would need to be provided for.

FAMILY DISABILITIES AND TREATMENT

Aims Today in Charity Work

The chief aim in modern charity work is to eliminate abnormal conditions of family life and promote normal conditions; also to keep families intact and aid them in ways that will restore them as far as possible to complete living, to say nothing of considerations of personal happiness and comfort. While direct material aid is often necessary, it is only a means to the end of family rehabilitation.

This obviously implies the belief that conditions can be changed and improved. The idea of any class of people being predestined and hopelessly chained to poverty and misery is repudiated once and for all. When family life is abnormal there must be some reason or reasons for it—reasons for the most part that are ascertainable and which past experience has proved in some measure to be removable. Here, for example, is a family in distress because the chief breadwinner has incipient tuberculosis and has been forced to give up his work; there are no savings or other resources, and outside aid is needed. Obviously the key to the situation lies in the father's restoration to health. As long as there is hope of restored health there is hope for restored family normality. Modern charitable effort, in addition to temporary

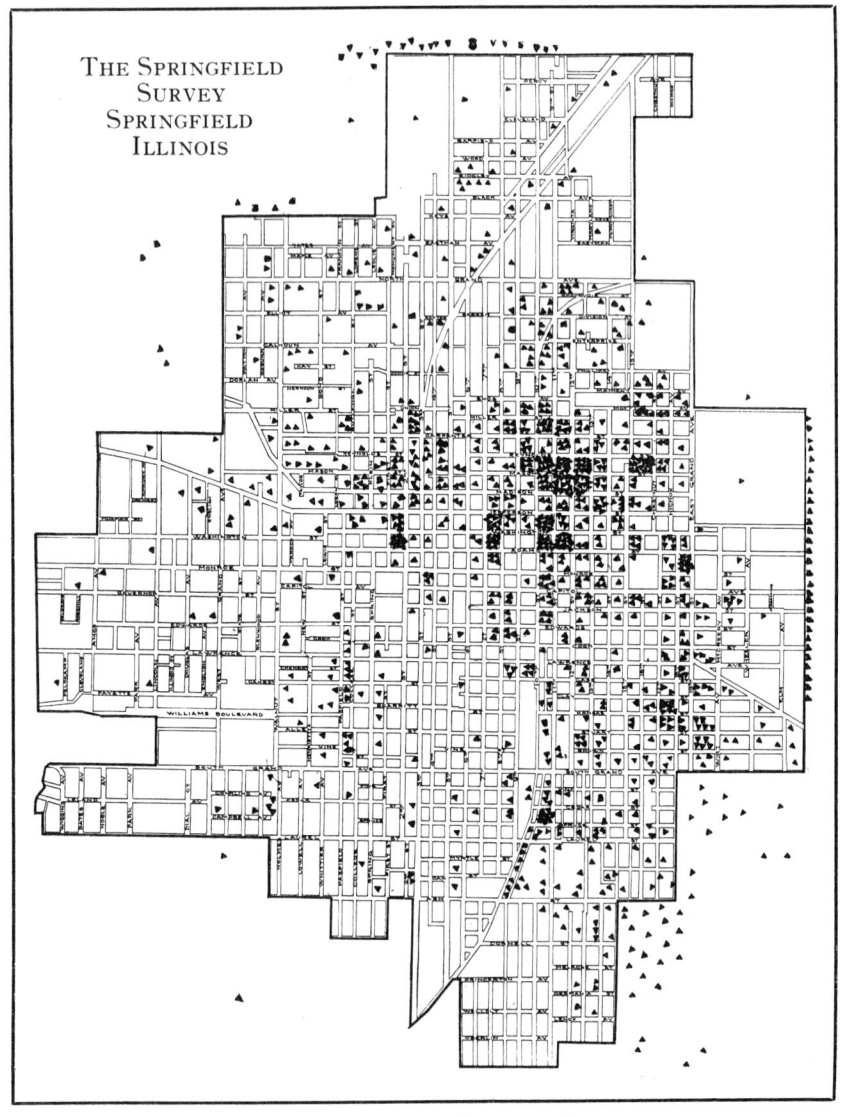

SIZE AND EXTENT OF THE CHARITIES PROBLEM

In 1913, 1,764 Springfield families received some kind of charitable service from public or private organizations. Each spot represents a family. (A few could not be located because of faulty addresses.)

aid, would be directed toward the father's recovery; it would thus help the family to the place where it could take care of itself.

In carrying out this ideal several things are imperative. First, there must be accurate knowledge of the difficulties in which the family finds itself. Facts are essential to a diagnosis of the family's problem and needs. Second, a careful plan of action to meet the needs must be decided upon and put into operation. Third, in most if not all instances the meeting of the needs of these families requires that social agencies work together, placing facts at each other's disposal and co-operating in a unified plan. And, fourth, there should be effort not only to remove the family disabilities already experienced but to take social action to prevent future disabilities; for example, to prevent the unnecessary deaths that cause widowhood, to prevent unemployment with its consequent reduction of family income, and so on.

These requisites necessarily involve good record keeping by social service agencies. Careful study of each case among the many handled daily, and treatment that will follow a plan once decided upon, are impossible unless the pertinent facts are put in form for ready and frequent reference.

Families Known to Agencies

In 1913, 1,764 families were known to have received some kind of social service. Not all were absolutely destitute, nor all in need during the entire year, but the figures mean that over 1,750 families were unable to function properly without assistance. For only 1,436 families, or 81 per cent of those helped, were the records complete enough to give some indication of the existence of the more common disabilities, such as sickness, unemployment, widowhood, desertion, and so on.

Although modern methods of co-operation in social work would presuppose that a very large proportion of these families would be known to at least two organizations in the city, the number known to only one agency was 1,467, or over 80 per cent of all. The Associated Charities, the usual center for co-ordinating work for families, knew only a few more than 200 families out of the total of 1,764, and some of these families were known only to it.

Family Disabilities

Records of the organization showed the factors in family conditions which signified subnormal conditions to be widowhood, tuberculosis, sickness other than tuberculosis, desertion, mental deficiency, intemperance, unemployment, irregular school attendance, crippled conditions, blindness, and non-support. In much the largest proportion of families only one disability was recorded per family, which in view of other local facts and of experience elsewhere in family work, immediately raised a question as to whether attention was being given to all needs of the families under care.

In the case of 169 families recorded as having two or more disabilities per family, sickness, widowhood, desertion, intemperance, unemployment, and irregular school attendance were seen to combine as important factors in family dependency.

Having classified the families according to their disabilities, a study was made of the treatment provided in each of the different disability groups, in the process of which all the records in each group were carefully read. Cases were found of widows with dependent children—among the most complicated cases to deal with—aided in the most casual way, without investigation as to whether the family needs were being adequately met, and without any attempt to assist them in utilizing their own resources. In cases of desertion—also difficult to treat—no examinations were made to determine the inciting causes or to formulate a plan by which reconciliation might be effected or support compelled.

A reading of the Springfield cases made it quite evident that there were no data upon which to form an opinion as to the amount of mental deficiency present in the families under study. Only first-rate family rehabilitation work of a kind not yet known in Springfield, with the keeping of first-rate records, would bring out this handicap and in any appreciable way show its proportionate seriousness in complicating family problems.

Intemperance is not by any means incurable, but its treatment requires thoughtful effort and resourceful planning. It must be fought with different weapons for different people. If in a given case it cannot be lessened, there may come a time when the breaking up of the family will need to be considered and undertaken. Very little constructive treatment was found in the matter of intemperance in Springfield.

With regard to tuberculosis, good co-operation was found to exist between the Associated Charities and the Tuberculosis Association, and in some instances efficient team work was being carried on. In cases of other diseases, however, there were numerous instances of inadequate attention.

Irregular school attendance, involving as it does problems of child labor, illness in the homes, family dependency, and other handicaps signifies subnormal conditions in families. In this matter there was obviously little co-operation between social agencies and the schools; and the work of each separately was below standard.

Non-support, too, was one of the serious unchecked evils in the social field in Springfield. Few cases reached the court, and those brought were not pursued to the end. This was probably due to the fact that there was no organization which was giving this matter careful attention and affording the wife moral backing for carrying the proceedings through.

Data on Living Costs

Records of family rehabilitation work in Springfield did not give sufficient data for estimating the cost of living except in a few cases with regard to rent. Questions of budget should be covered, both with reference to all families given assistance and with reference to those families in which continued material relief is necessary. This is true in general because of the vital connection between wages on the one hand and family well-being, physical and otherwise, on the other; and it is true of families receiving relief, in particular, because the determination of the right amount of supplementary relief depends upon an accurate summing up of income and outgo, and an estimate of what the family actually requires.

Finally, the study of treatment provided for disabled families in Springfield, together with facts such as above summarized, led to the formulation of the following general conclusions:

First, the data on record in the local agencies responsible for families were very incomplete.

Second, although recognizing that in many cases disabilities and other facts were probably ascertained but not recorded, it was evident that investigation of conditions in homes was not thoroughly and systematically made.

Third, inasmuch as comprehensive and intelligent treatment depends upon a broad basis of fact, it follows that this kind of family treatment was not possible with the insufficient investigations and record keeping found in Springfield.

And finally, in consequence, what was accomplished in actual rehabilitation—that is, toward the restoration of families to independence and normal living—was largely fragmentary.

PRIVATE AGENCIES PROVIDING SOCIAL SERVICE

The Associated Charities

Ordinarily the scope of the Associated Charities is very broad, and its calls for service are of many kinds. The staff of the Springfield organization was found to be insufficient to cover the field. Although a new trained worker had just been secured as general secretary, the staff needed the addition of an assistant secretary who, besides helping in case work under the secretary's oversight, should be responsible for the organization of volunteer workers and the development of a decisions committee.

The offices of the Associated Charities needed rearrangement and it was recommended that the clothing station be removed, preferably by transferring this service to some other organization in the city. The much-needed improvement in record keeping made between the field work of the survey and the issuing of the original report, needed to be extended to cover methods of confirming telephone orders on stores, the checking up of deliveries for orders, and the handling of special funds.

While recognizing many instances of excellent work, the conclusion was nevertheless inevitable that the treatment of families was very largely along lines of temporary material relief rather than rehabilitation. The society, moreover, had not taken an important part in movements looking toward the improvement

THE PLAYHOUSE AT THE EXHIBITION

A scene from "A Bundle or a Boost," a fifteen-minute play contrasting mere almsgiving and constructive family relief.

of social conditions in the city. An essential feature of the Associated Charities movement, and a policy to which all well-organized societies are committed, is that of leadership in developing preventive and community measures which the day-to-day family work shows to be necessary for the improvement of social conditions—measures, that is, which are not actively undertaken and carried on through other agencies.

It was recommended, therefore, that the general secretary should—in the Central Conference of Social Agencies, and after some progress has been made in the consideration of a decision upon the Springfield survey recommendations regarding the work of the different social agencies—take up, upon motion of the board of directors of the Associated Charities, any matters developed as a result of the case work which point to the need of undertaking some new social activity or of enlarging any already undertaken, or of effecting some administrative reform or legislative measure, or of educating the community. This to the end that there might be general participation in those most important social reforms whose need is bound to be revealed in the course of a really intensive, thoroughgoing family rehabilitation work. This kind of activity might very well be extended to matters in which executive direction was needed and was not elsewhere available for carrying out any of the recommendations of the Springfield survey.

The beginning made toward establishing a workable confidential exchange should be followed up to the end that the exchange would be developed and utilized.

The organization of a decisions committee which could give opportunity, in the treatment of family problems, for taking advantage of the wisdom of the group and for guiding action accordingly was strongly urged. Moreover, the work of the paid staff should be further strengthened and extended by a greater use of volunteer workers.

Finally, the work of the finance committee should be improved and the campaigns for funds should be better organized.

THE TUBERCULOSIS ASSOCIATION

As already indicated, the co-operation between the Tuberculosis Association and the Associated Charities at the time of the survey was very close; relations between these agencies had always been close. Nevertheless, the importance of early referring of all cases to the Associated Charities for social service where future destitution seemed at all probable was not always recognized. Such reference was strongly urged. In addition to cooperation with the Associated Charities there should be systematic inquiry of the confidential exchange about all patients as soon as they apply. The family records of the association were extremely good and were well kept.

HUMANE SOCIETY

The Humane Society was organized to deal with cruelty to and non-support of children, and with cruelty to animals. Our review of the charity work of the city and the discovery of work in the Humane Society's field which was not being handled led to the conviction that the society was not fulfilling a large function. The work should be radically reorganized to the end ultimately that all activities of the society relating to children sooner or later be removed to the juvenile court or to a central organization for child welfare, according to the needs of the individual case. The work for the protection of animals should continue to be handled by the police. It was expected, however, that for the immediate future the Associated Charities would need to act as originator of many non-support proceedings which otherwise would have fallen in the field of the reorganized Humane Society.

WASHINGTON STREET MISSION

The Washington Street Mission was carrying on three kinds of work: religious services, the maintenance of a lodging house for homeless men, and the distribution of clothing.

The lodging house for homeless men was the only institution of its kind in the city. Although the building which housed it and the church auditorium was not well adapted for lodging purposes, the equipment and management were relatively good. In 1913 a gross total of 6,743 lodgings were given, 1,182 suits were fumigated, 456 orders for meals were given away, 1,100 other orders were given out but paid for later. Employment, temporary or permanent, was found for 379 men, and 10 women in the neighborhood were also helped to employment.

Realizing the undoubted value of the work, the fact was to be regretted that a more systematic scheme of treatment and record keeping regarding the men was not adopted. The problem of the homeless man will never be solved until some constructive effort is made to understand individual cases, turn some of the men back to home ties left behind, or in the absence of home or other ties, to get them settled.

With regard to the giving of relief the only source of information was the record of 12,000 garments received. The giving out of clothing was considered an adjunct to the religious work of the Mission. This we believed to be a wrong basis of work, and we recommended that the distribution of clothing be separated from the religious work of the Mission.

We recommended further that more detailed record keeping of the work of the lodging house for homeless men be gradually developed, also of relief work done, that physical examination and treatment be extended to all applicants, and that a definite effort be made to replace men in their ordinary environments.

St. Vincent de Paul Society

The St. Vincent de Paul Society was organized November 20, 1913. A report made early in March, 1914, just before the survey was begun, indicated that it had 34 active members and 117 benefactors. The total number of families known to the society at that time was 77, 31 of which were Catholic, 29 Protestant, and 17 without religious affiliations. Relief had been given in the form of groceries, shoes and bedding, coal and other special forms. Far more important than the question of relief, however, was the fact that the society had recognized the necessity not only of adequate planning but of co-operative work, and had already established cordial relations with the social agencies of the city.

Day Nursery

A study of the day nursery which was started while the survey was being made was not possible, but such information as was obtainable at long distance indicated intelligent work.

CHARITIES

EARL GIBSON SUNSHINE SOCIETY

The local activities of the Earl Gibson Sunshine Society consisted of the support of national work for blind babies; the maintenance of a trained nurse for emergency work during the state fair week held in Springfield; special relief to families at the request of various social agencies of the city; providing flowers for patients in hospitals; and visiting people at the county poor farms. These local activities were commendable, but the society should follow a policy of doing no relief work except through existing agencies in the city.

SALVATION ARMY

The local branch of the Salvation Army was reorganized just prior to the survey and had not progressed far enough upon its new program of activities to warrant their study at that time.

KING'S DAUGHTERS HOME

The King's Daughters Home for the aged is for women over sixty, without serious mental or physical handicap, who are residents of Sangamon County. An admission fee of $300 was charged and anyone admitted must deed over all her property to the corporation. The house, which was well adapted for the purpose, was homelike and attractive, as nearly a home as such an institution can be.

We question seriously, however, the advisability of a home of this sort charging a fixed fee for admission and requiring the transfer of all property to the institution. The recommendation was that the home establish a sliding scale of charges for admission, setting a minimum if necessary; and also place in trust all capital sums received from inmates, demanding during the lives of the inmates only the income of their estates. The capital would go to the home at the death of the inmate, but in case of a desire to leave the institution, the trust could be easily dissolved and the capital returned.

ST. JOSEPH'S HOME FOR THE AGED

This is a home for aged men and women conducted by the Sisterhood of the Immaculate Conception and receiving general support through the Catholic diocese. A portion of the support came from Catholic citizens of Springfield. Only persons sixty years of age or over were admitted. At the time the home was visited it contained 23 women and 17 men, of whom 14 were non-Catholics. There was no fixed charge for admission.

Springfield Improvement League

This league which had been recently formed, aimed to work for a cleaner and more beautiful Springfield. It was made up of volunteer workers who served on special or standing committees which in general covered the fields studied by the Springfield survey. The league offered an effective channel for enlisting support in civic and social problems. It had already recognized the importance of putting social and civic endeavors upon a city-wide basis and dealing with them as community problems.

Public Agencies Providing Social Service

Sangamon County Poor Farm

The Sangamon County Poor Farm, which comprised 196 acres, was situated 15 miles from Springfield. The building consisted of two stories and a basement, with dormitories 22 by 28 feet containing from 3 to 11 beds each.

Of the 162 inmates 23 were insane, 3 sane epileptics, 1 insane epileptic, 4 consumptives, 2 blind, and 129 paupers not classified. None was under twenty-five years of age.

As far as certain bare comforts and necessities of life were concerned the inmates were fairly fortunate. It was apparently a peaceful institution, with no special methods of discipline or hard exactions.

A number of necessary improvements, however, needed to be made, and it was recommended that the Associated Charities and the Women's Club jointly take up the question of immediately effecting changes which need not be delayed, and that a special committee of the county board be appointed to consider the larger building problems involved. Among the changes which would make life in the county home more normal, cheerful, and comfortable were the following:

1. The most obvious suggestion was the transfer of its insane patients to state hospitals. This was already being urged by the local authorities but there was likely to be a residue for some time. Ultimately there should be a statute absolutely prohibiting almshouse care for such patients.

2. With the abolition of the cells for the insane in the basement, a rearrangement of space or provision for new space, such

CELLS AT THE SANGAMON COUNTY POOR FARM
These cells in the basement were used for insane persons. Such inmates should be placed in the comfortable and cheerful quarters of the state hospitals for the insane.

as would obviate the use of the basement for living purposes, should be worked out.

3. As soon as possible a special pavilion for the tuberculous and with provision for special diet, should be built.

4. Toilet facilities should be provided on the first floor.

5. Occupations should be provided for all except the bedridden. It could not be too strongly emphasized that an idle life in an almshouse is a most cruel infliction upon any human being.

6. A graduate nurse should be added to the staff.

7. There should be provision for a sitting room for women. The sitting rooms for both men and women should be provided with benches and chairs, among which should be a good proportion of rocking and easy chairs for the older inmates. . . . Good strong tables, one or two couches, and a few shelves on the walls for books and papers, should complete the furniture of the room. Good pictures, now available at small cost, should be provided for the walls of the sitting rooms.

8. A monthly entertainment of some sort in all except the summer months should be arranged by interested groups in Springfield.

9. The dining-room tables for all but the lowest grades of inmates should be covered with linen, not oilcloth.

Some of these recommendations involve immediate changes; and we would strongly urge that, if necessary, outdoor relief (that is, assistance given outside the institution) be reduced in amount so as to enable the county to meet these first responsibilities satisfactorily.

Overseer of the Poor for Capital Township

Capital Township is conterminous with the city of Springfield; and the field of work of the overseer of the poor was thus rendering assistance to those in need within the boundaries of the city. The office was appointive, and unprotected by civil service or by an adequate sense of responsibility on the part of the county board of supervisors in dealing with dependent families of the city along modern approved lines. A change of administration usually meant a change in the office. Under these circumstances obviously the office was not likely to be filled by anyone with experience or sufficient ability in the treatment of families. Such a state of affairs, unfortunately, was not regarded as criminal malfeasance in office, but the time will come when it will be so considered. It is as serious an error to assign to this position any other than a social worker with sufficient technical training and experience, as it would be to fill the position of city physician by appointing a man who had not studied medicine. Both deal with very vital matters connected with the promotion of normal living.

Relief Work Outside of Institutions

The service of the overseer of the poor has been almost entirely the giving of material aid. The expenditures for outdoor relief in 1913 amounted to $8,245.02, and for other purposes, $5,722.88, a total of $13,967.90. The amount was not extravagant for a city the size of Springfield, but the record keeping was so meager that there was no way of justifying or explaining any of the expenditures. Neither was it possible to study expenditures made on behalf of individual families to determine whether the amounts were adequate or properly adjusted to the family's need. In general, the amounts given were small; over 70 per cent of the cases received less than $25, and roughly, 60 per cent less than $15. There was a fair amount of co-operation between the overseer of the poor and social agencies of the city with regard to individual cases, but the giving of relief to a definite amount in order to further and form part of a predetermined plan was not practiced.

With regard to the transportation of dependents to other communities, the overseer was permitted to spend something for those asking for aid. In order to insure that the county or city was not doing some other community an injustice by shunting dependent individuals upon it and in no wise helping the person concerned, the overseer's office should be a signer of the Transportation Agreement of the National Conference of Charities and Corrections.[1]

In summing up the situation and needs in the work of public poor relief in Capital Township the survey recommended: First, that action of some kind be taken to secure experienced workers in the overseer's office. The Conference of Social Agencies should protest against the current procedure, and in succeeding elections should urge all parties to make public announcement of a policy pledging nominees for supervisorships to take this office out of politics and put in it a trained social worker under some kind of civil service restriction. Second, the record keeping with

[1] The Transportation Agreement for charitable institutions was drawn up in 1903. It now (1920) has over 800 signers. Copies may be secured by addressing the Charity Organization Department, Russell Sage Foundation, New York City.

reference to the essential facts of the cases cared for should be greatly improved. Third, the co-operation of the overseer with other social agencies should include the treatment of cases according to a mutually understood plan. Fourth, the cost of hospital and sanatorium care of the sick poor should be borne in larger part by the public—at least to the extent of increasing the payment of $4.00 a week to $6.00—and in all cases involving tuberculosis, special attention should be given to seeing that the relief provided was adequate, following a rehabilitation plan for the whole family.

Juvenile Court

At the time of the survey, 48 families were on the Funds to Parents List of the juvenile court. These grants to widows ran quite uniformly around $8.00 and $10 a month, although the variations in family needs were considerable. Despite the fact that good records were maintained there was practically no investigation made of applications in order to estimate what the minimum family income should be; what amount of work the mother should be expected to do—taking into account her physical, mental, and nervous condition, and other characteristics, whether there were any children of working age and what amount of their wages should go into the family purse; what amount was promised or should be expected of well-circumstanced relatives.

It was strongly urged that the court endeavor to secure a second officer who should give special attention to this work; for it required not only most thorough initial investigations but constant visitation. If it is worth while arranging for widows' grants it is worth while to see that they be really effective, for money relief in itself assures nothing. There should be not only better investigation of needs but careful planning of treatment, and if under the terms of the law a widow is not eligible for grant, she should be referred to the proper private agencies for attention.

School Attendance Bureau

Since problems of truancy and school attendance are intimately related to home conditions and are likely to be acute in families known to social agencies, this matter has been considered here as well as in the school section of the survey. With the thought in mind that the school attendance bureau may also serve as a social agency for dealing with families, the following is a brief summary of the suggestions offered as to methods of organizing and administering such a bureau:

Only when a satisfactory excuse cannot be obtained from parents by the use of inquiries sent through the mail should the case of absence be referred to the attendance officer.

The superintendent or the board of education should draw up written instructions as to what should be considered satisfactory excuses.

Excuse notes or forms on which are entered the parents' excuses, together with the action of the teachers thereon, should be filed monthly in the office of the superintendent.

Teachers should record the approximate date when pupils absent from school are normally due, so that inquiry may be made if the absence is unduly prolonged.

In cases of the transfer of children, immediate inquiry should be made by form letter or telephone to learn if actual transfer has been effected and if the child is duly registered.

It should be made clear to the parochial schools that the service of the attendance officer is open to them in following up unexcused absences, and their co-operation with the officer secured as far as possible.

Each year a comparison of the school rolls with the returns of the school census should be made, so that no children shall be lost track of at the beginning of the school term.

Habitual truancy generally indicates a family rather than an individual disorder. It points to weaknesses lying much further back, and is least often overcome by simply forcing a child into school again with a few new clothes, a new pair of shoes, and a grocery order. There are questions of family adjustment back of many unexcused absences of children from school which cannot be worked out by an attendance officer without the co-operation of the social agencies. This work should be considered a combination of school attendance and social service.

It was therefore recommended that the attendance officer be one with experience as a social worker and having a knowledge of the field of family rehabilitation. Whatever he does should be in accordance with plans worked out between himself and the officers or committees of the Associated Charities.

It was our opinion that the work of the mothers' clubs in the schools should be done entirely through the Associated Charities. Some of the members should be secured as volunteers in the working out of plans for rehabilitation and the raising of funds for individual families. We believed also that, in connection with the co-operative work of the attendance officer and the Associated Charities, many opportunities would be discovered where members of these clubs could tutor children who had suffered because of irregular attendance, thus rendering a most effective service to the children themselves and to the schools.

RECOMMENDATIONS REQUIRING UNITED ACTION

It was realized from the beginning of the survey, of course, that the various suggestions and recommendations growing out of the facts collected would affect not only individual organizations, but also groups of organizations; and as the field work of the survey began to draw to an end it became more and more apparent that a satisfactory reorganization of the Associated Charities would need to be worked out, together with some plan for bringing about much closer co-operation among all the social agencies. In anticipation, therefore, of such developments, and with a view to preparing the way for handling local social problems on a community-wide and more co-operative basis, a meeting was called by the sub-committee on charities of the general Springfield survey committee. To it were invited unofficially a number of persons vitally interested in the different agencies of the city.

At this meeting a resolution was carried providing for a conference of social agencies to follow the publication of the survey of charities, also to formulate a policy with reference to co-operation among the social agencies in Springfield.

With a view to facilitating the work of the Conference of Social Agencies, the following recommendations were offered with regard to developments requiring action on the part of more than one society:

CHARITIES

Confidential Exchange

The establishment of a confidential exchange by the Associated Charities was recommended. This meant that the following agencies should officially agree to use it and that each should make a contribution toward its support. These contributions should range from $50 to $5.00 a year.

Home for the Friendless.
Humane Society (until its work was reorganized as above recommended).
Tuberculosis Association.
Washington Street Mission.
City Physician (or his successor, a general dispensary).
St. Vincent de Paul Society.
Lincoln Colored Home.
Day Nursery.
Salvation Army.
Springfield Improvement League.

These were the agencies which were in daily need of a confidential exchange and which, except for one, were private in character, so that appropriations could be made for the support of the work. A committee should be formed in the conference composed of representatives of the organizations which agreed to support the exchange, and this committee should serve as an advisory committee to the Associated Charities in connection with the exchange. The contributions thus made to the exchange would not pay all the expenses involved.

Only one public agency was here listed, the city physician. We doubted whether the county board could be induced to make an appropriation for this purpose; but as long as the office of city physician was continued it would be worth $50 of the annual salary to the incumbent to have such an exchange, for he could regulate his legitimate city work thereby. A dispensary, when established, would inevitably use the exchange and should make an appropriation for that purpose.

The following agencies, public in character, would need it daily and should also make use of it:

Juvenile Court.
Overseer of the Poor for Capital Township.
Sangamon County Poor Farm.
School Attendance Bureau.

In addition to the above agencies which should use the exchange a great deal, the following private agencies would make use of it also, though not so constantly:

Orphanage of the Holy Child.
Earl Gibson Sunshine Society.
The Churches.

The churches should co-operate far more closely than most of them were doing.

Child Welfare Service

It was pointed out that a beginning should be made toward what would ultimately be a well-rounded county-wide child welfare organization which would stand firmly for comprehensive and sympathetic case work and for constructive measures for community betterment. Such an agency should make a thorough diagnosis of each application, socially, medically, and mentally, and should be prepared to supply treatment either through its own resources or through co-operation with other existing agencies. It should initiate an up-to-date placing-out work with departments for mothers with babies and a strong protective department ready to prosecute when necessary. It should be organically connected with the Illinois Children's Home and Aid Society, and should work in co-operation with the Department of Visitation of Children Placed in Family Homes of the State Board of Administration, also with those institutions of the county which deal with children. This work might start under the supervision of a child welfare committee appointed from Sangamon County by the Home for the Friendless.

Dispensary Service

The city should establish under its health department a free medical dispensary and take over the general medical service being performed by the city physician. The management of such a dispensary should be in the hands of a paid official, but a large volunteer staff of physicians should be organized. The responsibility for admission to hospitals on county charge should also be placed upon the dispensary. As a first move toward securing this dispensary service the Associated Charities should appoint a special committee to confer with the health department and county officials. The committee might later be enlarged to become a committee of the Conference of Social Agencies; in any case it should continue in existence until sufficient public backing has been secured to enable the public officials to act.

Movements for Community Improvement

The Associated Charities through its general secretary, and upon motion of its board of directors, should take up in the Central Conference of Social Agencies or elsewhere any matters developed as a result of its case work which point to the need of undertaking some new activity or enlarging some activity already undertaken, or of effecting some administrative reform or legislative measure, or of educating the community. An illustration of the need of such activity with reference to preventing violations of the child labor law was found in our special investigations of a few families, and also in the study of home conditions in the industrial section of the survey.

Similarly the co-operation of the Springfield Improvement League would be of great value in making for a more intelligent public opinion bearing upon current social and civic problems in the city and county.

The Ministerial Association should also be counted on in this connection.

County Poor Farm

The Conference of Social Agencies should ask a joint committee of the Associated Charities and the Women's Club to take up the questions, large and small, connected with the county poor farm, calling upon the conference for whatever other assistance may be needed in order to carry out an effective, and if necessary, long campaign for improvements. This campaign should include an endeavor to secure more adequate accommodations for the insane in state institutions and their removal from the almshouse. Some changes could and should be made immediately, but larger difficulties relating to the buildings may involve a far longer campaign to arouse public opinion.

Public Outdoor Relief

The conference was also advised to appoint a committee wherein should be represented the Associated Charities, the Tuberculosis Association, and the St. Vincent de Paul Society, to consult with the overseer of the poor of Capital Township as to the possibility of his giving especial attention to tuberculosis relief, the assumption of responsibility in all cases of non-residents, and other matters of mutual concern already pointed out. It was also recommended that the committee take up with the board of supervisors the question of increasing the rate of weekly hospital pay for the sick of the county. The work of the agencies indicated was distinctly affected by the policy of the overseer's office.

Moral Aid for Advance Steps

In addition the conference should lend its moral support, in public ways, to those agencies—the Associated Charities and the children's institutions, for example—upon which must fall the task of making extensive changes in their work, involving increased expenditure.

Secretary of Conference

It was recommended that when the reorganization of the Associated Charities should be effected that the new general secretary be asked to serve, if mutually agreeable, as secretary also of the Central Conference of Social Agencies.

Future Development

The organization of this unofficial conference of social agencies was suggested so that a center of co-operation might be in existence to take up the recommendations of the survey, and work them out with individual boards of directors or with joint committees and boards.

This advisory task in itself might require one or two years. It was hoped that long before the expiration of the period the conference would have succeeded in creating a demand which by mutual discussion and agreement would bring about the steady, related, co-ordinated, constructive development of social work in Springfield.

VIII

INDUSTRIAL CONDITIONS[1]

Purpose and Scope

To view industry in Springfield from the angle of social welfare and to examine the needs disclosed was the purpose of this investigation. Industry exists for people, not people for industry; and obviously industry can never be considered satisfactory until it serves effectively those who furnish capital and managing ability, those who furnish labor, and those who form the consuming community.

In what, then, in this connection, does social welfare consist? Few questions give rise to more conflicting views. There are, however, certain general principles and minimum standards in industrial matters upon which, as long ago as 1916 when the industrial survey findings were printed, there was considerable agreement among those who had given thought to these questions. As an aid in considering the problems to be dealt with in Springfield, and with a view to formulating a basis for evaluating conditions and needs, a statement of these general principles was found useful.

We are fully aware, however, of the danger that a listing of minimum requirements of any particular time for Springfield and Illinois might be taken as a statement of conditions that would be good enough, and thus be turned into a set of maximum requirements—in other words, the danger that they might be taken to represent the remote or ultimate rather than the immediate goals ahead. We would therefore make clear that the several propositions as we conceived them represented minimum requirements, and only such minimum requirements as appeared to have the approval of those who had given the matter mature

[1] Summary of report, Industrial Conditions in Springfield, Illinois, by Louise C. Odencrantz and Zenas L. Potter.

thought, and particularly of those who spoke neither for the employer nor the employe but for the public.[1]

First and elementary among these matters, as originally stated, were working conditions. These should be made as wholesome and safe as possible. Fire hazard should be minimized, machinery guarded, sanitary conditions maintained, industrial diseases prevented, and good light and ventilation provided. The maintenance of such conditions is a first responsibility of the employer.

Second, until children are sixteen years of age it is essential that they develop normally and receive training for the work of life. Any occupation is therefore objectionable which interferes with such development or training. Under fourteen, children should not be employed in gainful occupations.

Third, hours of labor should not be so long as to injure health or to deny workers opportunity for self-improvement, the development of home life, and an intelligent interest in public affairs. Eight hours for a day's work is a standard which is now widely accepted.

Fourth, every worker should have one day of rest in seven.

Fifth, women and children should not be employed at night.

Sixth, workers who give their full working time to an industry should receive as a very minimum a wage which will provide the necessities of life. This means, of course, that men with families dependent upon them should receive enough for the support not only of themselves but of their families. Otherwise family life will be undermined. If the business cannot provide this there is serious question whether it has a right to exist.

Seventh, either the "necessities of life" should include enough to allow workers to carry insurance and save something for old age, or else industry should provide directly for the care of incapacitated workmen and for the dependents of workmen who are

---

[1] For a statement of Social Standards for Industry, adopted as a part of the report of the Committee on Standards of Living and Labor of the National Conference of Charities and Corrections and presented to the session of the Conference held in Cleveland in 1912, see Appendix A, pp. 157-162 of the original report here summarized.

For a statement of principles adopted by the Federal Council of Churches of Christ in America in Chicago in 1912, see Appendix B, pp. 162-163 of the same volume. Later statements by the Council and other religious, social, and civic bodies are now available.

THE SMOKE NUISANCE

In the schools of Springfield the problem of adequate lighting was rendered difficult by the prevalent coal smoke in the air which rapidly deposits a bluish film on the surface of the window glass and seriously reduces its transparency.

This condition was universal throughout not only the school buildings but also residence and office structures, and added both to the problem of lighting and of keeping the city clean. In the picture are two of the many smokestacks responsible for the condition.

killed or used up at work, through payment made by the employer—the cost to be distributed over society by some form of insurance or other method.

Eighth, irregularity of employment should be minimized, and when workers lose their positions adequate facilities should exist to help them find new places.

Ninth, the bargaining power in settling the terms of the work agreement should be as evenly balanced as possible between the employer and the employe. This would recognize the right of employers and employes alike to organize or form unions.

If some may doubt the feasibility of requiring industry to meet these requirements now, few people we believe will question them as minimum conditions which industrial life must very soon provide and for which the community, because it is always an interested party, should strive.

In this report the endeavor was to show how far Springfield conditions measured up to or fell short of these standards, and, as far as possible when they failed, to suggest means by which they might be brought more nearly into keeping with them.

Time and Method

As stated elsewhere, the facts presented, unless otherwise indicated, describe conditions found in Springfield during the spring of 1914, the period covered by the field work of the survey. The time of the field work was limited to four and six weeks respectively for two investigators; and several additional weeks were devoted by them to the compilation of data from existing records. The general method followed was first, to visit factories and mercantile establishments in order to examine physical conditions and gather data regarding hours, wages, etc.; and second, to call on representative workers in their homes for the purpose of securing from them a full statement of their work conditions.

Information also was secured from labor organizations and from the Illinois free employment agency, from state reports containing industrial facts relating to Springfield, and from data gathered by the Springfield Commercial Association. Although the investigation had to do primarily with Springfield, special attention was paid to the planning and execution on the part of the state of methods of promoting industrial welfare, since through this channel public opinion is very potent in influencing industrial conditions.

PHYSICAL SAFETY IN INDUSTRY

Physical safety in industry is an elementary requirement. The problem of dealing with the industrial hazards to life and health, moreover, is rendered extremely important and serious because of the fact that workers, in Springfield as elsewhere, spend such a large part of their waking hours in the factory, mine, laundry, store, or other work places.

These industrial hazards are of three kinds: danger from accident other than fire, from fire, and from disease. For the purpose of discovering, as far as time permitted, the nature and extent of the hazards in Springfield inspections were made of all but one of the factories employing 100 or more persons, of several of the smaller factories, of the two largest laundries, and all of the larger and a few of the smaller mercantile establishments.

No establishment visited showed marked disregard for the safety and physical welfare of its workers. Some showed unusual care. Nevertheless, because of situations difficult to handle, such as old buildings erected before the development of modern factory construction, in certain other Springfield work places large numbers of employes were subjected to well-recognized industrial hazards, over 200 establishments, for example, being found to have unguarded machinery, fire hazards, or other dangerous conditions.

Work Accidents

Between 1909 and 1913, 36 Springfield individuals were killed by some kind of industrial accident, the largest number being among railway employes, mine workers, electrical workers, and men engaged in the building trades. Since the recording of causes of deaths was very faulty, and for other reasons, the real total was probably even greater. Thirty-six persons killed in industry, however, showed a serious situation—one demanding thoughtful attention.

As to non-fatal accidents, the available data again were very incomplete and did not include those occurring in establishments subject to the compensation law. Nevertheless 35 such accidents were reported for the single year 1913 These, particularly with the six fatal accidents of that year, were sufficient to show that grave accidents were occurring each year in Springfield and that these were resulting in more than enough suffering and economic loss to call for serious endeavors in accident prevention.

According to the Illinois Employers' Liability Commission, about one-half of the accidents occurring annually in industry are due to dangerous conditions which may be removed or to carelessness on the part of workingmen and which educational work regarding industrial hazards may greatly reduce. Up to the time of the survey, however, no energetic accident prevention campaign had ever been carried on in Springfield either by employers' associations, labor organizations, civic bodies, the public officials, or the great majority of employers, although such campaigns had yielded excellent results elsewhere. The consequence was many unnecessary injuries and deaths from work accidents.

Accident Prevention

An important requisite for carrying on campaigns of this kind is a knowledge of the facts of work accidents: how many, where and why accidents happen, how they may be avoided. These data were not available. The provisions of the Illinois statutes requiring the reporting of work accidents were confused and oftentimes overlapped, since in some cases similar establishments were obliged to report to entirely different authorities, because state officials were not compiling the facts for the same periods and because the data were not classified by industries or kinds of work.

It was impossible, therefore, to determine how many accidents happened in the state in any given year. It was even impossible to tell how many happened in factories, on railroads, or in bridge and building construction work. Moreover, only part of the data were presented by localities, and the reports offered no help in getting an accurate idea of the number of work accidents which occurred in Springfield or in any other city. One of the first moves for efficient accident prevention work in Springfield and Illinois clearly should be to replace these confused and overlapping statutes by an act requiring the reporting of all work accidents to one central authority.

Protective Legislation

Protective legislation going into considerable detail, applying to accident prevention in mines, on steam railroads, to building and construction work, and to factories, mercantile establishments, mills, and workshops, was found on the Illinois statute books. In this important railroad and mining state the work of the mine inspectors and railway safety inspectors who were charged with enforcing the law, however, was not well organized, and was not carefully checked up and reported on from time to time—no reports at all being issued to show the kind of work performed by the mining inspectors.

At the time of the survey the last published report of the chief factory inspector was two years old. It showed but one inspection to enforce the bridge and building construction safety law in Springfield in the two years ending June, 1912, and no inspections to enforce the act applying to factories, mercantile establishments, mills, and workshops. Unpublished records, however, for the year ending May, 1914, indicated much greater activity.

Occupational Disease

Illinois for several years before the survey had an occupational disease law. It was based upon studies made by the Illinois Occupational Disease Commission. The causes of occupational diseases enumerated by the commission were: vitiation of air with irritating or poisonous dusts and fumes; direct contact of workers with irritating and poisonous substances affecting the skin and producing eruptions; extremes of heat and cold; extremes of dryness and humidity; defects in lighting; abnormal atmospheric pressure; jarring, shaking, and deafening noise; and overstrain, fatigue, hurtful postures, and over-exercise of parts of the body. A number of these conditions were found by the survey in greater or less degree in Springfield. In some cases they seemed inherent in industrial processes, and in so far as that was true their bad effects could only be minimized. In other they were clearly removable.

Shortcomings in lighting, in the provision of exhausts on emery wheels, and in provision of seats for employes while at work, especially women, were particularly noted.

In the shoe factory, for example, practically all women workers except the operators were obliged to stand ten hours a day pasting, cutting, inspecting, or packing. Women laundry workers almost without exception stood at their work ten hours a day; and every such worker interviewed complained of tired and sore feet. The provision of seats was also inadequate for store employes; and a few employers provided seats to meet the legal requirement but would not permit their use. The law as to seats was vague and did not include all occupations. More definite legal provisions were needed.

On the other hand, it did not seem wise to try to cover by specific regulations all the varying and multitudinous conditions presenting health hazards which did not admit of clear-cut classifications. Instead, we recommended several measures affecting all of these questions: first, that the numerous independent bodies dealing with labor conditions be consolidated into a single department of labor and mining, with bureaus in charge of special work. These should include a bureau of inspection responsible for railroad, factory, and other inspection service except mining; of mining; of research and labor statistics; a bureau of workmen's compensation; and other bureaus recommended in later parts of this report.[1] Second, as a part of this reorganization plan, it should be provided that the reporting of work accidents should be centered in one authority—a bureau of the board which would make careful compilations, study the information, and then give wide publicity to methods of averting workshop dangers. And third, the plan of reorganization should provide for the establishment of a board or industrial commission in the new labor department, whose duty would be to confer with employers and employes in making special rules to fit each case which appears

[1] See pp. 201–203 for a fuller statement of the scope, organization, and functions of the proposed state department of labor and mining.

dangerous or hazardous to life, health, and safety. Wisconsin had found this a satisfactory procedure, and New York and Pennsylvania also adopted it.[1]

FIRE HAZARDS AND REGULATION

Some efforts to eliminate possible sources of the start and spread of fires and to provide adequate fire-fighting facilities were observed in many Springfield factories, but this could not be said of all. In a number of establishments provision for adequate egress had not been sufficiently looked after; in one establishment, for example, fully 500 persons, many of them women, worked on the second and third floors. The building is three stories high and has several wings which converge on a single wooden stairway about eight feet wide. Even under ordinary conditions, when workers passed out, the congestion was so great that the management let women go first before ringing the closing bell for men employes. While the factory was protected from spread of fire by an automatic sprinkler system, the danger of panic was great and it was entirely possible that escape down the stairway might be cut off. And panic even in cases where the buildings are low is one of the most deadly factors in fire hazards. The only fire-escapes on the building were antiquated ladders without platforms which did not reach nearer than 12 feet from the ground and which would be almost useless in case of fire. A modern stair fire-escape at the end of each wing of the building was clearly needed; but too much reliance should not be placed even upon these, for some of the recent factory fires have raised serious doubts as to the adequacy of protection afforded by outside fire-escapes—particularly where the fire-escapes must be near windows. A better plan is to put the fire-escape inside the building and wall it off completely from the rest of the factory.

In regard to fire, government regulation was again faulty and inadequate. Two statutes governed the matter. One provided for fire-escapes of a type to be determined by the local government, but in Springfield the type had not been determined. En-

[1] Similar industrial commission plans uniting in one authority the administration of workmen's compensation, factory inspection, and other labor laws, were adopted in 1915 in Colorado, Indiana, Montana, and Nevada.

forcement was left to the sheriff and grand jury, neither of whom inspected factories. The second statute stipulated that "sufficient and reasonable means of escape" must be provided, but this generalized requirement allowed too much room for disagreement over interpretation to permit very effective enforcement. A Springfield ordinance enacted many years ago also dealt with fire protection, but because of changes in the official machinery provided for carrying out the provisions and for other reasons, the ordinance was not effective.

But even if the laws had fully accomplished their purposes, they would still have been insufficient in that they did not include all the provisions that might be reasonably expected—among these being provisions for removing conditions which cause fires and help their spread, and provisions for fire-fighting facilities.[1]

Compensation for Industrial Injuries

Illinois, like many other states, had enacted a law within the last few years to compensate workmen injured while at work. This law marked a distinct step forward, for it eliminated the "assumption of risk," "fellow servant," and "contributory negligence" defenses against the recovery of damages by injured workmen. But it had three great weaknesses which must be eliminated before the injured workman will get just treatment. First, it was optional with employers; and many, especially in the most hazardous industries, had elected to be exempt. Second, health hazards in industry may result not only in accidents but in disease, but the law covers only injuries from accidents. And third, even where operative, the law as administered did not in all cases eliminate the drain of lawyers' fees. Not until these weaknesses have been remedied will Illinois have a law which establishes the basic compensation principle that industry should bear the losses from the inevitable hazards which it has introduced. A new law, or amendment to the present law, much more firmly establishing the basic principle of compensation should be secured;

[1] Some of the more important legal requirements suggested for enactment are detailed on page 30 of the full report. The New York law, though falling short of much that may be desired, was used as a basis for the more important of these suggested provisions.

and the administration of the act should be made a function of the industrial commission of the reorganized labor department.

But safety while at work should not be wholly dependent upon legislation. The employer, since he has a special responsibility, should see that dangerous conditions are eliminated as soon as recognized. The workers individually should feel the importance of using as much care as possible, and their co-operation through their unions should be expected. The public should assist through educational methods and campaigns for safety and industrial sanitation.

CHILD LABOR

As already seen, safe and sanitary work conditions are of sufficient community concern to make them the subject of legal enactment. Similarly the public through legal regulation in most states has recognized its responsibility in preventing child labor.

From conditions found in Springfield, however, it would appear that neither the child labor law of Illinois nor its enforcement was satisfactory. There were opportunities for fraud and evasion in the provisions governing the issuance of certificates to permit children under sixteen years of age to go to work, while violation of the provisions limiting the hours of work of children under sixteen seemed to be the rule rather than the exception.

The Child Labor Law

The child labor law of Illinois at the time of the survey had been on the statute books for over twelve years without alteration. When enacted it was considered a piece of advanced legislation, and even then ranked among the best laws in the different states. There were, however, certain weaknesses needing correction.

Important among these were the provisions for obtaining work certificates. It was easily possible that under them by a little sharp practice a child might prove himself fourteen years of age, though that may not have been the fact. The proverbial statement still holds true that a chain is as strong as its weakest link. So this proof of age provision was as weak as the least adequate of the proofs required.

Of the five kinds of proof enumerated three were open to easy evasion. In the case of the first—the record of the last school census, for example—a father desiring to put his daughter to work could give a false figure to the school census enumerator in order to prove the child fourteen years of age. The census figures so obtained become evidence of age which cannot be questioned. Second, if a parent went before the juvenile court and made affidavit that his child was fourteen years old his oath became proof of age; yet experience has shown that parents who wish to put their children to work before they are fourteen years of age are often not unwilling to swear falsely. Third, there was easy opportunity for evasion in the last requirement—that age according to the school record must be accepted. One hundred and thirty-five of the 138 children (almost 100 per cent) granted age and school certificates in Springfield in the year ending April 30, 1914, presented this kind of proof of age. We accidentally discovered one instance of a certificate improperly issued under this provision; and there was reason to think that this was not an isolated case. New York state in the requirements of the law covering the issuance of working certificates had proved the practicability of requiring real age evidence and rejecting the inadequate proofs accepted in Illinois. It was recommended that the Illinois statute be amended by removing its weak links and substituting the provisions of the New York law.[1]

In the amount of schooling required for the issuance of certificates the Illinois statute was also inadequate. The only requisite was that a child be able to read and write legibly simple sentences. The sentences did not even have to be in English. No test of his knowledge of arithmetic was required. Examination of the grades attained by Springfield children granted certificates in the year ending April 30, 1914, showed that of 131 children whose educational standing was given, only 26 had finished grammar school, while 64 had not completed the sixth grade. Twenty-eight children were in the fifth grade when they received certificates.

Finally, there were no requirements as to the child's physical condition before his working certificate was issued. An anemic or tubercular boy might require fresh air and sunlight, but that

[1] See the original report for an indication of the provisions on the proof of age in the New York law.

fact was no bar to his getting a certificate to work in a Springfield factory, or for that matter in a Chicago sweat-shop. That some safeguards should be set up in this regard is not a theoretical matter, for by the New York law already referred to, physical fitness must be determined through thorough examination by a medical officer of the health department in every case before an employment certificate is issued.

Child Labor Law Enforcement

So much for the provisions of the law. Its enforcement, aside from the work certificate provisions, was under the control of the State Factory Inspection Department. The results of our investigations indicated a very unsatisfactory situation with regard to enforcement at the time of the survey. In the time available 55 children between fourteen and sixteen years of age who had been granted working certificates in the past year, and selected at random, were followed up. These children, it will be remembered, might not legally work over eight hours a day or before 7 a.m. or after 7 p.m., or in any of an enumerated group of prohibited employments. Our endeavor was to determine how far these conditions were being observed. In addition, information was also secured from stores and factories and from home visits made for other purposes.

The results of these inquiries indicated that enforcement of the child labor law, especially those sections restricting hours of work, was decidedly lax. Among the 55 children concerned, it was found that 40, or over 70 per cent, had been illegally employed; and that there were only 15 of the number that had not worked illegal hours. Moreover, the majority of the 15 not working illegal hours were employed in union shops where the eight-hour day prevailed for all workers.

These violations of the hour law were not merely technical. Four of the children began work before 7 o'clock in the morning, while 21 worked in the evenings after 7 o'clock. Thirty-four worked more than eight hours a day, while 30 exceeded the weekly limit of forty-eight hours. In the employment of these 40 children *there was a total of 89 separate violations of different sections of the law on hours of work.*

These violations were not restricted to any one industry or occupation. Drug stores, however, were among the worst offenders.

In the group of 55 children there were three boys who were engaged in occupations absolutely prohibited to children under sixteen years of age. Two lads of fifteen were found who had worked as trapper boys until the mines had shut down. One expressed a desire to return to the work but said his father had forbidden it because "so many trapper boys get consumption." A third boy of fifteen worked in a bowling alley where flagrant violations of the child labor law existed. Several nights in succession the survey found *half a dozen boys not over twelve years of age, one or two much younger, setting up pins until 10.30 and 11 p.m.*, though under the law no one under sixteen might be so employed.

Reasons for this lack of enforcement of the law obviously could not be discovered without a thorough investigation of the State Factory Inspection Department, which was outside the scope of this investigation. Such facts as we gathered appeared to indicate the need among other things of a larger corps of factory inspectors. Until that could be done, however, the efficiency of the inspecting force could be increased, it was pointed out, through:

1. Better adjustment of the hours of inspectors' work to the character of their duties—especially with a view to their being on duty after 7 p.m., the hour beyond which children under sixteen are not allowed to work.

2. Revision of other methods for discovering violations of the hours of labor law for children.

3. Adoption of a regular policy of giving full publicity to successful prosecutions.

Finally, it would promote better child labor law enforcement and prevent children from using age and school certificates as licenses to loaf if the truant officer would follow up children granted certificates to find out where and under what conditions they secure employment.

WAGES AND REGULARITY OF EMPLOYMENT

The incomes of work people are a matter of community concern because they fix to a very great extent the standard of living of workers' families. Within certain limits they determine the kinds of houses these families live in, the quality of the food they eat, the kinds of clothes they wear, the amounts they are able to put by for a rainy day, and they have a clear bearing upon the family's present and future problems of self-support and economic independence. They also set limits to the educational advantages which many workmen's children may enjoy.

Workmen's earnings, however, must be measured with two things in mind: not alone wage rates, but also the regularity of employment—not to mention a third consideration, the cost of living. The family of a man who earns a high hourly rate, for example, but whose work is irregular, may not be as well off as that of a man whose wage rate is lower but who has steady employment the year round.

Income of Coal Miners

Coal miners represented one of the largest occupation groups in Springfield, roughly 2,500 residents in the city being so employed. Wage rates were determined biennially by agreements between the operators and the unions. The great majority of workers were paid by the ton of coal mined. Many of the miners (exclusive of miners' helpers and other mine workers) were able to make as high as $5.00 a day when there was plenty of work. But work was very irregular; out of more than 300 possible working days in the year ending June, 1913—the last year before this investigation—the mines in Sangamon County operated an average of only 181 days, or only three-fifths of the time. To the miner and his family this was a very serious matter.

Drivers, timbermen, and others paid by the day were earning less than miners whose pay was by the ton of coal mined, and therefore were affected even to a greater extent by the irregularity of the work. All were affected also by the fact that on many days when the mines operated they ran at less than capacity and did not give employment to all the men in their employ.

Some of the workers during slack periods were trying to fill in the time with other work, but there were difficulties against accomplishing much in this way, chief among them being that the free days were scattered irregularly through the year and that few of the men possessed skill in other occupations. The great majority found it either impracticable or impossible to combine much other work with mining. *The result was that wages for a large proportion of the men were below the minimum needs of an average family of five persons.*

The cause of the irregular mine work was found partly in the nature of the Illinois coal, which if left exposed loses some of its heat value and therefore production was made to vary with the varying seasonal demand. Another cause was found in the biennial agreements which resulted in overproduction in the months immediately prior to the expiration of old agreements. The operation of too many mines was also a factor.

For the improvement of conditions in the coal mining industry several suggestions have been made. Among these were: (1) extension of opportunities for miners to work in other trades through the development of efficient free employment agencies; (2) regularizing of the industry through encouragement of summer production; (3) governmental control, such as exists in some foreign countries, which would prevent the opening of new mines unless there is commercial need for them, and (4) the appointment of a commission to make a study of unemployment insurance. All of these seemed to the survey to deserve the fullest consideration.

Manufacturing, Mechanical and Other Industries

Irregularity of employment was found also in the manufacturing and mechanical industries. Out of something over 3,700 employes in 49 establishments for which data were available, about half had full-time employment in 1913; workdays for the other half ranged from 130 to 275 for the year. Over 400 employes were in establishments that operated less than 250 days. And some of the establishments did not operate on full time on all the days they were open. Brick making was the most seasonal of the industries in the manufacturing and mechanical groups.

In a few of these industries attempts were being made to reduce the irregularity of employment, but these had not got very far.

Wages in these work places varied so much from industry to industry and from one job to another that exactitude was impossible, except that *unskilled labor received from $1.75 to $2.00 a day—a large proportion not over $1.80.* This wage together with unsteady work kept men always on the borderline of poverty, with the result that in emergencies, sickness, accident, or unemployment, their families were forced to seek charitable aid. This amounts in many cases to the subsidizing by the community of establishments where wages are so low that the public and charitably inclined people have to make up the wage deficits.

In the groups above the unskilled workers the figures, as far as they permit classification, appeared to show that the great bulk of the employes received wages ranging from $2.00 to $3.75. A small proportion received as much as $5.00 and $6.00 a day. In a few cases where earnings were determined on the basis of piece work some dissatisfaction was found regarding the methods used in fixing the rates.

Work in the building trades, construction work, and in street paving is very much affected by weather conditions and change of season. One large company, for instance, from March until November was employing 200 men, chiefly unskilled laborers, at asphalt paving; but during the three or four months following, when outdoor work was impossible, only 15 were retained. Moreover, during these winter months the company reduced the rates of pay. For example, a skilled man who got $25 a week for nine months was paid only $12 a week for the three winter months. In choosing the few men who were to be kept on the payroll, men who were handy with tools had the best chance. In the busy months, too, the men lose a day's pay whenever it rains hard enough to prevent work; and there were occasional periods of idleness between jobs, although the company tried to transfer men from one job to another with as few gaps as possible. Even so, their total wage for the year fell considerably below $500.

Among men in the building trades—carpenters, painters, plasterers, paperhangers, plumbers, gas and steam fitters, sheet metal workers, bricklayers, and stone masons—who, in 1910, numbered about 1,100—irregularity of employment to a great extent offset the high wage rates which these workers had gained through their unions. Indeed the offset was such as to bring the yearly income down to a point where many families found it difficult to meet ordinary household expenses.

Among the 1,000 to 1,200 steam railroad and street railway employes there was much greater regularity of work. Wages among the steam railroad men who were organized into unions ranged from $12 to $30 a week. Wages of the street-car men who were not organized ran from $11.97 to $16.80 a week. *The seven-day week prevailed for both groups of railway workers.*

Laundry work was fairly regular through the year, but wages were very low, especially for the women workers who averaged about $6.00 a week. Here the wage rates were so low as to counteract to a considerable extent the advantages accruing through regular work.

Mercantile Establishments

In mercantile establishments work was also quite regular the year round but rates were low. The weekly wage for salesgirls in department stores averaged between $5.00 and $6.00. *A number of check girls and bundle wrappers received only $3.00 to $4.00.*

In three five-and-ten-cent stores the number of salesgirls varied from 21 in the first store to 30 in the second and 35 in the third. No check girls or bundle wrappers are employed in the Springfield five-and-ten-cent stores, but *the wages of salesgirls were very low. The average wage was from $4.00 to $5.00 a week.* One store started new recruits at $4.00, one at from $3.60 to $4.00, and the third sometimes started them at $3.50. The maximum rate for most positions was $5.00, but a few special tasks, like work at the music counter, which required piano playing, paid more. *After seven years' experience a salesgirl in one of these stores was earning only $5.00,* a rate which some of the store managers inferentially acknowledged could be maintained only because most of the girls lived at home and had no board to pay. The wage was clearly too low under any circumstances.

State Employment Office

Consideration of a number of measures for improving wage conditions in the mines has already been urged; among them, greater effectiveness in the work of public employment agencies. This applies in greater or less degree to other occupations also.

As far as income is affected by unemployment, some relief should be afforded through the development of efficient machinery for bringing together the man out of work and the employer needing workers. This, of course, is the function of the public employment offices.

In the eight public free employment offices located in the larger cities of Illinois, the state had thus made some provision up to the time of the survey for helping the man out of work to find employment; but the office located in Springfield at least had not reached a high state of efficiency.

The office was centrally located on the second floor of a business building. The staff consisted of a superintendent who was

WOMEN'S WAGES

5 & 10 CENT STORE

PAY $3.50 to $4.00 beginning wage
$5.00 maximum except for
5 out of 86 girls

A manager said:
"We choose girls who live at home because a girl can't pay board on what she gets and not go wrong or steal"

The Excuse Given
"Clerking in a 5 & 10¢ store is an apprenticeship for clerking elsewhere"

BUT WHAT DO THEY LEARN?

They don't make out sales checks
They don't judge or select goods
They don't display articles for sale

WAGES IN FIVE-AND-TEN-CENT STORES
Panel from Springfield Survey Exhibition.

formerly a mine manager, an assistant superintendent who was formerly a jail keeper, a woman clerk in charge of the woman's department, a stenographer, and a janitor. Only the janitor and stenographer were required to pass civil service tests. The others were appointed by the governor. Each new state administration, therefore, meant a new office force, a situation which almost necessarily interferes with efficient conduct of the work.

The class of labor served was almost entirely the unskilled. Of 3,773 positions reported to have been secured for men in the year ending September 30, 1913, practically half of the applicants, or 1,912, were recorded as getting jobs as "laborers," 315 as handy-men, 262 as farmers or farm laborers, while the positions of the remainder, about one-third of all the applicants, were divided in the main between those of dish washers, house men, porters, teamsters, and drivers. Almost no positions were secured in factories or offices and few were secured in the building trades.

Of the 1,194 positions reported as secured for women, 1,150, or over 95 per cent, were in domestic and personal service—chiefly as day workers, house workers, or laundresses in private families, hotels, and restaurants. A few positions were secured in offices, but none in stores or factories. While no one would dispute the importance of this kind of assistance to the unskilled, it was nevertheless clear that there were other important groups who needed the service also, and this was particularly true in Springfield, where there were no private employment agencies operating.

A further examination of the activities of the office revealed two vital weaknesses in its administration. first, that there was no follow-up work to see whether applicants referred to positions actually secured them; second, that in cases where no position was open for an applicant when he applied, no further effort was made to secure work for him.

The seriousness of the first condition is illustrated when an employer asks that a workman be sent him and the free employment agency sends a man who never shows up. When this happens once or twice the employer comes to look upon the employment office as undependable, and ceases to use it when he wants help. Indeed, we may go further. The duty of the employment office is to fill the position no matter how many persons need to be sent.

The importance of the second shortcoming of the Springfield agency is illustrated when an artisan applies for work and no request calling for a man of his trade is already on file. No record is made of this application for a job and thus he receives no help even though half an hour after he leaves the office an employer calls for just such an employe. The absolute necessity of keeping systematically filed and workable records of all applications for work, if the office aims at efficiency, and at handling a reasonable share of the work that ought to come to it, is too obvious to require argument.

Further evidence that the office was falling short of its opportunity and responsibility was found in the fact that as soon as application blanks had been entered in the register prescribed by law, the blanks were piled—not filed—in a store room where they had been accumulating since the office was opened five years before. If an applicant appeared a second time, a second blank was made out and he was compelled to answer again the same list of questions asked on his first appearance, and the method was the same for later visits. It is evident either that such an office procedure was not workable or that when used at all it involved an unnecessary waste of time.

Springfield and Milwaukee Employment Offices

Comparison of the Springfield public employment office with the public employment office of Milwaukee, Wisconsin, showed how the work in Springfield might be made more effective. There the janitor and stenographer were the only employes appointed by civil service tests; in Milwaukee all employes were so selected. In Springfield, except for a small entryway, there was no waiting room for male applicants; in Milwaukee separate offices were maintained for men and women and there were two waiting rooms for male workers, one for unskilled labor and farm hands, the other for skilled workers. Experience had shown that this latter provision was necessary if an office is to serve both skilled and unskilled workers.

INDUSTRIAL CONDITIONS

In Springfield, as has been said, applications for work were ordinarily accepted only when applicants could be referred immediately to positions; in Milwaukee effort was made to register all applicants and to find work for them. In Springfield application blanks were filed away in a store room; in Milwaukee they were placed first in a "waiting" file, and when positions were secured they were transferred to a permanent file, so placed as to be conveniently referred to by the clerk who received applications. In Springfield when an applicant was sent to a position his record was closed; in Milwaukee he was given an unstamped post card to be delivered to the employer, who was requested to post it after indicating whether the applicant was given employment. If in the course of a few days the card had not been returned, the agency communicated with the employer over the telephone to discover the result. Only after a position was actually taken was it counted among those filled. In Springfield no well-considered plans had been laid to gain the co-operation of employers and workers; in Milwaukee an advisory committee of representative employers, employes, and public officials had helped to gain for the public employment office widespread interest and co-operation. As a result of its methods large employers of labor were beginning to rely upon the Milwaukee bureau in selecting their help. On the other hand, of all the factory and store managers and other employers interviewed in the course of this investigation, and it was a goodly number, not one took the Springfield free employment agency seriously or thought that it was rendering an important service.

Changes recommended in order to improve the service were:

1. The selection of officers by civil service tests to secure more efficient management and to prevent a complete change of force with every change in state administration.

2. An advisory committee of representative employers and workers in order to secure better co-operation between employers, workers, and the bureau.

3. Rearrangement of office space so as to supply an adequate waiting room for applicants. Separation of skilled from unskilled workers would help the bureau to do more effective service for skilled men.

4. An adequate record system of applicants for work and for help.

5. All applications should be registered.

6. The scope of activities should be extended to include skilled as well as unskilled workers.

7. More adequate funds should be made available for advertising in Springfield and neighboring districts, and to provide salaries large enough to command first-rate ability for the staff.

The reorganization of the eight independent state employment offices under a bureau of a new department of labor was further recommended. But whether or not the recommendation is followed in its details, the need for some form of central control over these public offices was clear. Such control would not only promote more efficient administrative methods, but would make possible effective exchange of information between bureaus so that not only in the city but throughout the state workers could be sent where needed; and as far as possible, long periods of unemployment, which so greatly reduce the annual earnings of so many workers, might be eliminated. The institution of improved methods in the Springfield office should not, however, wait upon this centralization plan.[1]

HOURS OF LABOR

From two points of view hours of labor have bearing upon social welfare: first, because long hours of work seriously affect the workers' wellbeing, and consequently are intimately related to public health; second, because they affect the extent and possibilities of wage-earners participating in the civic life and activities of the community.

As to the first, fatigue is the result of the poisoning of the body by waste substances produced through physical activity. This has been demonstrated scientifically by running a dog until exhausted and then transfusing some of its blood into a dog that had not been exercised. The latter immediately showed signs of

[1] Other suggestions regarding methods of dealing with unemployment and inadequate wages among unskilled workers are made in the summing up of recommendations on industrial conditions beginning on page 194.

fatigue.[1] Work produces the poison of fatigue, and, as every one knows, if work is continued long enough a point of exhaustion is finally reached—the fatigue poison getting the upper hand. Of course the body attempts at once to rid itself of these toxic impurities. While work is continued, however, in most occupations at least, waste products are created faster than they can be thrown off. For this reason people are unable to work on indefinitely but are forced to take alternate periods of work with periods of rest. If good health is to continue, these periods of rest must be sufficient to permit the body, by functioning normally, to throw off the fatigue before taking up new work. Otherwise cumulation of fatigue will gradually exhaust vitality and undermine health, making the victim unusually subject to disease and premature old age. It is upon the basis of such facts as these that the United States Supreme Court has upheld laws restricting the hours of women and children as the legitimate use of the police power of the state for the protection of public health.

As to the effect of hours of work upon citizenship, it is part of the principle of democracy that people shall have leisure time to keep themselves informed and to maintain an intelligent interest in public affairs. The barrier against developing such civic interests set up, for example, by the twelve-hour day and seven-day week in the steel industry, which still obtain to a considerable extent, is one of the grounds upon which the industry has been severely condemned in recent years. With full allowance for all the mitigating circumstances, the fact nevertheless remains that such conditions, in addition to other unwholesome effects, destroy and prevent the best community life.

Hours in Manufacturing Establishments

As in the case of wages, comprehensive information regarding hours of labor was difficult to secure, for the working day varies not only from industry to industry, but from shop to shop, and between departments of the same shop. For wage-earners in the

[1] For a full discussion of the nature and effects of fatigue see Goldmark, Josephine: Fatigue and Efficiency. Russell Sage Foundation Publication, New York, 1912.

Springfield manufacturing establishments, however, fairly complete information regarding hours of labor was available.

The first fact to be noted was that the great majority of the workers in all establishments—85 per cent—were working nine hours or more a day. Only 13 per cent worked eight hours or less. It appears, therefore, that in manufacturing at least, the eight-hour day toward which the leaders of the labor movement throughout the country are working was still a good way from being achieved in Springfield.

On the other hand shorter hours were the rule in union shops. Among employes in these shops, for example, 54 per cent had an eight-hour day, while in the unorganized establishments only 7 per cent worked eight hours or less. Only 13 per cent of the men in the union shops, moreover, worked ten hours as compared with 37 per cent in the non-union work places. These figures tend strongly to support the trade unionists' point that organized workers are able to gain, and do gain for themselves, advantages which workers acting individually do not enjoy; and they refute the claim of many employers who oppose organization of their workers that they voluntarily grant all of the benefits which employes might secure through the union.

MINE, BUILDING, RAILWAY, AND OTHER WORKERS

As in manufacturing establishments, the majority of organized workers in other occupations had gained the eight-hour day. The strongest labor union group in Springfield undoubtedly was the miners, who had 10 local unions with a total membership of about 2,500. The mines of the vicinity were being run on a strictly closed shop basis, and since 1898, when the unions won a great victory in this industry, the eight-hour day had prevailed.

Most of the other trades, however, were not 100 per cent organized; and many workers in the trade were working longer hours. This was true, for example, of many boiler makers, machinists, iron moulders, and carpenters.

Employment on the railroad offered an illustration of a combination of long hours with work requiring strained attention, and with fatal results waiting as a penalty for relaxed watchfulness. Practically all of the 1,000 men connected with the various railroads running into Springfield were working a ten-hour day or night as the case might be. Irregular hours and the unbroken periods of work for week after week and month after month, without a regular day of rest, were other arduous features of railway employment. *Seven-day labor, moreover, was the rule among railroad employes.*

Conditions on the street railway were similar to those on the steam railroads, though the nine-hour day was more common and hours more regular. The conductors and motormen were working in two shifts, one from 6 a.m. to 3 p.m., the other from 3 p.m. until midnight. *Employment, moreover, was on a seven-day week basis*, although it was possible for men to get a day off now and then, with loss of pay.

Other instances of seven-day labor were found scattered throughout the city. Messenger boys were working seven days, and the same held true for bootblacks, whose hours were excessively long and who were working under something akin to the padrone system, the boys being boarded and housed together by their employers. At one stand the hours of the boys, who ranged in age from seventeen to twenty-one, were from fourteen and one-half to sixteen and one-half hours. In addition they worked two hours on Sundays, *making a work week of seven days and over ninety hours*. Seven-day labor, however, was not confined to male workers but was found also among women and to some extent among children.

Neither of the telephone companies, moreover, had seen fit to arrange its schedule so that every employe could receive one day off each week. Girl operators for both concerns were required to work at least every other Sunday and so received only one day off in every fourteen. Restaurant workers were in many instances also subjected to the seven-day week.

Certain tasks under our complex city life need to be performed for seven days a week, and there seem to be reasons which justify Sunday work in some instances; but there are few occupations in which it is not possible for an employer to adjust his force of workers so that each employe may enjoy at least one day of rest in seven, whether it be Sunday or some other day.

Hours of Women Workers

It was thus clear from our investigations that a much larger proportion of male than female workers in Springfield were enjoying an eight-hour day. The carpenters, painters, bricklayers, and other building trade workers, the miners, printers, cigar makers, and many other male workers had been able to make this gain. But their wives and sisters and daughters, whose physical resistance to the strain of industrial occupations was less than theirs, and who besides generally have home tasks after their exhausting day outside, for the most part were working in Springfield factories, stores, and laundries from nine to ten hours a day.

One reason for this undoubtedly was the fact that women workers were almost entirely unorganized. A few of them were members of a weak laundry workers' union and a few profited by the strength of the men's unions in the printing and cigar-making trades; but aside from these instances unionism had been very little utilized for them.

The women had, on the other hand, gained some protection from long hours of work through legislation, although much less than has been afforded women workers in many other states. The law, which set a standard much too low, seemed for the most part to be observed throughout the city—which observance in view of the ten-hour day legally allowed, employers could hardly in reason have failed in. More than a majority of the women workers engaged in manufacturing in Springfield were employed in three factories: the watch, meter, and shoe factories. The first two, at the time of this investigation, were operated on a nine-hour and on a six-day basis, with Saturday afternoons off the year round and two weeks of vacation without pay. Women workers in these factories were all provided with comfortable seats having backs and were seated at their work. On the whole, working conditions in these establishments were excellent and the tasks to which women were assigned did not require much physical exertion. At the shoe factory a six-day schedule of ten hours a day (nine on Saturdays) was being followed and working conditions were less satisfactory. About 400 women and girls were employed.

Women workers in the laundries, except on Saturdays when they left in the afternoon as soon as the clothes on hand were finished, were also required to work the full quota of ten hours a day allowed by the law. The conditions under which these hours were worked were often fatiguing. The majority of the women stood at their work, though experience elsewhere has shown that some of the tasks performed in Springfield in a standing position could be done quite satisfactorily sitting.

In the stores of Springfield where women were employed the ten-hour limit was reached on only one day of the week. A nine-hour day prevailed on the first five days of the week. No violation of the women's ten-hour law was found in any Springfield mercantile establishment—but so long a day would itself, in certain other states, have constituted a violation. One five-and-ten-cent store was giving all girls who had been employed a year or more a week's vacation on pay. A department store was also giving such employes a week's vacation on pay.

Night work was required of a limited number of telephone operators. A young girl of sixteen, for example, was employed by one company on the night shift from 9.30 p.m. to 7 the next morning; but her mother worried so much about her being away at night that she finally had to give it up. Hours of work did not exceed nine per day and in some cases they were seven.

Besides the telephone operators who worked at night, a few women were engaged in night work in restaurants and hotels. Unlike the law of New York state already held by the courts to be a proper measure for the protection of the health and morals of women, *the Illinois law permitted women or girls over sixteen years of age to be employed during any hours of the night.*

Thus in the industrial protection being given women Illinois was far from being abreast of the times. In failing to place greater restrictions upon the hours of women workers, it not only lagged behind the more progressive states but also behind the other great manufacturing states of Massachusetts, Pennsylvania, and New York.

ONE HUNDRED WAGE-EARNERS' FAMILIES

The main features of the industrial and work situation in Springfield—physical hazards, factory inspection, workmen's compensation, child labor, wages and irregularity of work, employment agencies, hours of work, labor legislation, and related matters—have now been reviewed. In planning the survey it was felt, however, that the investigations should be carried further—that as far as possible the effect of industrial conditions, particularly wages and unemployment, upon family life should be learned; for results in that connection are important not alone from the standpoint of the individual but also of the community. A study of conditions in 100 wage-earners' families was therefore made. These families included 573 persons, 272 of whom were employed in gainful occupations.

There is no claim that the 100 families selected are absolutely representative of Springfield's working population, for there is no known method by which 100 entirely representative families might be selected. The intention, however, was to make them as nearly representative as possible, and care was used to that end.

Proportions Gainfully Employed

The first fact which stood out in reviewing the results is the large proportion of persons over fourteen years of age who were gainfully employed. Of the males sixteen years of age and over, 96 per cent were in gainful occupations; and of the females of sixteen years and over, 45 per cent were so employed. Out of a total of 378 members of these 100 families who were fourteen years of age or over, 266, or 70 per cent, contributed to the family income. In more than half the families there were three or more contributors to the family support. Practically all who were able were obliged to help in order to secure moderately good conditions of life.

The proportion of wage-earning children was very large. Of the 57 between fourteen and sixteen years old, 41, or 72 per cent, were gainfully employed; and a number under fourteen brought in a few dollars now and then.

WAGES AND UNEMPLOYMENT

When employed, 10 out of the 70 fathers whose wage rates were reported received less than $12 a week; 32 received from $12 to $20; 28 received $20 or more; and the wages of the others were not reported or could not be estimated.

Of all the other males employed for whom information was available, one-third earned less than $7.00 a week, one-half less than $10. Among the women of sixteen years and over, more than one-fourth earned less than $6.00, and almost 70 per cent less than $8.00 a week.

Wage rates, however, are more significant in connection with regularity of employment. Of all members of these families who contributed to the family income, two out of every five reported irregular employment for the previous year—and irregular employment meant the loss of from several weeks to six months.

No accurate count of wages or days employed was kept by the workers interviewed. A few other tests were applied, however, as casting light upon the adequacy or inadequacy of earnings.

OTHER TESTS

Of the 57 families supplying information on rent, over half lived in houses which rented for less than $12 a month. They were mostly four- or five-room houses without city water, gas, electricity, or inside toilets. The insanitary surface well was the water supply. Some of these houses were crowded because of the necessity of taking in lodgers. Thirteen of the 100 families had to suffer infringement upon home privacy and the inconvenience entailed by taking boarders or lodgers, or both. One family of seven living in three rooms took in lodgers.

Of 56 persons discovered in the investigation who had left school before sixteen years of age, 25, or nearly half, had left because their parents had not felt able to continue them in school. It is true, of course, that many children, boys particularly, drop out as soon as possible because the school work as at present conducted is nowhere nearly as interesting to them as the work of the world; nevertheless the numbers leaving school because of the family's pressing need of income is large. There was reason to believe that a considerable number of Springfield children—running close to 100 per year—were dropping out of school for the latter reason. Most of the occupations they went into were "blind alley" jobs, which did not offer training or possibilities of advancement.

Over one-fourth of the mothers in the 100 families were earning money to augment the family income; and in some cases this meant neglect of children. One woman had done washing for twenty-six years until all her children were of legal age to work.

Thirty-nine of the families were saving in the form of payments on a home. A few more had bank savings; and five out of every six carried insurance, the amounts usually being only enough to cover burial costs.

It is a significant fact that of these families of Springfield wage-earners as many as 9 per cent were living so near the margin of dependency that death, sickness, or unemployment—events which may reasonably be looked for in every worker's family—had obliged them to seek charitable relief.

Finally, conditions found in Springfield showed clearly, as they have in other investigations elsewhere, the important part which low wages and unemployment play in the problems of bad housing, child labor, evasion of the laws as to compulsory education, neglected childhood, and the predisposition of families to physical and often moral breakdowns. No solution of these problems, therefore, will be effective that does not eliminate the great economic waste of unemployment and correct the evil of low wages.

INDUSTRIAL BETTERMENT IN SPRINGFIELD

Forces for Improvement

While, as we have seen, some industrial conditions in Springfield were found to be fairly satisfactory, there were many more that in important particulars failed to meet the minimum standards which the general public looks upon as reasonable. These needed improvement or correction. The immediate and important question was, what forces may be counted upon to forward this industrial betterment.

Three groups of interested parties have a share in determining industrial conditions: employers, workers, and the public. It is through these groups—employers acting together in some degree but for the most part singly, employes acting individually and through labor organizations, and the public acting through crystallized public opinion and the power of the state—that industrial improvement has been brought about in the past; and the same groups must be looked to for constructive action in the future.

Of the three, employers have the largest power and therefore the largest responsibility in determining industrial conditions. Except where labor unions force concessions, or where laws laying down definite requirements are enforced, employers have large latitude in fixing wage rates, methods of payment, hours of labor, conditions as to safety and sanitation, and regularity of employment. They may choose whom they will employ, and in a large proportion of cases may discharge workers when and for such causes as they see fit.

Economic forces, however, set substantial limitations to entire freedom of action by employers—particularly through the working of demand and supply in the labor market—and employers, therefore, are not always free to make the improvements that they are willing and ready to make. This, on the other hand, may not be accepted as a wholly valid excuse; for there are other economic forces, only now being discovered and experimented with, which when taken advantage of work toward freeing the employer to make some at least of the improvements that he favors. These are forces tending toward increased efficiency and reduced costs of production through greater consideration of the human factor in industry. Economies appear to be possible, for example, through shorter working hours that lower the accident rate, and that allow time for recuperation from fatigue; through the elimination of unemployment periods, thus escaping costs due to changes in the labor force; through increased wages—whatever the figure set by competition in the labor market may be—that would enable workers to raise their standard of living and thus maintain a higher degree of resistance against sickness; through larger participation of the workers in management; and through other measures.

Industrial Betterment by Employers

No employer in Springfield, as far as we were able to learn, was paying wages above the straight market rate. Neither was any case discovered in which an employer of his own initiative, for humanitarian reasons, had reduced the hours of labor of those in his employ. Even in safeguarding workers from industrial health hazards only one factory among those visited showed a definite effort to do more than the law required; and even in that factory legal requirements were violated in some particulars. Several employers, however, gave workers short vacations on pay, among them a telephone company, two department stores, and a five-and-ten-cent store. In most of these cases one week was given to employes who had worked a year or more. Other factories visited either gave no vacations or else allowed them without pay.

A considerable number of employers provided lunch and rest rooms for their workers, especially where many women were employed. These were found at the two laundries visited, at two of the department stores, in a telephone office, and in one large factory. Doubtless similar provisions were made at some work places not visited. Usually the lunch room was merely a place where the workers could go to eat luncheons brought from home; but one telephone company supplied a light luncheon free and employed a matron to look after the lunch and rest rooms. At the street railway car barns, where men were often idle waiting assignments, a library, club rooms, and baths were maintained. Aside, however, from these limited activities Springfield employers had done very little in the way of welfare work.

Industrial Improvements through the Workers

A girl earning $5.00 a week in a Springfield department store shortly before the survey asked for a wage increase. She was told that if she wasn't satisfied she could go elsewhere. To the store her loss was of small consequence. Another girl willing to work for $5.00 would take her place, and work in the store would move along as it had before. But to the girl the alternative was serious. It meant staying at less than a living wage, or possible temporary unemployment while seeking another place. Workingmen, moreover, with families to support, when placed in similar situations, hesitate a good deal before giving up employment, and many stay at a wage below what they think they deserve rather than venture on the uncertain hope of securing higher wages elsewhere.

The case of the girl illustrates the general truth that acting alone employes are practically powerless to win wage concessions, shorter hours, or better work conditions, for they have no means of enforcing their demands. Experience has shown that it is only by acting together that they can force hours down and wages up, or bring about other improvements. The labor union movement, therefore, offers an effective means by which employes may do something worth while toward industrial betterment.

Labor Unions

Although for many years there had been occasional activity toward organizing the workers, the labor union movement did not really get under way in Springfield until the 90's. The plumbers and the bricklayers and masons were organized in that year; the bakers, pressmen, and boiler makers in 1892. In June, 1893, representatives of the barbers, cigar makers, plasterers, printers, painters, mine workers, and hodcarriers met and established the Springfield Federation of Labor, securing a charter from the American Federation of Labor. From that time, although different locals had occasional setbacks, the growth of the movement in the city was steady.

At the time of the survey 52 different working groups were represented in Springfield's central labor body, classified under six main divisions: mining, manufacturing and mechanical industries, building and construction, trade, transportation, and miscellaneous.

There was also affiliated with the central body a women's trade union league and a federal labor union, the latter being composed of labor union sympathizers not then engaged in any trade. Besides the locals which make up the Springfield Federation of Labor there were also unions not affiliated with the Central Federation among locomotive engineers, firemen, conductors, and switchmen on railroads running into Springfield. Roughly speaking, at least 80 per cent of the workers in the organized trades were members of the union. The most marked exception to this was the laundry workers' local, which had been able to gain a foothold in but one establishment. The retail clerks' union was also rather weak.

It was not possible for us to state the exact percentage of workers in Springfield who were members of unions, for a number of the unions could not supply the data. From the figures prepared by some of the unions, however, it appears reasonably correct to put the proportion of the male wage-earners in the city who were union members (including the miners of course) at a little under 50 per cent, while of the female wage-earners less than 5 per cent were union members. Trades requiring a high degree of skill, and establishments largely patronized by working people, were generally well organized. Only about 12 per cent of workers in manufacturing establishments were members of unions.

Judging from the data supplied by over half of the various local unions, these organizations had been effective in increasing wages for their members. Most of the unions reported increases in the five years prior to the survey, the hourly rate for sheet metal workers, for example, having advanced from 45 cents to 50 cents; for journeymen stone cutters, from 50 to 56¼ cents; for ice men, from 20 to 25 cents; and on through practically all the list. There were no important decreases.

Similarly, as to hours, many of the locals reported reductions in hours per day or per week in the last five years. Sheet metal workers, for example, with an eight-hour day five years before, had recently reduced their hours per week from forty-eight to forty-four. Hours of journeymen stone cutters had been reduced in the same way; of ice men, from sixty-six to sixty. In a number of cases where there had been no reduction in hours, the eight-hour day had been gained five years before. In the majority of cases the improvements both as to hours and wages had been brought about without strikes.

Practically all of the unions provided benefits to members or their families in cases of sickness, accident, death, unemployment, or old age. Not all provided for all these contingencies, but practically all provided for some of them. On the other hand, though the need was evident, there were no important evidences of effectiveness on the part of the unions in improving the state inspection service into industrial conditions, or in securing through other methods better enforcement of the labor laws—particularly those relating to child labor.

Among skilled men workers the unions would undoubtedly continue to maintain their strength and perhaps increase it; but among unskilled men and among women workers, labor organization, though it should be striven for, nevertheless did not look so hopeful. In the skilled trades, therefore, male workers acting through their unions, might be counted on to play a part in industrial betterment, but among unskilled men and among women workers—where conditions were farthest from satisfactory—employers and the public must be relied upon chiefly for improvement measures in the very immediate future.

Labor Legislation

That the public has a stake in industrial questions and should shoulder its responsibility was recognized in a substantial manner in Illinois when in 1893 a State Department of Factories and Workshops was created and laws were enacted prohibiting employment of children under fourteen years of age, or of women, in the manufacture of wearing apparel, for more than eight hours a day and forty-eight a week. Previously, in 1877 and again in 1891 there had been efforts at child labor legislation, but failure to provide state inspectors to enforce the laws rendered the acts ineffective. Since 1893, the extension of state control over industry has been almost continuous. A listing of the more important enactments showed a fairly rapid extension of the field of labor laws and a gradual strengthening of requirements—but an extension that is not at all unique for an industrial state. Other states had legislated in fields not entered in Illinois, as seen, for example, in their establishment of minimum wage boards, the prohibition of night work by women, the limitation of the workday of eight hours for women, the guarantee of one day of rest in seven to workers, the enactment of compulsory compensation laws, and other measures. That the public will exercise increasing influence through legislation for improved industrial conditions appears certain, and should be encouraged, particularly with reference to the strengthening of the child labor laws, the reduction of the hours of working women, the protection of workers from physical hazards, and the establishment of minimum wage machinery.

OTHER PUBLIC ACTIVITIES

The influence of the community is potent in ways other than through legislation. Important, in this connection, is the existence of a public opinion that insists upon the fair and full *enforcement* of legislation touching industrial matters; that demands intelligent and even-handed treatment of the interests of both employer and employe before the courts and by court officers; that, in other disputed issues where no official tribunal has jurisdiction, will guarantee to both sides equal consideration before claims are decided; that would make it hard for industries and commercial enterprises maintaining conditions below a reasonable standard to do business in the community; and that would work through other channels as occasion demands.

Some of these may take form in the establishment and maintenance of agencies to furnish pertinent information on the quality of present law enforcement (through bureaus of government research, committees and commissions on public efficiency, industrial surveys, etc.); in the selection of persons for judicial positions who recognize the importance and complexity of industrial questions and have gone to some pains to make themselves intelligent upon them; in the creation of machinery for arbitration and conciliation of industrial differences; and in the organization and support of quasi-public institutions, such as consumers' leagues, civic improvement societies, and an independent press and pulpit, which afford opportunity in the public interest to thresh out acute industrial situations and to take organized action. This field of activity offers unlimited possibilities for public service; but in many regards it was still virgin soil in Springfield.

At the same time the community must be willing and expect to bear its share of the legitimate cost of maintaining good industrial standards. There undoubtedly are many cases in which employers are already doing all that they can. In such cases, where the cost of necessary improvements cannot be financed out of the reasonable proceeds of the business, the public, granting that the business satisfies a real need in the community, must be prepared to assume its part of the extra charges, which in most cases would take the form of increased prices. In other words, in addition to giving its preference to establishments meeting good standards as to work conditions, the public should be ready to pay its just share of the costs involved.

Let us look now at the more specific measures for improvement that needed to be adopted and the particular division or sub-groupings of these social forces that should give assistance.

Reorganization of State Industrial Bodies into a Department of Labor and Mining

The first and one of the most important conclusions regarding industrial conditions in Springfield was that the state bodies having to do with industrial conditions should be reorganized into a single Department of Labor and Mining. While the survey has dealt primarily with conditions in Springfield and Sangamon County, it was nevertheless clear that some of the remedies for local industrial evils must come through action by the state. Springfield cannot disengage itself from the state in these matters, and there was reason to believe that industrial conditions in many other parts of the state were no better than here. Springfield, moreover, had a special responsibility for assisting toward a better situation because of its natural position of leadership in the state and because it was no longer uninformed upon its more urgent needs.

It has been seen that much confusion prevailed in administering the labor laws (and in the laws themselves) because of the numerous unco-ordinated state bodies that had to do with industry and labor. For example, in the reporting of work accidents similar establishments were required in some cases to report to entirely different authorities, and the different state authorities did not compile these facts for the same periods. Again there was considerable difference in the methods and thoroughness in the work of the mine inspectors, railway safety inspectors, and those charged with inspecting factories, mercantile establishments, mills, workshops, and so on.

It was, therefore, recommended that the numerous independent bodies dealing with labor conditions be consolidated into one state department, to be called the Department of Labor and Mining, with bureaus organized to have charge of special work. These should include a bureau of inspection responsible for railroad, factory, and other inspection service, except mining; a bureau of child labor; of employment, including supervision of the public employment agencies; of mining; of research and labor statistics; and any other bureaus that may later be needed. The plan of reorganization should provide for the establishment of an Industrial Commission as an integral part of the new labor department, with the commission, instead of a single commissioner, acting as the executive head of the department.

This consolidation and co-ordination of functions was urged as of primary importance in improving labor conditions all along the line, insuring safety from accident and disease, reducing child labor and unemployment, prohibiting the extension of work periods beyond legal hours, and securing better industrial relations.

Industrial Commission

It was seen that safety from fire and other accidents while at work, and from disease due to work conditions, presented serious problems in Springfield. In some instances these were due to lack of law enforcement; in others to inadequate legislation. Remedies for poor enforcement have already been discussed. Where inadequate legislation was the cause two courses were open. In some instances it might be advisable to handle particular evils through specific legislation; but for the great majority of the varying, detailed, and multitudinous conditions presenting physical hazards it was not practicable to trust to specific laws. It was recommended instead that an act be passed laying down the general principle, as is done by the Wisconsin law, that all places of employment must be safe and that every employer must furnish and use safety devices and safeguards, "and shall do every other thing reasonably necessary to protect the life, health, safety, and welfare of employes." It was further recommended that, as a part of the plan to reorganize the state industrial agencies, an industrial commission or industrial board be created as a part of the new labor department, and charged with administering the law—the commission to be composed of three or five members having equal powers, one of whom should be chairman. For the assistance of the commission, advisory committees, upon which both employers and employes are represented, should be provided for. The commission should also be in executive control of the reorganized labor department.

The industrial commission should have jurisdiction over places of employment, and be vested with power to ascertain and prescribe standards of safety, to order safeguards and safety devices, to fix reasonable standards for the construction, repair, and maintenance of places of employment, and to issue orders designed to protect the life, health, safety, and welfare of employes, and to act as a board of arbitration, mediation, and conciliation. The law creating the commission should provide for prompt and full reporting of all accidents to this single body. Thus, instead of enacting special laws, the commission should, after an investigation and a hearing in each case, issue an order covering the point in question.[1]

Workmen's Compensation

Again, the investigations in Springfield showed that while the workmen's compensation law established greater justice in remuneration for work accidents, it failed, in many of the most hazardous occupations, because of its optional feature, to accomplish without litigation prompt and specific compensation for industrial injuries. A new law, or amendment to the old law, much more firmly establishing the basic principle of compensation—that industry should bear the costs of injuries due to hazards which it has introduced—should be secured. The law should thus make compensation compulsory. This would not

[1] See Industrial Commission Law, Laws of Wisconsin, 1911, Chapter 485.
For a full description and discussion of the industrial commission idea see report written by Prof. John R. Commons and signed by a majority of the members of the United States Commission on Industrial Relations in the final report of the commission.

only provide more adequately for injured workers, but would prove another powerful influence for the prevention of accidents.

The administration of the workmen's compensation act should be made a function of the industrial commission of the reorganized labor department.

Health Insurance

Conditions affecting health in Springfield industries have been shown to be of great variety and in many instances to constitute real dangers. Some of these conditions could be changed through preventive action either voluntarily taken by employers and workers, or required by state regulation, or through both means. Some of the resulting damages might be borne by employers through a broad interpretation of the compensation laws; but there would still remain a large amount of occupational sickness falling as a disproportionately heavy economic and physical burden upon the shoulders of the worker. It should not be his loss, but should at least be shared, if not entirely borne, by the industry and the public. A means to this end is found in health insurance. It was believed, moreover, as in the case of workmen's compensation laws, that health insurance legislation would act as a powerful force for prevention of disease. We recognized, however, that information on the actuarial questions involved and upon the proportions in which the various interested parties should participate in the insurance cost was still very limited as applied to conditions in the United States. It was recommended, therefore, that the first step be taken; namely, that a commission of the legislature be appointed to study and report upon the matter.

City Enforcement of Fire Regulations

In addition to a statute requiring "sufficient and reasonable means of escape" from work places in case of fire, a second statute stipulated that all factory buildings over two stories high must have fire-escapes of a type to be determined by the local government. Enforcement, however, was left to the sheriff and grand jury, neither of whom ever inspected factories. Moreover, the city government, as far as we could learn, had never determined what was a safe and acceptable type of fire-escape.

A Springfield ordinance enacted many years before also dealt with fire protection, but because of changes in the official machinery provided for determining the type of fire-escape to be required, the ordinance had not been effective.

The necessary steps should be taken in both cases to see that a standard type of fire-escape is determined upon, and that the laws are enforced. The consideration of other measures to prevent fires and to insure safety against them was urged as an integral part of the work of the fire department. This was especially important until the state industrial commission, here recommended, should cover the field.

Safety Campaigns and Co-operation for Safety

Safety for the worker while at work is not wholly dependent upon legislation and state action. It can be promoted by the employer who, out of a feeling of social responsibility and interest in his workers, makes it a point to be always in advance of the law, seeing to it that dangerous conditions are eliminated as soon as recognized; it can be promoted by the worker, who out of a due regard for the welfare of his fellow-workers, himself, and the interests of his employer, exercises as much care as possible in his work; by the public, which, recognizing its responsibility to the workers as well as its own stake in the injury problem lends its assistance through educational methods and campaigns for safety; and by all three through an appreciation of the importance of co-operation. This is not a new kind of activity, for many large corporations have engaged in it with gratifying results for a number of years.

With the exception of only one or two employers, however, no such accident-prevention work had ever been carried on in Springfield by any of the three main groups of interested parties. Such work should enlist the energies not of one or two exceptional employers, but of all, as well as the employers' organizations; for employers, because of their large powers, have a special responsibility in determining conditions in their establishments. It is a fruitful field also for labor unions, by instructing and encouraging the workers to use care, and by bringing hazardous conditions to the notice of responsible persons. Educational work by civic bodies and citizens' committees, and co-operation of employers, employes, and such public agencies are also recommended.

Enforcement of Child Labor Law

It has been seen that neither the enforcement of the child labor law of Illinois nor the law itself was satisfactory. Children under sixteen years of age were being employed for illegal hours or in prohibited employments. The remedy for this situation must come through the State Factory Inspection Department. The force of inspectors in this department should be increased to make effective law enforcement possible, and the chief inspector should then be held strictly responsible for the conduct of the work. Better adjustment of the hours of inspectors' work to the character of their duties, the adoption of a policy of giving full publicity to successful prosecutions, and better work by the truant officer were among the more detailed recommendations.

Under the reorganization plan recommended the enforcement of the child labor law should be in the hands of a bureau of child labor in the new department of labor and mining.

Child Labor Legislation

It has been seen also that the provisions of the child labor law governing age and school certificates were open to easy evasion. The remedy, of course, lay with the legislature. The law should be amended, making it more difficult to evade the requirements regarding proof of age, requiring at least a sixth grade education or its equivalent before a child under sixteen might leave school to go to work, and requiring that evidence of normal development and sound physical conditions be produced before a work certificate could be secured.

Wages and Unemployment

One important conclusion became clear. Springfield workers, except in a few trades, were suffering greatly reduced incomes because of a great deal of seasonal and irregular employment. One of the most important measures here recommended for reducing the amount and bad effects of this irregular employment, and one which has general application to practically all kinds of employment, was the development of greater efficiency in the work of the Springfield free employment agency. As a part of the reorganization plan, already recommended, by which the various industrial bodies of the state should be brought together in a department of labor and mining, it was urged that all state employment offices be put under a bureau of this new department. In the meantime, however, a number of improvements in methods in the Springfield office should be instituted.

In the coal mining industry a certain amount of irregular employment was artificially stimulated by biennial agreements between the operators and the union. To do away with as much as possible of this it was recommended that either negotiations between the operators and the men be started earlier, or that an arrangement such as was recently adopted in the anthracite district be made, which would provide for the continuance of work while negotiations are in progress or until it should become clear that a new agreement could not be reached. There was also a large amount of seasonal work due to seasonal demand for products, and the operation of too many mines was a factor. To mitigate the results of this it was recommended that the industry be regularized through as much summer production as possible. It was also recommended that careful consideration be given to the question of government control, which prevents the opening of new mines until there is commercial need for them.

Among skilled and semi-skilled workers in factories, the building trades, and on railroads, as we have seen, labor unions had an effective influence in increasing wages. In fact wage conditions among all union workers were generally better than among non-union workers in Springfield, though probably this fact was not due entirely to union influence. It appeared, however, that the unions offered one important measure for wage increases among the better trained and the skilled workers.

The wages of unskilled male workers in Springfield and of many women workers, especially in laundries, five-and-ten-cent stores, and restaurants, were very low—too low in many cases to permit the women to maintain themselves properly or to permit men to support an average family of five or six in decency. The pro[b]lem of increasing the wages of these groups, however, and of [re]ducing the irregularity of their employment is by no means simp[le]. Up to the present the labor union movement has made but lit[tle] progress with them. Union men should face this as one of th[e] serious problems and see in it both a responsibility and an opp[or]tunity for rendering service to a group less able to help the[m]selves than are the great majority of union members.

The wage problem, whether among skilled or unskilled, is [not] entirely a local problem; but its solution nevertheless depends [in] part upon the action of localities. A number of measures, ho[w]ever—some of them indirect in their influence—were reco[m]mended to citizens of Springfield as helpful toward improving [the] lot of low-paid workers. Among these were: the prohibition [of] child labor with the probable consequent increase in the dema[nd] for and the wage of adult labor; and as a corollary of this, [the] development of better industrial education for children now [of] school age, which shall prepare the coming workers for be[tter] paid and higher types of work; the establishment of better w[age] rates for manual labor on public works; and the establishmen[t of] minimum wage standards.

In the case of salesgirls in mercantile places, and other l[ow] paid women workers, some improvement might be brought ab[out] through organization of the workers—a measure which at [best] would be difficult but which should be thoroughly tried. A sec[ond] measure is the utilization of public opinion expressed eit[her] through constant objection to low wages in specific cases [or] through consumers withdrawing patronage from stores pay[ing] low wages. This has been worked out in some communi[ties] through the organization of consumers' leagues. In additio[n to] these, the establishment of a minimum wage board through w[hich] assurance may be had that wages at least adequate for the [decent] support of girls giving the whole of their working time to st[ores] or other work places was recommended.

Unemployment Insurance

As already stated, unemployment was found to be a ser[ious] problem in Springfield. The measures recommended to deal [with] it were aimed at as immediate relief as possible. The time when a system of unemployment insurance, if it should seem desirable, could be instituted did not appear close enough to offer an early improvement of conditions. It was recommended, however, that thorough study of the unemployment situation and unemployment insurance be taken up through a commission to be created by the legislature.

Seven-day Labor

Among both men and women a number were found working seven days a week. The courts of New York state had held a law prohibiting the seven-day work week in factories and mercantile establishments to be constitutional. A similar law was recommended for Illinois. It was urged especially that the churches and other religious bodies, which must at least believe that all persons should have one day of rest in seven, give this proposed legislation their vigorous support.

Hours of Work of Women

Many women in Springfield work ten hours a day—often standing—and a few women were night workers. Many other states, including all the great manufacturing states, were giving women greater protection from long hours of labor than was given by the state of Illinois. To correct the situation the law allowing women to work ten hours a day seven days a week should be changed to make it illegal to employ women at most for more than eight hours a day or forty-eight hours a week. This would merely be eliminating the seven-day week and reducing hours on the other six days to eight.

Moreover, the law should be amended to prohibit night work by women and girls.

Hours of Work of Men

The hours of labor of men in a few Springfield industries were exceedingly long. A majority of the trade union members, however, worked only eight hours. It seemed, therefore, that the union offered one important means—probably the most practical immediate means—to better working hours; and workers would do well to look into the accomplishments of the local labor organizations.

Since, however, unskilled laborers are difficult to organize and it was among them that excessive hours were most prevalent, it seemed likely, if long hours of labor were soon to be eliminated, that Illinois and other states must secure this result through legislation. There is a growing opinion that there is small reason to differentiate between men and women in restricting hours; and that there is ample reason for action by the state to regulate the hours of men's work. Illinois as a great industrial state had and still has an opportunity to lead in this advance movement.

In addition, and applying to the hours of both men and women, action by consumers through public protest and the withdrawal of patronage where hours of work are harmful, should be taken. Also a number of the indirect methods already recommended for dealing with low wages apply in some degree to the reduction of working hours that are too long.

IX

PUBLIC HEALTH[1]

The most definite index of the health history of Springfield is to be found in her death records. In general practice the number of deaths registered in a city includes all persons dying within the city limits, whether residents or not. In this survey, however, the study of death records was restricted to deaths of Springfield residents, the causes of these deaths, and their distribution throughout the city. On this basis the questions naturally arise as to what were the leading causes of death in Springfield and in what degree they were preventable. The survey's task, in general terms, also included an examination of the sickness records of the city and its sanitary conditions. The aim was to determine what losses were being suffered and in what way these losses might be prevented.

The principal cause in Springfield's death list was tuberculosis, a preventable disease; the second, pneumonia, is to a considerable degree preventable. With the third and fourth causes, heart disease and Bright's disease, the health authorities could do little of a direct nature, but the fifth, diarrhea and enteritis among infants under two years, offered great opportunities for life saving. Other opportunities for prevention were also noted in the records of typhoid fever, syphilis, the contagious diseases of children, and a part of the accidents and premature births. Altogether, the number of preventable deaths constituted at least a fourth, and quite possibly a third, of all the deaths. Summarizing the record of the city with respect to the principal preventable causes for the last six years before the survey, 1908–13, we found 1,405 preventable deaths—1,218 from diseases and 187 from accidents. These were conservative totals, as they did not include deaths from pneumonia among old persons, deaths of infants certified

[1] Summary of report on Public Health in Springfield, Illinois, by Franz Schneider, Jr.

under such titles as premature birth, marasmus, inanition, and a number of other causes where modern medicine argues that some

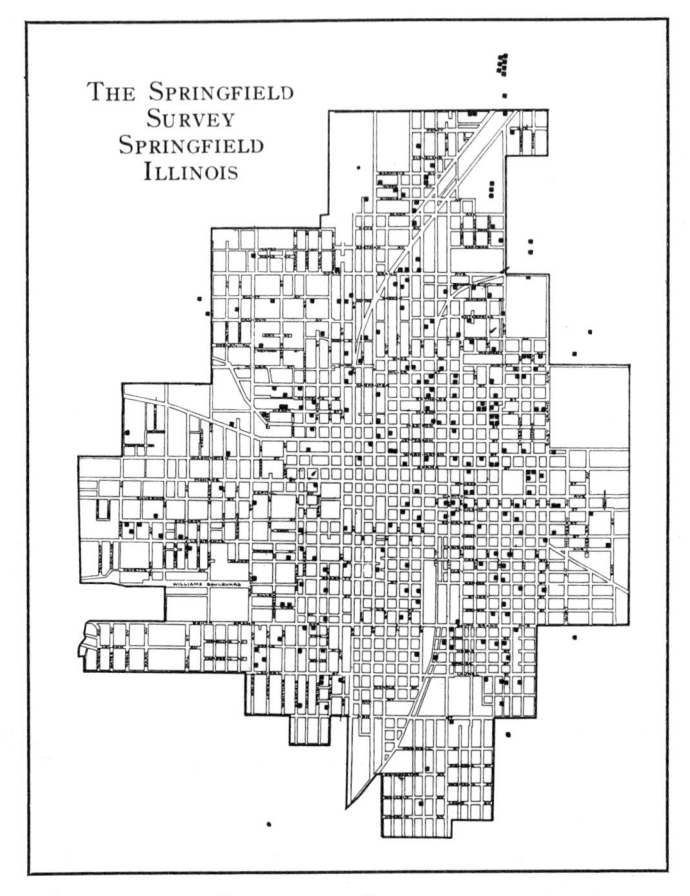

PNEUMONIA IN SPRINGFIELD

Deaths of residents under fifty-five years of age, 1908–1913. Pneumonia is another one of the important infectious diseases, and study of it by the health department, especially as related to the deaths it causes among infants, would probably be well repaid.

saving can be made. A life wastage of this magnitude demands the businesslike attention of the community.

General Facts Bearing on Springfield's Health

As already pointed out, the surface of Springfield, which occupies about eight and one-half square miles on the level prairie, is very flat. The city lies between two parallel creeks which flow in northeasterly direction to the Sangamon River. Spring Creek, to the northwest, receives about three-fourths of the drainage of the city; Sugar Creek, to the southeast, carries off the rest. Old Town Branch, a tributary of Spring Creek, is the city's principal drain and has been covered over and converted into a sewer.

Of the city's 51,678 people in 1910, 5.73 per cent were Negroes and 13.4 per cent foreign-born whites. While race and color were not important factors in Springfield, the clustering of these elements in certain districts had an important bearing on the city's health problem. Thus, while Negroes and foreign-born whites did not form a large proportion of Springfield's total population, 19.1 per cent in 1910, these two components together made up 36 per cent of the population in ward one, and 24 per cent of that in ward six, as compared with 11 and 10 per cent in wards four and five. Wards one and six had also the larger proportion of children of school age and a higher birth rate. The percentage of illiterates was 11.2 and 7.4 in wards one and six, as against 3 and 1.3 in the fourth and fifth wards. In short, the eastern and northern parts of the city contained the younger, poorer, and more foreign components of the population and most of the Negroes, while the southwestern section was more purely native white, was older, and its people were more comfortably situated. Thus the health problem was much more difficult in certain districts, demanding special activity on the part of the health authorities.

Infant Mortality

The best index of the intensity of infant mortality is a ratio, in a given year, of deaths of infants under one year of age to births. An efficient registration of births is necessary, however, for the computation of this rate and this status had not yet been reached in Springfield. Although the registration of births was a legal obligation, the acting superintendent of health estimated

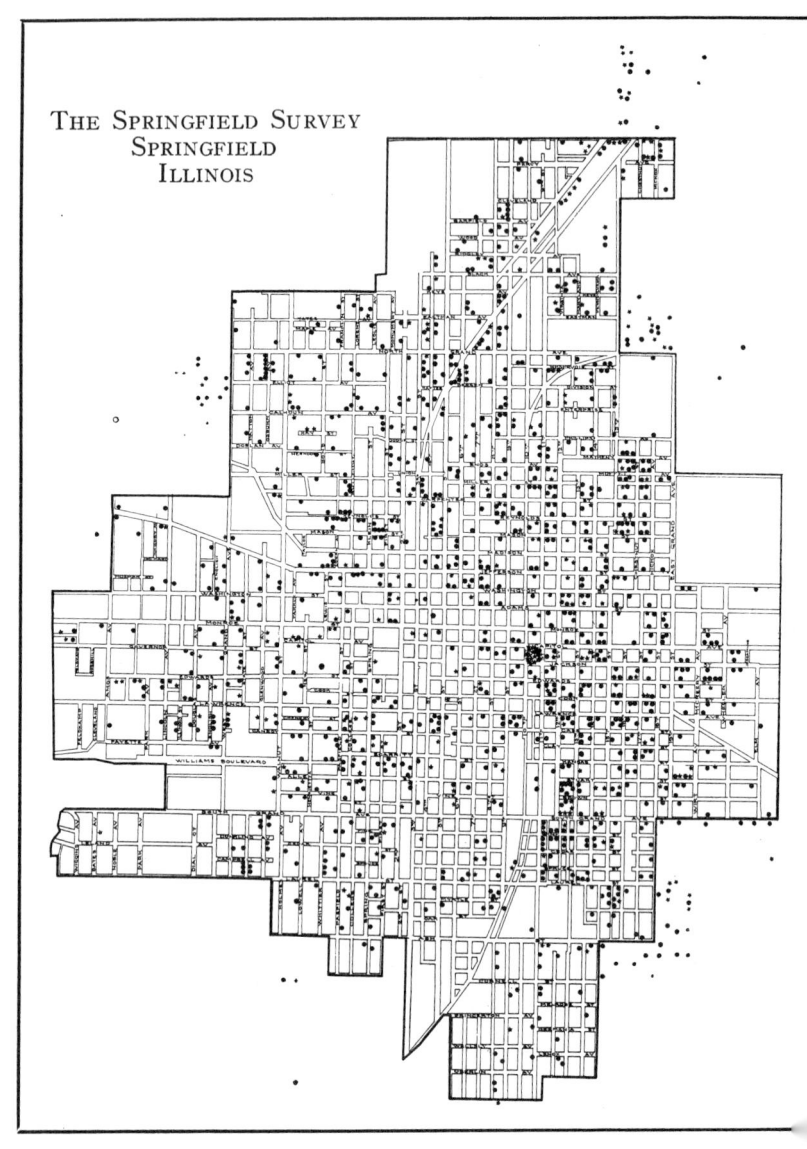

BIRTHS IN SPRINGFIELD, 1913

Round dots represent births registered at city and county offices during the last year before the survey. Stars represent unregistered births located by the survey. At least a fifth of the births were unregistered.

that the record of 1,373 births for 1912 and 1913 represented about two-thirds of those actually born.

During the survey a search was made for births not registered, and a study of these brought out the fact that failure in birth registration was not a sin of the poor solely. Twenty-five per cent of the unregistered births were in ward four, and 20 per cent in ward five, two of the best residential districts. Another fact of considerable interest was the low birth rate in wards five and seven, some of the best residence sections and the business section being in these wards.

Prompt and complete registration of births, already required by law, is essential to the computation of exact infant death rates and to the effective administration of preventive measures. Proper birth registration is also highly important to the child in later life; it establishes parentage, legitimacy, and age—facts which may be necessary in connection with school attendance, the securing of working papers, the right to marry or to vote, or relative to entering one of the government services or in obtaining an inheritance. Steps had already been taken to secure the cooperation of the public and the medical profession, and it was desirable that these efforts should be continued in a vigorous manner.

Such evidence as was available in the face of the incomplete birth returns pointed to about the ordinary rate of infant mortality for a city the size of Springfield. It must be pointed out, however, that the ordinary rate was an unsatisfactory one and that in certain parts of the city the problem was acute. When the infant death rate for 1913 was figured against the number of births for which any record could be found (including those for which no definite address was obtainable) the rate was 114.1 deaths per thousand births; when only those births for which a definite address could be obtained were used the rate was 129.9 per thousand. As a check on these figures, which were true infant death rates, the average number of infant deaths a year during the years 1908–13, i. e., the last six years before the survey, was compared with the number of infants under one year of age, the resulting rate being 127.4 deaths per thousand infants. In relation to Springfield's opportunities for saving life the problem is of prime importance.

Thus, out of every 100 infants born in Springfield about 10 died before becoming one year of age. In certain parts of the city, however, only about five died, while in certain other districts as many as 20 did not live to reach their first birthday.

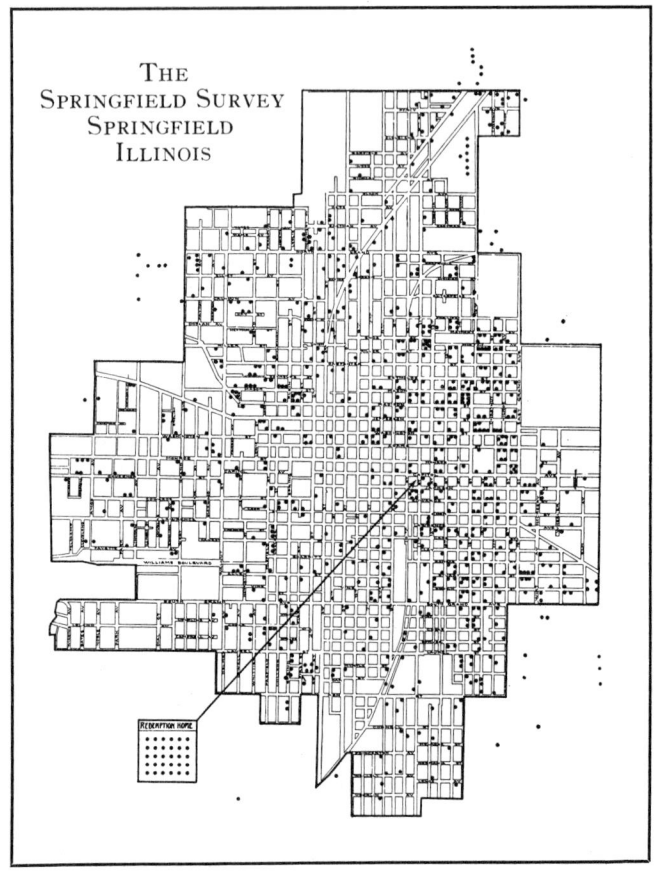

DEATHS OF INFANTS UNDER ONE YEAR. SPRINGFIELD, 1908–1913

The problem centered chiefly in the first and sixth wards in the eastern section, although there was reason to believe that substantial improvement could be accomplished in the third, fifth, and seventh wards. The wards to the east of Tenth Street, which in 1910 included 36.4 per cent of the population, were responsible for 45.6 per cent of the births located in 1913, and for 61 per cent of the infant deaths reported in that year. During the six years 1908–13 these wards were responsible for 57.5 per cent of the mortality. The infant deaths in these districts were due, furthermore, in a relatively high proportion of instances, to the diseases which modern sanitation has learned to prevent.

The principal causes of deaths of infants under one year of age were premature birth, the pneumonias, acute infections (including whooping cough, syphilis, measles, and the like), diarrhea, and enteritis. In examining this list with an eye to life saving, it may be conceded that a considerable proportion of the premature births were probably unavoidable, being due to constitutional defects. Prenatal educational and nursing work among mothers should, however, save many. The registration, examination, and regulation of midwives is also highly important.

In other cities the large group formed by the pneumonias, diarrhea, and enteritis have yielded to preventive efforts. Deaths from these causes are commonly the result of ignorance of the proper care and feeding of infants and the problem is that of teaching uninformed mothers. As a means to this end the employment of public health nurses who are qualified to visit homes and instruct mothers who would not ordinarily receive proper advice regarding the care of infants was recommended. This work might be carried on by means of infant welfare stations under the city health department, where instruction and demonstrations might be given mothers and at which a doctor should be in attendance during certain hours.

Moreover, prompt and complete registration of births, already required by law, should become an accomplished fact. Other steps, to be discussed later in this report, among them being improvement in sanitary conditions in certain parts of the city and improvement in the city's milk supply, should be taken.

No escape is possible from the conclusion that a steady and considerable life and health wastage was constantly going on among the infants of Springfield. If during the six years prior to the survey the other wards had but equaled the record of ward two, only 383 infants under one year of age, instead of 727, would have died. This would represent the saving of about 57 babies a year, or a total of 344. In other words, the lives of nearly half of these victims might have been saved by proper precautions.

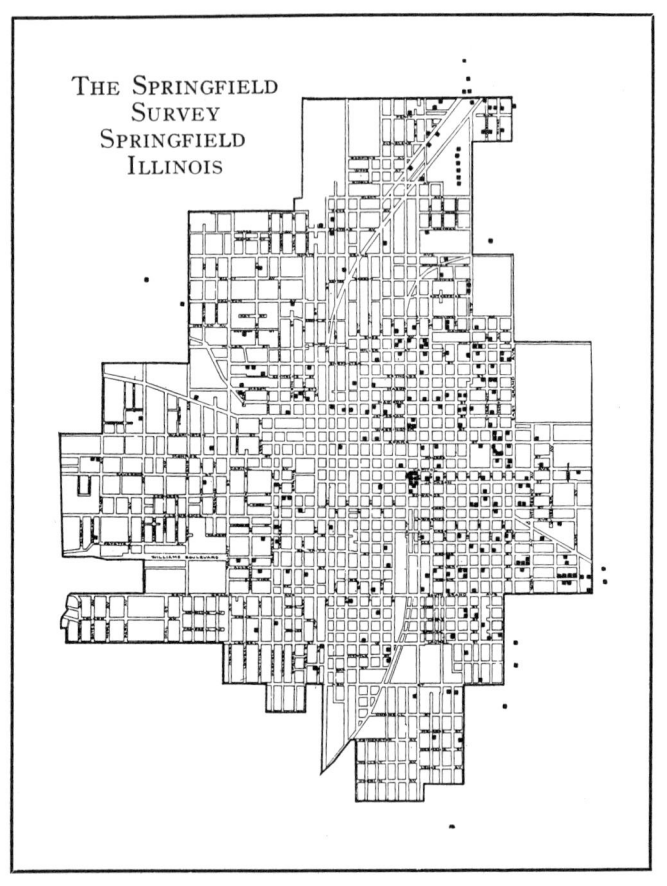

DEATHS OF INFANTS UNDER TWO FROM DIARRHEA AND ENTERITIS, SPRINGFIELD, 1908–1913
Note the preponderance in the east part of the city. This is one of the principal preventable causes of infant mortality.

CONTAGIOUS DISEASES OF CHILDREN

The most important contagious diseases with which children have to contend, if tuberculosis be excepted, are diphtheria, scarlet fever, whooping cough, and measles. Their importance is great, both as represented by the amounts of sickness and death of which they are the immediate cause and by the injurious effects they have on the kidneys, respiratory organs, and other parts of the body.

The number of deaths from these diseases in Springfield during the six years prior to the survey was 159, an annual average of 26. In the last five years 1,441 cases of diphtheria and scarlet fever alone had been reported. The October 1909 bulletin of the health department represented the situation truly not only for then but now, in these words:

> While it may be truthfully contended that Springfield has no more cases of scarlet fever and diphtheria than most of the other medium-sized cities of the Middle West, it is none the less true that we have too many such cases.

A study of the distribution throughout the city of diphtheria, scarlet fever, whooping cough, and measles threw light on their preventability and the problem of their suppression. As in the records of infant mortality, wards one and six were high, wards two and four low, and wards three and five in an intermediary position. The lowest rates of all were in ward seven. The ratio of deaths to cases reported by given diseases showed again that the east side ratios (those sections where Negroes, foreigners, and the poorer people were found in largest numbers) were excessive, although those for diphtheria in wards two, three, and four were higher than should prevail. While the general fatality in Springfield from these diseases, 8 per cent in a six-year period, was not uncommon, judged by the standards of modern hygiene, it was far too high. With regard to all four diseases under discussion, the situation showed no improvement in the last six years.

In recent years the best practice for the control of these diseases has undergone considerable change. Whereas great emphasis was formerly given to desquamation (peeling) and fumigation at the termination of the case, the importance of these points is now minimized and the emphasis is shifted to early recognition of cases, especially mild cases and "carriers" (persons who harbor the disease organisms but show none of the usual symptoms), and to the prompt and efficient disinfection of the discharges, particularly nasal and mouth, of infected persons.

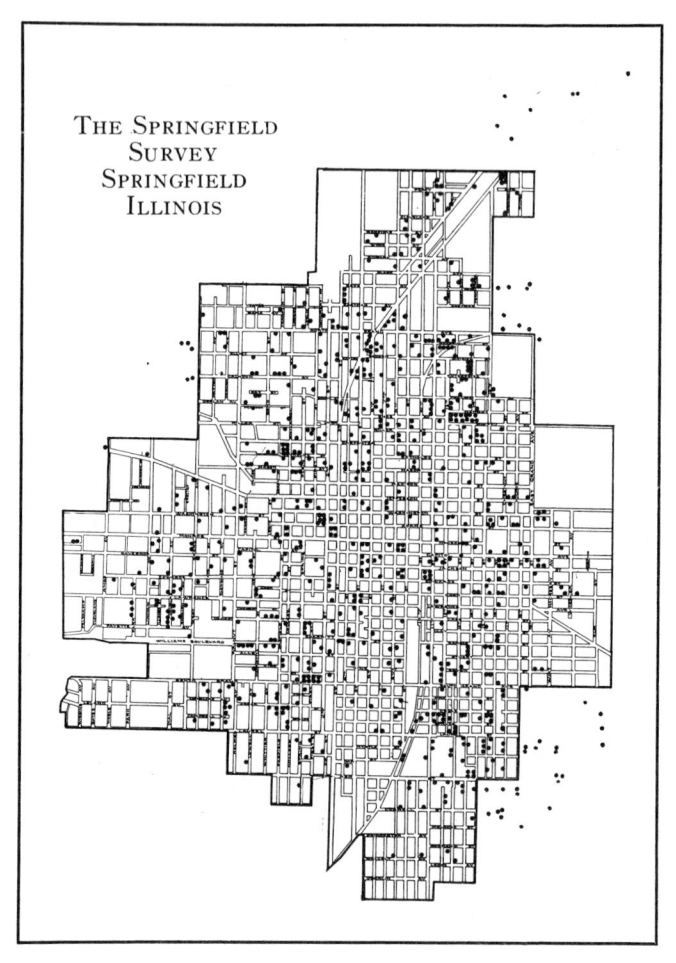

CASES OF DIPHTHERIA REPORTED TO THE HEALTH DEPARTMENT, SPRINGFIELD, 1909–1913

Cases of diphtheria were being released from quarantine by the attending physician. This is bad because there are usually a few physicians who will release cases too early and so expose other children to infection. Release by the health department only after negative cultures from the patient's throat and nose is much to be preferred.

In diphtheria, whooping cough, and scarlet fever much can be done by prompt isolation of patients with the first appearance of symptoms, and by searching for persons who have been in contact with such cases. In measles it is more difficult because a patient is infectious for as long as ten days before the appearance of symptoms. Health authorities can lessen the fatality of the disease, however, by calling the attention of parents to the necessity of taking great care of children for a considerable period after apparent recovery.

Additional health department activities demanded by the newer ideas include follow-up medical inspection of "contacts," better instruction of families as to the details of isolation, especially as regards the disinfection of discharges, and generous reinspection of quarantined cases. The savings incidental to the newer ideas include relief from the expense and annoyance of fumigation and, in a considerable proportion of cases, a material shortening of the period of quarantine.

The procedures employed in Springfield were those dictated by the older practices common to most American cities of similar size. These included reports to the health department of infectious and contagious diseases, the placing of a quarantine card at front and rear door, and the presentation of a state board of health pamphlet with regard to the care of the disease. Members of the family were required to stay apart unless there was satisfactory room isolation. The library and board of education were notified, and the family directed not to return milk bottles. Unless a complaint was received, the health department did nothing more until the attending physician notified the department that the case was ready for release. The inspector then took down the card and fumigated with formaldehyde. The usual quarantine period for diphtheria was fourteen days, and for scarlet fever the minimum period of isolation was twenty-one days, release being made on the word of the physician that desquamation was complete. In measles and whooping cough the patient was simply excluded from school, other children in the household being likewise excluded until they had had the disease or the patient was isolated.

A number of important suggestions were made, the adoption

of which would insure greater safety to the city's children. The chief improvements that should be instituted were:

1. Prompter and fuller reporting of cases. It is suggested that the health department furnish physicians with sets of postcard forms for this purpose, and that written confirmation of telephonic reports be required.

2. More detailed investigation of cases and of the possible relation between cases, accompanied by examination of persons who have been in contact with the case to discover mild and incipient cases and carriers. This would naturally require more complete history cards, the preparation of maps showing the distribution and spread of diseases, and the like.

3. Closer supervision of cases of diphtheria and scarlet fever, including a prompt initial visit by a medical inspector or specially trained nurse employed by the health department to issue detailed instructions as to the maintenance of the patient and the disinfection of his discharges; reinspection to follow at frequent intervals to see that instructions are being followed, with release only after a final inspection by a medical representative of the health department. In the case of diphtheria, release only after two successive negative cultures from the throat and nose.

4. The visitation of cases of measles and whooping cough to instruct the responsible parties as to the management of the patient and the disinfection of his discharges.

5. Transference of the present emphasis on fumigation at the termination of the case to bedside disinfection of discharges during the activity of the disease and general cleaning at its termination.

The Tuberculosis Situation: Extent

During the five-year period 1909-13, 346 whites and 72 Negroes, or a total of 418 resident men, women, and children, died in Springfield from all forms of tuberculosis. This was an annual average of more than 83. The tuberculosis death rate per 100,000 population during this time was 137.3 for whites and 470 for Negroes, making the rate for the whole city 156.3. This includes only residents of the city.

The ratio of white to Negro population in the city was 16.4 to 1; the ratio of white to Negro deaths from tuberculosis was 4.8 to 1. The Negro rate had varied from 1.9 times greater than the rate for whites in 1910 to 4.7 times greater in 1912, and 5.8 times greater in 1909. For the five-year period it was

3.4 times greater. The Negro rate, which is much higher throughout the country than the rate for whites, is generally explained by the personal habits and insanitary manner of living of the

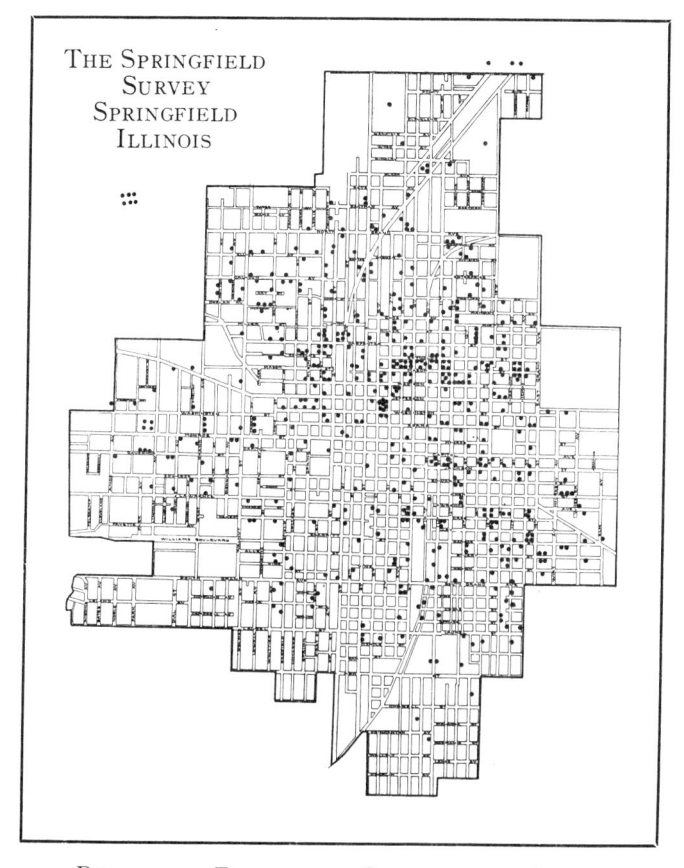

DEATHS FROM TUBERCULOSIS, SPRINGFIELD, 1908–1913

Tuberculosis killed 490 Springfield residents in the six years before the survey. It is one of the most important of the preventable diseases, but was receiving little or no attention from the city health department.

Negro. He presents an acute problem which is accentuated by the possibility of his spreading the disease to persons other than his own race.

The number of living cases of tuberculosis in a community may be conservatively estimated at five times the number of deaths from the disease during the previous year. Using the average number of Springfield deaths for the last five years (69 whites and 14 Negroes) there were probably at least 345 white and 70 Negro living cases in the city continuously—approximately 415 in all.

The application of this estimate was warranted by replies from Springfield physicians who reported the number of cases under treatment in 1913 as 546, and at the time of the inquiry 228. These figures did not include cases under the care of physicians not reporting, those persons who had no physician, and the probably very considerable number of incipient and moderately advanced cases who were unaware that they were afflicted. On the other hand, it is probable that some of the cases reported changed physicians during the time and were reported more than once.

Existing Agencies for Control of the Disease

Even a conservative view of the facts indicated wide prevalence of the disease in Springfield and the pressing necessity for controlling measures. The municipality, nevertheless, practically was ignoring the problem. Efforts to control the disease consisted of fumigation (at best of doubtful value) only on request, and distribution of a limited amount of literature. There was no enforcement of the anti-spitting ordinance.

Fortunately for the city during the past few years, the Springfield Tuberculosis Association had been conducting a campaign against the disease. It was maintaining one visiting nurse (two in 1912 and a part of 1913) who also did general nursing; was operating one free dispensary; bearing part of the expense of treatment of a few patients at the Open Air Colony, and was conducting a limited educational campaign.

The two general hospitals in Springfield were averse to accepting tuberculous patients although in the past St. John's Hospital had accepted a number of cases. This is the custom of general hospitals elsewhere which have no special provision for treating the disease.

The Open Air Colony, a private sanatorium of 24 beds for incipient cases, had cared for a few of the city's needy cases, the county and the Springfield Tuberculosis Association sharing the expense. The county almshouse had no adequate provision for tuberculous inmates, although there was hope of an appropriation for a special pavilion the completion of which was needed at once.

At the time there was no public institution where the citizens of the city of Springfield and the county of Sangamon, afflicted with tuberculosis, could receive care and treatment. Such an institution with special provision for children was not only desirable but necessary.

The physicians of the city were showing an increasing disposition to co-operate in the campaign against tuberculosis, which was necessary for its success.

Suggestions for an Adequate Campaign

The following measures, recommended for eliminating tuberculosis in Springfield, have received general approval throughout the county. Some of them were already partly in force in the city.

Bearing in mind that prevention of the disease should claim precedence over cure the first necessity was an adequate campaign of education. The entire school population should be reached about once every two years through lectures, preferably by a nurse and in connection with a small exhibit which might be secured at a reasonable cost. The board of education might well adopt the plan followed in an increasing number of cities of making instruction concerning tuberculosis part of the regular curriculum.

Meetings of women's clubs, labor, fraternal, social, and other organizations, and gatherings of all kinds offer opportunities for short talks. Sunday night stereopticon lectures in the churches would reach effectively a large number of people. In this connection the special celebration of Tuberculosis Sunday was urged. There are several good motion-picture reels on tuberculosis and other health subjects which might be shown in the motion-picture houses either at special performances or on the regular bill, and preferably with a lecturer to explain the details of the story.

Most of these reels could be secured through the regular exchanges at no additional cost to the motion-picture houses.

Local physicians should be invited to assist in giving the numerous talks necessary to the campaign.

Literature of a substantial and easily read nature should be distributed at the various lectures given. Pamphlets printed in large type with numerous illustrations are very effective, while cheap literature often is a waste of money.

The Red Cross seal campaign offers unlimited opportunities for the dissemination of information concerning tuberculosis and the necessary plans for its control.

An adequate educational campaign should include exposure of alleged "cures" for tuberculosis, of which "Nature's Creation," widely exploited in Springfield, might be taken as an example. It cannot be stated too emphatically that medicine in bottles will not cure tuberculosis. Fresh air, good food, and plenty of rest under proper supervision is the only known remedy.

Institutional Provision

A campaign to secure a hospital for tuberculous patients and to be maintained by public funds, undertaken without delay, was recommended. It is a sound and well-recognized principle of the tuberculosis campaign that the small sums which are raised by anti-tuberculosis societies may be spent to the best advantage in ways which will lead to more permanent and general relief of the situation by public authorities.

Such a hospital should accept patients from the entire county instead of from the city only, and should have 100 beds with additional provision for children. It was estimated at the time that the cost would be from $750 to $1,000 a bed for site, building, and equipment, depending largely on the cost of the site; the cost of maintenance would run from $1.35 to $1.50 a day for each patient. These figures would now need to be revised upward.

A hospital of this type is designed to prevent infection as well as to cure. Besides receiving expert care and treatment the patient is taught the danger of spreading the disease, also the precautions necessary to prevent his infecting those with whom he comes in contact.

Free Dispensary Service

An important step toward the control of tuberculosis is the discovery of patients before they have advanced too far for probable recovery, or recovery possible at anything short of great expense. One of the functions of the dispensary is to meet this need. The usefulness of the dispensary might be increased, it was pointed out, by urging people, through the educational campaign and the visiting nurses, to voluntarily come for examination at the slightest symptom of the disease and at intervals when no striking symptoms are present. The physician in charge should receive compensation for his services. The city might assume this expense as well as that for additional nurses. Complete medical and social information concerning all patients who visit the dispensary or who are visited in their homes by the nurses must be obtained and fully recorded.

Adequate Nursing Service

The visiting nurse must be depended on to visit the afflicted in the home, follow up discharged institutional patients, and bring suspected cases to the dispensary for examination.

An increase of the nursing service was undoubtedly necessary in view of the lack of hospital facilities, and especially should the suggestion be adopted of broadening the field of the Springfield Tuberculosis Association's work to include the entire county. While no definite estimate might be made of the number of nurses needed, it could be safely stated that at least two assistant nurses for the city and one for the county outside the city were required to meet the need at the time.

Reporting of Cases and Disinfection of Premises

In order that all patients may receive proper care and that necessary preventive measures be taken, every living case must be known to the health authorities. Physicians should report not only the living cases but the recovery, death, or change of residence of any patient; also the treatment he is able or unable to provide.

The least the municipality could do at the time was to pass

ordinances requiring the reporting of all cases of tuberculosis to the health department; requiring the disinfection, and when necessary the thorough cleansing, of all premises after the death or removal of a patient; and abolishing the common drinking cup and towel. It should also enforce the anti-spitting ordinance.

Open-Air Schools

Among the most encouraging features of the campaign against tuberculosis are the results obtained in open-air schools and fresh-air classes for tuberculous, predisposed, and physically subnormal children. Such schools and classes may be conducted with or without feeding, but experience has demonstrated that with feeding, children respond more readily. The board of education ordinarily supplies the teachers and paraphernalia for these schools and classes, and if possible the food, special clothing, and carfare for children who live at a considerable distance. These last three items may have to be supplied in Springfield by some other city department or by the Springfield Tuberculosis Association.

An examination of children in the Palmer School brought out the fact that 27 of the 456 children examined were probably tuberculous; 141 had enlarged tonsils; 91, adenoids; 140, enlarged cervical glands; 122, enlarged sub-maxillary glands; 139, apparent anemia; 43, discharging ears; and 63, temperature elevated above one degree. The study of this one school brought out the need for discovering physical defects in school children to be met by thorough medical inspection and the need for fresh-air classes and open-air schools for the anemic and those predisposed to or suspected of tuberculosis.

Partial Reorganization of the Springfield Tuberculosis Association

Since it appeared that the immediate burden of the campaign against tuberculosis would probably fall upon the Springfield Tuberculosis Association, it was recommended that the Association broaden its field of activities to include the entire county of Sangamon. The work might be facilitated by division among sub-committees somewhat as follows: Finance, hospital, nursing, dispensary, open-air schools, education and publicity, research, one of physicians, and one of Negroes.

Where the Responsibility Lies

Tuberculosis is essentially a problem in public health, and as such the responsibility for its control rests upon public officials. Hospitals, nurses, dispensaries, and other institutions for its suppression should be supported by public funds. There can be no permanent evasion of the responsibility, as tuberculosis is a preventable disease and must be stamped out. The question facing each community, therefore, is how soon it will take proper measures to achieve this end. The effective carrying on of this work by the public points to the necessity for a full-time paid health officer. Since state appropriations in sufficient amount to meet the needs of both incipient and advanced cases can hardly be expected very soon, local hospitals for advanced cases, near centers of population and within easy reach of patients and their families, seem to be the most desirable.

Tuberculosis is preventable, and curable especially in its early stages. These facts cannot be questioned. If true, why does Springfield permit the disease to persist and destroy so many of its people? In other words, why is this preventable disease not prevented? A decided beginning toward this prevention had been made in the city. There remained the necessity of broadening and intensifying the work.

Typhoid Fever

Typhoid fever is one of the best understood and most preventable of the communicable diseases. It is pre-eminently one of defective sanitation and its presence is a civic disgrace. Caused by a specific microbe, which dies rapidly outside the body of its victim, the disease may be eliminated by simply keeping the discharges of infected persons from entering the mouths of other persons.

Springfield had suffered severely from typhoid in the past, even as compared with other American cities. In 1907 the rate of mortality was 81.7 per 100,000 population, an exceedingly high rate; and in 1910, taking only deaths of residents, the rate reached 40.4. In the six years before the survey, 84 residents were killed by typhoid and several hundred more had been made ill. Although the condition had shown a tendency to improve, the city had no cause to be satisfied with the situation or with anything short of practical eradication.

The distribution of the disease throughout the city showed the east side of the city to have fared badly again, a distribution that corresponds in a general way to the larger numbers of wells and privies, which assuredly were playing an important part in keeping up the death rate. Since the use of raw river water had been abandoned there was no evidence to implicate the city water supply.

Another important way in which the disease is spread is through personal contact between infected persons and those coming into their immediate environment. The discharges of a person having the disease, even before the development of marked symptoms and during convalescence, are highly infectious. If the importance and methods of efficiently disinfecting the patient's discharges are not understood, persons may easily become infected, either directly when handling the patient or disposing of his discharges, or indirectly by handling articles which have become infected; and fingers all too often reach the mouth or touch objects that enter the mouth.

Because of the general lack of appreciation of the contagiousness of typhoid fever, once an initial case occurs in a family or neighborhood it is common to find secondary cases appearing in about the incubation period of the disease. Thus, in a manner less spectacular than that of the epidemic but in a way no less deadly, the disease will smoulder in a neighborhood.

In Springfield, upon receipt of a case report, an inspector would visit the patient's home and leave a copy of the state board of health circular regarding the disease. He attempted to learn the source of infection and gave some instructions with regard to minor preventive measures. An attempt was also made to get a history of the case from the attending physician by telephone, usually without much success.

Efficient bedside disinfection of discharges is the prime essential in preventing secondary typhoid, and it is doubtful whether the ordinary inspector, no matter how capable he may be in the matter of nuisance abatement or enforcement of the sanitary ordinances, is properly equipped to give instruction in the management of the patient, as was being attempted in Springfield. Similarly the history taking and study of the origin and relation between cases (epidemiology) is a matter for a person of special training or ability, and could not be expected of persons who had not made a special study of such matters.

Recommendations which were made for the reduction of the city's typhoid, aside from the elimination of wells and privies and total abstinence from the use of unpurified river water, related chiefly to administrative measures by the health department. These were much the same as in the case of the contagious diseases of children: a better reporting of cases; prompt visitation of cases by a medical inspector or specially trained nurse employed by the health department, with revisitation or removal of cases if necessary; and more thorough epidemiological work.

The Venereal Diseases

Springfield's death rate from syphilis in 1913, 23 per 100,000, was greater than its death rate from typhoid fever. The number of deaths certified under this title was probably far short of the actual number, because syphilis is seldom certified as a cause of death when any other can be substituted. Similarly we did not know the actual number of cases of syphilis in Springfield because the disease received no official cognizance.

The only information regarding these diseases that could be gathered from the local vital statistics related to syphilis. In the past six years the deaths of 30 residents had been recorded as due to this disease, besides 19 due to locomotor ataxia and paresis. While these figures probably did not cover the situation adequately, it is interesting to note that the majority of the deaths had been among infants and that all wards had a share of the mortality.

In order to get some further data on the actual amount of venereal disease, letters were sent to physicians requesting a statement of the number of cases under treatment during the previous year and at the time. Forty-nine individuals, about three-fourths of those addressed, replied that 346 cases were under treatment at the time and 1,264 in 1913. Since this list did not include all cases treated by physicians, specialists, nor untreated cases, there is ample basis for the statement that these were the commonest communicable diseases in the community.

A large part of the damage from these diseases is manifested indirectly. Thus syphilis can produce immediate suffering and injury of the most serious character; but it may also run a mild course or be apparently cured, only to have the victim break down in middle age with paralysis or softening of the brain. A very large proportion of the cases of paresis and locomotor ataxia are caused, according to the best medical opinion, by antecedent syphilis. Similarly, in gonorrhea the local symptoms at the time of the attack may be mild and the patient may apparently make a complete recovery; yet the microbe of the disease can lie dormant in such an individual for years, retaining its power to infect others who may be wholly innocent of any immorality. It is claimed that a large proportion of surgical operations among women are necessitated by gonococcus infections innocently acquired from their husbands. Gonorrhea seldom kills, but it blinds children and maims women. It is strictly true that the more we know of the venereal diseases the more we have reason to fear them.

Measures against the Venereal Diseases

Syphilis, chancroid, and gonorrhea are each caused by a specific micro-organism with whose characteristics the bacteriologist is familiar. Given the same privileges as in typhoid, diphtheria, and other infections, the health department could undoubtedly reduce the prevalence of these diseases to a considerable extent. The "conspiracy of silence," however—the unwillingness to speak of these diseases—is a factor that makes the complete reporting of individual cases and the institution of such preventive procedures impracticable. It even hinders the dissemination of educational material, and it is a condition which any plan of campaign must take into account.

Springfield could, nevertheless, undertake several methods of procedure that are valuable. Through its health department it could require the reporting of cases by number instead of name, the residence by district also to be given. This is the necessary first step toward acquiring an idea of the prevalence and distribution of infection. It could also, preferably through its health department, see that indigent cases are promptly treated and cured, thus eliminating these sources of infection. The city could also direct that adequate provision be made for the hospital care of cases of these diseases, and could arrange for free laboratory diagnoses of samples of blood and discharges, this service to be offered freely to physicians. Finally the city could, through its health department, educate the public, instructing how the diseases are contracted, how avoided and cured, and what precautions should be taken by patients to avoid infecting others.

City Water Supply

The Springfield waterworks is situated at a point along the south bank of the Sangamon River about two miles from the northern edge of the city and four miles from its center. The first works was built at this point in 1867, water being pumped direct from the river to the city through a 15-inch pipe. Although unpurified river water was dirty and unsatisfactory, it was more than two decades before it ceased to make up a major part of the local supply.

In 1913, after various experiments, a system made up of infiltration galleries and tubular well units was found satisfactory. The yield of these six well units was stated to average 1,000,000 gallons a day, a total capacity of 6,000,000 gallons. Compared with the average daily consumption of 5,500,000 gallons this yield would seem fairly adequate, but as the maximum rate of demand reached 8,500,000 gallons in the year ending February 28, 1914, and as the system had practically no storage reserve against possible conflagrations, and as the city is constantly growing, it was evident that the development, and experiments to determine the limitations of the possible development, needed pushing. The fact that during the summer of 1914, despite unusual drought, sufficient ground water was had was encouraging, but it was urged that the city be liberal in its allowances for further experiments and development, the need of which was conclusively shown by the shortage experienced at the very end of 1914.

The important need was that the supply be made entirely inde-

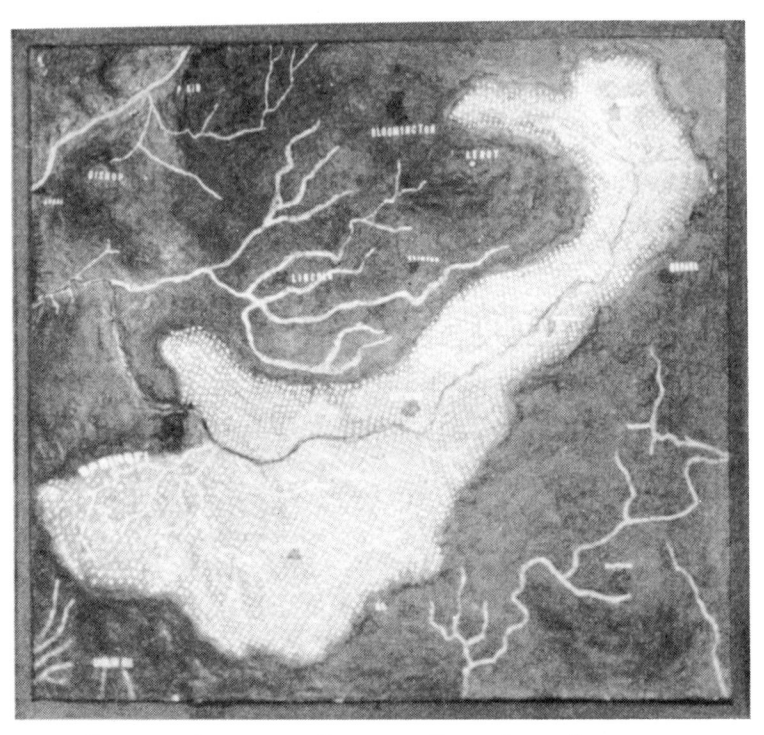

DRAINAGE AREA OF THE SANGAMON RIVER ABOVE SPRINGFIELD

A relief map showing why Springfield should not pump its water from the river. The lighter portion shows the area drained by the Sangamon River above the city works. This area in 1910 was inhabited by 191,000 people, of whom 110,000 resided in places of over 1,000 population. The river at Springfield was seriously polluted by the sewage of Decatur and parts of Springfield's own sewage, and water from it in an unpurified condition was unsafe. Map prepared and contributed to the Survey Exhibition by the State Historical Museum.

pendent of the river. The tubular well system should be developed to a point where the possible need of river water would be precluded, and the river intake should be eliminated because of possibility of leakage in the gate valve or of its being left partially open.

For the ordinary demands of consumers the pumping equipment, installed in 1913, was entirely adequate. But the force mains to the city then in use should be supplemented by one or more new mains to preclude the possibility of interruptions in the service on account of breaks in the existing mains, also to prevent excessive velocities in them such as give rise to objectionable turbidity.

The most important part of the distribution problem was to see that this water was available to all persons living in built-up parts of the city. At the time of the survey 30 per cent of the population in ward one, and 20 per cent of the population in ward six, had no mains in the streets, a serious situation in view of the dangers attending the use of wells and privies. New distribution mains were needed in the eastern part of the city if pure water was to be made available for all the citizens of Springfield. The city was to be congratulated on the improvements which had been made in the source of the supply and the equipment at the pumping station, but there was real need for further development.

Sewerage and Sewage Disposal

The sewerage of Springfield is of the "combined" type; that is, one set of sewers cares for both house sewage and storm water. The deficiencies in distribution were similar to those in the case of the city water system, but the sewerage situation over the entire city was somewhat worse. Fully 17.5 per cent of the city's population could not connect with sewers, as against 12.3 in the case of water mains. The presence of these very considerable unsewered areas was of prime sanitary importance. Lack of sewers compels the privy system, which in turn greatly increases the opportunities for fly infection.

Springfield was discharging her sewage in a more or less haphazard manner at some twelve points either within or a short distance outside her boundaries. According to inspections made by the State Water Survey, serious pollution, attended with nuisance objectionable to householders, was occurring at certain points in the streams receiving the sewage. There was also the added danger that must attend the discharge through populated districts of untreated sewage which may at any time contain infectious matter.

The city needed to look forward to the erection of sewage treatment works, both for her own safety and self-respect and because of the possibility of compulsion by the state authorities. In this event it would be a distinct advantage if the sewage could be treated at a single point and if separate sewers were provided for the collection of storm water and house sewage. The city should undertake a thorough survey of its sewerage equipment, and should utilize the results in formulating a plan for the rapid extension of the system to serve all built-up districts. Such a program should of course be attended by a policy of privy condemnation and city water main extension.

Wells and Privies

In 1910 Dr. George Thomas Palmer, then superintendent of health, made a sanitary survey to determine the number and location of all private wells, privies, cesspools, and premises otherwise insanitary in Springfield. He reported as follows:

1. There are 7,000 shallow wells in the city and the pollution of these is insured by 6,000 privy vaults.
2. There are 9,000 homes in the city, 6,000 of which are not connected with city sewers or water mains for sanitary purposes. The sewer and water systems of Springfield have cost the taxpayers approximately $4,000,000. This means that the public expenditure of $4,000,000 for sanitary purposes is utilized by but one-third of the population and the benefits which should be derived by the community are lost.

Extensive publicity was given to his findings and an ordinance was passed requiring all persons building, or rebuilding, to make proper sewer and water connections if within 100 feet of a sewer and a water main, and requiring all wells and vaults to be abandoned within thirty days of such connection. Owners of wells and privies not affected by this ordinance were at the same time strongly advised to abandon these appurtenances and connect with the city water and sewer facilities wherever possible.

Four years having elapsed it was thought desirable to bring the figures up to date. During the summer of 1914, with the cooperation of Dr. B. B. Griffith, at that time superintendent of health, a re-survey of the well and privy situation was made. It was discouraging and discreditable to the city to find the situation no better than in 1910. In fact the number of wells and privies had increased, as compared with the actual count of 1910,

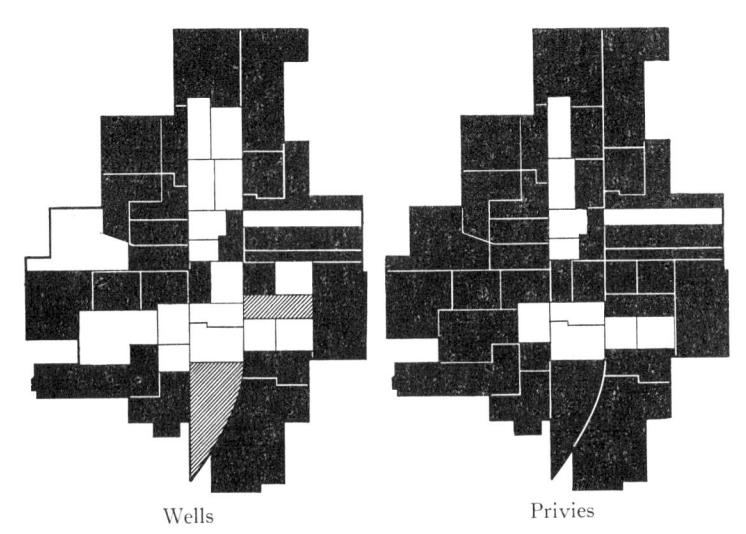

Wells   Privies

COMPARISON OF THE NUMBERS OF WELLS AND PRIVIES FOUND IN 1910 AND 1914
According to the enumeration districts used by the United States Census of 1910. Black areas indicate increases in the period; white areas decreases; and shaded areas no change in number.
Part of the increase is more apparent than real, as the survey of 1910 omitted certain sections near the city limits.
The actual change in the period, both because it was small and because some of it was in the wrong direction was discreditable to the city—particularly since the situation and its implications had been set before the community clearly in 1910.

the actual increases being probably due to the erection of new buildings where sewers and city water were not available, 400 cases of building and rebuilding having occurred during 1910–13.
The largest numbers of wells and privies were found in the sixth, first, third, and fourth wards. Over 50 per cent of the total, and approximately half of those that were absolutely unnecessary, were in the two wards east of Tenth Street, which in 1910 con-

tained 36 per cent of the population. Wards four and five, to the southwest, and ward seven, in the central business section, had relatively the fewest wells and privies in proportion to their popu-

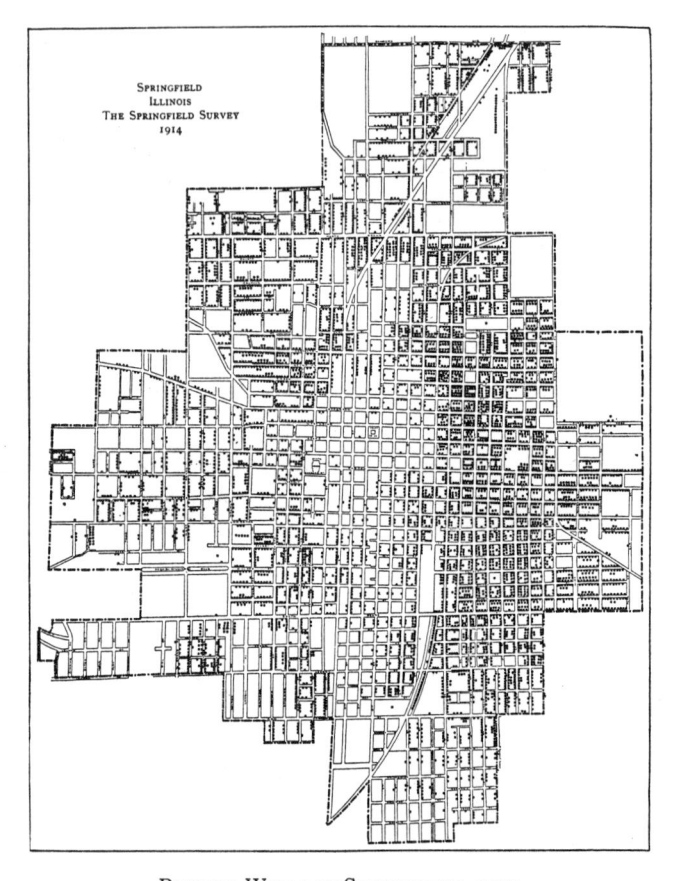

PRIVATE WELLS IN SPRINGFIELD, 1914

Each black square represents a private well. 7,530 wells were found, of which 78 per cent were at places where the city water was already in the street.

Enumeration by inspectors of the city health department; map prepared by the Department of Surveys and Exhibits.

lation. The southeast ward (six) had five times as many wells and privies per 1,000 population as the central ward (seven), the former having a well and a privy for each five persons. In other words, this ward, with its 11,500 odd inhabitants, was depending almost entirely on wells and privies, a situation which put this

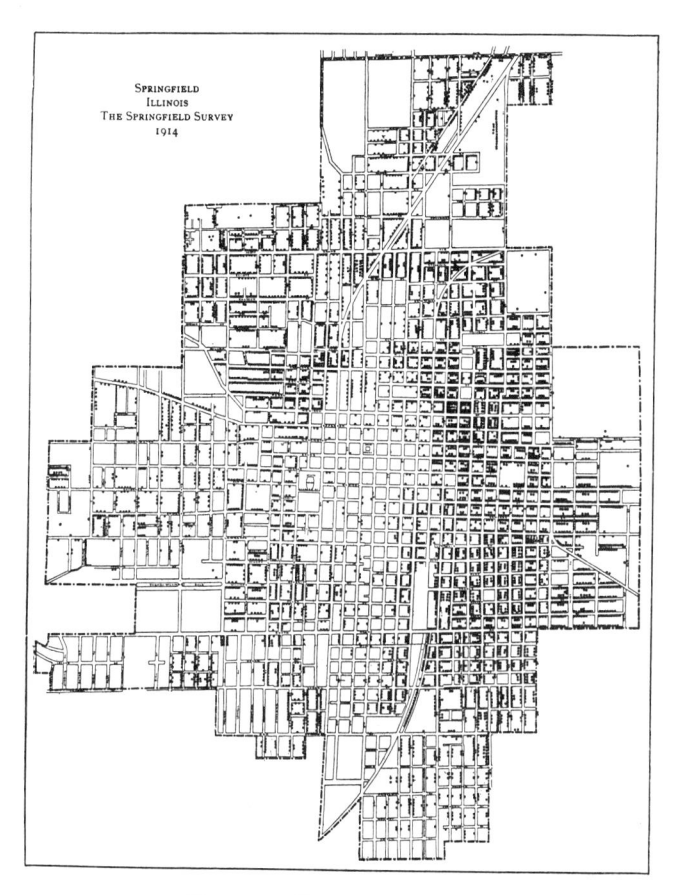

PRIVIES IN SPRINGFIELD, 1914

Each black square represents a privy. 7,431 privies were found, of which 74 per cent were at places where sewers were already in the street, and 63 per cent at places where both sewers and city water were available.

Enumeration by inspectors of the city health departments; map prepared by the Department of Surveys and Exhibits.

section of the capital city of Illinois in a class with those small villages of the state which still depend upon the insanitary makeshifts of pioneer days.

Privies in cities are objectionable because they pollute the ground water and allow flies and animals free access to human excreta. Many more persons are capable of discharging infectious matter in privies than is generally realized. Thus, in typhoid the danger is not limited to persons with a well-developed attack or to those coming down with the disease; some persons continue to harbor the germs and to discharge them in their urine and feces for years after recovery, while others become infected and discharge the germs without showing any symptoms of the disease whatever. Altogether in a city of Springfield's size and with roughly 7,500 privies, there is ample opportunity for some of the privies to contain infectious material from time to time; there is sure to be a supply of flies on hand at some of these times; and there is sure to be a supply of persons available for infection. Thus in the long run typhoid and other intestinal diseases are bound to arise from the privies. That such had actually been the case was indicated by the distribution in the past of typhoid and diarrheal diseases throughout the city. The liability for well pollution is very much the same.

Some wells, owing to the nature of the soil they penetrate and their location with respect to privies, will probably never be polluted. In rural districts, where the soil is of favorable quality and where it is merely a matter of protecting one's well from one's own privy, the situation can be controlled; but in the congested city, privies belonging to one's neighbors may be close at hand, the distances between the wells and the privies not sufficient, and the pollution of the ground water too heavy for the material to be cared for in the natural way. Wells in a city should always be regarded with suspicion, and always discarded when a pure supply of city water is at hand. Analyses of Springfield's wells gave ample reason for suspecting the polluted character of a considerable number of them.

A study of the availability of sewers and city water showed that 78 per cent of the wells could be eliminated without any addition to the existing water mains, while 74 per cent of the privies could be replaced without the construction of any new sewers. Nearly two-thirds of the privies were at places where both sewers and city water were available.

PUBLIC HEALTH

It is certainly folly for the city to spend millions on water and sewers and then neglect three-fourths of the sanitary advantages.

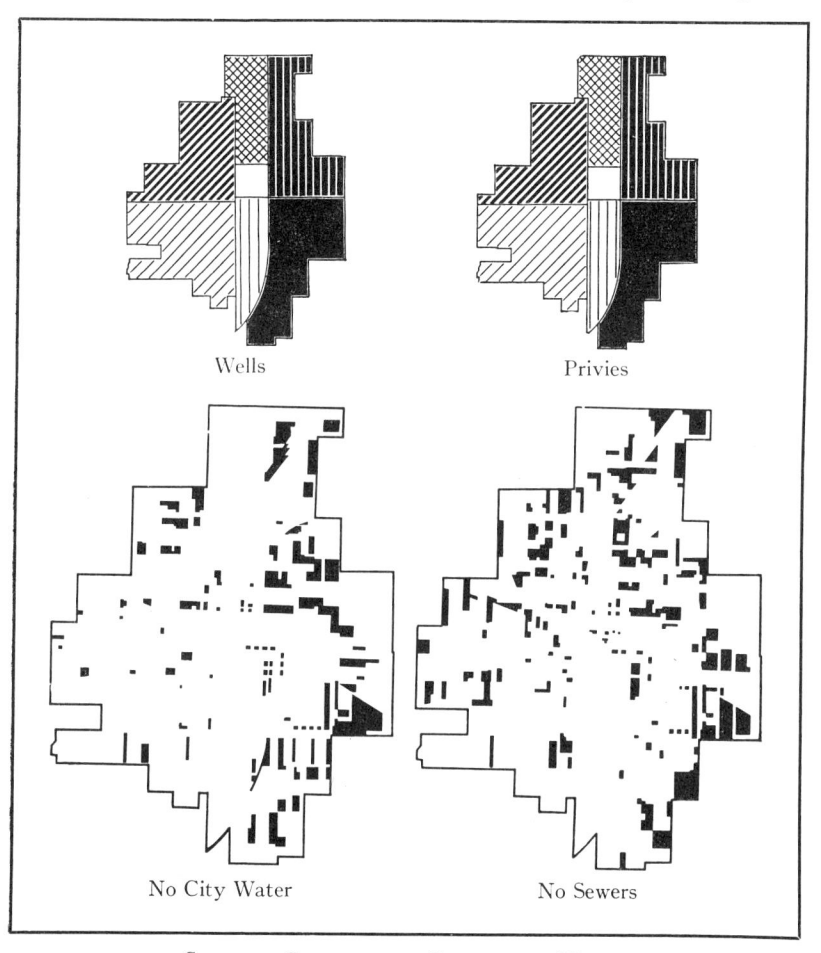

SANITARY CONDITIONS IN SPRINGFIELD WARDS

The darker shadings in the smaller maps indicate higher proportions of wells and privies per 100,000 population. The black areas in the larger maps indicate built up districts without sewers and without city water. Compare with illustrations on pages 251 and 253.

The presence of privies and wells, with the incidental communicable diseases, is a matter that affects more than merely the owners of these makeshifts. They are little short of a menace to all. Springfield should set about the elimination of both wells and privies, and should adopt a rational program working to accomplish this purpose. Until she makes marked progress on such a program she cannot hope to free herself of typhoid and diarrheal diseases.

Milk Supply

Springfield was being supplied with milk by some 100 producers owning about 1,055 cows furnishing about 2,355 gallons a day. Approximately a fourth of the farmers, producing a third of the city's supply, peddled their own milk; slightly more than half of them, producing a little less than half of the supply, sold to one large dairy company, this milk being pasteurized; the remainder disposed of their milk to stores and middlemen.

In the inspection of dairy farms made by the survey a modified government score card was used, but to make the test as fair as possible to small farmers who had but little equipment, only such essential points as cleanliness in all particulars, freedom from contaminating influences, cooling, methods of storage, and transportation were tabulated. Even with this modification, results were anything but favorable.

The average scores on all farms were 49 per cent on equipment and 44 per cent on methods. The average final score was 46 per cent, certainly a discreditable figure. Only three of the farms, less than 3 per cent of the total, earned the classification of "good," while 90 per cent of them scored "bad" or worse.

Information as to Springfield's milk production and dairy scores, classified according to the amount of milk produced and the manner of disposal, showed that the small farmer was one of the serious problems met with in seeking a sanitary milk supply. The man with three or four cows, kept largely for supplying milk for the family and because of the need of manure for fertilizer, usually made very small profits from his milk sales, could afford very little in the way of equipment, and often would quit the business rather than clean up. At the same time it should be said that the public should be prepared to pay a fair price for clean milk, and that experience in many places indicated that 10 cents a quart at that time was not an excessive figure. A still higher figure would probably be necessary now.

Dairies selling direct to the consumer made the best scores, those selling to middlemen were poorer and smaller, and the worst showing of all was made by those selling to the large milk company, to bakeries, confectioners, and the like.

In choosing a milk supply, however, cleanliness at the farm is not the sole criterion, as efficient pasteurization is highly desirable. Experience has abundantly shown that despite great efforts to secure cleanliness supplies may become infected, as by unrecognized carriers of communicable disease. Clean milk is certainly to be desired and striven for, but proper pasteurization is the final essential for safety.

The result of the milk survey indicated clearly that the milk situation was bad. It indicated emphatically that the city health department should be given a full-time milk inspector, competent to score dairies and examine milk. The activities of such an inspector should include the supervision of transportation and handling of milk, also the making of tests of its temperature and bacterial content in transit and storage. The inspector should be furnished with means of rapid travel from dairy to dairy and should be paid a salary commensurate with the ability required. The usefulness of such an inspector is indicated by the fact that reinspection of a number of farms several months after the original inspection, showed that considerable improvement had been made.

Granted an inspection system and a set of dairy rules, the other prime requisite was adequate publicity for the results of inspections. The health department should publish each month, or as often as practicable, a list of the inspections and analyses made, giving the particulars as to the name of the producer or dealer and whatever explanatory comment would seem necessary. Then every consumer would be able to know just what kind of place his milk came from and just how it compares with other milk on sale. At the same time we may reiterate that the public should be prepared to do its part by paying a fair price for a more sanitary product.

Food Supply

The sanitary handling of ordinary food products was a matter that had received more attention in Springfield than the sanitary production and handling of milk. The city had, for one thing, employed a meat inspector, while representatives of the state food commission had from time to time given more or less attention to conditions in the markets, groceries, bakeries, and the like. During the spring of 1914 one of the state inspectors devoted considerable time to Springfield, visiting some 134 places where food was handled or sold, and placed the results of his inspections at the disposal of the survey.

The general condition of the places visited was good. At the same time many dirty places existed in Springfield, and orders for improvement were issued in a very considerable proportion of the places visited. The most serious conditions disclosed by an examination of the state inspector's records were those relating to the toilet and washing facilities in the food-handling places. In a considerable proportion of instances the ordinary privy was in use, while many of the flush toilets found were either not enclosed or lacked outside ventilation. In view of the abundance of flies usually in the neighborhood of food-handling places and the opportunities the common privy gives to pick up infectious material, it is not only reasonable but important to require such places to make use of city water and sewer services wherever the latter are available.

The city meat inspector devoted about two-thirds of his time to the supervision of seven slaughter houses on the outskirts of the city and of a certain amount of killing in the outlying country, and the rest to the supervision of some 75 meat markets. Since limitations of time and place made it impossible for him to be present at all killing operations, this very impossibility pointed out the advantage of a central city slaughter house which would greatly economize the inspector's time, allow for a more efficient inspection, and result in much cleaner slaughtering conditions.

There was clearly need of another food inspector to keep closer watch of the various food shops, restaurants, candy and ice cream parlors, and factories. Such an inspector could co-operate with the milk inspector in his supervision of the handling of milk within the city and could relieve the meat inspector of much of the meat market and restaurant inspection that he was obliged to make.

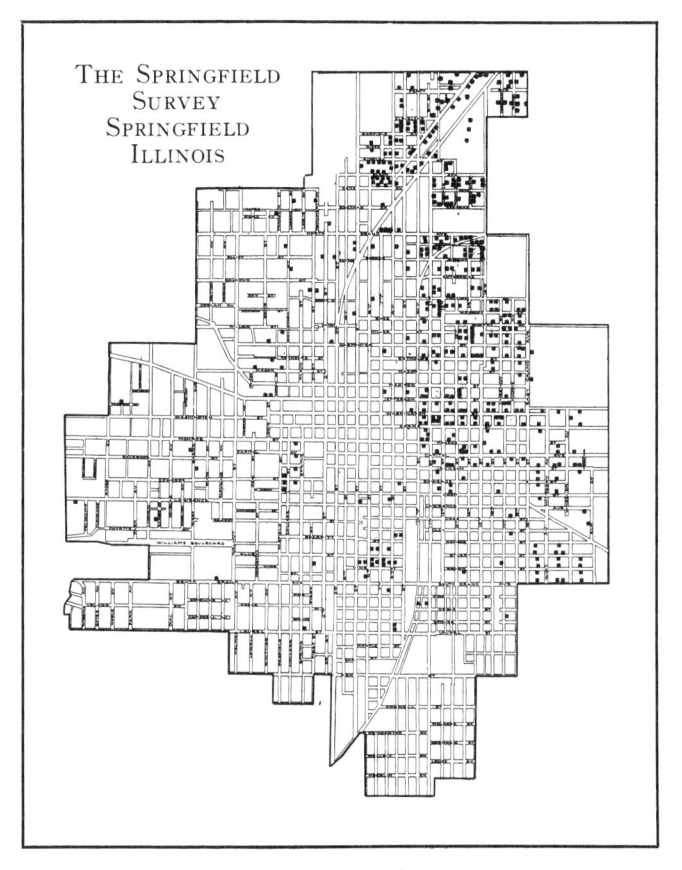

MANURE ACCUMULATIONS IN SPRINGFIELD, 1914
Each black square represents a manure accumulation found by the city inspectors—420 in all.

Other Sanitary Conditions

A matter of first-rate health importance is the handling and disposal of manure, because this material is the chief breeding place of flies. In the house-to-house canvass inspectors noted 420 open accumulations of manure, most of them in the northeast part of the city. The city should require tight containers for manure, stable floors and regular collection and disposal.

Although the importance of garbage as a breeding place for flies and as a source of vague deleterious effects on health has been the subject of great exaggeration, it must be acknowledged that the city should stand for decency; and it is indecent to tolerate alleys or yards littered with garbage, or haphazard systems of collection and disposal. Springfield at the time of the survey was in the somewhat anomalous position of maintaining a garbage incinerator but no collection system. Anyone might bring his material to the city incinerator and there dispose of it free of charge, but to do so was not compulsory.

The result was poor collection and disposal of garbage and considerable complaint over conditions throughout the city. The city was in fact without a system and action to this end was needed. It should be remembered, however, that the problems of collection and disposal of garbage are engineering matters, and before embarking upon a new plan, competent engineers should be consulted.

Present Health Department

The staff of the city health department consisted of a part-time health officer, a secretary-clerk, a meat inspector, three sanitary inspectors, and the matron of the contagious disease hospital. The department's physical equipment consisted of an office with a small laboratory in the city hall and the contagious disease hospital situated beyond Oak Ridge cemetery. The routine work of the department was represented largely by the activities of the three sanitary inspectors, and consisted principally in placarding and fumigating reported cases of contagious diseases and in abating nuisances.

Defects in the Existing Organization

The most serious defect in the organization of the health department that was not an out-and-out deficiency was the part-time employment of the health officer. The part-time system is a relic of days when health department work was regarded merely as an emergency provision in the event of epidemics, on which occasions the health officer could be called on for a heavy contribution of time. At other times he would presumably have nothing to do. Since those days we have come to know that a great health and life wastage is going on even in the absence of epidemics, and that the health department can and must prevent this steady wastage. We have also come to realize that health departments should prevent epidemics and not merely curb them after they are well established. These modern ideas of the health department's usefulness and functions call for a continuous, ever-watchful campaign against disease—and for the full-time health officer.

One of the most important recommendations for the improvement of the health department was the employment of a full-time health officer, appointed for a definite term of years, removable only for cause and given free rein over his department.

Two great opportunities for life saving—campaigns against infant mortality and tuberculosis—were being quite neglected by the city health service, while the work to control communicable diseases was open to radical improvement. A recommendation hardly second to that of the employment of a full-time health officer was the employment of public health nurses to carry on work against tuberculosis and infant mortality. To reinforce the work of the nurses a free tuberculosis clinic, such as was being maintained by the Anti-Tuberculosis Association, and a free baby consultation station to which sick infants might be brought, were necessary.

There was need for an epidemiologist to study the progress of communicable diseases and to check up on measures to be taken for their control. Such a person might also act as medical inspector in contagious diseases, and with the public health nurses supervise isolation against typhoid and the contagious diseases of children. A milk inspector was greatly needed, and only somewhat less urgently a food inspector. The probability of the ultimate need of a laboratory man for the examination of milk and water and for the laboratory diagnoses of communicable diseases was indicated for the not-distant future.

Another line of work pointed out for the department to develop was that of health education and publicity. For its most effective labors it is essential that the public have a sympathetic understanding of what the health department is trying to do, and that

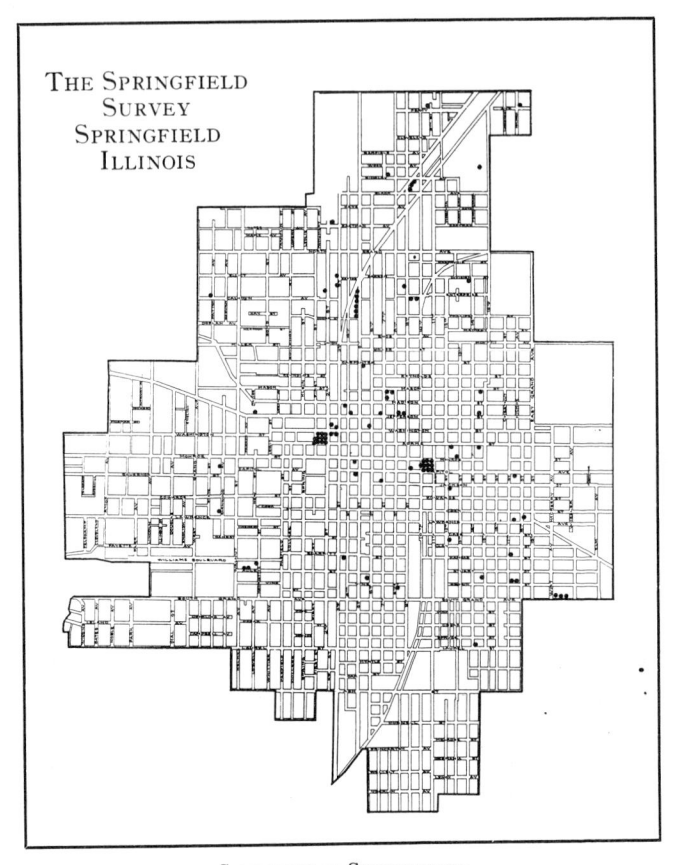

THE SPRINGFIELD SURVEY
SPRINGFIELD
ILLINOIS

SMALLPOX IN SPRINGFIELD

Cases reported to the health department in 1909–1913. Smallpox is one of the most contagious of diseases and is extremely hard to control by ordinary methods of isolation. Vaccination is by far the most effective barrier to the disease.

the public receive advice on the best ways to avoid infection and on other subjects of public health importance. To this end many departments find it advantageous to distribute a bulletin understandable to all—not merely a compilation of unintelligible and insignificant statistics. The co-operation of the newspapers should be secured, lectures and exhibits arranged, and moving pictures utilized. Some such efforts had been made in the past by the Springfield health department, but they should be continued and greatly extended.

The importance of an adequate annual report should also be emphasized, the form preferably to follow in general one of the excellent standard forms prepared by certain public health associations. In this connection a word of praise may be given to some of the department's past reports, which were certainly creditable as compared with the department's resources and deserved to be published with greater regularity and in fuller form.

The record keeping of the department was rather better than the average found in cities of similar size. Minor improvements could be made in the manner of keeping and filing some of the records, but the most radical suggestions related to new and fuller records, as in the case histories of communicable diseases.

The registration of vital statistics was another important branch of the work in which improvement should be made, although in this case the responsibility rested more particularly with Springfield's physicians. There should be greater insistence on more accurate certification of death, and greater realization on the part of physicians of the importance of this.

The contagious disease hospital was meeting fairly well its present purpose—that of a boarding house for persons with contagious diseases. It took infectious patients out of homes where proper isolation could not be maintained or where patients could not have decent care. Its isolated location, however, was a disadvantage, both as it affected the transportation of patients and the securing of medical service. Renovation of considerable of the equipment was needed, and measures needed to be taken to add to the attractiveness of the place. If funds are available, a new contagious disease hospital, centrally located, should be provided. Such a building, properly maintained, is no danger to its immediate neighborhood.

With regard to communicable diseases there should be a shifting of emphasis from quarantine of the premises and fumigation to early recognition of all cases and efficient bedside disinfection of the patient's discharges. There should be greater strictness in the matter of release from quarantine, in diphtheria by the culture method only, and in scarlet fever only after inspection of the patient by a medical representative of the health department. Work against venereal disease, such as has been instituted by progressive health departments in other cities, should likewise be organized.

One other point regarding the organization of health work in Springfield may be noted—the possibility for advantageous coöperation between the city and county. The county was carrying practically no public health work, which was a serious disadvantage to county residents outside of Springfield and to residents of the city itself. The county residents needed protection on their own account, and many of them were living just over the city limits so that infection among them was a danger to residents of the city proper. This last point was recognized by the city in setting up its jurisdiction, as far as quarantining contagious diseases is concerned, for a distance of a half mile beyond its borders. Under similar conditions a number of American communities have established joint city and county health departments. Such departments are financed by both city and county and exercise equal jurisdiction and supervision over both the city and the rest of the county. The arrangement is desirable because it secures for the county the nucleus for a strong service and for the city a stronger department because of the additional funds available. The result is better health in both county and city. Springfield and Sangamon County are of a size to make such an arrangement economically desirable. The formation of a joint department would very probably be advantageous to the community and such a step is recommended.

Springfield was spending 98 cents per person on police protection and $1.72 per person on fire protection, but only 16 cents per person on the much needed health protection. Most authorities at the time were recommending the expenditure of from 50 cents to $1.00 per inhabitant as the proper figure for adequate work by a well-rounded health department. In order to permit the adoption and proper administration of the measures recommended here, the city must increase its altogether too inadequate and scanty appropriation of the health department.

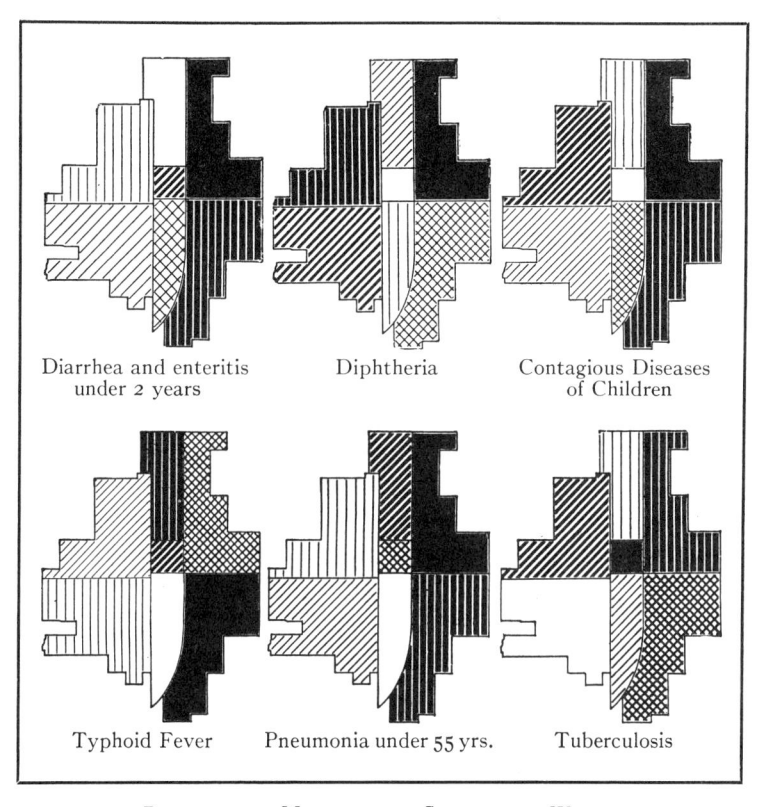

Diarrhea and enteritis under 2 years

Diphtheria

Contagious Diseases of Children

Typhoid Fever

Pneumonia under 55 yrs.

Tuberculosis

PREVENTABLE MORTALITY IN SPRINGFIELD WARDS

The darker shadings indicate higher death rates. The rates on which the rankings are based are per 100,000 population, except in the case of diphtheria and the contagious diseases of children in which cases they are per 100,000 children of school age. The figures are for residents only. Compare with illustrations on pages 241 and 253.

SUMMARY AND CONCLUSION

Thus it is seen that Springfield had a well-defined and clearly localized public health problem. A serious life and health wastage was constantly going on. During the last six years 1,218 residents died from the more common communicable diseases and several thousand more were made ill. At least a fourth of the deaths from all causes may be laid to these preventable diseases.

The greatest single agent in this devastation was tuberculosis, responsible for 490 deaths during the previous six years and for 11 per cent of all the deaths in 1913, the year studied in detail. The diseases of infants formed another great contributing group; 727 infants under one year of age died during the six years, deaths of such infants amounting to 18 per cent of all deaths in 1913. Nearly half of these infant deaths were from the ordinary preventable causes, such as diarrhea and enteritis, pneumonia, and acute infections. Other important contributory factors in the preventable mortality and morbidity of the city were the contagious diseases of children, typhoid fever, and the venereal diseases.

The toll exacted was much heavier in certain sections of the city than in others. Thus the tuberculosis death rate in the wards east of Tenth Street was over twice that in the two southwest wards. Corresponding differences were found in the death rates for typhoid fever, the contagious diseases of children, and infant mortality. The east wards, which had these high death rates, were the ones that contain the greater proportions of Negroes, foreign-born whites, and illiterates. They also had the highest birth rates and the highest proportions of children and people of working age, and they were the districts which had called for the largest amounts of poor relief. The plain fact is that people were dying in parts of the city because they were ignorant; because they were poor; because they were surrounded by inferior sanitary conditions; and because the city did not give them a proper health department service.

What was needed at once to meet Springfield's public health problem was fairly obvious. The city should do away with wells and privies; should perfect its water supply and sewerage, making the mains of both systems available to all; it should also see to it that the benefits of such improvements are denied no one simply because he is too poor to afford them. Then the city should set to work, through its health department, to overcome popular ignorance with regard to sanitary matters. Finally, it should provide its health department with proper equipment in the way of staff and funds, so that the department may adequately cope with the various administrative phases of the needed preventive work. The health department expenditure needed at least to be trebled or quadrupled. Even then it would be moderate as compared with health department expenditures in more progressive cities, and small as compared with what Springfield was spending on

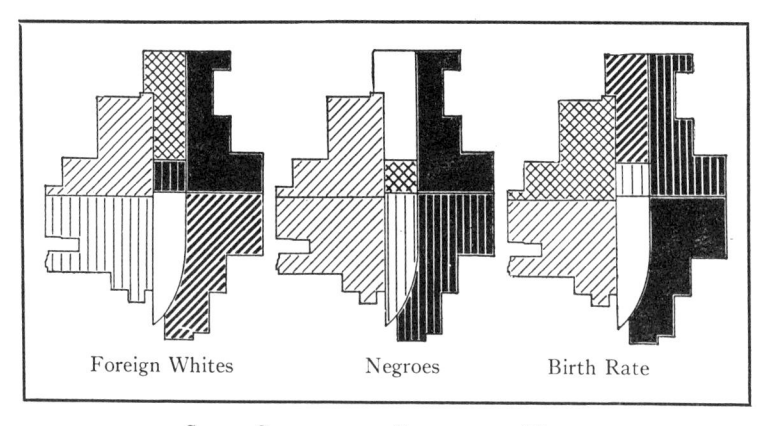

SOCIAL STATISTICS OF SPRINGFIELD WARDS
The darker shadings indicate higher proportions of Negroes and foreign-born whites, and higher birth rates. The east wards evidently have the higher ratios. Compare with illustrations on pages 241 and 251.

other departments of the public service. The health department need was urgent.

That public health is purchasable has almost become a public maxim. Springfield had a splendid opportunity to buy—to save 200 or more lives a year and to prevent much additional sickness. Realizing that the safety and welfare of its citizens are involved to this extent, there ought to be no question of the willingness and determination of the city to find the funds needed and to buy wisely.

X

THE CORRECTIONAL SYSTEM[1]

Out of Springfield's population of about 52,000 in 1910, as already indicated, 13.4 per cent were foreign born and 5.7 per cent colored. The police records did not show arrests by nationality, but they did separate colored people from whites. The former in 1913 contributed 10.2 per cent of arrests, or nearly twice as large a proportion as they formed of the city's population.

Situated halfway between Chicago and St. Louis, Springfield is a convenient stopping-off place for tramps, "yeggs," and other semi-criminal classes who swell the jail population as lodgers and prisoners. The annual state fair also offers opportunity for pickpockets, swindlers, and professional beggars who usually crowd the jails until the fair is over.

The city at the time of the survey had some conspicuous features of a wide-open town—a segregated district marked with glaring red lights; gambling carried on under cover and not vigorously suppressed; 220 saloons,[2] one to every 263 persons. Sunday closing was not enforced.

Between two and three thousand of its male workers were employed in seasonal occupations, with periods of enforced idleness which undoubtedly were a factor in the crime problem of the city. Public recreation, an effective preventive of crime, as seen in the chapter on Recreation, was undeveloped, and there was little adequate control of commercial amusement.

The Problem Stated

Springfield's correctional system is a part of the state system, organized and regulated by state law. Therefore the list of correctional institutions included state and county as well as muni-

[1] Summary of report on The Correctional System of Springfield, Illinois, by Zenas L. Potter.
[2] This count was made in April, 1914.

cipal agencies. For the apprehension of law breakers the community had the police department and the sheriff's force; for temporary detention pending trial, the city prison, county jail and the detention home, the last being for children; for prosecuting cases before the courts, the city attorney and state's attorney; for trial and sentence of those arrested, the justices of the peace, city magistrate, county and circuit courts, and the juvenile court for children; for detention on sentence, the city prison and county jail; for probationary supervision, the juvenile probation officer, for children only.

How were these correctional agencies and their methods protecting Springfield from law breakers? Punishment and reformation are only a means to an end. The real test of correctional work is the protection of the community. To apply this to the activities of the above-mentioned agencies and to suggest remedies for the weaknesses discovered was the purpose of this division of the survey.

As to the size of the delinquency problem a few figures are indicative. In 1913 there were 4,909 arrests with some specific offense charged. Of this total, 3,312 were arrests by the police department made within the city limits, while 1,597 were arrests by the sheriff's force largely outside the city. In addition to these the police took 521 and the sheriff 284 persons into custody upon suspicion, but later released them without entering specific charges. During the same period there were 1,271 convictions in criminal actions, of which 1,119 were in the justice of the peace and city magistrate's courts, and 152 in the county and circuit courts. Of the 66 children arrested, 39 were found delinquent by the juvenile court.

A considerable proportion of the arrests by the police and the sheriff in 1913, 1,447 out of 4,909—almost 30 per cent—were of "repeaters." The number of persons involved in these arrests and thus taken into custody two or more times was 548. Three hundred and sixty-six were arrested twice, 98 three times, 45 four times, 25 five times, 5 six times, 3 seven, 1 eight, 1 nine, 2 ten, 1 twelve, and 1 as many as sixteen times.

These figures include out-of-town persons as well as residents of the city. Many non-residents arrested were professional beggars, hoboes, and yeggs who travel from city to city. Because of their transient habits they are less likely than local persons to be of the repeater type. A truer idea of the part played by chronic offenders in the crime problem of the community is obtained if arrests of residents only are considered. Since sheriff's records do not give residences, police arrests were here considered.

Arrests of residents of the city by the Springfield police department in 1913 totaled 2,414. Of these, 934, or 39 per cent, were of persons arrested more than once during this single year. Those arrested two or more times numbered 353, and formed 19 per cent of all Springfield residents taken into custody. Two hundred and twenty-four were arrested twice, 81 three times, 28 four times, 11 five times, 2 six times, 3 seven, 1 eight, 1 ten, 1 twelve, and 1 thirteen times.

Since these figures covered a single year only, and undoubtedly a number of persons arrested in 1913 were old offenders, conditions are probably understated. Even so, the fact that at least 39 per cent of Springfield arrests in a normal year were contributed by repeaters raised serious questions as to the effectiveness of correctional methods in use. Apparently, among the persons who knew better than anyone else what to expect from Springfield's police, courts, and jails, these methods had been weak in deterrent and reformative effect. The treatment received had neither frightened repeaters from the commission of further offenses nor instilled in them a desire to be law abiding.

THE HANDLING OF ADULT OFFENDERS

Disposition of Cases of Arrest

In order to know, as a starting point, how many cases came to trial, how many resulted in convictions, and how many led to payment of penalties, the 3,312 arrests on specific charges made by the police department in 1913 were studied. Of these only 34 per cent, or two out of every five, resulted in conviction by the justices of the peace and the city magistrate. In 32 per cent of the cases there was no prosecution, while 21 per cent were dismissed; thus, a total of at least 53 per cent of all police arrests on charges resulted in no penalty being imposed.

THE CORRECTIONAL SYSTEM

In addition, however, to the 1,744 arrests which make up this 53 per cent and in which payment of a penalty was thus escaped, 192 of the arrests which resulted in convictions also did not lead to payment of a penalty. In all there were, therefore, not counting the 206 cases bound over for the grand jury, 1,936 cases, or 58 per cent of the year's total of 3,312 police arrests on specific charges, which resulted in no penalty.

To test the effectiveness of the correctional methods in protecting the community at a vital point—against those already known to be dangerous—attention was given first to the treatment of the adults proved guilty. There were 1,119 such persons —192 guilty who escaped punishment and 927 others.

The large facts which stand out in this test were: First, that the favorite method of these courts in disposing of those found guilty was to impose a fine, 791 out of the 1,119, or 71 per cent, having been disposed of in that way, and that by far the most common assessment was $3.00; second, that the next most usual method was to impose a jail sentence, 171 being thus dealt with; and third, that in many cases an attempt was made to rid the community of offenders by giving them a fixed number of hours to leave town.

The tabulation of these facts, however, did not in all cases tell how sentences were finally executed. For instance, of the 171 receiving jail sentences seven escaped going to jail—one by appeal and six because the court suspended execution of their sentences. In five of the six cases sentence was suspended pending good behavior. In the sixth case the offender was given hours to leave town. Moreover, of 732 persons who were fined and whose method of payment is known, but 475 paid their penalties and only 337 paid them fully in cash. Seventy-five had not the money to pay and were forced to spend a day in jail for each dollar of their fine. Sixty-three others were not able to raise the full amount of their fines and spent some time in jail. One hundred and forty-nine had their sentences suspended "pending good behavior." Thus the actual disposition of the cases of those fined did not entirely correspond with the statement of formal sentences imposed.

Summing up the penalties actually paid by the 1,119 persons proved guilty before the justices of the peace and city magistrate, we found that 337 paid fines in cash, 239 spent terms in jail, 63 paid fines part in cash and part by terms in jail, 219 were given hours to leave town, and 154 received suspended sentences. One hundred and seven others paid or escaped penalties in other ways.

County and Circuit Court Sentences

In order to get a more complete picture of the disposition of offenders, the study of sentences imposed by the justices of the peace and city magistrates must be supplemented by those given in the circuit and county courts. The total persons involved were 152.

The most frequent penalty in these courts was a combination of fine and jail sentence. Fifty offenders received such sentences, ranging from a fine of $3.00 and one hour in jail to $150 and six months in jail. Twenty offenders received fines only, which ranged from $5.00 to $750. Nineteen were sent to jail for from one day to four months. Twenty-three were sent to the state penitentiary, the shortest term being one year, the longest for life. Nineteen of these 23 received indeterminate sentences subject to the decision of the state board of parole. Eight younger offenders went to the state reformatory, also with indeterminate sentences. Thirty-two persons were placed on probation, nine of whom were men convicted of non-support and one of whom was a man convicted in a bastardy case. Probation in these ten cases was granted on condition that payments be made for the support of wives or children or both.

Fines and Community Protection

Fines were by far the most usual method of disposing of Springfield offenders. Of the 1,119 sentences imposed on persons coming before justices of the peace and the city magistrate, 71 per cent, as we have seen, were fines, and of these fines 60 per cent were $3.00 or less.

There are three ways in which the treatment to which offenders are subjected may serve to protect the community: First, by deterring people through fear from breaking the law; second, by regenerating through upbuilding treatment those who break the law; third, by permanent removal of confirmed criminals from society. Fines, of course, do not accomplish the last named purpose. The extent to which they protect the community will be measured, therefore, by their effect, first, as a deterring influence from law breaking, and second, as a means of reformation. We shall discuss their use from these points of view.

FINES AS A DETERRENT FROM LAW BREAKING

The facts regarding the rearrest and reconviction of persons fined in Springfield in 1913 indicate that fines were not effective in deterring people from crime. The records showed that they had not protected the community against repeated offenses by the large group of persons of the repeater type. Twenty-three per cent of all fines levied during the year were assessed against persons who were again arrested before the year ended, while 13 per cent were assessed against persons who were not only rearrested but were again convicted. These figures, moreover, understate the failure of fines to prevent law breaking, for many persons fined during the latter months of the year were not likely to be rearrested or again convicted before the year closed.

Detailed examination of the use of fines revealed some of the reasons for their failure as an effective deterrent. Most of the fines assessed were for small amounts, $3.00 or less. Except to the unskilled laborer such fines were not a serious penalty, even though costs of 60 cents or $1.35 were added. To the man earning $5.00 a day they meant little or nothing. The pettiness of the majority of the fines assessed failed to give the offender any serious impression of the necessity to obey the law.

Moreover, a number of fines were levied for offenses in the commission of which the offender made more than the amount of the fine. Estimating that the average earnings of a woman in a house of ill-fame were $25 a week, it is unlikely that she would give up such a life through fear of having occasionally to pay a small fine. During the year four persons were fined for keeping disorderly houses; one $3.00, one $10, one $25, and one $100. One man was fined $3.00 for running a gambling house.

A second group of offenses were due to the liquor or some other clinging habit. Probably half the arrests in Springfield were made either for drunkenness or some other offense in the commission of which drunkenness was the immediate contributory cause. The 869 arrests in 1913 in which drunkenness was specifically charged formed 26 per cent of all police arrests on definite charges. The ineffectiveness of fines in these cases is demonstrated by the fact that in 1913, of the 93 fines assessed for drunkenness or drunkenness and disorderly conduct, 36, or nearly 40 per cent, were levied against persons who during the year were arrested two or more times for intoxication or other offenses in the commission of which drunkenness was probably a factor.

In the same class with crimes due to the liquor habit are those wherein habit-forming drugs are a factor. It was not even illegal under the Illinois law to sell opium, morphine, heroin, or laudanum, some of the drugs used most commonly by drug victims who often resort to trickery, forgery, or larceny to get their supply. To fine a person who has stolen to get money to buy morphine is useless.[1]

INEFFECTIVENESS OF FINES
Panel from Survey Exhibition.

[1] It has been estimated by authorities that fully one-third of the inmates in the New York City correctional institutions are drug users.

THE CORRECTIONAL SYSTEM

Gambling possibly may also be classed with offenses stimulated by some kind of habit; in fact gambling itself appears with many people to be a habit with a psychological hold on its victims. In the cases of 38 men who in Springfield in 1913 were fined $3.00 each for gambling, it seems hardly probable that the fear of repetition of such penalty would be sufficient to lead them to give up the practice, or that others learning that three-dollar fines were being assessed would be led to do likewise.

Besides the law breakers under the grip of some habit, there are others with confirmed tendencies toward delinquency on whom petty fines have but little deterrent effect. These, for instance, include persons so much below normal mentally as to be classed as mental defectives. Dr. Goddard estimates that from 25 to 30 per cent of persons in prisons are mentally defective.[1] There are, too, besides the mental defectives, probably a few bold crooks—more than likely the product of misdirected "gang" spirit when they were boys—who regard a life of crime as a game to which the possibility of being caught and made to suffer only adds zest. Fines in these cases and in those previously cited are not likely to prevent further law breaking.

FINES AS A REFORMATORY INFLUENCE

Much that has been said about the relatively small influence of fines in deterring from crime applies equally to fines as an upbuilding influence. They cannot change the offender's desires, his abilities, his habits, or his point of view toward life. The truth is that fines were never intended to reform offenders but to act as a deterrent from law breaking, a matter in which, as we have seen, they are likewise often ineffective.

FINES FROM THE STANDPOINT OF JUSTICE

As a means, moreover, of providing just punishment as between offenders, the fining system is also open to attack. Where petty fines are much used, as in Springfield, the general tendency is to assess them in large or small amounts in proportion to the seriousness of the offense and not after taking into account also the

---

[1] Goddard, Henry H., M.D.: Feeble-mindedness: Its Causes and Consequences. New York, Macmillan, 1914.

ability of the offender to pay. To a man of some means a fine of $3.00 or even $25 is slight punishment, but upon the laborer earning $1.75 a day it falls heavily. The offense may be the same and yet in the payment the poor man may suffer the rich man's penalty many times over. One hundred and thirty-eight persons in Springfield in 1913 went to jail because they were not able to pay their fines, in whole or in part. Many of the largest fines were assessed against vagrants who had no money at all. In such cases fines result in nothing less than sending people to jail for being poor.

Where Fines are Useful

Yet fines, in spite of their weakness as a general means for dealing with offenders, are not without their uses in preventing the repetition of minor and technical offenses in which non-compliance with the law is largely a matter of failure to take pains, as for instance, violating the dog ordinance, obstructing the street, speeding, violating the school law or the traffic ordinances. They may in such cases serve to call attention to the law in a forceful way, especially if the amounts are adjusted to the means of the offenders. In no case in 1913 was a person fined twice for such offenses, which suggests that the fine was all that was necessary to secure observance of the law.

Fines may also serve a useful purpose when they are large, if execution is suspended during good behavior. But it should also be pointed out that in connection with suspended sentences they are not, with a certain class of offenders, superior to the more dreaded jail sentence.

Hours to Leave Town

Two hundred and nineteen offenders in Springfield, most of whom were beggars, vagrants, intoxicated and disorderly persons, in 1913 were given a certain number of hours in which to leave town. This method of protecting the community from undesirable characters is very common throughout the country. The net result is that a large class of men become the prey of police departments, being shunted from one city to another and back again, finally ending as members of the army of hoboes or as professional criminals.

THE CORRECTIONAL SYSTEM

In the long run no city gains in this process, which serves only to confirm pauperism and delinquency. At the same time no one city can put a stop to the practice. The remedy must come through national co-operation of police departments. Until some solution of the problem is brought about, Springfield, in self-defense, will probably continue this abominable practice. But there is no excuse for Springfield courts ridding the community of its own resident and proper local charges by giving them hours to leave town as they did in several instances in 1913.

Suspended Sentences and Probation

A third means used in Springfield in disposing of offenders was suspension of sentence "pending good behavior." The justices of the peace and city magistrate in 1913 suspended execution under this condition on five jail sentences and 149 fines. Since these offenders were sent back to their old environments with no form of supervision, it is not surprising that 23 out of the 154 suspended sentences had to be revoked within the year, while in a number of other instances those whose sentences were suspended were again convicted on new charges.

A suspended sentence cannot be effective without such control over released offenders as will help in overcoming law-breaking tendencies. The state law authorized the use of probation for first offenders in all courts, subject to certain restrictions, and provided for the appointment by the circuit court of a probation officer. The circuit court, however, had not chosen to make such an appointment; so that all those placed on probation by the circuit court and all so placed by the county court, save those proved guilty of non-support, had been put under the charge of voluntary officers, in a number of cases of relatives. Though this was an improvement over the suspended sentence, it did not take the place of a well-organized probation department.

Jail Sentences

Persons arrested by the police in Springfield were being held temporarily, and those unable to pay fines for violation of city ordinances, on sentence in the city prison. Persons arrested by the sheriff and those held for the grand jury were confined temporarily, and those receiving jail sentences or fines for violation of state laws which they were unable to pay, on sentence in the county jail.

The City Prison

On December 12, 1912, the Springfield city prison was inspected by the Illinois State Board of Charities, and the report, published in the *Institution Quarterly*, describes the jail as follows:

The Springfield city prison is a disgrace to any community. The main section for men, located on the first floor, is dark and ill

Springfield Police Headquarters
City jail at the rear of the building and the city magistrate's office upstairs.

ventilated. The room has only a few windows on one side, and they are covered with iron sheets perforated by small openings.

The cage has only three small cells which are ventilated by bar fronts and backs. Each cell has two bunks, provided with old mattresses and comforts. As there are always more than six daily prisoners, many men sleep on the floors or on top of the cage.

Toilet and bath facilities are placed in the corridor.

Women are placed on the second floor in a department which is fireproof. The only approach, however, is a stairway of wood. Cots with mattresses and blankets furnish the rooms. There is one iron cell, ventilated by means of bar openings, which is rarely used.

A section on the second floor is used for male prisoners whom it is desirable to segregate. Minors are placed in this department.

Juveniles are sent to the annex to the county jail. Minors held at the city jail are segregated from older offenders.

Tramps, "drunks," etc., are herded together in the dark section on the first floor. The city should provide work for men held in jail.

The officials deserve praise for the cleanliness of the place and for observation of the law providing segregation for minors.

Since that time a few improvements in sanitation had been made, but on the whole the above was a fair description of the city jail as we found it.

The dishes in which prisoners received their food, which was fairly satisfactory, were of tin. Drinking water was supplied by a common drinking cup. No hospital ward was provided either for men or for women. Dangerously ill prisoners were removed to St. John's Hospital, four having been taken there in 1913. Others were treated at the jail by the over-busy city physician, who kept no record of his cases.

Male prisoners over seventeen years of age and females over eighteen, both those held pending trial and those serving sentence, were kept in the city prison. The terms of confinement in 1913 ranged from a few hours to two hundred and eight days, the latter being rare. The average confinement pending trial was usually not more than a day; the most common term of sentence was about two weeks.

The law provided for the appointment of a matron, but this statute had not been observed and women prisoners were in charge of men keepers. There were also provisions regarding classification of prisoners which applied both to city and county jails. In the Springfield city prison, however, female prisoners regardless of age, color, offense, or guilt were confined together;

good women and girls with confirmed prostitutes; those held on suspicion with those proved guilty.

To provide proper classification for male prisoners the jail authorities made some use of the extra ward for men, but it was clear that in many instances even two wards did not permit complete observance of the law. It was not uncommon, therefore, to find thrown together in the "bull pen" those held on suspicion or for

INSIDE THE "BULL PEN," CITY PRISON, SPRINGFIELD

The cage furnished the only bunks for sometimes as high as 50 prisoners. The jail exists to protect the community from law breaking; but unless prisoners' treatment is upbuilding instead of degrading, those taken into custody are likely to go out merely to break the law again, as many did in Springfield in 1913.

trial, the guilty, first offenders and old rounders, those guilty of technical or of serious charges, clever crooks and drunks, drug victims, highwaymen, murderers, and lodgers.

The situation was aggravated, moreover, in the Springfield city prison, by the fact that save for a few trusties the prisoners spent the days in idleness, lying about their cells, playing cards, telling vile stories, swapping criminal adventures, and passing the time as best they could.

The County Jail

The county jail comprised a main building and an annex. The main building was divided into two parts, the first serving as the sheriff's residence, the rear as the jail which was divided into a

The County Jail, Springfield

Jail in the center; sheriff's residence at the right. Conditions in the jail and the treatment received by prisoners—many of them held for weeks and months in complete idleness—were in no sense reformative.

ward for women and a ward for men. The annex was used for the confinement of insane persons, alcoholics, and children.

The days of detention of prisoners in the county jail ranged in 1913 from one to two hundred and seventy-three days. While the largest numbers were held only two days—most of these being suspects and destitute lodgers—many served extended terms, 417 having been imprisoned for thirty days or more, 147 for sixty days or more, 77 for ninety days or more, 15 for one hundred and twenty days or more, a number as long as six months, and two for over two hundred days each.

Men's Ward

In the men's ward there was unusually good general light and ventilation but cell ventilation was not adequate. The words "dark and ill-ventilated stone cells" used in 1911 by the State Charities Commission still held true. The ward was divided into two sections, one for white and one for colored prisoners. The ward for white prisoners was always overflowing, and many whites were kept with the Negro prisoners, transfer to the Negro section being used sometimes as a disciplinary measure.

Each section of the ward had a bath tub, two sinks with hot and cold water and soap, and a toilet. No towels were furnished and the tin drinking cups were used in common. After nine o'clock at night all men who had cells were locked in them, and buckets were used for toilet purposes. Aside from the lack of provision for the regular washing of bedding, the ward was in a comparatively good state of cleanliness. It was nearly always overcrowded, however, and many men were forced to sleep on the floor without coverings.

Women's Ward

The women's ward was situated on the second floor in a part of the building not fireproof, entrance to which was gained by a flight of wooden stairs. The ward was immediately over the kitchen and, since the windows were barred, in case of sudden fire it would be difficult, to say the least, to rescue women prisoners.

The ward consisted of one large room with windows on two sides. Heavy bars running from floor to ceiling separated off a good-sized cage which was formally the women's ward, but at the time of our visits women prisoners had the freedom of the whole room. Within the cage were four beds with clean bedding. At one end were a flush toilet and a clean bath tub. The sheriff's wife was employed as matron, but the keys to the women's ward were kept by the male jailer who thus had free access.

In the same room with the women, in a cage with three sides solid and a front of bars, was an extra ward for men who were United States prisoners or who for some reason needed to be separated from other offenders. In this cage were a bed with mattress and blankets, a porcelain bath tub, and a flush toilet. The cage faced away from the women's compartment, but as women prisoners had access to the whole room there was no adequate segregation of female prisoners and men held there.

No regular hospital ward was provided for either men or women, though sick prisoners were frequently sent to the annex to be kept with the children, or when seriously ill were transferred to some hospital. They were attended, as in the city prison, by the city physician, who, as stated before, was already overburdened.

Feeding of County Prisoners

The ordinary menu of county prisoners consisted of cereals, coffee, soup, boiled meats, beans, potatoes, and bread. The sheriff received 30 cents a day for each prisoner fed, which made it clearly to his advantage to provide food as cheaply as possible. To the credit of the incumbent at the time of this investigation, it should be stated that the food furnished was not bad. The system, however, of paying the sheriff a salary and then paying him for feeding county prisoners, is unquestionably wasteful to the taxpayers, and as it was working out, most unjust to the prisoners. In the city prison, where the feeding of prisoners was not delegated at so much per diem, the total cost to the city was $917.64, or 9.68 cents per man a day, if one counts days as the county authorities do. If the sheriff did as well in reducing costs, and there was every reason to think that he could, he must have cleared some $6,611 out of the $9,761.30 which he received for feeding prisoners in the year ending November 30, 1913.[1]

[1] As the earlier detailed report of the correctional system went to press, the Springfield newspapers announced that the new sheriff, John A. Wheeler, had publicly declared that he would not accept any profit for feeding the prisoners in jail. He estimated that the amount turned back into the county treasury would be about $7,600 a year.

Classification of County Prisoners

Classification requirements of the state law were even less observed than in the city prison. Offenders in all degrees of degradation were herded together. As in the city jail, there was no work for any but a few trusties, and the majority of the prisoners passed the days, weeks, and months in complete idleness.

Jail Sentences as a Deterrent

A study of the records of 1913 showed that the jail sentence was seriously ineffective as a deterrent. Forty-five per cent of the jail sentences imposed were of persons arrested two or more times during the year. Nine persons were sentenced to jail twice, 1 three times, and 1 four times, so that in all, 63 persons were involved in the 77 jail sentences of repeaters. These included many of the worst "rounders" in the city and contributed a total of 199 arrests during the year, 63 of which were made of offenders who had once suffered jail sentence. In 32 instances those who served sentences were again convicted before the year was up. When one considers that 30 per cent of these

FEEDING PRISONERS

The County pays the Sheriff for being Sheriff
Then it pays him handsomely for feeding the prisoners

What County Pays for feeding prisoners / What City pays for feeding prisoners

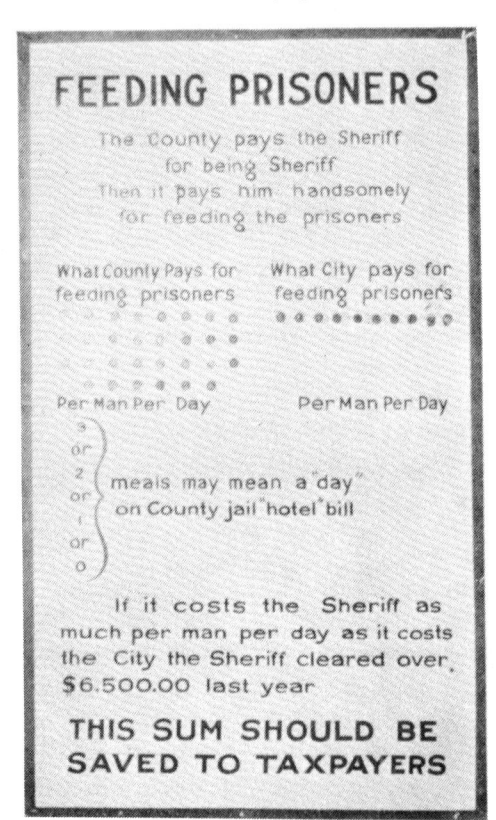

Per Man Per Day / Per Man Per Day

2 or 2 or 1 or 0 meals may mean a "day" on County jail "hotel" bill

If it costs the Sheriff as much per man per day as it costs the City the Sheriff cleared over $6,500.00 last year

THIS SUM SHOULD BE SAVED TO TAXPAYERS

Cost of Feeding Prisoners in Springfield
Panel from Springfield Survey Exhibition.

sentences of repeaters were imposed during the last three months of the year, so that arrest and conviction were not likely to recur within the period studied, the ineffectiveness of such sentences in preventing law breaking by offenders of this type is further emphasized.

Why the Jails Fail as Deterrents

There are in general two classes of offenders: those not confirmed in delinquency who still retain some self-respect and standing in the community, and those whose reputations and self-respect are so impaired that a jail term will harm neither. To those in the first group the jail sentence has some effect as a deterrent; they fear the discomforts and associations of jail, and they fear for their reputations.

Persons of the other type, however, with nothing to lose, make up the bulk of the jail population. Such individuals, as records of repeating show, find a jail sentence quite bearable because it offers them a bed, regular meals, warmth in winter, and the companions they prefer without the necessity of working. The truth is that the only kind of jail which can have any real deterrent effect on this class of offenders is one which provides good hard work.

Were the Springfield Jails Reformative?

Conditions in the jails of Springfield not only were weakening and corrupting prisoners but they were sending them out more likely than before to be a danger to the community.

No physical examination was made, and unless prisoners were acutely sick their physical needs received no attention. Prisoners had no opportunity for exercise, and their already weakened bodies became still weaker. Drunkards and victims of drug habits were given no help in breaking their habit nor any kind of a "cure."

Nothing was done for the mental training of prisoners, and except occasional efforts at religious influence by outsiders, nothing was done on the moral side. In fact each term of enforced idleness made it less likely that the prisoner would become a self-supporting, law-abiding citizen upon release.

First offenders received exactly the same treatment as long-time offenders. Workingmen were serving time in enforced idleness, while their muscles were growing flabby and their energy was being sapped. Men and women free from venereal disease were using toilets, bathtubs, and drinking cups in common with others when the city physician estimated that 50 per cent of the prisoners in both jails were infected with syphilis. Good girls and women were thrown in with prostitutes. Young men who had "pulled off" their first exploit were thrown into daily contact with embezzlers, forgers, highway robbers, and murderers.

Such conditions and treatment are not reformative. But even if the jails were of an entirely different sort and were designed primarily for the regeneration of offenders, it is doubtful if a great deal could be accomplished in the short periods for which most prisoners were being confined. No one was sentenced for more than six months, and 61 per cent received sentences of thirty days or less. If the community is to receive protection through the regeneration of law breakers, prisoners must not only be subjected to upbuilding treatment but must receive it for a sufficient period to make it reasonably effective. Therefore not only a new jail system was needed but a new plan and a new purpose in sentencing offenders.

Further, when prisoners left the jail they went back to their old haunts, under the same conditions that caused arrest, without help or guidance. In any plan for the development of a more effective correctional system, some provision must be made for parole supervision of released prisoners.

Conclusions Regarding Present Methods

The conclusion is unavoidable that Springfield's correctional methods were in large measure ineffective in protecting the community. The more important facts leading to the conclusion are briefly:

Fines, the most used method, were employed in many instances where in the very nature of the case they could not act as effective deterrents. Nor were they effective as reformative agents.

Giving offenders a limited number of hours to leave town produced no results when other cities were also following the same vicious practice.

Suspended sentences "pending good behavior," when used as here without probationary supervision, were not particularly productive of the desired results.

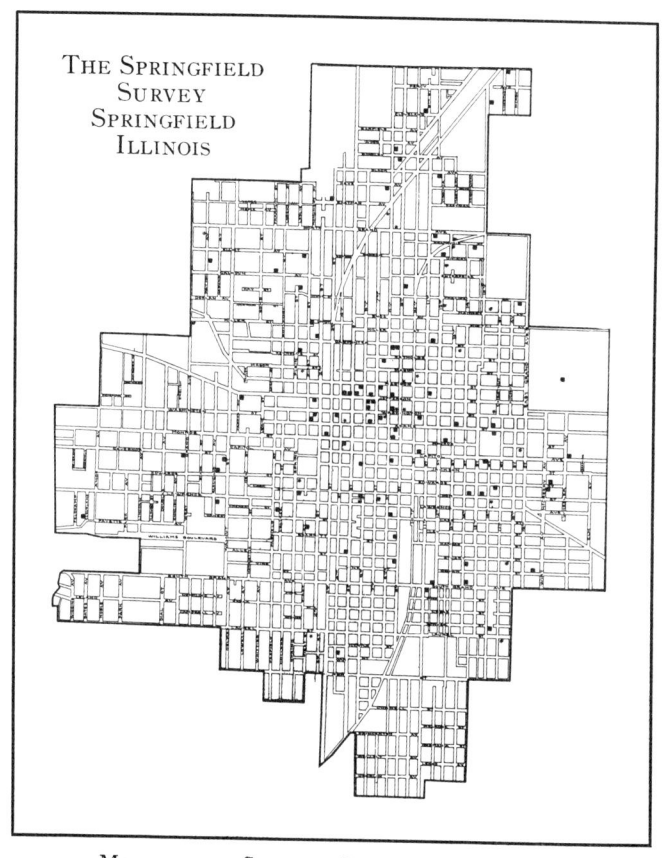

MURDERS AND SUICIDES, SPRINGFIELD, 1908–1913
A total of approximately 100 deaths.

Conditions in city and county jails were such that prisoners were less likely to become law abiding citizens upon release than they were when they entered.

Free board without work was not deterring prisoners of the repeater type. The short terms, moreover, made impossible any adequate reformatory treatment, even had the jails been able to give it. Failure to aid released prisoners was a distinct community neglect.

Springfield was relying upon only one means in trying to protect itself. It was holding to the traditional belief in the deterrent effect of punishment—this to the utter neglect of efforts to fit law breakers to lead normal lives. The call was clear for bringing all means of protecting the community into play and for developing a correctional system which would furnish for each offender treatment that not only might deter him from future law breaking but develop in him law-abiding habits and a distaste for crime.

A New Jail System Outlined

For reconstruction of the jail system two alternatives deserved consideration:

1. The state might be persuaded to undertake the care of misdemeanants in state institutions conveniently located near the larger cities.
2. The city and county might take advantage of the Illinois house of corrections act and unite in the establishment of an institution for the care of city and county prisoners.

State Care of Misdemeanants

Authorities on criminology are pretty well united in believing that the ultimate solution of the problem of handling misdemeanants is to provide state institutions for their care, just as is done for felons. As compared with county jails most state penitentiaries and reformatories are of a superior type. Moreover, local care in comparison is grossly extravagant. If the state of Illinois can be persuaded to undertake the care of misdemeanants in state institutions, that would, we believe, be the best solution of the jail problem. Instead of the 102 county jails caring for misdemeanants a quarter that many state district jails for the detention of persons pending trial, none of them larger than the average county jail, and perhaps three or possibly four state institutions for misdemeanants confined on sentence, would better serve the needs. There should be a woman's reformatory, and two or three farm institutions for male offenders, one to be located near Chicago and the other one or two to be located so as to serve adequately the central and southern parts of the state.

If, however, the state declines to undertake the care of misdemeanants, Springfield and Sangamon County should unite in an endeavor to provide for prisoners locally in a more adequate manner.

A Springfield House of Correction

A state law enacted as long ago as 1870 provides for the establishment of houses of correction by municipalities. Another statute authorizes cities to purchase not to exceed 40 acres outside of the city limits for the purpose of establishing houses of correction. These statutes together form an excellent basis for the development of a correctional institution of the right kind.

Plans for the development of a house of correction were laid by the Springfield City Commission in 1913, but the project was never completed. In order that prevailing jail conditions should continue no longer than absolutely necessary we would recommend new legislation and action for the completion of these plans. Whether, however, the jail situation is to be met locally or by the state there are certain standards representative of the best and most recent thought which should govern the development and management of institutions for misdemeanants and other petty offenders. The more important details follow:

Correctional Institutional Standards

1. The institution should be located in the country where farm work will be available for prisoners.

2. The superintendent should be a man of good business ability who has also an understanding of prisoners' needs. A salary adequate to attract a thoroughly capable man should be offered, for a poorly qualified superintendent will prove a great extravagance in the long run.

3. Besides the superintendent there should be in control of the institution a matron, if women are to be detained, an agriculturist, and guards, the last named being selected for their ability to take charge of blacksmith, tailor, shoe, carpenter, or other shops and to teach the prisoners trades.

4. There should be also a special institution physician, paid and required to give adequate time to the work, and a trained nurse in charge of the hospital ward. In large institutions a corps of physicians who are specialists and more than one nurse are necessary.

5. Buildings should be durable and fireproof and should provide a separate room for each prisoner with plenty of light and air, and warmth in winter. The women's ward, if women are to be held, and that for men, should be entirely separate. There should also be four divisions of each ward to permit separation of prisoners whom it is not desirable to confine together.

6. The building for the housing of prisoners should furnish, besides sleeping quarters, a dining room—suitable also as an assembly room—a kitchen, modern laundry, hospital ward, and a bathroom (with shower baths only). In addition to this main building and those for farm purposes, quarters for shop work to aid in the upkeep of the institution and to give prisoners employment during the winter months should also be provided.

7. Buildings should be constructed as far as possible by the prisoners. The feasibility of this has been repeatedly demonstrated. It will save the taxpayers money and furnish wholesome work for the men.

8. When prisoners are received they should be given a bath and supplied with institution clothes of plain, durable material (not striped). Their own clothes should be taken from them to be sterilized, patched, and pressed so that when released, prisoners may be presentable candidates for work.

9. As soon after arrival as possible prisoners should receive a thorough physical examination, and definite treatment should be prescribed when needed. If the institution physician himself is not fitted to handle unusual cases, consulting physicians should be called in. Too much emphasis cannot be placed upon physical treatment, for a sound body is the first essential to regeneration.

10. Special attention should be given to administering the cure to victims of the liquor or drug habits. Every precaution should be taken to make sure that while in the institution prisoners do not receive supplies of either drugs or liquor unless on the physician's prescription.

11. Provisions should be made for religious and other educational instruction. In local institutions the former may generally be had without expense if churches of different denominations are invited to supply regular religious instruction to prisoners of their

faith, while the latter may well be furnished by the board of education as a part of the regular evening school work.

12. Food for prisoners should be wholesome and adequate. Needless to say, the exact expense of feeding and no more should be paid for by the government. The New York State Prison Commission is wisely recommending the use of crockery dishes in all jails and penal institutions because of their effect in stimulating the self-respect of prisoners.

13. Work for prisoners should include fruit growing, truck gardening, stock raising, dairying, and other kinds of farm work; brick making, quarrying, possibly canning, besides other work necessary in the upkeep and management of the institution. Women prisoners, if kept there, may be employed in farm work and in making clothing. The problem of finding work for men in the winter may be met in part by reserving improvements in buildings and equipment for winter months, and in part by quarry work which may be carried on in cold weather. The construction and improvement of the institution will provide excellent work for several years.

14. As far as possible men should be assigned to perform the kinds of work for which their physical and mental capacities best fit them. A man desiring to be a carpenter should, if qualified for the work, be put in the carpenter shop. Those with anemia or weak lungs should be sent out of doors.

15. No contract labor scheme should be entered into, and as far as possible competition with outside labor should be avoided.

16. The products of the institution should as far as possible supply not only the institution's needs but those of other city, county, or state departments.

17. There is considerable opinion favoring the payment of regular wages to prisoners after deducting the cost of their keep. It is claimed that this not only leads to greater productiveness on their part but tends to increase self-respect, which is perhaps the community's greatest protection from law breaking. It also prevents prisoners' families from suffering while they are confined, or supplies prisoners themselves with small funds to tide over the precarious days without work immediately following release.

18. A careful cost-accounting system should be developed for each department of the institution. All goods disposed of to other departments of the city, county, or state governments, should be credited to the institution at market prices, and an annual report should be published showing both financial results and results obtained in fitting prisoners for normal life.

Temporary Detention

The establishment of state care or of a farm institution will not, of course, provide for persons who need to be held temporarily, pending trial, awaiting transportation to the institution in which they are to serve their sentences, or awaiting the action of the grand jury. For this purpose the maintenance of two jails would be a needless extravagance, and if possible some method should be worked out by which the county jail, which was superior in physical equipment to the city jail, could be used.

INDETERMINATE SENTENCES

When is a prisoner fit to be set free?

The judge at the trial can weigh the single deed but he can't weigh the whole man

In ILLINOIS PENITENTIARIES prisoners are confined on indeterminate sentences

The penitentiary authorities decide when prisoners are fit for freedom

If indeterminate sentences are good for serious offences they're even better for minor ones

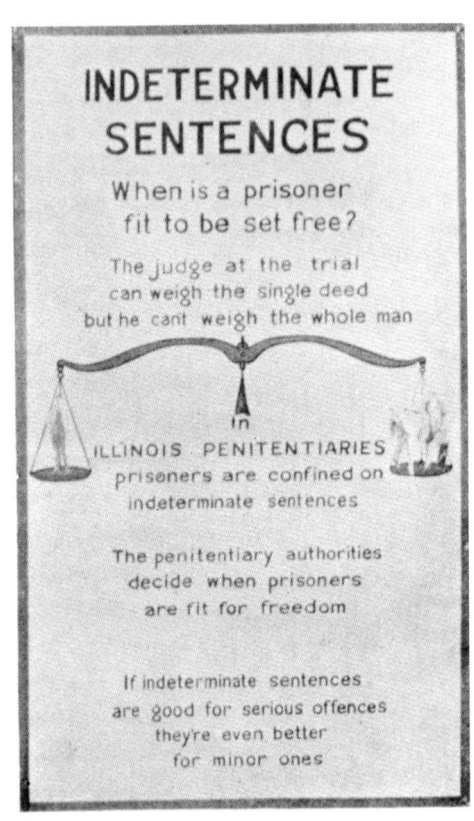

INDETERMINATE SENTENCES
Panel from Springfield Survey Exhibition.

Indeterminate Sentence

However upbuilding a jail may be, its success in regenerating offenders will be hampered unless prisoners are sentenced for sufficient periods to permit effective treatment. For this reason, as has already been indicated, jail sentences in Springfield were too short. At the time, however, nothing could be gained by subjecting offenders for longer periods, but under a new jail system sentences would need to be lengthened before any effective work of regeneration could be carried on.

THE CORRECTIONAL SYSTEM

For the protection of the community, no sentences are better than those indeterminate in length, which permit the holding of prisoners until there is some likelihood of their making good when given their freedom. With some exceptions persons guilty of felonies were committed to the Illinois penitentiaries for indeterminate periods, and if such sentences were desirable for them, how much more so for those guilty of less serious offenses and among whom the possibility of reform was consequently greater. With the development of better jail facilities there is therefore every reason for applying the indeterminate sentence to misdemeanants.

The existing indeterminate sentence laws set a maximum term beyond which a prisoner might not be held, and a minimum to be completed before he might be paroled. Restrictions on indeterminate sentences applied to misdemeanants, however, should differ from those which applied to felons. It would probably be wise to give the board with paroling power authority to release a prisoner on parole at any time after commitment when, in its judgment, he or she gives satisfactory evidence of a purpose and ability to live at liberty without violating the law. It would also be wise to have a graduated maximum term dependent upon the number of times the prisoner has been convicted.

Parole Supervision

Even with upbuilding jails and indeterminate sentences, work for the regeneration of the prisoner will often break down if prisoners are sent from the jail with no help or supervision. Quite often the offender has lost his job and needs to find employment; often he needs a new environment and different associates or friendly encouragement in his effort to make good. If correctional work is really to put offenders on their feet, help and direction to released prisoners must be given and a parole department with capable, paid parole officers should be established.

The failure of the state law to provide for the paroling of misdemeanants, when such methods were almost universally admitted to be successful and were already being used in dealing with those guilty of felonies, was but another example of the neglect to which those guilty of minor offenses have been subject.

Adult Probation Needs

Thus far we have dealt with the treatment of law breakers requiring institutional treatment. A majority of offenders, as has been shown, were fined instead of being sent to jail. We have recommended, however, the abandonment of the general use of fines. What, then, should take its place? The answer is probation—of a sort that will mean another chance under the guidance of an officer whose business is to do all in his power to help offenders keep the law.

But there were no paid probation officers for adults in Springfield, and those persons placed on probation by the county and circuit courts were placed under the care of volunteer officers, often relatives or friends. While volunteers are undoubtedly of great service, the best results are obtained through trained officers or when volunteers work under the direction of paid probation officers.

Under the provisions of the Illinois law it was possible to appoint one probation officer. If probation should largely replace petty fines, Springfield would need not less than three probation officers to serve the county and circuit courts, the city magistrate, and the justices of the peace. The present statute provided also that the chief officer should receive $1,200 a year, and other officers $800. These amounts were even then too low considering the qualifications needed. There was need, therefore, for amendments which should not only permit the employment of a larger number of officers but allow the payment of more adequate salaries.

The statute restricted the use of probation and permitted it only when the offense fell within certain specified groups. In order to obtain the most beneficial results it would seem wiser if courts were given entire discretion in the use of probation, for experience has shown that they are inclined to be conservative and are very unlikely to abuse such power.

Reorganization of Minor Courts and Revision of Sentences

Under the minor court system of Springfield the city magistrate and five justices of the peace had concurrent jurisdiction in all criminal actions punishable by a fine of $200 or less. An offender would first come before one justice, then before another, each dealing with him in his own way, regardless of the plan of the others. In a number of cases in 1913, offenders were fined large amounts by one justice and given suspended sentences pending good behavior, only to receive fines much smaller than the suspended ones when brought before another justice on new charges. It is obvious, under these circumstances, that no effective constructive program could be put into operation.

Unfortunately the salaries and honors attached to lower court judgeships are generally small and the qualifications do not even include legal training. Since the lower courts for the great majority of citizens who cannot afford the excessive costs of appeals are, in fact, courts of last resort, it is highly important that the standards there prevailing should be more nearly equal to those of the higher courts than they were.

The justice of the peace system is a relic of a more or less pioneer period of small communities which in Springfield had ceased to exist. The law permitted cities to establish city courts, but these had concurrent jurisdiction with circuit courts and did not replace justice of the peace and city magistrate's courts. Neither did they solve the minor court problem. The Municipal Court Act of Chicago offered the best suggestion for new legislation to meet the situation. This act provided for the abolition of city magistrates and justices of the peace in Chicago, and gave the municipal court jurisdiction in all criminal cases in which punishment was by fine, or imprisonment otherwise than in the penitentiary, and in all other criminal cases which the laws in force from time to time might permit to be prosecuted in other ways than on indictment by a grand jury.

A municipal court of this type for Springfield would offer definite advantages over the prevailing system, as follows:

1. It would permit the outlining and carrying out of a careful plan for the treatment of each offender.

2. It would tend to attract to the bench men of a superior type.

3. It would command more respect from the public and from law breakers than the present system. This is especially impor-

tant if the correctional activities are to aim at the regeneration of offenders.

4. It would abolish the current pernicious system by which the city magistrate and justices received their remuneration from the fees they were able to collect.

The fact is worth noting that under the fee system the justice ordinarily receives nothing if the person is set free. There is a temptation to find people guilty whenever possible. Moreover, entries in the police docket for 1913 show that justices sometimes went so far as to collect fees for cases dismissed, for cases bound over to the grand jury, and for others in which no charges had been proved.

Court Sentences

Under these proposed changes in correctional methods court sentences will need to be altered to suit the new conditions. It will be more important to provide treatment that will transform the offender into a law observer than to find suitable punishment. Fines will be restricted to minor offenses which do not indicate well-grounded delinquent tendencies. Cases which are not serious and are likely to respond to probation will be put under the care of the probation officer. If the case is more serious and the offender needs special treatment he will be sent to an institution where every influence is wholesome and where physically, at the very least, he may prepare himself to take up a normal life. His term, moreover, will be largely dependent upon the changes brought about. When he goes out he will be a presentable candidate for a job and will have the advice and help of a parole officer in re-establishing himself, with the necessity, if he fails to do so, of returning to the institution. As a means for community protection from law breakers the superiority of this proposed treatment over that then operating must be evident.

Special Legislative Inquiry Recommended

Conditions which were found defective in the correctional system of Springfield were not unique but were fairly representative of the situation throughout the state. In fact many of the most fundamental weaknesses of prevailing methods were traceable more to state than local regulations and could be eliminated only through state action. We were convinced, therefore, that in spite of improvements in correctional methods which might and should be brought about through the activities of Springfield people, still greater results could be secured if inquiry into Illinois correctional methods could be conducted on a state-wide scale.

The survey therefore recommended that the people of Springfield seek the support of those interested in correctional reform in Chicago and other parts of the state, in an endeavor to have the legislature establish a commission to investigate methods used in the handling of petty offenders throughout the state. Such an investigation would enable the citizens of Illinois to establish substantial improvements in their correctional system and thus to go far in eliminating those weaknesses handed down from past generations and which are the common inheritance of all the states.

THE HANDLING OF JUVENILE DELINQUENTS

Complaints Against Children

The attitude of the state toward children who break the law is entirely different from its attitude toward adult offenders. Delinquent children are not dealt with under the criminal law, but are, to quote the juvenile court act, "considered as wards of this state subject to the care, guardianship, and control of the court." The endeavor is not to punish, but to protect them from growing up to lives of crime, and the important consideration is not so much whether a specific act of delinquency has been committed, as whether, by assuming guardianship over a child, the court may save it from further delinquency.

Springfield had recognized the possibility of constructive work with juvenile offenders to the extent of designating a special policeman known as the humane officer, establishing a juvenile court and detention home, and employing a juvenile probation officer. But for one cause or another the benefits reasonably to be hoped for from these provisions had not been fully realized. Radical changes were not needed, however, so much as strengthening the work already established.

As compared with the number of adult offenders, juvenile offenders were few, only 71 children having been brought before the Sangamon County juvenile court in the fifteen months before the survey. Most complaints against children in Springfield were made by citizens not to the court directly but to the police department. They were then investigated by the humane officer, who made arrests when he thought cases warranted it. Arrested children were then taken to police headquarters in some instances in the patrol wagon. Here their names were formally entered upon the police docket along with those of adult offenders, and they were lodged in the annex of the county jail. As far as the police department was concerned, children were treated as if they were adult offenders, and no appreciation of the state's attitude toward such children was apparent.

Cases in which complaints were made by the humane officer were, in 1913, greater in number than cases coming before the juvenile court through any other channel. We believe, however, that the practice of having so many complaints pass through the hands of the police before reaching the juvenile court was an error in procedure. Except in cases in which there is danger that children may run away, the police department should refer cases to the juvenile court without making arrest, and thus permit the probation officer to investigate whether court action is necessary. When immediate arrest is necessary the police should take children to the detention home for confinement.

Detention of Children

Delinquent children, like adults, often need to be held temporarily pending hearing of their cases or waiting transportation to state schools. Although the city provided a detention home for children, the real detention home of Springfield was the annex of the county jail. Here, in 1913, 203 children were held, most of them delinquents, while only 42 children were kept in the detention home.

The County Jail Annex

The annex of the county jail was bare, cold, and unattractive, with barred windows and doors, a typical "jail." In the six rooms that it contained there were five beds, and many times, boys, if not girls, were forced to sleep on the floor; on a certain night 18 persons were known to have been confined in the building. There were no toilets in the rooms and when persons were locked in them, buckets served the purpose. The rooms were

SANGAMON COUNTY JAIL ANNEX, SPRINGFIELD

In this building were held children, insane persons, and those with delirium tremens. On crowded days it was impossible to provide adequate segregation. Since the county was paying out money for a detention home, supposedly for the detention of delinquent children, there was no excuse for keeping delinquent children here under the disgraceful conditions which existed.

Seventy-eight insane persons and 88 suffering with acute alcoholism were held here in 1913—some as long as twenty days. Neither the insane nor alcoholics should be detained in such a place; instead, they should receive hospital care until the state provides sufficiently for their treatment.

separated only by bars, and persons confined in one room could readily see into the others.

On crowded days, even though the authorities were careful in their efforts, it would be impossible to provide adequate segregation. As it was, boys and girls—the investigation showed that some were as young as nine years—were confined with insane persons, those with delirium tremens (generally the last stage of degradation), and occasionally a sick prisoner suffering from some other trouble. The presence among these children of the insane and alcoholics was not a chance happening but the rule. No amusement was provided for the children who were being held for periods of several days, a few as long as a week, ten days, or a fortnight, and one boy for thirty-seven days. The matron of the jail and annex was on duty during the day, but at night, when a woman was most needed, a male keeper was in charge.

Such conditions, which offend common decency, were inexcusable. Perhaps the least inexcusable thing was that children were being confined in such quarters, when the county was paying for a detention home for those boys under seventeen and girls under eighteen years of age who came under the jurisdiction of the juvenile court.

The Detention Home

The detention home was a seven-room residence in a good state of repair, but not suitable for a city the size of Springfield. An experienced woman superintendent, with an assistant, seemed to be making the best of the building facilities and providing as good care of the children as the circumstances permitted. The place was clean and homelike, the children neat and apparently happy.

The facilities, however, did not permit proper classification of the children. Although the usual sex classification was observed, it had been impossible to classify by age groups or to separate dependent and delinquent children. It was also difficult, if not impossible, to hold children who might try to run away.

The detention home could not provide treatment of an educational or reformative character which institutions holding delinquent children for more than temporary periods are expected to provide. The court continued, however, to use it for purposes of more than temporary detention; five out of eight delinquent boys were detained two months or more, two being held more than a year, one as long as nineteen months, while quite a number of dependent children were held more than a month, and nine more than two months.

Under the arrangement at the time the superintendent of the home and her assistant received $50 a month each, also whatever they could save out of the regular appropriation of $75 a month for maintenance, which did not vary whether there were one or a dozen children to be kept. This allowance of a stipulated sum for monthly expenses and for which the superintendent did not give account, was thoroughly vicious, and while we do not believe it led to abuse by the superintendent then in charge, it offered a constant temptation to economize at the expense of the children. Such an arrangement sooner or later is almost certain to lead to abuse of a serious nature.

Briefly, the detention home, while well administered by the superintendent, was not serving its purpose and was not fitted to do so; and conditions in the jail annex where most delinquent children were held, as we have seen were unspeakably bad. The county was thus maintaining two inadequate institutions, when one, organized and administered on right lines, could serve the same purpose a great deal better and at probably no greater expense.

The abandonment of the practice of holding children in the annex of the county jail and the provision of an adequate detention home were recommended. For the acquirement and management of such a home, suggestions were offered as follows:

1. The home should be planned and managed as a place for temporary detention, not for institutional care.
2. It is desirable not to have delinquent and dependent children housed in the same institution, and if arrangements can be made by which the Home for the Friendless will hold dependent children temporarily, pending their disposition by the court, the detention home should be planned for delinquent children only. Otherwise it should be planned for delinquents and dependents.
3. The home should provide for the holding of all delinquent boys up to seventeen years and delinquent girls up to eighteen years of age.
4. Building a new detention home rather than remodeling some present structure is recommended. The money is available, the voters having given consent to a one per cent tax levy for the purpose, and a more satisfactory home will thus be ob-

tained. It also will be economy for the county to own the home rather than to rent, for this is to be a permanent county institution.

5. The home should be located, if possible, within six or eight blocks of police headquarters and the sheriff's office, so that it will be conveniently accessible.

6. Plans for the building should provide a section for boys and one for girls entirely apart from each other. A separate sleeping room, which need not be large, should be provided for each child. There should also be in each section a dining room, a living room, and a bathroom with shower baths only. Quarters will also need to be supplied for those in charge of the home, and it will be advantageous if provisions for juvenile court hearings can be made.

7. If the home is maintained for delinquents only, it should be planned to accommodate not less than 10 boys and five girls. The number will usually run much below this figure, but provision should be made to meet emergencies and future needs.

8. As far as possible the institution should have the appearance of a home rather than a jail, and should therefore be attractively and comfortably furnished. It will be necessary, to prevent escapes, to cover the windows with heavy wire screening firmly fastened on. Bars should not be used. Adequate locks should be provided on all doors, also hinges of a kind which cannot be removed. All these features should, however, be as unobtrusive as possible.

9. Children who have passed the age of adolescence should be kept apart from other children, save when one of those in charge of the institution is present.

10. A yard at the rear, extensive enough to permit play, should be enclosed with a high board fence, with in-turned barb wiring at the top to prevent ready scaling, so that in good weather children may enjoy outdoor exercise.

11. There should be in charge of the institution not only a house mother to look after the girls, but a house father to look after the boys. In fact the latter is absolutely necessary to care for older delinquent boys. The present policy of having trained persons in charge of the home deserves to be continued.

12. The superintendent of the home should be required to keep a record showing the name, sex, age, and address of each child detained, the cause of detention, the day and hour received, the person received from, and the person discharged to. A record now kept by the probation officer gives most of this information, but it should be kept by the manager of the home as required by law. When the present record book is used up, a card catalog should replace it.

13. Accurate financial records should be kept, as required by law, and the exact expense of the home should be borne by the county.

THE SANGAMON COUNTY JUVENILE COURT

From January 1, 1913, to April 1, 1914, the docket of the Sangamon County juvenile court showed that 71 children had been brought before the court charged with delinquency. Conditions found and recommendations made with regard to the juvenile court may be briefly summarized as follows:

Court dockets showed marked carelessness in the records of children's cases. That the court see that the names and disposition of all cases of children coming before it are entered fully upon the court docket was recommended.

The judge reserved Saturday mornings only for juvenile hearings. This necessitated holding some of the children for several days in the county jail annex or the detention home, awaiting the convenience of the court. We recommend that an hour each on Tuesdays, Thursdays, and Saturdays be set apart regularly for the hearing of juvenile cases.

Most of the hearings, held in the judge's chambers, were informal and private, as they should be. In four instances, however, attorneys were present and in one of these there was a trial by jury, a most undesirable procedure. We recommend that the court do all in its power to discourage the employment of attorneys and trial by jury in juvenile cases.

An unfortunate condition in Springfield was the newspaper publicity given to children's cases. Among their companions this often makes delinquent boys heroes, while on the other hand, it injures their good name, and often injures their chance of getting employment. Since accounts of childish exploits and misfortunes have no news value, newspapers in many cities have agreed to omit such items. We recommend that the court in person request the owners and editors of newspapers to refrain from publishing items regarding the delinquency of children.

The state legislature had empowered the court to appoint probation officers to investigate and furnish such information and assistance as the judge might require, but the probation officer had never been requested to make a single investigation of this kind. Most decisions of the court had been without adequate

JUVENILE OFFENDERS IN THE SPRINGFIELD PRESS
Publicity of this kind hinders efforts of court and probation officer to save children from lives of crime. In some cities newspaper editors have agreed not to publish articles on child delinquency.

knowledge regarding the children's homes, their school records, health, use of leisure time, employment, or other matters which throw light upon the causes of wrong-doing; or regarding the constructive forces which might be brought to bear, such as interested friends or relatives, churches, or boys' clubs. A detailed study made of several cases where lack of information led to mistaken or inadequate treatment, illustrated the impossibility of meeting or understanding children's needs without more facts than the court was getting.

To correct this situation, before any case is disposed of, a report should be required from the probation officer showing as fully as possible the cause of the child's delinquency and the constructive forces which might be brought into play; and further, the court should examine the facts presented in such report with great care and decide the disposition of each child on the basis of the kind of treatment that will tend most strongly to prevent the child from committing further acts of delinquency.

In some cases boys were transferred to the jurisdiction of the circuit court for indictment by the grand jury. Since the juvenile court had authority to commit boys to state industrial schools and reformatories or to place them upon probation, there was no need or excuse for bringing them into contact with the criminal machinery of adults. The court should refuse to allow any child coming under its jurisdiction to be proceeded against according to ordinary criminal procedure.

There were instances recorded where it seemed that juvenile offenders were placed under the guardianship of persons concerning whose character and ability the court had little information. We would recommend that when delinquent children are placed in private homes rather than in institutions, the court insure by having careful investigation made that the homes selected are entirely above question.

In neglecting to utilize the possibilities of conditional probation, such, for example, as the restoration of property destroyed, the court had apparently overlooked an important means for helping delinquent children. Our recommendation was that use be made of conditional probation where it seemed desirable, and that the probation officer be required to see that the conditions imposed were fully complied with. Further, if probation to parents is resorted to at all, it should be used only when homes have been proved satisfactory and when children's delinquent acts have been casual mishaps, not likely to be repeated.

There is a growing belief among juvenile court authorities that more satisfactory results will be obtained if cases of delinquent girls are heard by women. Whenever the court deems a woman probation officer fitted by character and experience to perform the function, it was recommended that she be assigned to act as referee in cases of delinquent girls.

Juvenile Probation Work

Juvenile probation work, as has been seen, is intimately connected with the work of the juvenile court and directly under court supervision. A detailed study of it in Springfield indicated that in many ways conditions were far from satisfactory. This was due to four main causes:

1. The work had not been properly organized or administered, the court not requiring the degree of efficiency which should be demanded. To remedy the weakness of organization the court should adopt and enforce rules laying down the duties of the probation officer in detail. A set of such rules is presented in Appendix C of the full report here summarized.[1]

2. There were four successive officers in 1913, which thoroughly disorganized the work.

3. The officer at the time was, when appointed, without previous training to fit her for the position and had never been adequately instructed in the duties of the office.

To remedy the difficulties in the way of efficient service and to prevent their recurrence, it was recommended that the county board of supervisors raise the salary of the first probation officer to $100 a month to attract persons of experience—a figure which would now need to be still further increased. In order to secure probation officers who are at least fairly well fitted for the position and familiar with the duties, a competitive examination should be given, open to residents and non-residents. The judge should pledge himself to appoint one of the three persons standing highest in the ratings.

[1] Potter, Zenas L.: The Correctional System of Springfield, Illinois. (The Springfield Survey.)

4. The tasks falling to the lot of the officer were greater than could be performed, even by a trained person, with the degree of thoroughness which the work required.

The probation officer was being asked to perform the following tasks: (a) probation work with delinquent and neglected children; (b) investigation of petitions filed under the Widows' Pension Law; (c) record keeping for these two kinds of work; (d) keeping of detention home records; (e) answering telephone for the court and for the court stenographer.

The first duty was imposed by law and could not be escaped. The second was placed by law upon "some officer of the court," the probation officer being the most logical person to perform it. The third was a necessary accompaniment to the adequate performance of the first two. But it was possible to shift the last two, one to the superintendent of the detention home where it properly belonged, the other to the court stenographer or bailiff. Such action should be ordered by the court. But even if a little time could thus be saved, the duties of the probation officer in supervising the children, investigating probation and widows' pension cases, and keeping adequate records made more work than one person could perform satisfactorily.

There was only one way to change the condition and that was by the employment of a second probation officer. The county board of supervisors, upon the recommendation of the judge, was empowered by law to provide for the appointment of a second probation officer. The survey strongly recommended that this power be used, that the salary of the second officer be fixed at a figure which would secure the proper qualifications, and that he or she be assigned to handle, under the supervision of the other paid officer, that part of the work which deals with widows' pensions. Without the adoption of this suggestion there was no way in which the probation work for children, with all its possibilities for crime prevention, might efficiently be carried on.

Legislative and Administrative Needs

The Illinois Juvenile Court Act, as amended by the legislature of 1907, was one of the best in the country. It provided for civil, not criminal, procedure. It granted the court jurisdiction over all delinquent, dependent, and neglected boys under seventeen years of age and girls under eighteen years. It constituted the judge of the county court also judge of the juvenile court, except in Cook County in which Chicago is situated, so that children of smaller places were protected from contact with ordinary criminal procedure. It authorized the court to appoint one or more paid probation officers.

In certain respects, however, the law could be improved. Tentative drafts of amendments that would do this and increase the effectiveness of the court will be found in the original of the report here summarized.

These amendments provide for the release of children who need not be detained during court hearing; prevent children from coming into contact with adult offenders by providing proper places of detention; place definitely upon the court the duty of making rules for the proper organization of its work; provide the court with adequate funds for forms and blanks necessary for its efficient conduct; and assure the publication of an annual report so as to bring the largest public interest to bear upon the important task of caring for delinquent and dependent children.

Other amendments suggested define in detail the duties and powers of probation officers; provide a means by which cases of delinquent girls may be heard and decided by a woman; also provide means by which the court may discover the physical needs of children; and when parents cannot or will not provide adequate treatment, a way by which such treatment may be secured.

THE POLICE DEPARTMENT

Size of the Force

The Springfield police department in April, 1914, was made up of 52 persons, all men. There were 34 patrolmen, 8 detectives, 3 patrol wagon drivers, 3 alarm operators, 3 sergeants, and the chief. As compared with police forces of cities of approximately the same size, Springfield's force was below the average in numbers; in fact it was a quarter smaller than the average force for the 16 American cities having from 53,000 to 63,000 inhabitants.

Department Control

Control of the police department was nominally vested in the commissioner of public health and safety, who appointed the chief. Other members of the force were selected through examinations by the city civil service commission, which, except in cases of promotion, certified a single name for each appointment. Those so appointed might be removed by the chief within six months without review. After six months, tenure of office was secure unless a member was removed by the civil service commission. That commission, therefore, through its power to control selections and removals, determined to a greater extent than the chief or commissioner of public health and safety the make-up of the department, and in this way to a considerable extent controlled its policy.

The commission, however, is appointed by the mayor, so that control of police affairs in large measure is divided between the mayor and the commissioner of public health and safety. In another particular, also, responsibility was divided. While law enforcement in saloons and other licensed places was in the hands of the commissioner of public health and safety, the mayor issued licenses and had the power to revoke them, which was one of the penalties attaching to violations of the law by saloon keepers. The result was that responsibility for law enforcement might easily be obscured.

Direct control of the Springfield police department, where definite accountability of one official is more needed than in any other municipal department, should be returned to the mayor, where it formerly rested. By such action only, under the city charter, could responsibility in police affairs be definitely fixed.

Selection of the Force

The most important factor in securing efficiency in the police department is the appointment of competent candidates. To attract men capable not only of seizing law breakers and taking them to jail but also able to help in a program of crime prevention, men who cannot easily be led into alliance with law-breaking elements but who can gain and hold the respect of law breakers and the community, the city must pay adequate salaries with increases for long and efficient service.

Springfield was seeking $75-a-month men for her police force, with no chance of advancement except that of becoming a sergeant at $85 a month. The result was that the city was attracting to her police force men who graded in ability below the skilled mechanic and not much above the unskilled laborer.

Fitting Men for Duty

Another way of securing greater efficiency is to use every means of fitting men for their duties. There were opportunities in this direction which Springfield had not utilized. If it does not seem practicable to have recruit schools similar to those in larger cities, new members of the force might be given instruction in first aid, in crime prevention, in the primary facts of sex hygiene, in legal evidence, how to present their cases in court, and ways in which the police may co-operate with other public and private agencies. At the time, new recruits merely patroled their beat a few days with other patrolmen and absorbed knowledge of these matters as best they could.

Appearance of the Force

The appearance of Springfield's force was by no means bad, but by requiring uniform neckwear and providing in headquarters for the men a shoe-polishing stand and equipment for pressing uniforms, improvement could easily be made.

Discipline and Honors

Discipline in Springfield was divided between the chief and the civil service commission, and consisted of reprimands, fines, and dismissals. Under the chief then serving, no nonreviewable penalties had been inflicted, and but two of many charges against officers by private citizens were pressed. There was marked indifference to charges of an alliance between the police force and the segregated district—one of the most serious charges that could be made against the department—and an investigation was requested by the men accused.

For the reward of meritorious service no system of honors was in use by the department. Such a system is a stimulus to esprit de corps and good service and may also be used effectively as a disciplinary means—revocation of honors being attached to violation of police rules. The plan of granting arm bands, stars, or other insignia for each year of meritorious service or for special acts of courage is worthy of adoption.

Efficiency Record

If the requirements of the police book of rules had been met, 28 different record books would have been kept by the police department. As a matter of fact, only one, an arrest and disposition book was kept. The survey recommended keeping the following records: (1) efficiency record book; (2) book of lost, stolen, and recovered property; (3) complaint book, showing all complaints received, with action taken whether against members of the force or other citizens. In addition, files for correspondence, daily reports, notices of persons wanted, and official orders were desirable. Moreover, a new compilation of city ordinances was greatly needed.

Police Pensions

For retirement of men who had seen long service, a police pension fund was established under an act of the legislature of 1910 amended in 1913. The administration of the fund was in the hands of a board of three, one appointed by the mayor, one by the police, and one by the pensioners. Persons who might receive pensions, together with amounts were:

1. Men retiring who have served on the force twenty years receive one-half the last year's salary but not over $900 or under $600. Retirement after twenty years' service is optional.
2. Men injured while on duty receive, until reinstated, grants at the same rate as those retiring.
3. Widows, and children under sixteen, of men killed in performance of duties, receive the same amounts as men retiring.
4. Widows, and children under sixteen, of men who have

served ten years and die or become insane, receive one-half of above amount but not over $900.

The purpose of this law was admirable, but the law itself was an example of very bad legislation.

In the first place, men who have served on the force twenty years may be perfectly competent to continue as wage-earners. They may in fact, if they began work early, be just in the prime of life. There is no reason why a policeman should retire with an annuity if he is still able to serve the city. Under the law, at that time, 19 of Springfield's 51 policemen would be eligible to retire when under fifty years of age—6 of them under forty-five—and be paid $600 a year by the public the rest of their lives. The state law should be at once amended to make this impossible.

A second bad feature was that it created a financial tie between the police department and the saloons. The heaviest contribution to the pension fund came from the payment of licenses; thus the fund was largely dependent upon the continuance of the saloons of the city.

The law was bad, finally, because it violated a principle of sound public finance, making, without data on how it would fit the need, a set appropriation to a fund the demands upon which will vary from year to year. It would be infinitely wiser and more satisfactory if the state law, instead of diverting certain revenues from the city treasury to the pension fund, were to require the city to pay annually from the general revenues pensions to members of the police force who have been retired according to the pension law. Should it be deemed advisable to have a reserve fund planned on an actuarial basis to meet accident emergencies, this also could be raised in the same way. Under this arrangement, too, men could continue to contribute 1.5 per cent of their salaries for pensions, demands being met from these contributions until such amounts were exhausted. It was strongly recommended by the survey that efforts be made to have the state law in this particular amended.

We also recommend that the police pension board make a better disposition of the pension fund of $19,849.77 (April, 1914) than that of deposit in a city bank at an interest rate as low as 2.5 per cent.

Police Policy: The Making of Arrests

That every person found breaking the law should be arrested is a commonly accepted point of view which in practice is never followed. Policemen do and should exercise discrimination in making arrests. A warning, for instance, is sufficient for the contractor who unwittingly obstructs the street, for the housewife who dumps ashes within 10 feet of a building, or for others whose violations are technical in nature. In cases of offenses against chastity, property, the person, and some of the more serious offenses against public policy, arrest should follow. To make the distinction clear between minor and technical offenses and those which indicate delinquent tendencies, it was recommended that the chief of police definitely designate offenses for the commission of which arrest must always be made. Since there is always danger in the use of discretion by individual patrolmen, care should be taken to insure the enforcement of these rules set up by the chief and to insure the wise use of discretion.

Crime Prevention and Police Policy Toward Saloons

Prevention of crime by the elimination of conditions which foster delinquency is the responsibility of the entire community, but the police have an important part to play in preventing the development of crime.

More careful regulation of dance halls and commercial amusement places was recommended in the recreational survey.[1] The police department should enforce the ordinances passed for this purpose. A policewoman to deal with such problems and assist with female offenders would be of great service, and such an appointment was recommended.

At the time of the survey when Springfield had some 220 saloons another opportunity for crime prevention lay in the power of the police to regulate the conduct of the saloons and to suppress to some extent at least vice, gambling, and the sale

[1] See Recreation in Springfield, Illinois, by Lee F. Hanmer and Clarence A. Perry, pp. 5–22, 87.

of drugs. In enforcing laws governing these matters the Springfield police had shown great leniency.

On July 1, 1914, the number of licensed saloons was reduced from 220 to 198, the reduction being due mainly to business laxity, though in a few cases keepers who were in the bad graces of the police department did not apply for renewals. There had been no policy of restricting the number of saloons in Springfield and practically every person applying for a license could get one upon making proper representations. Under the keen competition which existed, in order to keep going and pay the high license fee every year saloon keepers were often led into other activities than liquor selling, such as the introduction of gambling devices or alliance with vice. Moreover, under the stress of financial need the temptation to encourage drinking in artificial ways, to sell to minors and habitual drunkards, and to break other regulatory statutes was unusually great.

In 1913, 869 arrests were made in which drunkenness was specifically charged, and these represented only a part of those in which arrested persons were intoxicated. Eighty-six cases of alcoholism were treated at the county jail. However, no arrests were made during the year for selling liquor to minors or for selling to confirmed drunkards. The Sunday closing law was a dead letter. The need of more vigorous enforcement of regulatory laws and ordinances and of those prohibiting the sale of liquor to confirmed drunkards, intoxicated persons, or to any others in sufficient quantities to cause intoxication was quite apparent. While this need, as far as it relates to local enforcement, will presumably be greatly changed by national prohibition, a certain amount of watchfulness and co-operation on the part of the local authorities will still be desirable.

Drugs

The use of cocaine, opium, and their derivatives, according to statements of the jailers and the city physician, was common in the underworld of Springfield. In view of the fact that the use of drugs tends to weaken will power and make succumbing to temptation easy, and also since it often leads to trickery, forgery, or other illegal means to secure supplies of the drugs, the subject demands attention. In this connection the police should co-operate in enforcing the recently enacted federal habit-forming drug act which places restrictions upon the sale of such drugs in Illinois.

POLICE ATTITUDE TOWARD VICE

Segregation rather than suppression was the policy of the Springfield police department toward vice. But vice was not entirely confined to the segregated district, for clandestine prostitution flourished in many hotels and rooming houses.

In the district at the time of the survey, there were 33 recognized houses of prostitution containing white women, with a total of about 143 inmates, also a considerable number of Negro houses with something like 60 inmates. It was estimated that the total yearly earnings of recognized houses, black and white, were between $140,000 and $185,000. The extent of the profits of such traffic makes it clear why the suppression of commercialized prostitution is so difficult.

When this investigation was begun the segregated district was indicated by red lights, house names painted on the doors, and soliciting from windows. Later, however, names were removed and open soliciting and street walking were largely abolished. Still later the district itself was abolished.

The two chief methods of dealing with this evil are segregation, the plan followed in Springfield, and vigilant suppression. Advocates of the segregation policy claim that the district brings business to the city, but opponents reply that it brings business of an undesirable sort. Advocates of segregation claim that the district localizes crime and makes it easy to control, but opponents claim that toleration of vice attracts persons of delinquent or criminal tendencies, creates an alliance between the underworld and the police department, and undermines the whole city government because of the political activity of the vice interests.

Advocates of segregation claim that abolition of the district will subject all women to greater moral and physical dangers, but opponents state that in cities where segregated districts have been abolished, the facts do not support the claim.

Those favoring segregation contend that the existence of the district diminishes the spread of venereal disease, but opponents say that established houses are important conveyers of venereal disease, and that a real policy of suppression diminishes prostitution and reduces the spread of the disease to a minimum. The investigation of venereal disease in Syracuse, New York, before and after the abolition of the segregated district, while based to a considerable degree on estimates, made a convincing showing as to the reduction in gonorrhea and syphilis.

Advocates of segregation claim that such a policy reduces the evil to a minimum, for attempted suppression only spreads it over a city. Opponents answer that vigorous suppression has largely freed cities from professional prostitutes, and that clandestine prostitution goes on always, even when there is a segregated district.

Apart from arguments of those who favor segregation, opponents claim that the worst feature of the whole matter is the great financial profit which vice interests make by drawing girls into prostitution. The abolition of the segregated district destroys, to a great extent, the commercial advantages of organized vice.

In answer to the argument of those favoring segregation, that men's "personal liberty" should not be restricted because of the moral views of others, it may be pointed out that all laws restrict the personal liberty of the few for the benefit of the many.

As to our own view, we believe that most of the arguments in favor of a segregated district cannot stand the light of searching investigation, and that the commercial aspects of vice—its worst feature—can never be destroyed or minimized until the policy of segregation is abandoned. Significant is the fact that of the vice investigations made by municipalities, states, and private organizations during recent years—some 15 reports of which had been issued—each condemned segregation in severe terms.

Suppression, however, will never suppress if a police department is friendly with vice and unfavorable to suppression. Any effort to change the policy of the city with regard to vice must be well organized and followed by the constant vigilance of citizens who realize that the vice interests have thousands of

THE CORRECTIONAL SYSTEM

dollars at stake and are willing to spend money freely, when and where needed, to keep the business going.

Recommendations on the Police Department

The recommendations made concerning the work of the police may be summed up as follows:

1. That control of the police department be returned to the mayor where formerly it was vested.

2. That after more pressing needs have been met, the city consider the advisability of a general increase in the police force.

3. That the city civil service commission adopt definite rules applying to the arrest of children.[1]

4. That when possible salaries in the department be raised and that a graduated scale be adopted.

5. That more care be exercised in fitting policemen for their work.

6. That means be adopted for helping policemen maintain a neat appearance.

7. That complaints or rumors regarding the alliance of the department with vice be carefully and thoroughly investigated by the civil service commission when men in the classified service are involved, otherwise by the city commission.

8. That an honor system be developed.

9. That a more adequate system of records be adopted.

10. That a new compilation of city ordinances be undertaken.

11. That efforts be made to have the police pension law altered by the state legislature along the lines suggested.

12. That the police pension board endeavor to secure payment of a higher rate of interest on the pension fund.

13. That official recognition be given to the use by patrolmen of discretion in making arrests and that safeguards be adopted to prevent its misuse.

14. That the police co-operate with the federal authorities in enforcing the laws against the sale of drugs and intoxicating liquors.

15. That in dealing with vice the policy of segregation be replaced by a policy of suppression through vigorous enforcement of the state law.

[1] A suggested set of rules is presented in Appendix B of the original report. See Potter, Zenas L.: The Correctional System of Springfield, Illinois, pp. 174-175. (The Springfield Survey.)

XI

CITY AND COUNTY ADMINISTRATION[1]

Since the reports on the other divisions of the survey, in dealing with the local needs and with the agencies designed to meet the needs, necessarily took up important phases of city and county administration related to them, consideration of these phases was omitted, in the main, from this investigation and report. In other words, this division of the survey deals chiefly with the work of public agencies not covered in the other divisions. Further, because the work of the city of Springfield and Sangamon County was found so interrelated and interdependent, this division deemed it best to examine and report, as far as possible, upon what was being done in both.

The data gathered fell along four main lines:

First, the plans on which the local governments were organized and administered—a general view of the machinery set up for providing public service.

Second, the organization and efficiency of the particular departments of the city charged with furnishing this service—the methods used in spending the taxpayer's dollar.

Third, the assessment and collection of the government income—the methods of raising the money to be used for all current public purposes.

Fourth, the methods of handling the special funds of the city—the practices followed in public borrowing, in levying special assessments, and in meeting other than current expenses.

Thus the survey of city and county administration was concerned with the methods used in securing the funds and in purchasing public service through still other local agencies than those examined in the previous divisions of the survey; such agencies,

[1] Summary of report on City and County Administration in Springfield, Illinois, by D. O. Decker and Shelby M. Harrison.

among others, for example, as the fire department, water department, street-cleaning, street-lighting, and building departments.

General Organization and Administration of the City Government

Springfield adopted commission government in 1911, when only about 30 American cities had taken similar action. Its commission is composed of the following members: the mayor, who at the time of the survey supervised the work of the comptroller, city attorney, corporation counsel, civil service commission, and the inspectors of weights and measures; the commissioner of public health and safety, who supervised the fire, police, and health departments, the city prison, isolation hospital, and the work of the building and electrical inspectors; the commissioner of public property, who directed the work of the municipal lighting plant and of the waterworks department and had charge of the city hall; the commissioner of streets and public improvements, who had charge of the streets, sewers, sidewalks, garbage, and the work of the city engineer and of the superintendent of special assessments; and the commissioner of accounts and finances, who was accountable for the work of the city clerk and city treasurer.

The mayor's power to appoint members of the city civil service commission gave him considerable control over the personnel and policy of the police department; and through his power to issue and revoke saloon licenses he could exert influence toward the enforcement or evasion of liquor laws. The other activities of the commission dealt with general public policy and included the raising and apportionment of budget funds.

Election of City Commissioners

The mayor was the only commissioner elected for his particular duties. The others decide among themselves after election what department each shall administer. Thus a man may be assigned to work for which he is not fitted and with little chance of being given more suitable duties later. Should he grow fit through practise, the present system does not guarantee his continuance in the same office after he has become proficient. A better plan would be to elect men for clearly defined places in the public service.

Moreover, election to definite duties would also tend to separate issues now confused. For instance, law enforcement is one among many questions relating to efficient administrative work by the government, and it at least should be separated from the other issues. Any doubts as to the policy on law enforcement could, under the plan suggested, be settled in the case of Springfield by the avowed policy of the candidates nominated for commissioner of public health and safety. The system prevailing in Springfield lends itself to a misdirection of the attention and thought of citizens, by bringing to the front in each election campaign one or two issues at the expense of all others. No consistent progress can be made while such befogging of real issues is possible.

City Manager Form of Government

Indeed, the city manager form of government, which is in many respects superior to the commission form, goes further. It provides for the *election* of the officers who determine programs and enact laws, and for the *appointment* of the officers who, chosen because of special fitness, do the administrative work. This form of government regards administration as a profession. It assumes that the responsible head of a government may become expert in choosing competent administrators, and that a first-class man can be more easily retained in service if appointed by a responsible officer who has been elected on a platform of efficient administration, than would be the case if his tenure of office depended on the uncertainties of a general election.

Springfield, however, had been comparatively fortunate in its election of commissioners, and a radical change in its form of government did not seem necessary. If any change were contemplated, however, the city manager form was recommended for consideration. Certainly the recently advanced suggestion that the city return to its former large-council system should not be followed.

CITY AND COUNTY ADMINISTRATION

The Short Ballot

The city wisely was using the short ballot, which presented only the names of candidates for the mayoralty and for the four commissionerships. This centralizes public opinion and allows care in selecting the officers, who in turn are more likely to make appointments of a higher type than could a larger, and therefore less responsible, group, as was the case in the older large councils.

Appointment of Department Heads

The commissioners, following the principle involved in the appointment system, choose their subordinate department heads. There appeared to be no good reason for changing this procedure.

All minor officials in the departments, except a number of employes appointed by the executive heads, were appointed by the commission as a whole. Only part of the city employes were under civil service regulations.

Civil Service Commission

The city had a civil service commission of three members, each of whom, in addition to a chief examiner who did practically all the work and was merely supervised by the commission, drew an annual salary of $1,000. In 1915 the expense of the commission was $4,292; and 31 persons were certified and received appointments, the average cost for each appointment being $138.45, or, if promotions are included, $116—an excessive amount. The duties of members, except examiners, are no heavier than are those of the unsalaried library and school boards, and should be performed without compensation or for nominal amounts.

Civil Service Appointments and Dismissals

The civil service commission could improve its methods by submitting for appointment the two or three names standing highest, as it did for promotions, instead of the one that headed its list. This would give opportunity to take personality into account.

Springfield's former practice (with its defects eliminated) of keeping efficiency records for civil service employes should be resumed. It is essential to have full information on ability, performance, and character in passing upon promotions, demotions, and dismissals.

Removal of civil service employes was being made through charges by the employer to the civil service commission, which then conducted a trial. With the possible exception of policemen and firemen, better administrative results would be obtained if public employes could be removed by a department head after he had given the reasons in writing to the employe and afforded the latter an opportunity to explain. This method would not destroy the main purpose of civil service reform; for since the appointing power through this system has presumably been removed from politics, one of the chief causes of the abuse of the power to dismiss, the dropping of workers in order to appoint political friends, has been eliminated. Enough publicity would ordinarily attend such removals to enable the public, in case the plan should be abused, to hold the department head responsible at the next election—a final recourse which is at the bottom of the theory of commission government.

INDEPENDENT GOVERNMENT BODIES: NEED OF CENTRALIZATION

In addition to the city government proper—the body presided over by the mayor and the city commissioners—several other public boards or commissions, with independent taxing powers and in most cases financed by their own tax levies, namely, the board of education, park board, library board, and the city cemetery board, were furnishing public service in the city. These were in addition to separate township and county government bodies operating in the city. The existence of so many largely independent boards made local government administration in Springfield very complex. To increase the confusion, the legislature had fixed by law for each board a limit which it could not exceed in appropriating money from the city revenues for its need, and had stipulated how parts of other revenues should be distributed.

Obviously this method of furnishing the various boards of

the city with funds is faulty, since the income which it provides for may sometimes be too large, and sometimes too small, to meet the varying needs of a board. The budget for all public purposes in the city—indeed we would add, the budget also for public service furnished by the township (Springfield and the township in which it is situated, Capital, are co-extensive) and the county—should be fixed by one body, which, however, must be composed of able persons if the plan is to succeed. All revenues should then go into a general fund, and the distribution of funds should be made on the basis of a unified program that would take all factors and needs into account. Tax limits for special purposes should be removed, and the city and county, which know local conditions best, should be allowed to decide their own tax levies to meet their needs instead of allowing the legislature to fix by guess, and for several years in advance, the program of the community.

Budget of the City of Springfield

Meanwhile, until the various governing boards are combined in a unified system working on a flexible budget basis, and even afterward, the same care as heretofore should be exercised in making the city budget, which was found to be superior to that of most cities of similar size and character and to that of the county. Among the few defects of the budget was the fact that its total figures were about double the probable expenditures. This was unavoidable under the system prescribed by the state laws, since if it were uncertain which among several projects necessitating the expenditure of money would be adopted, money for *all* had to be appropriated, although only one was to be chosen. This was because money could be obtained only through a vote for a definitely specified purpose, and if something different was later chosen in its place, the funds for the one finally selected could be secured only through a new vote taken the following year.

The budget should therefore be further improved by a change in the law allowing transfers of items, after the adoption of the budget, on a unanimous or four-fifths vote of the council, providing that the grand total is not increased. Until the law is altered a budget something like the one being used, carrying all probable extra items, should be adopted and then this should be supplemented by an informal working budget, totaling exactly the amount of the estimated needs and revenues.

Classification of Budget and Monthly Reports

Modern city budgets have been developing along uniform lines of classification. Should Springfield change its present budget, it would be advisable for officials to examine some of the latest budget forms and adopt standardized classifications.[1]

In a monthly report on the status of budget appropriations the city comptroller of Springfield was giving the city commission a statement showing important data under five separate columns. A sixth column showing the unencumbered balance of appropriations was needed, since without it, to know the final figure usually desired, the outstanding obligations had to be deducted from the balance left in the appropriation. Such a monthly report was found in comparatively few cities. Its use should be universal. Springfield was to be congratulated upon being one of the first cities that took this step.

Centralization of Expert Advice

Springfield possessed expert knowledge and experience among its public officials which it was not using fully. The comptroller's experience, for example, should have been taken advantage of in the bookkeeping of every department and he should be responsible for the installation of all accounting and financial systems. That is his function and his specialty and he should have expert assistance when needed. He should be continuously available also for advising the departments; for his office is properly more than merely a bookkeeping center. It should be charged with systematizing the records of all the city work. Similarly the experience of the engineer's department should have been

---

[1] For detailed suggestions on approved methods of budget formulation see Appendix A, page 149, of the original report, City and County Administration in Springfield, Illinois. For further discussion of the purposes and requisites of budgets, see pages 135–140 of the same report, where the subject is considered in connection with the administration of Sangamon County, which had no real budget.

more generally utilized. The department should even be strengthened with this end in view.

Such a plan would correct another weakness in the city administration of Springfield, namely, the lack of full information; and it would make available to the commission needed data concerning matters upon which they are required to act. Cost accounting, better budget preparation, the use of the comptroller's office to organize accounting and financial systems and to supply statistical aid for each department, would much improve the situation.

Service and Cost Records

Moreover, the available data should be increased by the installation of service and cost records—a system of record keeping that will put the cost of work done and the amount of service rendered into comparable units for use locally and elsewhere. Aside from the waterworks department and the city lighting plant, there were no cost data reckoned by any city department in Springfield; and no department kept service records.

The cost data need not be elaborately worked out, although to have them so usually proves an economy; but a moderate amount of cost calculation is a necessity. It is particularly needed in street and sewer work. For example, in repair jobs the calculations should show the cost of each job based on the square yard or on some other unit; in street cleaning, the cost based on each street or on a definite number of blocks; in refuse disposal, the cost per ton destroyed; and so on. The system should be installed by the city comptroller.

Time records showing the actual number of hours devoted to work by all employed, from mayor down to office boy, and how it was used should also be kept. These data give a basis on which to estimate service and efficiency, and would be useful in tests for civil service promotion. They automatically tend to hold workers to proper standards. Though it was not possible for us to make tests of work done, the grade of service in a number of cases was clearly as high as is found in the ordinary well-run private business. At the same time in other cases very little at all was being accomplished. The favorable experience of other cities has its suggestion as to the practicability and the usefulness of such record keeping for Springfield.

City Accounting System and Audit

Springfield's accounting system was good. Its books were found to be in good condition; the accounting methods followed were above the average; and its practice of having an annual audit was especially to be recommended, although the facts shown by the audit needed more publicity.

Letting out the audit by competitive bid, however, was not a good practice. The price paid, moreover, was not sufficient to enable the necessary checking-back of accounts to be done properly, and the best results could not be expected. The annual audit is too important to run the risk of a superficial examination of details. And indeed the service purchased was not as good as it should have been, for serious errors were found in the auditor's report for the last year before the survey. A more careful audit was an obvious need.

Inventory of Property and Equipment

Up to the time of the survey no inventories of city property and equipment had been compiled annually nor kept up to date, although a commendable beginning along this line was soon afterward made. Such a listing should be further developed, and should include from each official or employe, quarterly or at least annually, a schedule of all equipment under his control, goods or supplies on hand at the beginning of the period and their condition, what had been received or purchased, what disposed of, and what remained at the end of period, its condition, etc. Department records of this kind would make it possible to compile a general inventory for all the city; and this should be kept up to date.

City Purchasing

Springfield's charter requirements for city purchasing, in theory at least, were excellent. As the plan worked out, however, the commissioner of accounts, who supposedly made all the city purchases, in reality often merely approved the order of purchase as made out by some other city officer. This procedure developed because the head of the city department was usually better informed than the commissioner of accounts regarding goods likely to be needed, their cost, quality, and so on. The commissioner needed to familiarize himself with such matters, keep service and cost records of all prior purchases, and, in purchasing, combine his data with those of the official specially concerned. He should also take more initiative in the annual purchasing contracts, which should be let after competition based upon standard specifications. Indeed, the introduction of the full procedure followed in a modern city purchasing bureau would undoubtedly effect large savings to taxpayers.

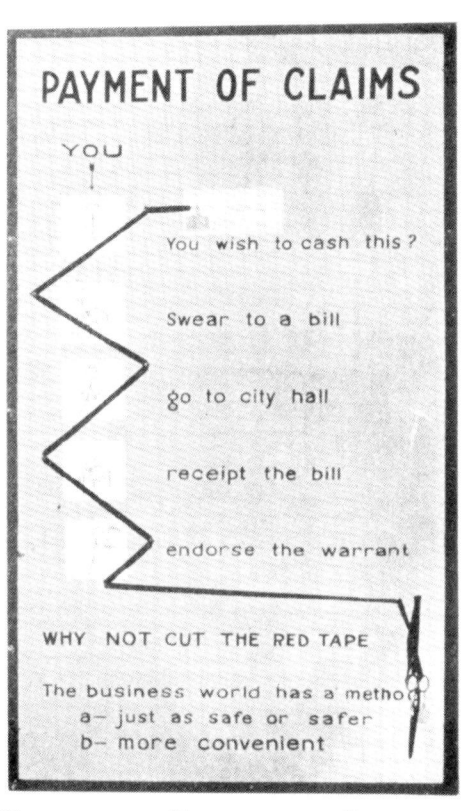

UNBUSINESSLIKE METHODS IN THE PAYMENT OF CLAIMS AGAINST CITY AND COUNTY
Panel from Springfield Survey Exhibition.

PAYMENT OF CLAIMS

Springfield's oversafeguarded system of paying its debts was cumbersome and unbusinesslike. The procedure did not benefit the city and was laying an unnecessary burden on its creditors. To secure payment of his claim the city required a creditor to (a) swear before a notary to the claim; (b) wait one week for its audit; (c) go to the city hall for his warrant;

(d) receipt the bill prior to receipt of the warrant; and (e) exchange the warrant for a city check. If the money called for by the check was not ready, he must go again. A more efficient plan, outlined below, which is finding general acceptance elsewhere, was recommended as follows:

1. Claims are certified to but not sworn to. The commissioner of accounts and finance and the comptroller should know whether the claims are correct.
2. The comptroller prepares and orders paid a list of vouchers which, properly signed and presented to the treasurer, is itself a warrant.
3. The treasurer prepares and mails to creditors voucher checks which themselves constitute receipts for individual claims.

In contrast to the city's overcareful method of paying claims, its laxity in approving bills was particularly surprising. It made no provision that a person familiar with services rendered and goods delivered should certify to that effect upon the claims before their audit. Without such certification they should not be approved unless the department head himself knows these facts.

Central Information and Complaint Bureau

Requests for information about and complaints registered against city service were being handled in the various departments and bureaus. Much detailed work would be saved officials if a plan were devised for receiving all such communications and bringing them together, say at the clerk's office. Complaints, recorded on cards, should be answered promptly by telephone or letter through this bureau. To insure prompt service and develop popular confidence in the city's method of conducting its business, an automatic follow-up system by means of metal tabs attached to the cards is recommended.

Reports and Publicity

Knowledge of what the government is doing is essential to real government by the people, and its necessity cannot be overemphasized—particularly in a commission-governed city, since one of the chief purposes of commission government is the centralization of duties and powers to such an extent that officials can be held responsible. And the plea of economy on the cost of printing reports cannot be accepted, for it is obviously shortsighted to spend thousands of dollars in elections and then in order to save a few hundred dollars fail to give voters the information they need to make the best decisions.

The Springfield city government failed to put fully before citizens the essential facts regarding its activities. There was no general report on all departments and except for the water department, which was issuing good monthly and annual statements, the departmental reports were so few and so irregular that their usefulness was very slight. The monthly summaries of "Receipts" and "Expenses Vouchered" were not related nor brought together at the end of the year, and therefore told the layman but little.

The auditor's report of the city would be Greek to most voters, even if they could be persuaded to wade through its detailed schedules. The auditors, or some impartial expert, should prepare a short statement for the public which would give, first, a picture of general financial conditions; second, show comparative tendencies; and third, refer to supporting schedules which would verify conclusions if more intensive study is desired.

This statement should then be given the widest publicity in the local press, and should be included later in the annual report which the city was urgently advised to publish. The issuing of quarterly reports, so arranged as to be comparable with other quarters and other years, would be another good practice.

COMMUNITY SERVICE THROUGH THE MUNICIPALITY

The foregoing discussions relate more particularly to the city government as a whole. Let us look now at the functioning of some of the departments of the local government.

FIRE DEPARTMENT

According to the insurance records of the local fire department, property worth over $700,000 was destroyed in Springfield during the five years prior to 1915, the annual losses varying from $94,000 in 1914 to $313,000 in 1913. The number of fires per year ranged between 272 in 1911, and 336 in 1910. The average loss for each fire, slightly above $500, was a moderate figure; but the average per capita loss for the five years, $2.88, was comparatively high. The average annual number of fires, about 5.6 for each 1,000 people in the city, was also high.

Indeed, the loss was still greater, for much was destroyed that did not appear in the insurance records. Such annihilation of values annually demands that the public give greater attention to work against fire, particularly since the underwriters' analyses of the causes of fires in Illinois in 1915 showed over 62 per cent to have been either wholly preventable or partly preventable.

Organization and Operation

Executive control within the department, which itself was under the general supervision of the commissioner of public health and safety, was administered by the fire marshal or chief, who was appointed by the city commission for a four-year term and was removable for cause. The force was under civil service regulations, although the commissioner might make temporary appointments when no eligible applicants were listed. New members were on probation for six months.

Although no age was set for compulsory withdrawal, members might be retired on a pension of half pay after twenty years' service. Dependents in the deceased members' families and totally disabled members were also pensioned.

The assistant fire marshal and over 80 other men, 77 of whom, including the chief officers, in 1915 were members of the active fire force as captains, engineers, etc., formed too small a department to provide sufficient protection. Their number should be large enough to insure continuous service notwithstanding necessary absences.

The rules, discipline, and general administration of the department were comparatively good. The chief or the commissioner might suspend members for thirty days or less, pending civil service action. Though capable of suspending without pay or imposing fines, the commission was obliged to delay dismissal until the evidence had been reviewed by the court. Trials by the department head, not subject to court review, are preferable.

Fire Engines and Equipment

In 1915 hardly half of the department's vehicles were motor driven. As rapidly as possible horse-drawn apparatus should be replaced by motor-drawn equipment. General experience shows the immeasurable importance of saving every moment in

FIRE DEPARTMENT EQUIPMENT

Of the five fire engines, six hose reels, two chemical engines, two ladder trucks, two chief's wagons, and two other wagons owned by the fire department in 1915, only three—an engine, hose wagon, and one of the chief's wagons—were motor driven. Complete replacement of horse equipment by auto apparatus was recommended in the survey exhibition and printed reports. A start has since been made toward such replacement.

reaching a fire. And Springfield's own experience had shown that motor-drawn apparatus was far superior to horse-drawn. Furthermore, it is cheaper to operate. The city could also partly compensate for a shortage of firemen by purchasing an auto-squad wagon, which carries from four to eight men, thus enabling the present force to guard a larger area.

Since the five-minute zone for auto apparatus is two or more times as large as that for horse-drawn, when the equipment is completely motorized, station houses need not be so near together as they were then. Changes in the location of stations may very well wait such motorization, unless a thorough study of the station house question with a view to a station house plan for the whole city were immediately instituted.

It should be stated that in accordance with the recommendations of the first summary on this report, presented in the Springfield Survey Exhibition, the citizens voted (in April, 1917) to motorize the fire department completely, and appropriated $50,000 for the purpose. This action was opportune, because much of the apparatus was unfit for use. The usable pieces might still be kept for emergencies.

The survey revealed the need of other equipment, including hose couplings to meet national standards, better charts showing the location of water plugs, explosives, etc., and the need of searchlights.

Fire-Alarm System

The fire-alarm system of the city, which was combined with the police signaling system, was decidedly inadequate in equipment, distribution of boxes, and general maintenance. The matter was important and demanded careful consideration. Pending the installation of a fire-alarm telegraph system, or the making of some sort of improvement, alarms may be sent by telephone, as was being done very largely; and as, indeed, will always to some extent be done.

There are several difficulties connected with telephone transmission of fire alarms, such as the fact that in emergencies the telephone system in a large section of a city may be entirely disabled, the difficulty that a person who does not own a telephone may have in reaching one at night, and also the danger of error in transmitting alarms. While all of these objections can be met in part at least, that fact should not relieve the authorities of the obvious necessity of careful attention to the fire-alarm question.

Water Supply for Fire

The two lines of pipe, one 15 inches in diameter and the other 24, which were conducting all water from the pumping station to the city, although sufficient for ordinary needs did not insure the city reliable protection against fire in emergencies. Since both were laid close together, in many places over coal mines, a cave-in or other accident might easily disable one or both during the progress of a fire, which might then result in a great disaster. The water department should provide another pipe, laid along a different route, as soon as possible.

The large water mains should be joined by cross mains at frequent intervals, and numerous gate valves should be installed so that in case of a break in a large main the water could be supplied by other mains through the cross mains.

Springfield must always be prepared to use pumps on all large fires. Not only were the ordinary pressure of streams direct from the hydrants too low for fire fighting, but the great public and private expense involved in a reconstruction of old water mains and pumping facilities to assure high pressure everywhere, made any change in this respect prohibitive.

Additional hydrants should eventually be installed so that they will nowhere in the city be over 300 feet apart. More sprinkler systems were desirable, too. Less than ten were found in the city.

Instruction of Members

The department was weak on the training and drilling of its members. Besides the practise provided in the operation of engines and the harnessing of horses, the men should be instructed through lecture and reading courses and through drills, supervised by a competent instructor who is familiar with similar work in other cities. The drills should include the following:

Use of the scaling ladder	Handling of ladders
Use of the jumping net	Resuscitation and first aid
Knotting of ropes	Opening locked doors
Emergency repairing of hose	Use of fire helmets
Use of chemicals	Selection of hose and nozzles of particular sizes
Use of various couplings and connections	

The lectures should be on such subjects as:

Building inspection and fire prevention
Laws and ordinances on fires
Care of fire apparatus
Combustibles and explosives
Water system
Personal hygiene
Salvage of property
Modern fire fighting

The men should also have daily physical exercise.

Records of the Departments

The department was compiling valuable data on its work, but these data and their significance were given very little of the general publicity necessary in enlisting the proper support and co-operation of the public, which is essential to successful fire prevention.

More clerical help and assistance from the comptroller's office was needed in order to improve the record keeping of the department. For example, captains of all stations should file weekly reports regarding the men's time on duty and these should ultimately be compiled. Also, details should be kept regarding delays and accidents, names of the senders of alarms and methods of giving them, apparatus used and its effects. Duplicate sets of such records should be forwarded to headquarters. Furthermore, regular routes to be taken in caring for the territory of other companies whose own apparatus is in use somewhere else should be indicated on printed sheets.

Fire Prevention

In March, 1915, the department received 29 alarms due to chimney fires, and 33 in February, 1916. Notwithstanding the number of these calls, Springfield was paying little attention to fire prevention work or to the education of owners and occupants of buildings regarding fire dangers. The situation demanded the amendment of the building laws to cover modern requirements for safety and construction, for amplification of regulations for the handling of inflammable materials, for more frequent inspections, for fuller enforcement of the regulatory rule, and in general more educational work among owners and occupants in regard to fire dangers.

BUREAU OF BUILDINGS

The establishment of the bureau of buildings as a subdivision of the department of public health and safety and the consequent centralization of all matters relating to building construction had certain advantages. A further improvement would be to appoint the building commissioner from persons certified to by the civil service commission.

Our investigation showed the need of more systematic and continuous building inspections, to prevent fire hazards and poor construction generally and to meet recognized housing standards, than were then being made. A new housing code was the necessary first step toward the satisfactory prosecution of a modern program for the building bureau. The second step was the appointment of sufficient building inspectors.

To prevent depreciation in land values in residential districts, the city itself should follow the example of progressive real estate dealers in restricting the types of buildings to be constructed in certain areas. The city should be divided, or zoned, into districts of specific types, so that factory districts, for example, will not encroach upon residential sections, and vice versa. Such restrictions might be considered in the formulation of a new housing code, or the park board or any other local body interested in city planning might deal with them.

WATER DEPARTMENT

The city owns its own water-supply system, which is supervised by the commissioner of public property. The 25 employes, except the department superintendent who was appointed by the commissioner, were, when the survey was made, under civil service regulations.

The records of this department indicated that the value of the waterworks system was approximately $1,000,000. The department had paid out of net receipts from water rates about $500,000, thus leaving about $500,000 of the city debt due to expenditures for the system.

All things considered, the pumping equipment was adequate. But the insurance underwriters' report of needed changes should be heeded; for the most part they were very important. The proposed new trunk water main, to be laid along a new route from the pumping station to the city, would then have cost about $150,000. It was a clear necessity, however. Probably a total sum of $50,000 would sooner or later be required to replace mains which were too small because of the city's growth, and possibly $100,000 more to meet some of the other suggestions of the underwriters. The whole city, however, should bear part of these costs, and the necessary funds raised by general taxation or through city bonds.

The water department was facing still other costs, for people were applying for extensions of the water mains into new sections of the city. Though desirable as health measures, it was impossible from a business point of view to comply with all these requests. A way suggested by the survey for the settling of the problem was to install mains in new districts which requested them, and to charge each lot owner a flat rate of, say, $15 for each 40-foot lot. The amount would probably need to be more now. The large feed mains should be paid for by a general charge over the entire city.

Water Consumption and Rates

The very general introduction of meters probably was one of the chief causes of the reduction in annual per capita consumption of water from 125 gallons in 1906 to 85 gallons in 1915. The department had also begun to make periodic (biennial) tests of the accuracy of meters, thus saving the city considerable loss in this way also.

Many factors must be considered in passing judgment on the fairness of water rates. A comparison of rates in different cities is significant only as showing whether the particular ones in question are within the bounds of general practice. Compared in some detail with those of 640 other American cities in 1915, Springfield water rates were considerably below the average.

The water service of the city at the time of the investigation compared favorably with similar enterprises that were privately owned. The state engineer, in an official report on the waterworks of Springfield in 1913, stated that the initial cost of the city's waterworks system was comparatively low, and that the unit costs, already moderate, were being gradually reduced.

Our examination confirmed his conclusions. Data were being kept showing the cost of (1) operation, (2) fuel used, (3) oil used, (4) waste used, (5) number of gallons pumped, (6) nature of services on every meter and repair job and the cost, and (7) a record of each connection made for supplying water service. In addition, the uniform system of accounting and cost data required by the State Utilities Commission for privately owned waterworks had been voluntarily installed since our study.

Water Rate Making

Although the charges for water rates were reasonably low, a few inconsistencies remained to be equitably adjusted. According to the 1915 rates, under certain circumstances the use of an unnecessarily large amount of water would decrease one's bill instead of increasing it! Thus in December, 1915, a domestic consumer was charged $7.50—10 cents a hundred—for using 7,500 cubic feet in the preceding three months. In February, 1916, the same consumer paid for 6,900 cubic feet at the rate 11$\frac{2}{3}$ cents, and his bill was $8.05, or 55 cents more than the preceding quarter, although he had used 600 feet less of water.

This and similar inconsistencies were due, under the old rates, to the whole plan of the rate schedule. Their remedy did not demand changes in particular rates, but a general readjustment of the rate plan. A popular method of correcting this difference is to charge an amount determined according to the size of the householder's meter and a certain maximum allowance of water for the year; water exceeding this quantity is paid for by the gallon. The rates should be computed, of course, after a careful study of the cost of supplying water and the local method of cost distribution to consumers.

Another method is to charge for each connection with the water system an amount varying with the size of the meter; and then to charge a uniform rate for all water furnished. Exact rates could and should be computed from the water department's very excellent cost data and from an operation statement similar to the one now being issued at the time by the department.

The cost of furnishing service, reading meters, and all other overhead charges should be covered, to a large degree if not entirely, by the flat meter charge suggested in this second method. After that, all persons should pay at the same fixed rates for the water used. This principle underlies all regulation of rates, and any substantial deviation from it savors of rebating and is particularly obnoxious in municipally owned utilities.

The water department as a whole, in the opinion of the investigators, was being efficiently managed.

City Light Plant

For a number of years the city had owned and operated a small electric light plant. Until within a few years the service was used entirely for lighting streets and public buildings, but by 1916 some 700 domestic consumers were being supplied.

The survey exhibition and the first draft of this report pointed out that the installation of modern equipment in the city light plant would save something like one-third of the operation cost, and that consolidation with the waterworks would reduce the cost of construction and operation and facilitate supervision. Furthermore, the surroundings of the water-pumping station were favorable to probable future extensions of the lighting plant. The city later took these steps and the vacated electric station became available for a much-needed city storehouse.

The municipal rates charged to consumers before the electric light and waterworks plants were consolidated were from 25 to 60 per cent less than those of the privately owned lighting company of the city. In the opinion of a Chicago expert, these rates could easily be maintained after the combination in equipment was effected, and the first seven months of operation after consolidation (up to February, 1917, before costs had been greatly affected by the war) tended to confirm that opinion. The question, then, of extending the service to private consumers became largely a matter of efficient management. If the citizens believe, as there was some evidence to think they did, that the new lighting plant could be as well managed as the public waterworks system, that is sufficient reason for wanting the city plant to furnish private consumers with its surplus current, and to build its plant for future development accordingly. No current should be sold to private consumers, however, until the city, the school district, and probably the county, also, have an adequate supply.

GAS AND ELECTRIC METER INSPECTION

Springfield had an excellent equipment for testing gas and gas meters, and was employing a well-qualified inspector to do this work. But no meters had been submitted for tests for two years, and the inspector's duties were thus largely confined to the testing of newly installed meters. The gas company was required to test and mark the date on each meter when installed. The city inspector also tested these. In the fiscal year 1915-16, only six of the 2,222 meters examined were over 2 per cent incorrect.

No one but the inspector seemed to be aware of the fact that the gas that was supplied to the city did not measure up to the 600 British thermal units of heating value required by ordinance; there was no publication of the facts brought together by the inspector's tests. Such information should at least be brought to the attention of the city commissioners or of the State Utilities Commission promptly and the meaning of the figures made clear.

No tests of electric meters were being made. These should be made if the gas and meter inspection department is continued. The city's record in furnishing gas-testing service, however, made the advisability of continuing any testing service seem doubtful. It was therefore recommended that the city abandon this service and that the work be turned over to the state. For a small sum the work of the state could be periodically checked. This would probably be desirable, since in that way the city officials could keep in touch with what was being done.

BUREAU OF WEIGHTS AND MEASURES

The city was not giving sufficient attention and support to the inspection of weights and measures. The sealer was hampered by incomplete equipment and by insufficient salary. His equipment and salary should be covered by the budget, since there was enough work to warrant a living salary for full-time service.

The weights and measures laws and ordinances were not adequate. The state law, which made the county clerk sealer of weights and measures for the county, was too brief to be an effective guide. Indeed what was needed was a new state law, with adequate state inspection through a state bureau of weights and measures. This would insure uniformity of requirements in all cities and counties. In the meantime Springfield needed constantly to test local dealers' weights by buying and weighing of commodities, and should forbid the possession of unreliable brands of scales. It should teach the public how to secure full weight, and should give publicity to the work of the inspector and to the convictions obtained. To obviate the present difficulties in securing convictions in cases of violation of the law, a special procedure and special rules of evidence in trials for violating the statute or ordinance applying to weights and measures should be instituted.

City Law Department

The city council should eliminate the office of either the city attorney or the corporation counsel from the law department. One person, empowered to appoint and discharge first and second assistants if necessary, should control the department, which should handle all the legal work of the different city departments and boards. The work of the department at the time demands but one assistant; but additional counsel might be advisable in technical cases, and would be necessary when all the legal work of the city is centralized in this department.

Department of Streets and Public Improvements

At the time of these field investigations, Springfield had slightly under 161 miles of streets. About 93 miles, or 58 per cent, were unpaved. Of the paved streets, by far the largest proportion were covered with brick.

Many factors must be taken into account in choosing paving materials; such as the grade of the street, the amount of shade, soil conditions, volume and nature of the traffic, the character of the district and its probable future development, and the use of the street for car tracks. To meet these varying conditions, pavements differ as to their original cost, probable life, repair costs, the possibility of proper repair-making, riding surface, cleanliness and the cost of cleaning, noiselessness, and slipperiness. Thus it is obviously impossible to lay down any generally applicable rule as to any one best pavement. What is

ALONG A WELL-PAVED AVENUE
Showing one of Springfield's newer and attractive types of street lights.

best under certain conditions may not be best under others. In order to determine what is best for Springfield, a careful study should be made to learn what would most adequately suit district conditions. Such a study would be quite within the province of the city government; or it could be a valuable contribution by some civic or commercial organization. In the meantime only some general observations on the pavement situation are possible.

Paving Materials

The streets unpaved in Springfield in 1916 were still more than half of all. As already stated, on the paved streets brick was very largely used. Asphalt, macadam, asphaltic concrete, and a small amount of mineral rubber, dolarway, and wood blocks was also used.

Brick is cheap and serviceable in Springfield. Asphalt, too, if well laid and promptly repaired, especially where the traffic is not heavy, usually shows good results for the money expended. Macadam was little used in Springfield, and its further extension was not desirable. Concrete, laid under certain precautions, is fairly satisfactory. It was recommended that increased attention be given to asphaltic types of pavement for medium- and light-traffic streets, and to improved granite block and wood block for heavy-traffic streets. These were suggestions for immediate consideration. Beyond these, the study of the pavement question, recommended above, should be made, and it should be supplemented by or include a survey of the need of pavement repairs.

Pavement Repairs, Openings, and Replacements

Prompt repairing of pavements is most important. To facilitate intelligent estimates of the city's needs, charts should be made indicating the general condition of the streets. If the charts are made of material from which pencilings may be erased, the marks may be destroyed after repairs are computed, and the charts thus remain a correct record of street conditions. The pencil data thus shown are often very important in compelling prompt repairs by contractors.

Pavements were being opened and replaced by individual persons and companies not connected with the street department. The uniform experience of other cities has proved the necessity of confining this work to the street department, and this policy has been adopted by Springfield since this report was first drafted. The street repair gang should do refilling and replacement, and the city department or persons responsible for the opening should pay the cost. This will insure definite responsibility for the work, and the experienced workmen will give the best results possible.

CITY AND COUNTY ADMINISTRATION

To prevent for as long as possible the opening of pavements, notice of the laying of a new pavement should be served by the commissioner of assessments upon the superintendent of sewers, the commissioner of public property, and other persons likely to be concerned, as soon as new pavement construction is reasonably certain. Work requiring later cuts in the street could then be anticipated and useless controversy as to the person at fault could be eliminated.

The ordinance prohibiting private individuals from opening a pavement until it had been laid five years or more was too un-

A RAILROAD AND STREET CROSSING

Six railroad lines enter Springfield and three of them cut through either the full length or breadth of the city. A very large number of the railroad crossings are on the street level. Many of these were rough and dangerous, and called for vigorous action to compel the railroad companies to put and keep them in better condition.

reasonable to be enforced. Moreover, its legality was doubtful. Owners of abutting property should be allowed to have openings made, but they should be charged for the privilege according to a sliding scale, the amount decreasing with the age of the pavement and depending on the size and character of the cut.

STREET CLEANING AND FLUSHING

Considering the condition of the pavements and the comparatively small annual expenditure for cleaning, Springfield streets were as clean as could be expected. The methods used were good and the work of the street gangs was well managed. The department was considering needed improvements in general surface conditions of the streets, however; and this was essential to really efficient cleaning work.

Sprinkling makes a pavement slippery if there is any dirt on it, and it may eventually impair asphalt pavement. It is recommended that sprinkling be discontinued and flushing substituted, since the former merely makes mud which catches more dust; and soon all turns into dust again.

It would probably be desirable to buy several street-flushing wagons or an automobile flusher, for use at night on main streets and by day on side streets. This sort of cleaning will still need to be supplemented in the business section by that of men who pick up refuse by hand and shovel. More refuse containers should be placed on street corners.

City Dirt Roads

A large proportion of the citizens of Springfield live along its 90 miles (in 1916) of unpaved streets. Obviously, these dirt roads should be at least as good as the dirt roads outside the city, but this was not the case.

Ultimately, all the streets should be paved. Meanwhile, their condition can be greatly improved for nine or ten months of the year by providing adequate road drainage at slight additional expense, and by doing the spring work as early as the soil is workable.

The road should first be smoothed and crowned to a height at the center or crown of 18 or 20 inches in most cases, by a scraper or road machine. It should then be thoroughly rolled with a five- to 10-ton roller. The smooth surface and crown should be restored after showers, but not until the ground is no longer sticky, by dragging with a split-log drag, and should be so treated several times during the summer. If this treatment is applied when freezing begins, as well as when thaws are over, the roads should remain in good condition through much of the winter.

The method described is best adapted for quick results and

in cases where considerable soil needs to be moved. The split-log drag is better and cheaper than scrapers and rollers for use when extensive grading is not necessary.

Wooden Cross-walks and Sidewalk Inspection

The wooden street crossings of the city were undesirable. The application of the treatment recommended for dirt roads would probably make them unnecessary, or at least replaceable by cinders or other filling.

Ruts in a City Dirt Road
At certain seasons of the year the unpaved streets of the city are in bad condition. The short stretch of dirt road shown in the picture is illustrative of a number of roads which, while not in extremely bad condition, were in worse shape than necessary. By a small amount of attention they could be greatly improved. The importance of the subject is apparent when it is recalled that 93 of the city's 161 miles of street were improved.

Springfield had a sidewalk inspector who also inspects for weeds and nuisances between the property line and the curb. His work was handicapped because in Illinois the cutting of weeds between the curb and the walk and the removal of snow from the sidewalks could be enforced only through special assessments. But weeds *in a private lot* were construed a menace to health and therefore subject to police power. The city thus could usually force attention to these nuisances, if not compel their removal; but constitutional and legislative changes were needed to facilitate legal action in the matter. Meanwhile, pres-

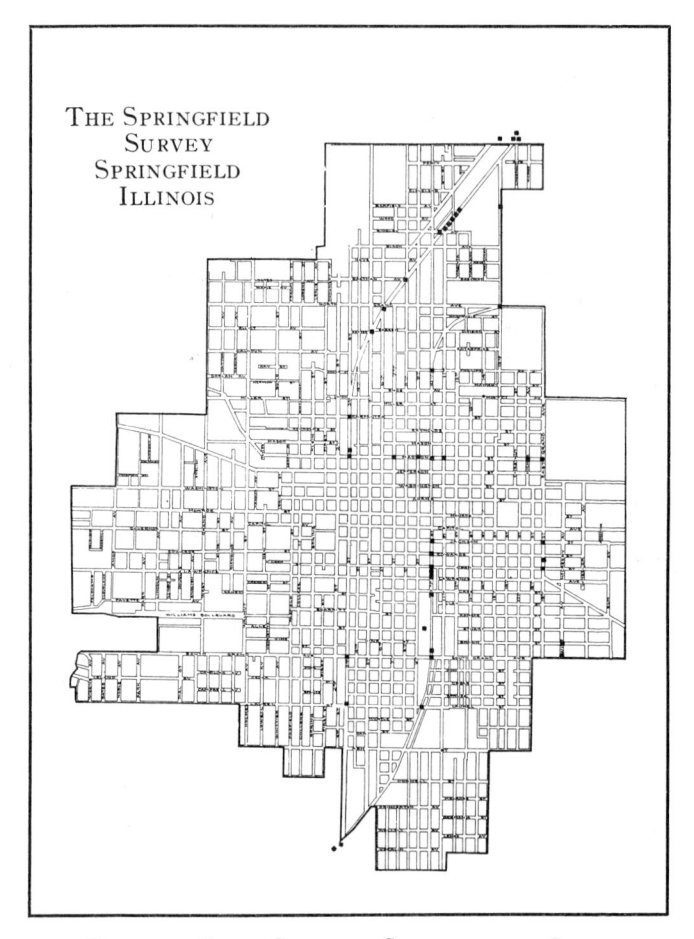

DEATHS AT GRADE CROSSINGS, SPRINGFIELD, 1908–1913

Grade crossings in Springfield were very dangerous, as is witnessed by these deaths numbering nearly 50. The grade crossings should be done away with; in the meantime the railroads should be required to guard the crossings more effectively.

sure might be exerted on owners of abutting property if, upon their neglect to comply with notices to cut the weeds along the street, they were heavily penalized for allowing weeds to grow on any lot they possessed.

The sidewalk inspector was doing little toward compelling lot owners to cut weeds. The police were supposed to report cases needing attention, but they did not do so to any great extent. All curb conditions should be inspected and checked up by the sidewalk inspector, together with conditions as to snow and weeds in vacant lots.

The records and follow-up system of the department of streets were unsatisfactory, and in general a thorough reorganization of the method of sidewalk and weed control was recommended.

The city has a great asset in its multitude of shade trees, but practically nothing was being done at the time of the survey for their preservation and renewal. The city should have a tree warden, and until his appointment the sidewalk inspector should constantly report dangerous trees or limbs and take measures for their removal.

Refuse Collection and Disposal

Springfield had a garbage incinerator but no collection system. People might bring refuse to the plant and have it disposed of free of charge, but this was not compulsory. The amount brought for disposal was not large. A broad city collection system was needed.

A study that would take into account the many varying factors, such as the quantities of refuse to be disposed of, salvage qualities of each sort of refuse, relative costs of different systems, etc., was recommended as a basis for a permanent program of disposal. Until such a program can be determined, the use of the dump system for disposal might be continued. Even though it was still near the city, its objectionable character might be largely removed if the emptying of refuse were done from movable platforms, so that only a few square yards of garbages which should be daily disinfected and covered with fresh earth, are "open" at one time.

Cemetery Administration

The management of the city cemetery was not covered by the law providing for the new commission government. It is controlled by its own board appointed by the mayor, and the city clerk does its clerical work. It logically should be under the supervision of the commissioner of public property.

Much work for lot owners was being done on credit; many charges were uncollectable or disputed; and the collector was receiving 10 per cent for collecting all bills not paid in advance. The improvement introduced since our survey, which provided that only those whose prior bills were paid should be allowed credit, was not sufficient. Cash payment should be required for all work done. Work for the indigent should be charged to the proper charitable agency, either public or private. If accurate records of all cost charges were kept, a superintendent would soon learn to make estimates very close to the proper amounts to charge, and to gauge the efficiency of work done.

To improve the general administration of the cemetery it was suggested (1) that all orders contain a schedule of prices; (2) that no work be done until payment is made or guarantee offered; (3) that the superintendent be supplied with registered orders (i.e., orders numbered consecutively in advance); and (4) that employes be required to keep time and cost records.

Elections

If even a minor official, such as a justice of the peace, should resign, a special election costing about $3,000 was necessary in order to fill the vacancy unless his unexpired term was less than a year. In 1914, a not unusual year, 10 elections, all cailing for a force of election officials, were held; and all but two required the use of polling places. The cost in time and money was not inconsiderable.

In order to improve the situation, several suggestions for constitutional changes were offered. Provision should be made (1) for the general use of a short ballot, thus creating more appointive and fewer elective offices; and (2) for appointments to fill all unexpired terms in judicial offices. In addition, legislative changes should be made providing (3) for nomination of township and judicial officers on petition; (4) for the combining of special elections on propositions, and any other elections occurring within ninety days; and (5) for reducing the number of registrations at polling places and for substituting registration at the office of the local election commission.

SIZE OF POLLING DISTRICTS

The increased number of voters in the election districts at certain elections since women were given the vote in Illinois, made it seem advisable, for economical and other reasons, to amend the law that made the standard number of voters in each district 300 and restricted them to 450, so that more voters could be handled in each instead of increasing the number of districts.

Too many reserve ballots were being supplied for each district. Ten per cent more than the registered number of voters would probably be sufficient. In addition, the board of election commissioners might supply themselves with an additional reserve of 20 per cent of the total required for the city. The designation of the district should be omitted so that any district might use them by filling in its name with a rubber stamp. This would materially reduce printing costs.

Printers should be required to send in competitive bids for ballots. This was not always done. The city's use of public buildings for election purposes is commendable. In general, the administration of the election board seemed satisfactory.

CURRENT INCOME OF THE CITY GOVERNMENT

The corporate revenue of the city during the last few years had been approximately $400,000, of which about $270,000 came from city taxation and about $110,000 from retail liquor licenses. The remainder (about 4 per cent) came from other license charges, from franchise moneys, interest on deposits, fines, and miscellaneous smaller collections. Of the $270,000 derived from local taxes, nearly three-fourths was raised from real estate assessments, about one-fourth from personal property, and the remainder from a small capital tax and an insurance tax.

ASSESSMENT OF REAL ESTATE

The total assessed value for the county (including the county seat) during the last half-dozen years had averaged about

$36,000,000, Springfield's share of which had varied between $11,000,000 and $13,000,000. These figures represented only about one-fifth or less of the actual value. Existing Illinois laws prescribed that the taxable value should be 33⅓ per cent (previous to 1909 only 20 per cent was required) of the full value, but in actual practice it worked out that the amount of which 33⅓ per cent was taken was not the full or 100 per cent value, but approximately 67 per cent. No one knows exactly how much. This reduced the amount upon which taxes were assessed to 20 or 22 per cent of the true value.

The same situation, with consequent complications, prevails throughout the whole county. With the valuation only about one-fifth of what it should be, the nominal tax rate was of necessity about five times as large as it should normally be. The following dictum by Professor John A. Fairly was strikingly exemplified in the county's methods of assessment: "When once a departure is made from the standard of full value, it appears to be impossible for assessors to adhere to any definite standard; and the inevitable result of undervaluations is not only an unnecessary increase in the nominal tax rate, but also marked variations in the standards of valuation between different classes of property and different individuals; and a pronounced violation of the constitutional requirement that taxation shall be in proportion to the value of property."

A change in the state law to require assessments at 90 to 100 per cent of actual value was strongly recommended; also better qualified assessing officers were needed.

Assessing Officers and Board of Review

Sangamon County had 26 local assessing officers in addition to the assessing officers for Springfield. Their terms of office were usually short, and for the most part they possessed no special aptitude for tax work. A county assessor, with provision for deputies to assist, was recommended, as well as a reorganization of the county board of tax review in order to allow for the inclusion of one of the county tax officers among the membership. The reorganization of the state board of equalization, to be made

CITY AND COUNTY ADMINISTRATION

up of trained individuals giving their full time, was also needed in the interest of better local tax administration.

Assessment Method in Springfield

The Somers system of making assessments, which was adopted by the city several years ago, was an important step ahead. It was founded upon certain front-foot values which had been agreed upon as fair and which were used as bases in working out tables of local values, from which all lot values in the city were in turn computed.

Similarly, in assessing the improvements put on land, rules based on the square feet of foundation and the height of improvements were being used in valuing buildings, a definite cost unit being assigned to each different class of construction. The gross value thus

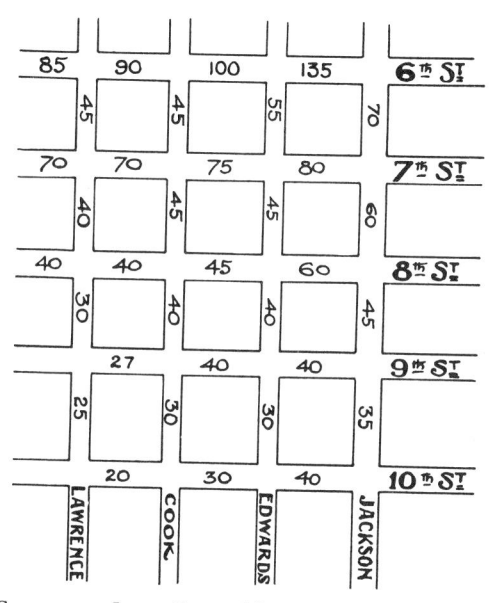

SECTION OF LAND VALUE MAP IN COUNTY CLERK'S OFFICE IN SPRINGFIELD

The figures show front-foot valuations placed upon real estate for purpose of tax assessment in 1914. The map was on file in the county clerk's office but was not published. Its reproduction in brief pamphlet form, section by section, showing the bases for assessed valuations in all parts of the city, would be a very desirable step in the direction of full publicity in tax matters.

obtained was then depreciated by other tables, by scaling down according to age of the building and the amount of upkeep it had received or required. By using such definite rules, the assessor could closely approximate absolute fairness, which of course is a first requisite of assessing.

Still more equitable assessments could be obtained, however, by using the fixed rules applied to land more as guides than as inflexible standards or absolute determinants. It is obvious that the desirable or undesirable use to which an adjoining lot is permanently put, and the grade and "lay" of the land, particularly if it is very different from other land in the district, will be a more nearly correct measure of valuation of a particular lot than will the arbitrary computation of the tables, however correct they may be in general.

The rules used in Springfield had a provision for flexibility called "local influence," which allowed additions or subtractions from the computed value of a lot; but in practice the provision was seldom employed. It should be used extensively.

As pointed out in the first edition of this report and in the survey exhibition, corner lots were being assessed too high in proportion to the valuations placed on the intermediate lots. The corner "influence" rules were later improved in this respect however. Again, the survey found no one who knew what difference was made in applying the corner-lot rules to business and to residential sections. Such lack of full details as to the working of the system was fatal of course to the best results. Moreover, all rules should be simple enough for comprehension by a very high proportion of the people; they should be made public and should be used, as already suggested, only as guides and not as absolute determinants.

Assessing Buildings and Improvements

The tables and rules used for valuing buildings and improvements since the Somers system was installed in 1911 were by 1916 no longer used exclusively, nor were they officially open to the public. In fact no complete set of mathematical tables was being used in that year nor were they shown in justification of assessments. The first reason given for this partial abandonment of the system—that the original rules were not correct for Springfield—did not appear to us sound, for the rules could be changed until at least approximately correct for a given community.

The second objection to the system—that depreciation of

property depends upon the lack of upkeep and repair, and that with the limited time available for assessing it was impossible to determine all the facts necessary if the tables were to be used for computing the depreciation—had some merit. The trouble, however, as far as it concerned real property, could be obviated by administrative action and without legislation. An all-time force was recommended to do the work which, with time for more systematic study of all new improvements and for rechecking all old buildings could, by using the fixed rules, reach very uniform results; and such an assessing method would be as inexpensive and more efficient than that of the part-time force.

Land and buildings or other improvements were being valued separately in Springfield—a method which general experience is tending strongly to approve. In accordance with the state law, however, property valuations were being made up only once in four years, except in the cases of new buildings or of additions, destructions, or injuries to land or personalty, which of course comprised a very small proportion of the whole. Obviously the cash value of real estate fluctuates considerably during so long a period. In this connection it was recommended that consideration be given to the plan in use in several European countries and in several American and Canadian cities by which such an additional tax is placed on land as would claim a part, at least, of the increased land value which is due to the general growth of the community. Meanwhile, real estate valuations should be made by competent assessors annually.

Publicity of Assessments

Besides the method of giving publicity to assessments then in use—that of merely keeping the assessors' books open to public inspection—the city was advised to publish annually and circulate a set of large maps, showing the front-foot assessments for every block in the city, as a means of securing greater equity of assessments.

Personal Property Assessments

The administration of the personal property tax in Springfield and Sangamon County, as in any other localities in this

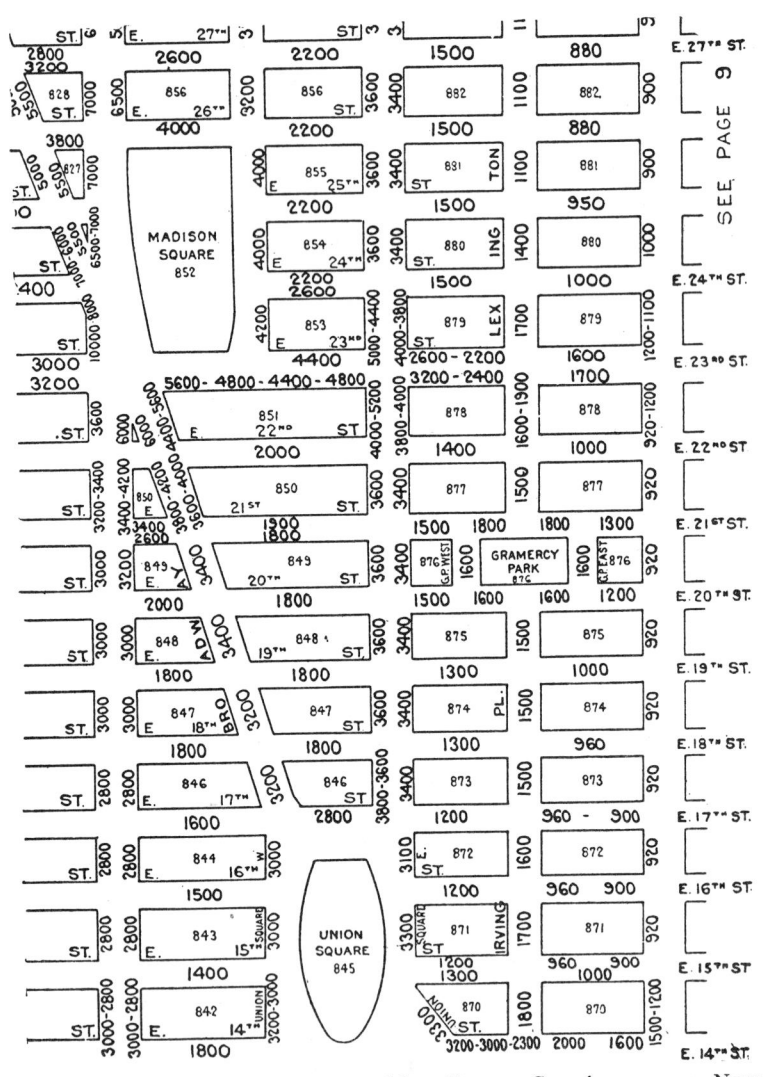

SECTION OF ONE OF THE LAND VALUE MAPS USED BY CITY ASSESSORS IN NEW YORK CITY IN 1917
(Section reproduced in exact size of original)

In order to secure publicity to its tax valuations, the department of taxes and assessments of the city of New York publishes annually a volume of land value maps showing the front-foot valuations for all parts of the city. In view of the importance of full publicity as a means of securing greater equity of assessments, methods similar to those followed in New York are recommended for Springfield.

340

country, was extremely unsatisfactory. Its undervaluation was even worse than that of real estate. Indeed a large proportion escaped assessment entirely. The result was that a small number of property owners paid the personal property tax —property owners who were so burdened not by any just process of selection, but because they were honest in listing their holdings, because they were small investors with but little opportunity to place their funds in untaxed districts outside the state, or because they were corporations whose books were open to inspection.

Experience throughout this country indicates the impossibility of taxing personal property, especially intangible personalty such as stocks, bonds, mortgages, etc., at the same rates as those applied to real estate. A fairer and more practical method is the laying of a more moderate tax on personal property, say a tax at about one-fourth or one-fifth of the rate applied to realty. Further, the centralization of the assessment work, with a more expert assessing staff, already recommended, should also help the situation.

COLLECTION OF TAXES

Outside of Springfield taxes were collected by town collectors, one for each township, up to a certain date; after that by the county treasurer. In Springfield (Capital Township) all taxes were being collected by the county treasurer.

State and county taxes collected by township collectors were paid over to the county treasurer. All other taxes collected in the township were paid to the proper township official; that is, school taxes were paid to the proper school officers, and so on.

Because of prompt and well-managed tax sales, the county treasurer was collecting practically all real property taxes. The results in the more difficult task of collecting personal property taxes were almost equally good. In 1914 and 1915 the amounts uncollected were only about 2.5 per cent and 2.2 per cent respectively of the total personal property taxes.

The township collectors outside of Springfield were not able to collect so large a proportion of the total levy. Since the county treasurer must then collect the large remainder for the township, the survey recommended that the township collectors be abolished and that the work be put in the hands of the county treasurer. For the convenience of rural taxpayers, the deputies of the county collector might sit in the various townships on certain previously advertised days.

Transfer and Safe Custody of Tax Funds

The county treasurer was not turning over to the city every ten days, as required by law, all the tax money collected by him. Neither were the books kept so that the city balances could be readily ascertained. Only after considerable computation was it possible to discover that during a five-month period just prior to the survey field work, he was withholding from $5,140 to $72,795 balances belonging to the city school district, park board, and other government bodies. Meanwhile the city was borrowing money at 6 per cent interest, and might have saved nearly $700 and retired the certificates drawing 5 per cent interest had this money been turned over at the proper time. The practice being followed by the county treasurer deserved severe condemnation and required immediate correction.

The Illinois law made the county treasurer liable under all circumstances for money under his control. He must give a very large bond—in 1915 it was for $773,000—but might then deposit the money wherever he chose. A better law would provide for the naming of depositaries where he might deposit and be relieved of responsibility. The depositaries could then be required to give security for their deposits and pay interest on daily balances, as they were doing on city funds which they were holding.

The special funds and state moneys held by the treasurer should also earn money, which should go to the county or be added to the funds themselves.

THE HANDLING OF THE SPECIAL FUNDS OF THE CITY

Borrowing for Current Purposes

Because the funds raised by taxation for paying the expenses of the city government were not available until next to the last month of the fiscal year in which they had been incurred, the city was borrowing heavily to pay for a large part of its current work. These loans in anticipation of tax returns were bearing interest at 5 per cent. At the same time the city had certain funds on deposit in the banks which drew 3 per cent interest. Both of these rates were fair under the circumstances, but the difference between them, which was a loss to the city, should be saved by temporary use by the city of parts of these bank balances. Also the dates for assessment of taxable property and the collection of taxes should be set ahead from six to eight months, with provision for penalties for delinquency in payments.

Such a plan would greatly relieve the situation. With an efficient collection procedure, it has been found that the plan of collecting taxes at two periods in the year does not add sufficiently to collection expenses to materially reduce the savings otherwise effected. This should prove to be true in Sangamon County, as the county treasurer's force was not being largely increased at tax collection periods.

To make these changes it probably would be necessary to change the fiscal years of counties and other tax districts, and generally to revise all revenue laws. Such a revision is desirable in any event.

City Bonds and Sinking Funds

The total city bonds outstanding at the end of February, 1915, was $727,700, a moderate amount in view of the value of the public property alone. Very little was known as to how this indebtedness was incurred, the bonds then outstanding having been issued to refund earlier issues regarding which the records were incomplete. The bonds for the purchase of the waterworks were probably still unpaid.

In order to provide a more systematic method of paying the city's bonded indebtedness, a sinking fund ordinance was passed on April 5, 1909, which appropriated funds for the retirement in 1925 of city bonds to the amount of $487,000. Although this would leave a debt of $238,700 still unpaid at that time it was a fairly liberal provision, since the bonds were partly the debts of former generations and the citizens who are paying for them have not enjoyed any special benefits from the original expenditures.

At the time of the survey the city commissioners were not exercising their powers of determining the kind and maximum price of bonds to be purchased through the sinking funds in a way to net the city the greatest possible saving. They should advertise for offerings of bonds, and should direct that those be retired first which would give the city the best values when interest and market price are considered. On the basis of 1914 prices they could, by this method, have been saving the city from $1,200 to $1,600 a year.

Bond moneys collected by the county treasurer were not being paid over to the state auditor on the dates required by law. If this were done and bonds were retired as soon as money was available for their purchase, the city could thus have been saving $300 to $400 more.

Bonding Procedure

Obligating the future residents of the city for the payment of debts made in the present is a matter of sufficient importance to call for careful consideration of all the factors involved and for the following of certain principles which experience has approved. A city should issue bonds only as a last resort when current requirements of the community cannot be met through current taxes. Moreover, the Illinois law providing that bonds be used for no other purposes than those for which they were issued should be strictly enforced.

Experience more and more favors bonds being made serial in form; that is, in the case of twenty-year bonds, one-twentieth should fall due and be paid from current taxes each year. Postponement of the first instalment to the end of the third or fourth year after issuance of bonds should not be provided for. Only the later issues in Springfield were serials.

Bonds should all be retired before the end of the life of the improvement for which they were issued, or, preferably, in three-quarters of that time since the upkeep charges toward the end are excessive. Some of the serial bonds for riot judgments should have been made to fall due before 1918.

Every precaution should be taken to make the absolute validity of bonds unquestionable, else their market value will be impaired. Their increased marketableness would fully compensate for the expense of employing a nationally recognized bond expert to approve them and manage their issue.

It has been found a saving to cities and an advantage to local investors to issue bonds in small denominations of $50 or $100.

Special Assessment Funds

Special assessments are special taxes assessed for public improvements. The property owners who particularly benefit by the improvements pay part of their cost; the city pays for the remainder. Residents of Springfield might complete settlement immediately or might contribute their share of the expense in five equal instalments. In the latter case the city, which was acting as agent for property owners in the matter, paid the contractor with serial bonds which he usually sold. The city wisely (we believe) maintained the value of the bonds by meeting the deficits—between $2,000 and $3,000 a year—which usually exist between the money collected from the owners and the funds expended in paying the bonds and interest as they fall due.

These deficits in the collections were due to several largely preventable causes. First, since most of the overdue assessments were collected by June 15th, the county treasurer might have turned them over to the city at that time; but (at least in the last year previous to the survey) he did not do so until September 22d, and the city was thereby delayed in retiring its bonds and was thus obliged to pay longer than was necessary the 5 per cent interest which they drew, at a yearly loss to the city of $400 to $500. The county treasurer, in complying with the law to turn over funds every ten days, for convenience could do so on account and present his complete report with the final payment.

Second, even after the funds were turned over to the city by the county treasurer the delay in retiring bonds caused a further loss of interest, since the city continued to pay the 5 per cent interest due on the bonds until their retirement and meanwhile received only 3 per cent interest on the funds in the bank. It was possible to work out an equitable system of prompt retirement without seeking any new legislation. Care needed to be taken, however, that the methods used to call in bonds were not unfair nor unpopular, since such methods would affect the marketableness of future bonds.

Third, the county treasurer retained 1 per cent of overdue collections for his services in securing them, and the city suffered an annual loss from this source of $250 to $300. The city should charge the cost of making overdue collections to the property owners at 5 per cent of the amount due, as a penalty for delinquency.

Finally, the maximum of 6 per cent which the law allowed for the services of engineers and of the general supervision of the work did not always cover the actual cost. The law should be changed in order to allow an adequate appropriation for this purpose.

CERTAIN PHASES OF SANGAMON COUNTY GOVERNMENT

The county board of supervisors, consisting of 21 members from Capital Township and one from each of the 26 other townships, was the governing body of Sangamon County. Its work was done very largely through some 15 or 20 standing committees which dealt with such matters as asylums and hospitals, claims, and other county matters. In addition there was a long list of elective officers chosen to render certain other administrative services through the agency of the county.

Long Ballot

With several candidates running for each of these numerous offices the ballot was long and confusing; furthermore, the element of centralized responsibility, recognized as necessary for efficient government, was lacking. It was recommended that the county follow more closely the method of the city of Springfield in elections. A county commission of three or five members should be elected to take charge of certain definite functions, such as finance, poor relief, and so forth. This commission should replace the present county board of supervisors, and township government should be done away with. All the administrative officers (the county clerk, county treasurer, etc.) should then be appointed by the commission, or preferably by its president or popularly elected chairman. The advisability of appointing county judges is probably still doubtful, but in any case the court officers should be appointed by the court.

Another improvement would be the adoption of a non-partisan election procedure similar to that used by the city. It is absurd to allow questions of national politics to continue as important factors in these strictly local elections.

Civil Service

County officers were not subject to nor protected by civil service regulations. The county needed such regulations quite as much as the city. A good civil law should be formulated and adopted as soon as the other legislative changes can be made. Citizens would then find the problem of electing the right man to office less difficult, since whoever is elected will have a trained and efficient organization and staff for the continuance of the work of the office.

THE LONG BALLOT
One of the many cartoons used in the survey exhibition to illustrate points brought out in the investigations. The cartoons were by A. S. Harkness of Springfield.

County Budget

Sangamon County had no real budget. As a makeshift basis for the annual tax levy, each year an estimate or apportionment of funds needed to carry on the county work was made up.

This schedule of figures had been used for a long time as the chief guide for expenditures during the year.

This tax levy schedule, although later somewhat improved, was still weak in the following particulars in comparison with a real budget:

(1) It is not based on the total revenue actually receivable or even accurately estimated; (2) it is not used as a guide in making expenditures, since a large deficit would sometimes ensue if it were followed; (3) it is not properly classified as to functions nor itemized in detail; (4) there is no adequate control of accounts to prevent overcharging, as would be the case if a ledger specially arranged for the handling of the different funds were used; and no record of liabilities is kept.

A budget should be prepared under standard, detailed classifications and should be accompanied by proper budget-accounting and control. It should show a total in excess of estimated revenues from all sources and should cover every expenditure, including even the cost of offices that depend upon fees for part of their support. The items should be controlled and no expenditures made nor liabilities legally incurred until the auditor had vouched for the fact that funds were available.

The law should be changed to meet any legal difficulties that would interfere with such a budget. Meanwhile an informal working budget should be used.

Two of the main reasons for adopting the budget system are that it forces officials to formulate intelligent programs for their departments' future work and saves public funds. The experience of many cities and counties proves the soundness of this policy. Other results at which budget-making procedures aim are: the lessening or elimination of "log-rolling," informing the public on the city's financial aims; furnishing a formula to guide and check administrative officers; providing a framework for a proper accounting system and adequate reporting on public work, and furnishing a basis for purposes of comparison.

Accounting System Needed

The account keeping of the county contrasted poorly with that of the city. Except for improvements brought about at the end of 1912 by the creation of the office of auditor, the situation was practically the same as that described in the following excerpt from the report of O. R. Martin, of the University of Illinois, of his investigation of the county's business methods:

No central set of books for the business of the county as a whole is to be found, and such books as there are are kept on the single entry basis. The county treasurer has a cash book, a duplicate of which is kept in the office of the county clerk. This and a register of the county warrants kept in the county clerk's office constitute the most comprehensive records, but they are by no means satisfactory for the purpose of presenting, in a complete manner, the financial business of the county. Each officer keeps a number of records and accounts which relate directly to the work of his office, but these are nowhere brought together to show their relation.

The system was complicated and its efficiency was impaired by the existence of practically three fiscal years, for the supervisors' year began on September 1st, although they do not take office until April, and the other county officers began their fiscal year on December 1st. They should all use the same fiscal year. The system was further complicated by the fact that the fees received in some of the offices constitute a large part of their income.

The account keeping needed to be thoroughly overhauled and reorganized.

Purchasing and Payment of Claims

The somewhat limited duties of the county auditor, whose office was created in 1912, were: auditing claims and recommending their payment or rejection; collecting statistical information; approving all orders for supplies before the order was placed; keeping a record of county offices and officers. He also purchased some supplies. The great difference in prices paid by different county officials in the past showed the need of such a central agent, and the saving effected through this method of purchasing had been estimated at $2,000 a year on only a small proportion of all the purchases made for the county.

The best results, however, will not be obtained until such handicaps as the poor account keeping and the limited power of the auditor over inventories of county officers, over the making of the budget, and over county purchasing are removed.

As soon as the necessary amendments to the law are obtained, the county's cumbersome and unbusinesslike system of paying claims should be simplified in a way similar to that suggested for the city.

County Reports and Publicity

Finally, Sangamon County was publishing no annual reports that were in such form as to give citizens any clear idea of the county activities of the year, their costs, and the general status of county matters. Indeed, except for the auditor's statement, which was limited by the deficiencies in the county accounting system, practically no reports at all were issued. The situation urgently called for a change. The public must be informed upon public matters. The issuance of readable annual reports, with the facts explained and so grouped as to be easily understood, is essential to the intelligent participation of the public in their government, and is necessary if officials are to be held to the full performance of their duties.

PART THREE
PUTTING THE FACTS TO WORK

XII

THE EXHIBITION OF SURVEY FINDINGS

The people of Springfield took over the survey, so to speak, during the preparation and course of the survey Exhibition in the fall of 1914. The Exhibition at one stroke placed them in possession of the leading facts, ideas, and recommendations of the surveyors; and in addition afforded an opportunity, grasped by nearly a thousand, to participate personally in the venture and in this way not only to feel a sense of proprietary interest but to be in fact part owners. Here was a new broad channel through which many citizens might help to put the survey's information and suggestions to work; and through 40 and more exhibit committees they took up the task.

In addition to the opportunity for a wider sharing of the work and responsibilities, and to the opportunity to present the major findings in such simple, graphic, and entertaining ways as to gain the attention and be understood by the many, particularly those who are not habitual readers of periodicals or printed reports, the Exhibition, as has been pointed out in an earlier chapter, would create an event in the community, lasting ten days and preceded by two months of active preparation, which would give further "news" value to the survey's facts and conclusions. It provided the occasion for focusing the attention of large numbers of people upon the data at one particular time and gave added timeliness to discussions of the material in meetings of clubs and societies and in other gatherings. It moreover presented the information and suggestions which the survey had to offer as a unit —in the form of a great picture or a panorama spread out in a way to bring new aspects, emphasis, and freshness of interest to conditions in the city which too great familiarity or occupation in other matters had obscured, even from the many who regularly frequent the city's streets or take part in its daily routine.

A Tour of the Exhibition Hall

Perhaps in a tour of the exhibition hall, using the floor plan and the pictures scattered through these pages to aid, an idea of the Exhibition may best be secured. The reader may then see it as the "average" citizen saw it. At the same time a glimpse behind the scenes will show something of the great co-operative effort that added so much significance to the picture.

The state of Illinois is the co-operator first in evidence as you approach the exhibition hall, for the state has given the use of the huge and imposing First Regiment Armory and with it, light and heat for ten days. Great stores of equipment have been moved out to make room for building the elaborate framework which will enclose the exhibits. As you enter the hall, your first impression is that of a big achievement in decoration and construction alone. The national colors are used with fine effect to give dignity and beauty to the Exhibition and to soften the harshness of iron beams and brick walls. Large flags hung from the ceiling take away from the great height of the building which would otherwise overawe the low exhibit booths. Long rows of booths line the walls and form a double row down the center of the hall. These have walls of buff-colored panels framed in green. Red, white, and blue bunting is draped in fan shapes over the hall's balcony, the latter forming the ceiling of the booths.[1]

The center of first interest, aside from the general effect, is likely to be the attractive pavilion directly opposite the entrance, with white pillars supporting a canopy top of red, white, and blue and tall palms flanking the arch of the stage at the back. But we will get to this again later. In the meantime it suggests other co-operators. A number of busy men gave much time to planning and building appropriate settings for the exhibits. It is especially interesting, incidentally, and fairly typical of the spirit of the whole enterprise, that the architect who planned the decorative features and the manager of the public utilities corporation who supervised the construction were both in disagreement with certain important findings of the survey. Like a great many other public spirited citizens, not knowing "where the lightning would

[1] See illustration on page 13.

Floor plan of The Springfield Survey Exhibition—"One Way" Exhibition—Follow the Arrows

The "One Way" Route

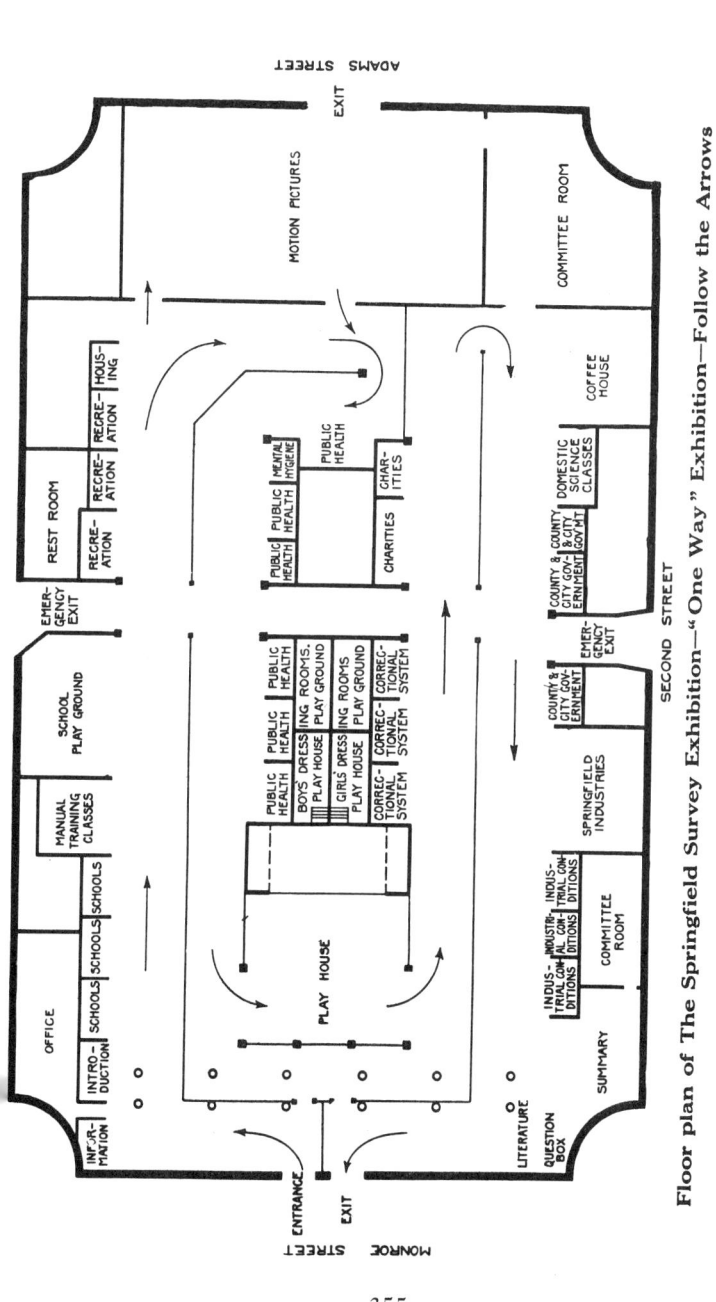

The floor plan was so arranged that all visitors went in the same direction in touring the Exhibition hall. Copies of the floor plan were distributed in advertising the exhibits and as a help in understanding the scheme as a whole.

355

strike," they willingly endorsed the project as a whole without regard to any quarrel they might have with some part of it.

A committee on drayage provided trucks and automobiles to haul a large amount of equipment and exhibit material. A furniture committee secured the chairs, tables, and rugs you will find in the rest room, rest spaces, office, stage settings, and restaurant, if you drop into byways and places "behind the scenes" along your route.

FIRST REGIMENT ARMORY AS EXHIBITION HALL
The state of Illinois co-operated by turning over its huge armory, with light and heat, for ten days to be used as the Exhibition hall.

THE ONE-WAY ROUTE

But you may not make a tour of the hall in any haphazard way, dropping in here and there. For at the entrance an usher directs you to turn to the left (even if he were not there a sign and a guide rail would start you in that direction), and thereafter you have little choice but to follow the one-way route that is marked by the guide rails, reinforced by ushers at those points where it is necessary to have an opening for fire protection. The ushers committee brought in one large group of co-operators, high school boys in the afternoons, and members of the National Guard in the evening. What better way than through a chance to be of service could there have been for bringing these young men in contact with the survey?

You come first to a booth labeled "Information" where several women workers are very busy, but are ready to answer any questions and to be of help in other ways. All ushers, explainers, and other helpers report here, receive badges, and are marked "present" on a large chart that hangs on the wall. Each day postal cards are sent out from the information and management committee to the helpers who have been scheduled for the next day, reminding them of the hours assigned to them. Here also is the outpost of the office of the Exhibition directors, from which the

"INFORMATION" AT THE EXHIBITION
The first booth you come to; every visitor had to pass it on the way in. Here several women volunteers were regularly on duty ready to answer questions and to help visitors get a right start in making the round of the hall.

directors and managing committees, working together, keep the machinery of the Exhibition running, not always smoothly to be sure, but with remarkably good results for a temporary and volunteer organization.

AN INTRODUCTORY DEFINITION OF THE SURVEY

And now for the exhibits. Next beyond "information" is the "introduction" to the exhibits. If you came without much advance information (as you probably did, representing as you do the majority of visitors) you wonder what it is all about; what is a survey anyhow; who is doing this and why? Your questions are answered in the form of a dialogue between "Father Springfield" and the "Wise Owl," lettered in large type on panels covering one wall of the booth. Their conversation runs as follows:

WHAT IS A SURVEY?

FATHER SPRINGFIELD: "I feel a bit run down; I guess I need a tonic."

WISE OWL: "Maybe you do, but you need a Survey first."

FATHER SPRINGFIELD: "A Survey? What's that?"

WISE OWL: "You call in specialists to examine you, weigh you, and test your heart and lungs. They make notes about you and take them back to their offices to study. Then they prescribe for your real trouble."

FATHER SPRINGFIELD: "That sounds fine. But where can I find these specialists?"

WISE OWL: "Ask the Russell Sage Foundation to send them. But remember! They'll tell you the facts whether you like it or not."

FATHER SPRINGFIELD: "I'm not afraid. You send for them."

So the specialists were sent for and they came.

Father Springfield will become a familiar figure in the course of the tour. He was the inspiration of a local artist and expressed in his strong, determined bearing, and the dress and beard of the elderly responsible citizen the type of middle westerner who, as a pioneer, built cities like Springfield and felt a real stake in making them good places in which young and old might work and play and otherwise live their lives to the full.

You are assured in this same introduction that the survey belongs to you as a citizen. On the exhibit panels it was put something as follows:

THE SURVEY IN THREE WORDS

SPRINGFIELD	WELFARE	CO-OPERATION
It is Springfield's enterprise. Started by Springfield. Backed by Springfield.	It is for Better Health. Schools. Recreation. Morals. Working Conditions. Home Conditions. Government.	These matters affect you. They need your interest, co-operation, and action.

THE SCHOOL EXHIBIT

If you are like most visitors you will spend ten minutes at least on the next exhibit, but you will gather in the short time a surprising amount and variety of information about the public schools of your city. You are likely to tell about it afterward, too, because the amusing and expressive pictures and devices impress the facts and their importance upon your mind. For example, there is the panel on "Overheated School Rooms" showing the temperature found in 170 school rooms during a day in March. Your attention is especially attracted to this because of the thermometer over four feet high in which red "mercury" rises to 80 degrees, drops and rises again, while a series of sketches show a child growing drowsier as the higher temperatures are registered. Another panel called "Arithmetic Tests" gives illuminating information on the strong and weak points in the class room instruction. You learn that Springfield children stand almost at the head in addition, above the average in multiplication, just above the average in subtraction and division, way below the average in problems calling for reasoning, and almost at the foot in accuracy. Rows of silhouettes of children are cut of gummed paper, 27 figures in a row representing the school children of 27 cities. All the figures are green except one representing the Springfield child, which is red.

Again, 300 Springfield boys of thirteen years tell you what they would like to do when they grow up. One-half of them chose occupations for which industrial training is needed, and you are chagrined to find that at present they cannot get such training in the most helpful form in the public schools.

A diagram which moves up and down next attracts your attention; in fact, it must be admitted that it was made to move for no other purpose than to get your attention. It shows by columns of varying height and color that about half of the children who leave school at fourteen have not completed the sixth grade; and this is related to the laws regulating attendance.

In one of the school booths there is a working model of a school door with a self-releasing fire exit latch. You will probably stop there longer than otherwise if it happens that one of the most enthusiastic explainers, a real fireman from the city fire department, is on hand to demonstrate the advantages of this door. He is here very regularly, so you are not likely to miss him. Although he is especially enthusiastic about fire protection, he will not let you neglect any feature of the school exhibit.

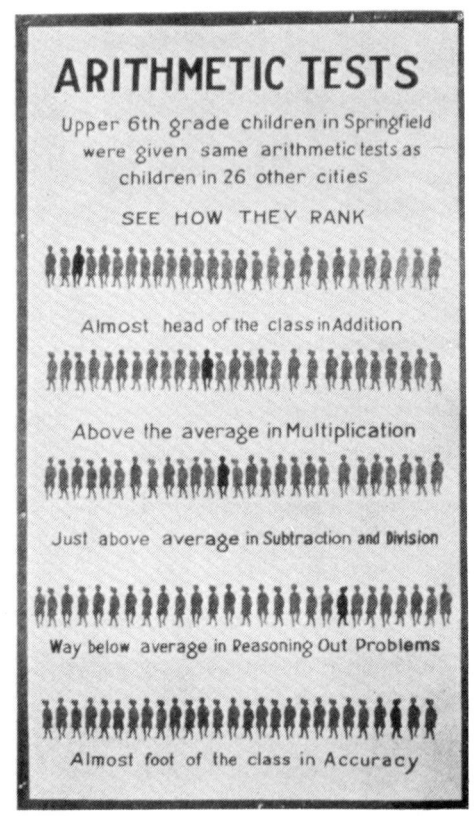

How They Rank in Arithmetic
A panel from the Exhibition. The figures in silhouette representing the school children of 26 other cities were in green, and the one representing Springfield was in red.

Extending clear across one side of the last booth in the school series is a description printed in large letters. It shows the progress made in improving the schools in the eight months since the

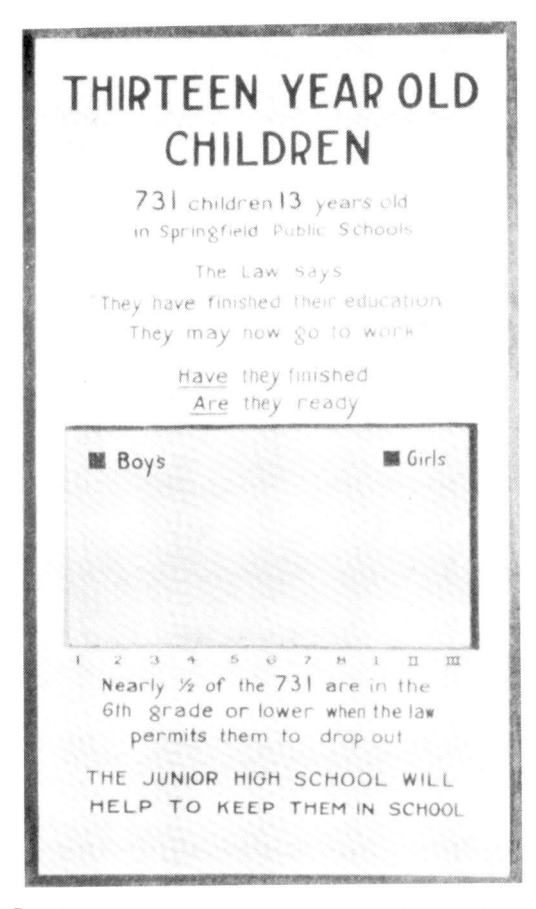

> **THIRTEEN YEAR OLD CHILDREN**
>
> 731 children 13 years old
> in Springfield Public Schools
>
> The Law says
> They have finished their education
> They may now go to work
>
> <u>Have</u> they finished
> <u>Are</u> they ready
>
> ■ Boys   ■ Girls
>
> 1 2 3 4 5 6 7 8 I II III
> Nearly ½ of the 731 are in the
> 6th grade or lower when the law
> permits them to drop out
>
> THE JUNIOR HIGH SCHOOL WILL
> HELP TO KEEP THEM IN SCHOOL

GRADES OF BOYS AND GIRLS THIRTEEN YEARS OLD
In the blank space of this panel at intervals columns of varying heights and colors automatically moved into place to show the distribution by grades of children reaching the limit of the compulsory attendance period when large numbers may be expected to drop out of school.

facts were gathered in March, 1914, and in the five months since June when they were first published. The list makes a very encouraging showing and as a beginning gives promise for the survey as a whole.

The school exhibit, only a few of whose 18 or 20 main points can be touched upon here, presents a good example of the way in which local talent was commandeered. The survey staff and the commercial exhibit makers were responsible for facts, copy, layouts, construction, and lettering of panels. But the electrical devices (there were two in this section) were made by volunteer electrical engineers, members of the model committee; sketches on eight or ten panels and the cleverly designed silhouettes were contributed by as many amateur or professional artists, all the arrangements being made by the art committee. The faithful services of the member of the fire department was another illustration of the wide range of interests that united in giving the survey message to the people.

THE SCHOOL PLAYGROUND DEMONSTRATION
Each day of the Exhibition a different group of children, 20 to 30 at a time, played games here under the direction of a play leader. During the ten days every school and every grade was represented.

MANUAL TRAINING AND SCHOOL PLAYGROUNDS

By the time you have studied all of this part of the school exhibit—and even with the pictures, models, and other enlivening features this exhibit does, after all, require close attention—you will find some mental relaxation in a visit to the manual training department and the school playground. Here the exhibits are all action.

THE SURVEY EXHIBITION

In the manual training booth there is a different class present each session, taken from the eighth grade or the high school. They are demonstrating drawing and bench woodwork. The large open space just beyond is called the playground, and here 20 or 30 children are playing games under the direction of a play leader. They are so absorbed as to be quite unconscious of the crowd of visitors in front of the rail. There is no doubt that they are having a good time and that it is wholesome fun.

But why a play director? And why playgrounds in a city of generous outdoor spaces like Springfield? There are answers to these questions in the recreation exhibit which comes next. Before going on, however, you may be interested to learn that there is a different group of children on the playground every day, and that during the ten days every school and every grade in the city will be represented here. And of course nearly every child who takes part brings parents and neighbors to the Exhibition.

The Recreation Exhibit

In the recreation exhibit, the first object to attract your attention is a remarkably realistic model of a school building and playground. You will easily recognize the building, as it is an exact reproduction of the Enos School, but the grounds have been transformed from a bare and unused space to an attractive playground equipped in one part with play apparatus, planted as a garden in another, and with one section reserved as a ball field. You may never guess that those shade trees are sponges dyed green; and you probably will agree that the play apparatus is worthy of a professional toy maker. The children of the Enos School made the model from a plan furnished by the survey. Now that they have pictured so vividly the possibilities, they are all the more eager to have the real playground. You, for one, may be ready to help get it for them too; and after you have seen the panels at the back of the booth, having a play director does not seem a mere frill. For example, there is a photograph of a crap game with the reminder, "Left to themselves, children sometimes play wrong"; and in contrast, boys playing basketball and dodge ball with the caption, "Rightly conducted sports develop character."

A BOOTH IN THE RECREATION EXHIBIT

The model is an exact representation of the Enos School, except that the school grounds have been replanned to show the plans for the use of school playgrounds recommended by the survey. The model was made by children of the Enos School.

You pass the section on "Parks," glancing at the pictures and brief labels that suggest more use of the parks for holiday celebrations and organized sports, for you are a bit curious to know why so many people seem interested in lingering at the booth next beyond.

Full of novelty as well as of practical suggestion is this next section, which shows what Springfield does and fails to do to provide good times for its young people. There is always a crowd here and you have to wait your turn to see what is in that large mysterious box with an opening at about the level of your eyes. While you wait, you are attracted by the brightly lighted street scene at the back of the booth, and a moment's observation convinces you that here is a sensible and practical idea. After seeing the gay and inviting theaters, dance hall, and pool room flanking the dark and deserted church and school house, you read the question, "Why not light up the schools and churches for evening recreation?" and you echo, "Why not, indeed?"

But it is your turn to look through the peep hole of the box and here you see a toy model of a school room standing idle, just as all Springfield school rooms were doing at the time for eighteen hours of every day. Obeying the directions on the box to "switch the handle and see an empty school room changed to a school center," you see in the place where the empty school room stood an instant before a similar room with the seats pushed back and young people dancing or seated in groups. If you still have any doubts about the need for school centers, there is food for thought in the map of Springfield dotted over with pool rooms attached to saloons which are called "Youth traps in the heart of Springfield." And there is also the discouraging record of "Springfield's theatrical offerings" during two months when all but four of 401 performances were slap-stick, farce or burlesque and coarse, cheap humor.

On another panel, showing pictures of activities in school centers in other cities, you are reminded that, "In the movie you only *look on* at life. At the social center you yourself *live.*" So the street scene takes on new meaning as you see it again. But your attention will hardly fail to be called to this street scene also as a work of art. The ingenious and painstaking work of the art com-

WHY NOT LIGHT UP THE SCHOOLS AND CHURCHES?

The buildings in this street scene taken from the recreation section of the Exhibition were made in three dimensions by one of the local co-operating committees. No effort was spared either in color or in looking after its many details to make a faithful reproduction. Even the shadows of the dancers could be seen against the windows of the dance hall. The scene contrasted the motion-picture houses, dance halls, and saloons which were lighted up and inviting attendance with churches and school houses which were not being utilized as places for social life.

mittee in this scene well deserves your appreciation, for in color and in looking after its many details they have spared no effort in making it a faithful reproduction. You can even see the shadows of the dancers against the windows of the dance hall. And the crowds on the street, which are figures cut from magazines and painted, are by no means crude and unconvincing, as amateur work of this kind is likely to be. You cannot help having faith that the Springfield volunteers who worked so faithfully and well to present this recreation program to their fellow-citizens will not fail to see that it is carried out.

The Housing Exhibit

The last exhibit on this aisle is on Housing. There is one booth, and in the main the exhibit confines itself to one idea, namely, "Family Homes for Family Life." You may have some doubts that those models represent houses that would be safe out on the prairie. The roof of one is very insecure, and they all look as though even a light wind would blow them away. But the large and attractive photographs are perhaps convincing enough to offset the crudeness of the models—for along with the remarkable achievements of the volunteer organization you will observe, of course, that there was an occasional failure or part-failure.

Father Springfield is found here again and his counselor, the Owl, who warns against welcoming "Mr. Tenement" to Springfield. There are examples of evils that come in with multiple dwellings if citizens are not watchful, such as dark rooms, lack of fire protection, insanitary conditions, and the "borrowing of light and air from neighbors" by building on all of the lot. There are also pictures and facts about the bad housing conditions found among Springfield's colored population.

High School Printing and the Motion Picture Hall

Your floor plan shows you a small empty space at the end of the aisle. There is just room enough here for the high school boys to set up their printing press and show you what they can do. They are making themselves very useful to the publicity committee,

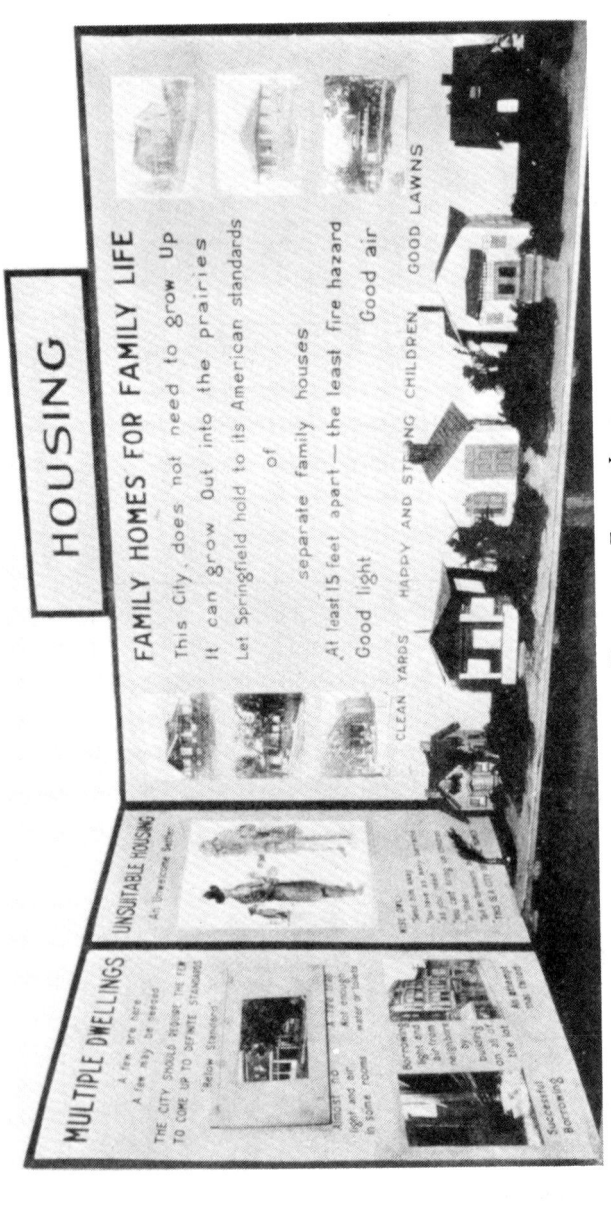

FAMILY HOMES FOR FAMILY LIFE
Father Springfield advises Mr. Tenement to settle somewhere else, as Springfield is a city of family homes.

for they are printing and distributing colored cards bearing such messages as:

*Please invite your friends to come
to the*
SURVEY EXHIBITION
and see the
SPRINGFIELD HIGH SCHOOL
demonstrate printing

Springfield High School Press

At this point in your tour you can either go into the motion picture hall or, if you are especially energetic and serious minded, you will scorn the movies and continue along the exhibit route. But, both as a rest from continuous standing and as a matter of interest, it is worth while to spend fifteen or twenty minutes here. It will be a welcome change from the scrutiny of still pictures and reading matter. Even if you are a movie fan you will not stay longer than this because the same picture is repeated at twenty-minute intervals throughout each session of the Exhibition, so that the picture may not compete with exhibits for your attention. A new picture is shown each afternoon and each evening. The subjects are in keeping with the survey topics, chiefly health, sanitation, safety in industry, and industrial training. Most of the few good films on civic and health topics available at the time will be shown during the ten days.

The films were collected by a business man who took the entire responsibility for this feature of the program. In the back of the guide book, among acknowledgments of contributions of "materials and professional services," you will find listed the Motion Picture Operator's Union, whose members contributed their services in showing the films for the entire period of the Exhibition. Before you leave the hall one of the directors takes a few minutes to invite the audience to bring or send their neighbors and friends to the Exhibition and to take part themselves in carrying out its purposes.

Milk Exhibit of State Department of Health

Leaving the motion picture hall, you find yourself facing the Milk Exhibit of the State Department of Health. This exhibit is more permanent in form than the other exhibits, for it was made with a view to touring the state after its display here. The model of good and bad dairies is made like a stage, set with miniature buildings, fences, wagons, animals, and farmyard in the foreground and a painted background of fields and trees. Below the model, all of the elements that go to making a clean milk supply for the city consumer are named on the links of a chain with the title, "The milk chain is not stronger than its weakest link." Facts about Springfield's milk supply are given on panels on either side of the model.

The Mental Hygiene Exhibit

Now you round the corner and start toward the front of the hall, coming first to the Mental Hygiene Exhibit. Here the facts are striking enough, but most of the panels have too many words and too few pictures. The amount of attention you give to this booth may depend on whether or not a good explainer is present. The "Kallikak family" is the conspicuous feature, with its sketch in color of the two lines of descendants of Martin Kallikak demonstrating the fact that feeble-mindedness is inherited. That, although insane persons are really sick, "Springfield does not treat them, but jails them," is illustrated by records of insane persons held in the county jail from one to even twenty days. The need of special classes for mentally defective children is pointed out in other panels.

In an exhibition on so large a scale there is bound to be unevenness in the quality of the work for any one of several reasons: the imagination of the "copy" writer and designer runs dry; or the execution of a good idea is bad; or the facts do not lend themselves readily to graphic forms; or, most commonly of all, the time for preparation is too short. But you do not think about why an exhibit looks dull; you merely give it a casual glance and seeing that it lacks color and movement you pass on, since there is much to see that does not make a severe demand on your attention. Fortunately, the Mental Hygiene Exhibit, which you have somewhat slighted, will get its full share of public attention later because of a political battle that is waging around some of the facts shown here.

The Health Exhibit

Five sections are devoted to health and, very naturally, the section on babies comes first. Flashing lights are used here, both to catch your eye and to make the facts more impressive. As you look at a large map of Springfield tiny green lights scattered over its surface flash up, and as they disappear tiny red lights appear in

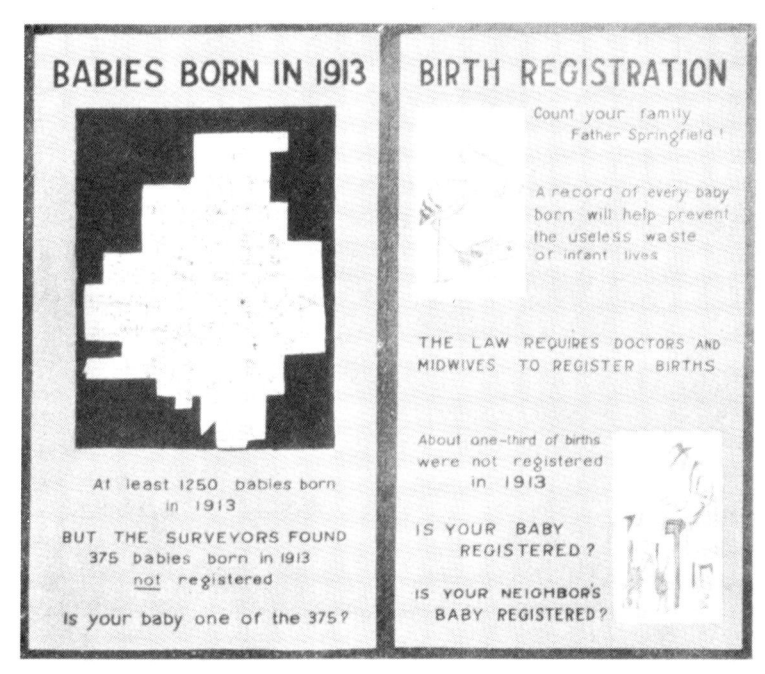

BABIES BORN IN 1913

At least 1250 babies born in 1913

BUT THE SURVEYORS FOUND 375 babies born in 1913 not registered

Is your baby one of the 375?

BIRTH REGISTRATION

Count your family Father Springfield!

A record of every baby born will help prevent the useless waste of infant lives

THE LAW REQUIRES DOCTORS AND MIDWIVES TO REGISTER BIRTHS

About one-third of births were not registered in 1913

IS YOUR BABY REGISTERED?

IS YOUR NEIGHBOR'S BABY REGISTERED?

BIRTH REGISTRATION
Three hundred and seventy-five unregistered babies found by the surveyors are placed on the map, and Father Springfield is warned to count his family more carefully hereafter.

other places. Then both green and red lights are flashed together. Each light represents the home of one of the 1913 crop of 1,250 Springfield babies. No really proud parent would care to be represented by one of the 375 red lights, for these stand for the unregistered births, nearly a third of the total.

At least 20 or 30 volunteers can claim a share in producing that interesting map. There were those who helped in the survey, examining church christening records, interviewing ministers and doctors, and following up various sources of information to find the unregistered babies. A group of patient high school girls dropped into the exhibit headquarters daily after school and punched holes and pasted green and red paper over them at points where the lights should shine through. When all this was done, electricians planned and set up the apparatus that would make the widely scattered green and red lights flash alternately and then altogether.

Next to the map is a panel with a headline reading, "Count Your Family, Father Springfield." One cartoon on the panel shows a row of storks bringing babies for the doctor and nurse to examine, and another shows Father Springfield industriously at work at an adding machine; and the caption says that a record of every baby born will help in preventing the useless waste of infant lives.

What happens to the 1,250 babies, registered and unregistered? That is perhaps the saddest story the Exhibition has to tell. Water-color sketches of ten winsome baby faces are grouped as you see them in the panel or page 373. One face is painted on ground glass, and the sudden flashing and gradual fading out of a light shining through the glass calls your attention to "the tenth baby" that does not reach its first birthday. On another panel there are photographs and explanatory statements to show how, by providing instruction for the mothers, the city could save many of these babies.

The remaining sections of the health exhibit will invite and hold your attention if you are interested in maps. The information on these maps explains some of the most important reasons why Father Springfield felt "all run down," as he told the Wise Owl. For these maps are really charts of Father Springfield's health, showing the weak spots in his system, and the reasons why they were serious liabilities and should be looked after.

There is much about the water supply and sewerage system. On a panel appropriately ornamented with two rows of shiny brass faucets (here the much maligned plumber made his contribution), is the reassuring statement that "Springfield apparently has on hand an adequate supply of pure ground water," but several improvements are needed, including protection

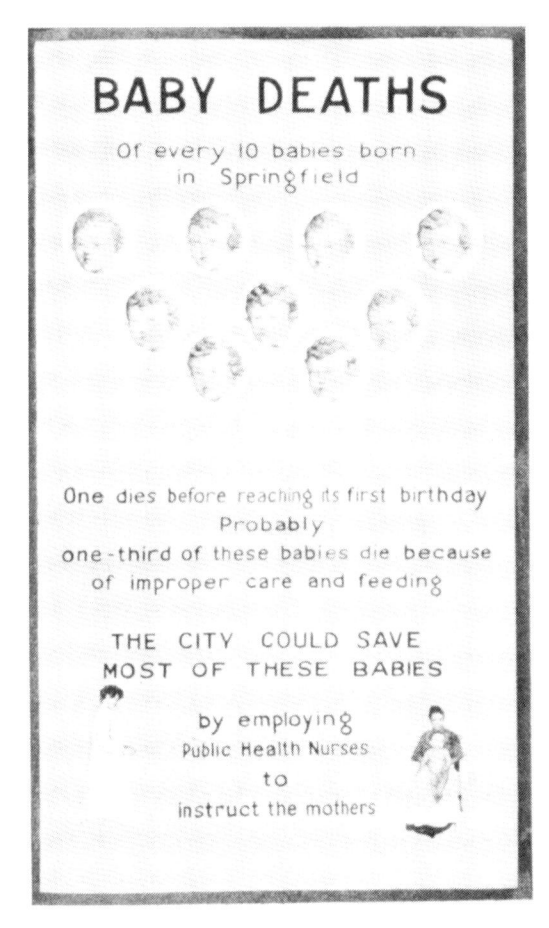

BABY DEATHS

Of every 10 babies born in Springfield

One dies before reaching its first birthday
Probably
one-third of these babies die because of improper care and feeding

THE CITY COULD SAVE MOST OF THESE BABIES

by employing
Public Health Nurses
to
instruct the mothers

THE TENTH BABY
The face at the bottom was painted on ground glass. The flashing out of a light behind this face at regular intervals called the visitors' attention to the fact that one baby in every ten in the city was not reaching its first birthday.

against the possibility of pumping polluted river water. Two relief maps in color show the sources of contamination of the Sangamon River which runs through Springfield. The maps were prepared by the State Historical Museum as a contribution to the Exhibition.

A section also is devoted to tuberculosis, the disease which was found to be responsible for more deaths than any other one cause. The exhibitors have made quite an elaborate attempt to show the battle against tuberculosis as a real modern battle with all of the community represented in fighting units. But perhaps those who collected the toys, the sign painters and other collaborators, did not have quite enough of the fighting spirit and so the battle may not thrill you as it should. This is indeed unfortunate, for the good work being done by the Tuberculosis Association, as shown in pictures and words, certainly needs and deserves the reinforcement that you might be persuaded to give.

The Playhouse

While you are viewing the health section you are on your way to the playhouse, and the amount of time you devote to health may depend on whether you are disturbed by the megaphoned voice announcing that the performance is about to begin. If you happen to be just a little early for a performance (given twice each afternoon and evening), you may be glad to rest here for a few minutes while an enthusiastic worker tells you about the playhouse. There are seats for about a hundred people, and the stage is built high enough so that all those who are seated and those who stand at the back of the pavilion can see.

Five different playlets are produced here with over 100 actors taking part. One young woman, recently out of college and with an abundance of energy and organizing ability, gathered together the players and with a few associates to help her, drilled them and provided costumes and stage settings. For some of the plays two casts were trained, so that it would not be necessary for any of the performers to appear for more than two or three sessions. It would be hard to say which was the biggest single undertaking of the many big feats of construction and management carried through by the Springfield people, but certainly the successful organization and management of the playhouse with its seven or eight groups of players made up of children, young people, and grown-ups was a big achievement all by itself. Not that there were not plenty of mishaps and the usual number of trying moments, but the percentage of smooth performances was high.

Plays Presenting Survey Findings

The playlets, all of them about fifteen or twenty minutes in length, were written especially for the Exhibition and dealt with conditions and recommendations contained in the survey. They were very simple and the moral always stood out frankly and boldly so that you couldn't escape it. Indeed, the intention was to make these performances little more than the acting out of

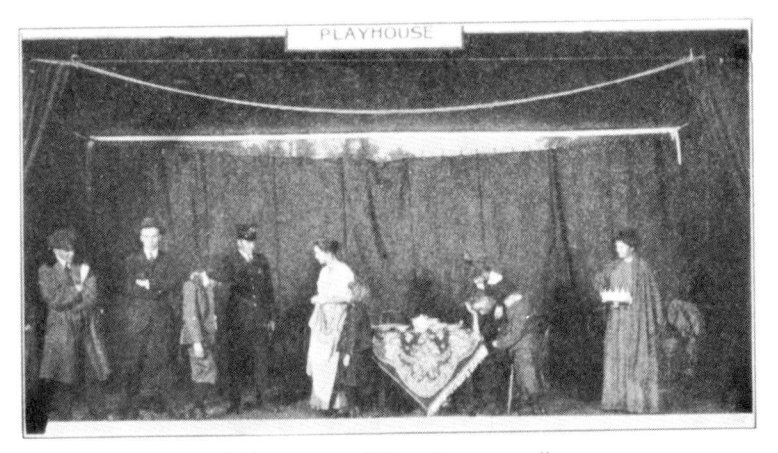

A Scene from "Two Birthdays"

Five different playlets dramatizing survey facts and recommendations were produced in the playhouse, with over 100 amateur actors taking part. "Two Birthdays" deals with the effect on the family of the irregular employment of miners. See page 147 for an illustration showing more of the setting of the playhouse.

some of the things the surveyors saw in the everyday life of Springfield people and the contrasted changes that might come about if survey recommendations were followed. For example, the play now about to begin is intended to boost the school center idea. The title printed on a placard at the left of the stage is, "Why the Gang Broke Up—A Pantomime in Five Scenes." The curtains are drawn back and the gang appears, looking very tough and evidently seeking trouble. A boy carrying a notice of the school center appears. The gang stop him, read his sign, hold a whispered conversation and start off, evidently bent on mischief.

The stage setting for this scene is merely a painted back drop showing an outdoor scene and borrowed from a local theater. By running a curtain in front of this drop an indoor setting for scene two was had. (These two backgrounds served for all of the five plays.) In scene two a gymnasium instructor and some boys are boxing and wrestling. The gang burst in aggressively and then stop short, somewhat surprised by what they see. Soon they are keenly interested, and one of the boys begins to strip off his coat ready to get into the game. Immediately the instructor shakes hands with him and invites him to come and join them. The other boys back off the stage trying vainly to take their companion with them. In successive scenes the fast dwindling members of the gang visit a dance, a rehearsal of a play, and a glee club—and one member succumbs to the allurements of the entertainment each time. This loosely built story made a good entertainment, and the very simple plot merely told in action what had already been told in printed words, pictures, and models in the recreation exhibit.

The plots of the four other plays are outlined in your guide book as follows:

The Playmaker

The school recess bell rings and boys come running out in a disorderly manner. Some stand around idly, others shout and run, and some of them are fighting. Then the playmaker comes and interests several different groups in games, until they are enjoying wholesome, lively, and worth-while play.

A Bundle or a Boost

Father Springfield, benevolent and kind-hearted, listens to tales of distress from the poor and gives them the things they ask for. Mr. Better Helper watches for a while, and then goes out to investigate the cause of their poverty and troubles and tries to remedy that. He refuses to give them baskets, but they are soon able to help themselves.

The Imps and the Children

The "Handicap Imps"—"Weak Eyes," "Sore Throat," "Can't Hear," and the rest—attack the unprotected school children, and glory in their success is a mad "Dance of the Imps." But when the school board is told how dangerous the Imps have become, they call doctors and nurses—"Test Tubes" and "Air Pumps"—and drive the Imps off in a patrol wagon. Then the children who have dropped like tired flowers, spring up and dance with gladness.

The Two Birthdays

There is joy in Mrs. Brady's little home for her Joe is a man with a steady job, and it is Tim's birthday, and Tim has won honors at school. But the mine closes, leaving Joe without a job. Mrs. Brady and Tim go to work, so that on Nannie's birthday the home shows neglect, the children have become unmanageable, and the purse is empty. At last, Joe gets a job that will support them until the mine opens again, and their troubles are over—for a while. So is the home affected by seasonal employment.

The Exhibit on the Correctional System

Following the arrow as you leave the playhouse, you come to the "Correctional System," an exhibit that has more dramatic interest than its dull sounding title would imply. Your first glance shows you a rather bewildering array of words, pictures, and devices, and many of the titles such as "Indeterminate Sentence" look rather technical.

If you were as docile in following directions as the exhibit planners expected you to be, you would begin at the left and read to the right, getting the story in its proper sequence and finding it, after all, easy to understand. You are not likely to do this of your own accord, however, being an average visitor. While you are trying vaguely to get some meaning out of it, an explainer comes to your rescue and gathers you and a dozen others into a group to be personally conducted through the section. You find yourself following with close attention his interpretation of the panels. He directs your thought first to the question, "Why are thousands of dollars spent each year for police, jails, prosecutors, and courts?" By way of helping you remember, you are requested to find the answer for yourself; and turning a handle on a disk you bring into focus out of a confused mass of letters this brief reply: "To protect the public!"

Well, you know you want protection for your family and your property. The explainer points to the next question, "Does Springfield's system protect?" It seems that it does not deter certain offenders from crime, and so it follows that it does not

BULL PEN VERSUS PRISON FARM

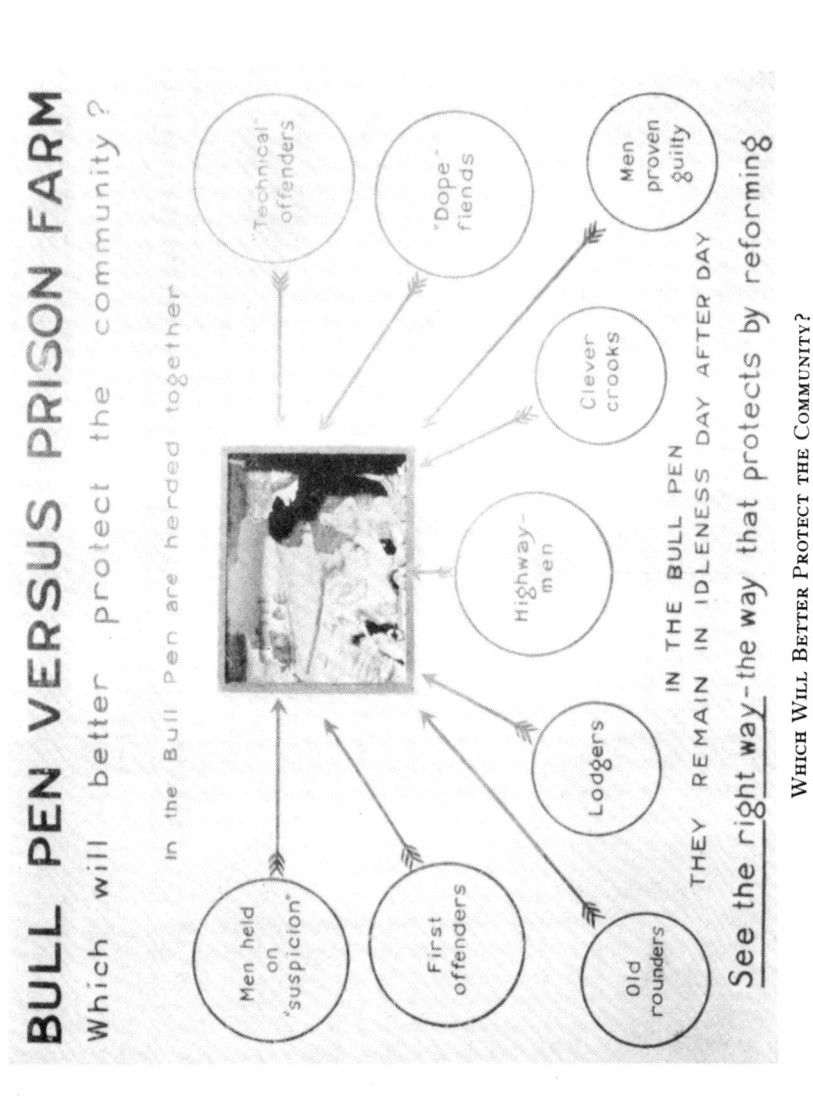

Which will better protect the community?

In the Bull Pen are herded together

- Men held on "suspicion"
- First offenders
- Old rounders
- Lodgers
- Highwaymen
- Clever crooks
- Technical offenders
- "Dope" fiends
- Men proven guilty

THEY REMAIN IN IDLENESS DAY AFTER DAY IN THE BULL PEN

See the right way—the way that protects by reforming

WHICH WILL BETTER PROTECT THE COMMUNITY?
A mechanical device revealing alternately a panoramic view of a model penal farm and a photograph of the "bull pen" in the Springfield city prison.

protect you. To make this point clear to you, you are first introduced to "the repeater." You see him repeating endlessly a tour of the same circle of court, jail, streets, and saloon. Springfield in a year has had over 1,400 arrests of these repeaters, for whom the correctional system has done nothing. The modern methods that do correct and prevent repeating are described and illustrated; probation, indeterminate sentence, and parole. Instead of these, Springfield has petty fines; 65 per cent of all sentences in one year were fines and many of these were only three dollars.

For those who go to jail and those held awaiting trial, the demoralizing jail conditions serve as anything but a corrective influence. If you will look at this picture of the "bull pen," which is a large iron cage where a number of men are confined together, you will know where to place responsibility for making repeaters of many first offenders. While you are looking at this photograph it moves upward like a stage curtain and reveals a pleasing scene, a landscape and buildings in the background and men working in the fields in the foreground. This is the prison farm, which you are told is "the right way, the way that protects by reforming." After a brief glimpse of this hopeful picture, the "curtain" is lowered and you are again faced with the reality, the cages, well called "bull pens," where men are herded together like beasts every day in your town.

You have seen how the adult offenders are treated. But what of the children? One booth is devoted to the methods of dealing with juvenile offenders. On one panel are the words "The Bad Boy—'What made him do it' is more important than 'What he did.'" A door mounted on the panel arouses your curiosity. Beyond this courtroom door, the explainer says, are found the things the juvenile court judge needs to know before deciding a case. He turns the door back, revealing pictures that suggest some of the causes of juvenile delinquency: a vicious home, bad companions, no place to play, and others. But the judge does not have these facts, or at least does not take advantage of them, as the story of one boy shows. There are four brief illustrated chapters to the story of "John, aged 12—Delinquent." Chapter One tells of a drunken mother and a neglected home; Chapter Two of John's petty offenses; Chapter Three of his being placed by the court on probation, under the control of his irresponsible mother. The last chapter is "Arrested again—What next?" The juvenile court system at present apparently has no answer to this question, so it seems that the courts are beginning with twelve-year old boys in the process of making repeaters.

But there is even more to the tale of this wrongly named "correctional system." Here is a cross-section of the county jail annex, showing its six rooms and five beds. One day's record shows that eight boys under seventeen, one girl under eighteen, four insane persons, and one case of delirium tremens were kept in these six rooms. You are invited to solve the puzzle: Can *you*, or anybody, distribute the 14 so that eight boys and one girl, or any of them, would not be demoralized?

When you come to the last panel the explainer leaves you and goes back to the beginning to perform the same service for the next group of visitors. How simple it all was to understand with his help, and yet he did little more than call your attention to

COUNTY JAIL ANNEX

WHO ARE KEPT THERE

Insane   Boys under 17
Delirium Tremens cases   Girls under 18

ONE DAYS RECORD
8 boys   1 girl   6 rooms
4 insane 1 "D.T."   5 beds

PUZZLE: How distribute the 14 so that 8 boys and 1 girl are not demoralized?

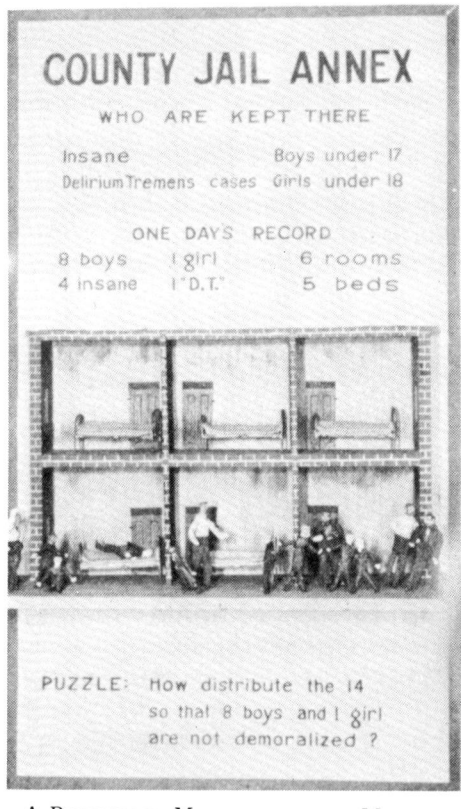

A PROBLEM IN MATHEMATICS AND MORALS

A combination panel and three-dimension model used in the Survey Exhibition for bringing home to citizens the demoralizing situation in the jail annex, where sometimes as many as 14 persons were held in the six rooms. In this case there were eight boys, four insane persons, one girl, and one suffering from acute alcoholism.

what was before you, contributing in addition his own enthusiasm for better methods of correction. He is a busy lawyer who is giving generously of his time to help Springfield citizens to see what the jails and courts which they never visit are like.

Many other volunteers have helped to make the picture vivid. The art committee produced that cleverly painted scene of the prison farm, the doll figures for the jail, and about a dozen cartoons that illustrated various panels. The model committee has made devices to work by hand or electricity, calling on carpenters, a manual training class, and electricians for contributions of service. The photograph committee has worked hard to get pictures that furnish clear evidence of the conditions that are described.

The Charities Exhibit

"Charities" comes next. Here, you are told first about what sort of a chance the handicapped have in Springfield; what happens to those who are in want because of illness, unemployment, widowhood, or desertion; and what sort of a substitute for family life is provided for children who for one reason or another are homeless. "What the yard stick says" is the title of a panel on which the care of dependent children in Springfield is measured by modern standards and found to be far from satisfactory.

It has seemed best to the surveyors, however, not to dwell at much length on what they have found in their study, but rather to take this opportunity to give you a brief and elementary lesson in the meaning of organized charity; and so half of the space is devoted to an exhibit of nine panels loaned by the Charity Organization Department of the Russell Sage Foundation. This exhibit gives in cartoons and a few words convincing answers to the usual criticisms made against organized charity. It makes clear something of the difference between "helping the poor *in* their poverty" and "helping the poor *out of* their poverty." A few people who are keenly interested in the charitable work of the city are making the exhibit the occasion for enlarging the circle of sympathizers, and though the crowd at this section may not be large, there are usually several there engaged in earnest conversation with the explainer, potential recruits, many of them, for the movement to put the charitable work on a sounder basis.

Now you pass around the end of the fence dividing the up-and-down aisles and you are started on the last lap of the tour. You pass somewhat regretfully the now deserted "coffee house," an attractively decorated and roomy space filled with chairs and tables. The only refreshments to be had in the evening are the boxes of home-made candy, which high school girls are selling to raise money for a school gymnasium. A placard announces that lunch is served at 25 cents,.dinner at 50 cents, and tea at 15 cents. The school girls who serve tea in the afternoon are now busy in the next booth showing the practical value of this branch of school work, and the spaghetti and tomato sauce that they are preparing certainly look appetizing.

The Government Efficiency Exhibit

City Housekeeping comes next, giving a bird's-eye view of city and county government. Just a glance at the titles bring home to you how much a matter of practical housekeeping city government is, and how important it is to the everyday life of all the people. There are panels among many others, on fire protection, garbage disposal, street lighting, trees, and pavements. Many accustomed inconveniences or dangers take on new significance by being taken out of their familiar settings and presented to you as matters that you as a citizen should take action upon. For example, that bad railroad crossing; the neglect of the valuable trees that are the pride of every citizen; the lack of a city system of garbage disposal. Concise and clear suggestions are given as to what to do about these things.

There is a map of the city spotted thickly with red arrows indicating the "jogs" in the street and the "dead end" streets which are a great nuisance to everyone. The map gives point to the cartoons on city planning, showing the old method of developing additions to the city in a haphazard way, in contrast with the new way in which Father Springfield is seen standing with his blueprint in hand directing the distribution of dwellings and factories and the opening of streets according to his well-thought-out plan.

There are other things here that you ought to know as a taxpayer. Space does not permit describing them all; but by a glance at random your eye is attracted to a subject to which you

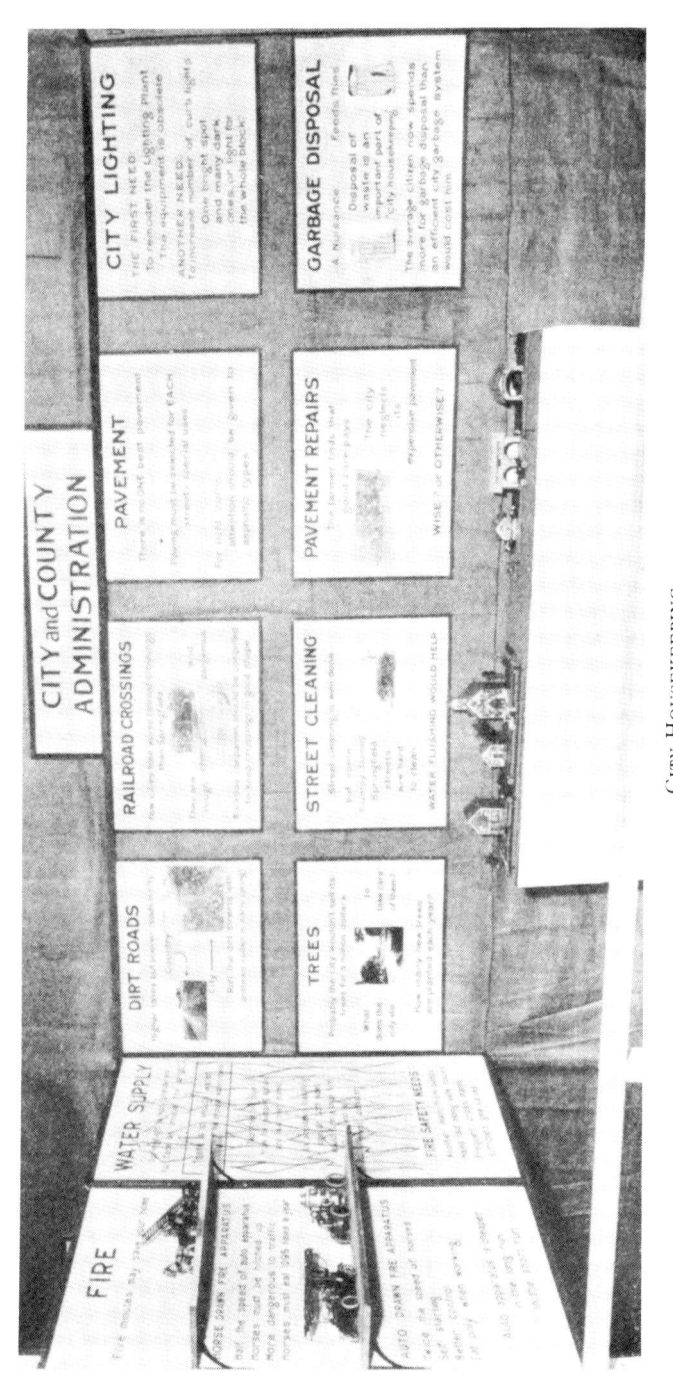

CITY HOUSEKEEPING
A corner in one of the booths of the City and County Administration exhibit.

have never given much attention. The method, or rather the lack of method, in buying city supplies is here illustrated. On a shelf is a row of five identical articles, each labeled with the price paid for it at retail. The prices vary from $2.75 to $4.00. The lowest price represents what the surveyors themselves paid at the nearest drug store. The other prices are taken from the records of city and county institutions. Any business conducted on as large a scale as the city government would have a central purchasing department; but in Springfield each department or institution head does his own buying, often at top prices.

The Industries in Miniature

You come now to a large booth more imposing than its neighbors. In large letters on the broad arch above the front opening are the words, "The Spring in Springfield." You look down at a miniature industrial city, its buildings ablaze with light. There are factories, stores, and office buildings and even a railroad with a train of cars making a continuous run on the track that loops the cluster. The walls of the booth are lined with panels, each carrying information about one of Springfield's industries. This exhibit is the contribution of the manufacturing and business firms whose names appear on the panels. Here you see something of the economic understructure upon which much of the city's life and future progress depend. The exhibition committee has not overlooked the advertising value of such a feature as this, for each model proves to be of interest to a large group of people who are workers in the particular plant so represented.

The Exhibit on Industrial Conditions

Next door to the industrial city is the exhibit on Industrial Conditions. You have seen the fine buildings and read the record of output and sales and of the excellence of the products. Now it is appropriate to give some attention to the workers in these plants. What of their working hours and wages? Do they have regular employment? Can they maintain a decent standard of living? Are their surroundings comfortable and safe? Are the children obliged to drop out of school to go to work at an early age? If you are eager to know these things you will not hesitate to tackle the rather heavily worded exhibit; but fearing that you might not be in a questioning frame of mind, the exhibitors thought it best to work out numerous methods of attracting and holding your attention. Thus if the exhibit seems dull in appearance, that circumstance is offset by the very "live" explainer who is usually present. Here a young poet of Springfield with a gift for picturesque expression and a real interest in the cause of the workers brings before you vivid pictures of the homes that fall below "An American standard of living." He shows you diagrams, figures, and statements that tell why.

INDUSTRIAL SPRINGFIELD IN MINIATURE
This booth represented in models of factories, stores, office buildings, and railroads some indication of the economic foundation upon which Springfield was being built.

One great cause of poverty, aside from the low wages paid to a large proportion of the workers, is irregularity of employment. The miner (there are over 2,500 of them in Springfield) earns as much as five and six dollars a day, but his yearly wages are likely to average about $500. The miners hold the center of the stage in this exhibit both because of the striking facts that are brought out regarding their working conditions and because of the ingenious device which lends fascination to otherwise dry statistics. A box about four feet high and six feet wide has on its face a chart showing "the working days in Sangamon County mines" during one year. Those miniature miners that you see following a path up and down across the chart are attached by a wire to the electric motor which keeps them continuously in motion. Each worker reaches the top of the employment peak in October when he has twenty days of work, and from that irregular time on he continues down hill to almost total idleness.

"The law aims to protect growing children" is the heading on another panel. Below are silhouettes of 55 children with dinner pails. These are the working children found in a brief search by

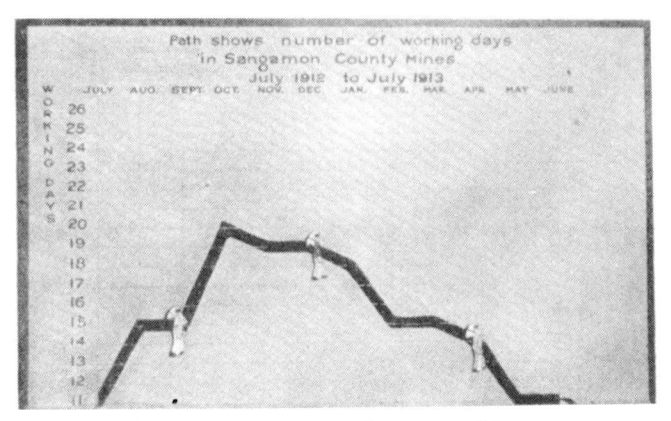

SEASONAL EMPLOYMENT AMONG THE MINERS

The curve, showing the working days in the mines of Sangamon County during the last year before the survey, was represented graphically in the Exhibition by this device. The course of employment was represented by a path traveled up and down and across the chart by these miniature miners attached to an electric motor which kept them continuously in motion. See page 385.

the surveyors. Only twelve of them were obeying the law as to the hours of work. As to hours for grown-ups, the figures for 72 establishments show that 85 per cent are working nine or more hours a day, also that organized workers are far ahead of unorganized workers in securing better hours.

THE LAST WORD SECTION

Beyond the Industrial Exhibit is a large open space invitingly furnished with chairs, tables, rugs, and palms. Here you may drop in for the "last word" before you go. You have spent perhaps an hour and a half traversing the length of the hall four times, but it is still early and you may as well respond to the invitation on a placard to "Rest a Minute." Another says, "Attend the Silent Lecture on Next Steps." A variety of ways to spend the time here is offered. You may talk over what you have seen with your friends; or you may sit down at one of the tables where pencil and paper are provided and write one or more questions about things that were not made clear; or there may be sug-

THE "LAST WORD" SECTION
Here in a large open space invitingly furnished with chairs, tables, rugs, and palms, the visitor might stop for the "last word" before leaving the hall. Opportunity was thus afforded for talking over what had been seen, learning of follow-up plans of the survey, asking questions, and offering suggestions.

gestions that you care to offer. These may be dropped in the question box and you will find the reply in one of the morning papers the next day. Or you may join the group standing around a leader mounted on a chair and bring your question into the discussion that is going on there. Once or twice every evening impromptu meetings are held here. Sometimes questions found in the box are read and someone especially qualified to answer them is placed "on the stump"; more often questions are asked from the floor. Always the meeting breaks up with an urgent request to send your friends and neighbors to the Exhibition.

Then there are survey reports on the table; four of the nine sectional reports are in print, and you can look them over here or buy them to take along home.

But the "Silent Lecture" is the most important feature. A series of lantern slides describing the follow-up plans for getting results from the survey are shown on the small screen that you see in the back of the room. The lecture was planned as a silent one, but it was found much more successful in holding interest to have a member of the committee talk with the slides. On the slides a scheme of organization of a citizen's committee is outlined and offered for criticism and amendment. Above all, the aim is to get citizens to join in taking over the survey as an enterprise that they are from now on to be responsible for. It is thus hoped that, in leaving, visitors may feel some impulse stirring to carry out the "co-ops' oath," displayed on a placard in this room, which reads:

> "We will transmit this city greater, better, and more beautiful than it was transmitted to us."

Attendance and Methods of Securing it

The "average citizen," through whose eyes you have seen the Exhibition, was one of about 15,000 who came during the ten days of the show. The sort of people who made up this audience and the methods by which they were recruited are much more significant than the numbers. The group of promotion committees made it their business to see that every interest in the community and every neighborhood should be well represented.

That nearly everyone in Springfield belonged to some organization was evidenced by the "directory of organizations," a card catalogue in the exhibition office which contained the names of 400 local organizations. That meant that for every 150 men, women, and children in Springfield there was one club, a church, society, lodge, union, parents' association, or a literary, musical, athletic or social club. These groups were bombarded from many angles. Ten-minute speakers attended their meetings and explained the plan and purpose of the Exhibition. About 25 speakers were kept busy in this way for a month. The committee on co-operation invited the groups to appoint co-operating committees to represent their organization in all relations with the Exhibition. These co-operating committees were also offered their choice in a long list of assignments of special work that their organization might undertake, thus bringing them still more closely in touch with the Exhibition. The special-days committee asked them to name the day and hour when their group would attend in a body. If desired, any club could hold its regular weekly or monthly meeting in a room at the Exhibition set aside for this purpose. They could come for luncheon, tea or dinner. When all these arrangements were carried out, attendance was further aided by the announcement in the daily papers each day of the organizations expected on that day.

Most of the larger organizations responded to these invitations and many small ones. The Ministerial Association, Knights of Columbus, Rotary Club, Bar Association, Eastern Star, and several church and literary societies were among those which held luncheon or dinner meetings. On these occasions a member of the Exhibition executive committee outlined the plan for follow-up work. Some immediately offered to co-operate, and others agreed to devote a session to some phase of the survey later. The Catholic societies came in such large numbers that they filled the hall one evening. Missionary societies, organizations among the colored people, the medical and dental societies, supreme court judges, and many lodges also came for an afternoon or evening. "Labor Day" was the afternoon of Thanksgiving Day, and many of the unions turned out in full force.

The efforts of the promotion committees spread far beyond the city. A county committee carried the news through public addresses and other methods to the rural districts. One Saturday was "County Day," since many farmers would be in town then and the rural teachers could also come in. The committee on out-of-town organizations worked chiefly through letters. At the committee's suggestion the chamber of commerce sent messages on its own stationery to similar organizations in all towns within a radius of one hundred miles inviting them to send delegations. Similarly, the mayor wrote to other mayors; the superintendent of schools to other superintendents; the club women to other clubs; and so on. Many individuals and some officially appointed delegations came in response to these letters, and the visitors' book showed names from towns scattered over the whole state, and indeed, from a number of other states.

School Children at the Exhibition

The educational value of the Exhibition for the school children was fully appreciated by the school authorities, and the advertising value of their attendance was equally appreciated by the publicity committees. The morning hours from 10 to 12 each day were given over almost exclusively to the children from the fifth grade up through the high schools. They came by classes, in charge of their teachers, and were received by members of the parents' associations from their own schools. These reception committees brought the parents' associations into direct relation with the survey, and also added a neighborhood interest to the many other group interests represented.

As the children knew that they would be expected to write up the Exhibition afterward, they came as reporters looking for a story. Two sets of prizes for the best essays on the Exhibition, one for grammar school and one for high school students, had been offered by a citizen who was especially interested in the teaching of civics in the schools. Many of the children were eager to win a prize.

An excellent plan was devised for getting rid of confusion both in the touring of the hall by the children and in their search for material that they could describe. The children of each school as they arrived went directly to the motion picture hall where they saw a one-reel film and then heard a five-minute talk on how to see the exhibit. Bits of red ribbon had been attached to the exhibits that would be of special interest and value to them, and they were told to look especially for "red ribbon exhibits." Needless to say it required no labels to attract their attention to the models, the pictures in color, and the moving devices. Compositions written later showed not only that the flashing and moving objects had caught their eyes but that they had understood and remembered the ideas so conveyed. A further detail of the arrangements that saved a great deal of time and confusion was the method of distributing the children around the big hall. When they left the motion picture hall they marched in double files until they were spread out over the entire circuit. Then the order to halt was called out and they broke ranks, going thus in small squads to the exhibits nearest them. After that they moved around the complete circuit just as all other visitors did.

Each child was delegated as a special messenger to carry the news of the Exhibition to his parents and neighbors. These 5,000 bearers of news were probably the best single advertising agent the Exhibition had.

Newspaper Publicity and Advertising

Although the attendance was promoted chiefly through the personal efforts of committees in setting aside special days, writing letters, giving talks, sending messages by the children, and getting the Exhibition widely talked about, this personal effort would have amounted to little if it had not been backed by generous newspaper publicity and advertising. For several weeks a continuously swelling volume of news in the four daily papers gave evidence to the readers that the Exhibition was the event of the hour, that it was enlisting the real enthusiasm of a great many citizens, and that it was something quite different from anything Springfield had ever seen before. Not only in the news columns, but in club notes, society column, and on the editorial pages the survey and the Exhibition had conspicuous place.

Three papers carried special features of their own. The State *Register* published the "Survey Question Box" on its editorial page for about ten days. Questions of all kinds about the survey and the Exhibition were invited by this department, which was edited by a local journalist with the help of exhibition directors. The State *Journal* carried several signed articles by local writers on such topics as health of school children, playgrounds, and printed comments on the art and other aspects of the Exhibition. Other series were planned for other papers, such as "Why Teachers should See the Exhibitions" and similarly, why lawyers, parents, business men, ministers, and others should go; but they were not carried out.

Paid advertising was not used very extensively, partly because the funds were not available and partly because the local committee placed much reliance on the effectiveness of the free publicity secured through news and personal efforts. The city was well placarded with window cards, and large illuminated signs were displayed in windows at several of the busiest corners. A good four-page folder containing the floor plan of the Exhibition and a list of attractions was very widely distributed. A leaflet was used in the campaign to secure workers and subscribers to the Exhibition budget, and a window card called for volunteers. It cannot be said that any of this material was particularly distinctive, however. Perhaps the best advertising was secured by the committee on advertisement mention, which did its work so thoroughly that more than half of the local advertisers in daily papers carried an announcement in their own ads of the Exhibition one or a number of times for almost two weeks.

More effective advertising undoubtedly would have increased the attendance. But the limited amount of money and service that it was possible to secure was probably much better invested in the personal work of committees directed toward obtaining a widely representative attendance.

Spirit and Value of the Volunteer Work

We have reviewed the Exhibition as a picture and as an event which reached practically every household of the city with the survey facts. But, for permanent value in getting action on the survey recommendations, the bringing together of a large body of exhibition workers was at least equally important.

When the exhibition project was launched about one hundred were actively interested in the survey. At the close of the Exhibition at least a thousand people had taken some part in presenting the survey to their fellow-citizens.

It was as much a part of the exhibition plan that work should be found for volunteers as that tasks should be accomplished. The scheme of organization devised for carrying on the enterprise is chiefly interesting for the way in which it provided for getting the essential work done by people of known ability, and for extending indefinitely the opportunities for service that would help the

THE SURVEY EXHIBITION

Exhibition if carried out and not hinder it if omitted. A small and energetic executive committee took the entire responsibility for the project and worked closely with the Exhibition director in the administrative work. Four of its members headed the four groups of committees into which the forty were divided and were responsible for getting the work done in each group. These leaders did their work so well that the director was left free to give much time to making plans, meeting emergency situations, and advising with committees about all sorts of details without carrying the whole burden of the administrative machinery.

Committee work was made more efficient also because the advance plan, which was turned over to the executive committee at an early stage in the preparations contained a brief typewritten statement of the assignment for each committee. Such an outline was prepared for each of the forty committees.[1] In addition, there was always to be found at headquarters a list of special assignments that any group of volunteers might undertake. These usually went to the co-operating committees already referred to as a feature of the promotion work. For example, one woman's organization came in as a co-operating committee and took entire charge of a rest room which was maintained for women and children and for workers at the Exhibition. A club of high school girls took charge of the sale of guide books.

Another feature of the committee plan that was of importance in paving the way for future co-operative effort was the way in which the committees were made up. "A Census of Useful People" was the title for the card list of names which was prepared and classified according to the ability and interests of about 700 men and women. The committee chosen to make up this list included a member of the school board, a labor leader, a minister, a business man, a lodge member, and enough others to insure a committee having wide acquaintance among people of a great variety of interests. This census was used by the committee on committees, whose work took about a month.

The activities of committees were made as interesting as pos-

[1] Eight of the committee outlines used in Springfield are reproduced in Appendix B, beginning on page 199, of The A B C of Exhibit Planning, by Evart G. and Mary Swain Routzahn, Russell Sage Foundation, New York.

sible both to the workers and to the public. A large vacant store in an excellent location was secured for headquarters. A great many people passed and stopped to wonder what was going on, for at most hours of the day there were meetings at several of the tables scattered over the large room; and many office helpers were seen addressing and stamping envelopes, clipping newspapers, and coming and going on numerous assignments. The broad display windows were used for posters and announcements and there was always an invitation to come in and learn about the survey.

Perhaps the most useful experience for future work in using the survey data was given to the explainers' committee. The chairman of this committee was responsible for selecting, training, and supervising about one hundred men and women to act as interpreters in each of the exhibit booths. The explainers were grouped in sub-committees, one for each topic, and they were selected, as far as possible, because of their interest in and general knowledge of their topic. Each group met once or twice to learn what the exhibits would tell. Several meetings of all explainers were held to discuss methods of attracting and holding the interest of visitors; and the chairman toured the hall frequently during the Exhibition to see that her helpers were taking the initiative in getting attention for the exhibits and not waiting for visitors to ask questions.

Finally, a feature of the organization work which tended to bring about that esprit de corps so much needed in getting results from the survey was the series of three rallies held at times when there were good reasons for bringing the workers together. About two weeks before the Exhibition opened, a committee rally was held to spur the workers on to a big final effort. Spirited talks, refreshments, and practical information about the progress of the project were the ingredients from which new enthusiasm was created at this meeting.

On the Saturday night preceding the formal opening of the Exhibition a private view was held to which were invited 1,500 workers, public officials, reporters, teachers, ministers, and all others who in any way had helped or would be expected to help in making the show a success. This occasion was a fortunate one

THE SURVEY EXHIBITION

in stimulating the get-together spirit. As everyone expected to come again they did not examine exhibits in detail, but obtained a general impression of the thing as a whole and spent the evening in meeting friends and rejoicing over the general attractiveness of the hall, the fine attendance on this first occasion, and other indications of a satisfactory opening. The hospitality committee, whose members had worked many hours in compiling the list and getting out invitations, received the visitors.

The third rally came toward the end of the Exhibition. It was a dinner meeting of explainers and all others who had taken any part up to this time or were ready now to join in the plan of follow-up work. Vachel Lindsay, writing of the Exhibition, said of this dinner:

"The most contradictory factions in the town were represented at the explainers' dinner the last evening. There assembled here people destined to take opposite sides in many a future argument or political campaign. If there was as much faculty for co-operation among hostiles in the whole nation of Mexico as there was under that arsenal roof, there would have been a government down there some time back. This spirit of co-operation showed itself early in the survey and was not confined to the local workers —residents of Springfield."

APPENDICES

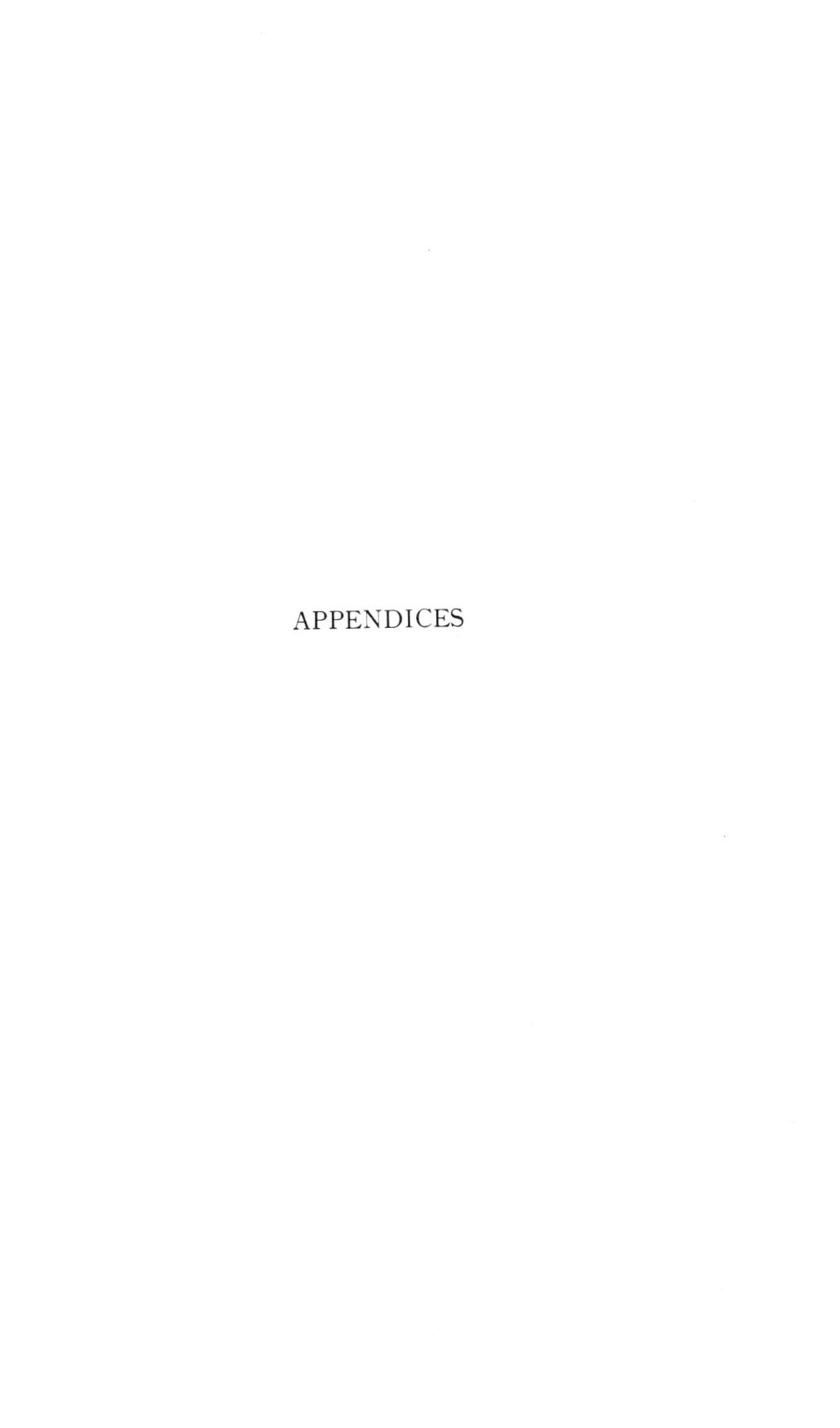

APPENDIX A

RESULTS OF THE SURVEY

The question is often asked whether surveys such as this one made in Springfield actually lead to constructive action; whether results in fact did follow in Springfield. It is a fair question; but, as has been pointed out in Chapter I, instead of attempting to answer it ourselves by making up a list of developments which appear to have had their beginning in the survey, it seems better to take the answer from the testimony of citizens of Springfield —particularly since a number have expressed themselves on the subject and since, also, their statements were not made at our solicitation. The statements came into our hands after they had been given out to the public. They are printed, except for the letter of inquiry and the reply, in the order of their dates.

I

RESULTS OF THE SPRINGFIELD SURVEY[1]

By A. L. Bowen

Executive Secretary, Illinois State Charities Commission, Springfield, Illinois

The results of any great campaign are of two kinds: the tangible and the intangible. The intangible results of the Springfield survey are worth more to our community than those which we can actually see with our eyes or touch with our hands. I would say a new community conscience, or perhaps more truthfully an aroused and stimulated community conscience, is the most noteworthy effect of the survey. Our attitude of a community toward all questions affecting its well-being has radically changed. We see new meanings in them and react to them in a different manner. Our sense of duty in many cases where it formerly would have been dormant, now asserts itself and prompts us to action. There is a new spirit in our work. Our ideals of humanitarianism have undergone revolutionary process. All this has occurred quietly, gradually, and we have been almost totally oblivious to the changes.

[1] From an address on this subject delivered at the City Conference of Charities and Corrections, held in Springfield, March 17–19, 1916, as reported in the Illinois State *Register*.

The survey has taken from us at least much of our smug provincialism, that notorious state of mind and attitude which regards those things which we have created or possess as right, correct or perfect, and the critic of them as a rogue and public enemy. The greatest obstacle to any progress is this provincialism—known to some as loyalty to home and local pride. With this complacency and satisfaction which we feel in our own possessions and prowess there is always present the spirit of abuse for those who try to reveal these faults or failures, or deficiencies against which we have closed our eyes.

A community has won a victory over self when it becomes able to stand criticism of its own institutions and habits and to change them to meet the ideas of constructive critics. It is difficult to look at a competitor and acknowledge that his methods are better than ours. We frequently refuse to do so, even though we lose by it.

Narrowness was Evident

When the first survey report arrived we immediately began to display to the world our narrowness of vision and character. Dr. Ayres told us some unpleasant things about our schools, and at once we ruffled up our feathers and began to denounce him as an unmitigated defamer of our fair name, an enemy of Springfield, and withal a long-haired reformer and a short-haired liar. Unfortunately there are some among us who are still in this frame of mind. But it is to the everlasting credit of our city that we had a few present with sense, poise, and courage sufficient to march heroically to the front, to demand that this report be read and studied dispassionately. It is susceptible to proof, they said. We can determine whether he has told the truth. We can compare ourselves with others and decide whether other cities are getting more for their money or are spending more money to get more than we have.

The agitation was short lived. We found that Dr. Ayres had not lied about actual conditions. We made comparisons with other cities of our class and we have found we do not have all that we should have, and we have begun to acquire them. And we are going to continue the acquisitionary processes until this city has a complete, modern, up-to-date school system, capable not only of absorbing the good ideas that others originate but competent to contribute to the world some original ideas. We must do this because neither capital nor labor will settle in a community whose educational system is not fully abreast of the times.

Each Brought its Flare

So one after another the reports came in, and after each one there was a flare-up. They were not altogether complimentary. They did reflect upon us. Our correctional system, our poor farm, our jail and city prison, our poor relief, our associated charities, and the rest of our institutions suddenly took on a sacredness undreamed of. Before, we had considered them first class, veritable world beaters. But we had been measuring them by a rule which we had made ourselves. We were judging them by the amount of money we were putting into them and not by the quality of the work they were doing. This gave us excuse to flatter ourselves with our gross and vulgar liberality.

Among the tangible results of the survey, some are directly due to it. We can hardly say that the closing of the segregated district was a direct effect, but we know the survey attacked this infamous evil and presented its wrongs so vividly that it must have made a deep impression. It must have been responsible in large degree for the creation of that public opinion so necessary in uprooting an institution forty years of age.

We know that there is better spirit of co-operation among all our private agencies and between our private and public agencies. This meeting and the organization of the Central Conference of Social Agencies are sufficient demonstration of the new spirit. I feel that there is better feeling between our local welfare organization and our city and county officials. The old distrust of each other has passed to a large extent, and it is well that it has. The agitation for a new jail and the demand for facilities whereby petty offenders may be treated and cared for in a better institution than a jail are valuable, not only to our county alone but to the whole state. There is some difference of opinion among us as to just what should be done on the jail question, but we are a unit that our system is wrong. It is going to be changed. Whether we make the change as a county or wait a little for the state to assume its duty, the main point is that the change is coming and the survey may be directly credited with our new interest.

We Know Our Needs

We have been awakened to the need for better attention to our insane.

There is a marked improvement in our handling of children in the courts. Our juvenile detention home has been greatly improved, and our juvenile court deserves credit for the many progressive methods it has adopted. Undoubtedly good may be expected from improved means of garbage and sewage disposal. This problem is a long ways from solution, but it is noticeable that there has been serious consideration of it within the past year. We find our milk dealers appealing to the public on the cleanliness, purity, and freshness of their supplies. Our milk situation is far from satisfactory, but the survey and the exhibit inspired some of the dealers with a new idea.

Our school system has undergone many changes for the better—junior high school, new high school building, new buildings in the districts; more attention to fire protection, health precautions, ventilation, and sanitation;

the use of the buildings as social and civic centers, as meeting places for pleasure, education, political discussion, and the like; night schools for adults for the time being suspended for lack of funds, and many things yet undone because of no funds but agreed by all to be necessary functions of a complete school system; as well as special classes for backward children, vocational schools, continuation classes and open-air school rooms, and a wider and broader use of the physical plant. Perhaps someone will say the survey deserves no credit for these, but we must not forget that what has actually materialized, has materialized since the survey report. Prior to that time we had talked about them. The survey gave them a shove across the line.

Charities Work Improved

The work of our Associated Charities has taken new directions. Let me just mention this fact as a complete proof that something has happened. Last year we had difficulty in raising $2,500. This year we have already raised $4,000 and will gather in $5,000 before its close with no more labor and anxiety than was expended the year before.

It is more than a year since the survey was made, yet today we are just beginning to understand its importance and magnitude, just beginning to feel some of the beneficial results and to see some of its immense possibilities. It is to remain with us permanently, to prod our conscience, a light to our feet and an inspiration to our effort to make Springfield the best place in the land in which to live.

II

WHAT IS A SURVEY?[1]

HOW SPRINGFIELD, ILLINOIS, FOUND OUT

By Grace Humphrey

Springfield, Illinois

When the general manager and directors of a factory realize that things aren't going as well as they might and their score is below one hundred per cent, they summon an efficiency expert to go over their plant from A to Z. This may be a task of weeks or months, for it involves a careful study of conditions in workrooms and office and selling force, of raw materials and finished product, of insurance and welfare work. Then comes his report, pointing out the weak spots, making definite suggestions for improvements, the next steps to be taken immediately and others to run over several years.

[1] Reprinted by permission from *The Outlook* (New York) of December 27, 1916.

The same thing can be done for a community, which is only a factory of another kind, for its product is citizens ready to do their work in the world. Their one hundred per cent depends on schooling and public health and recreation, and all the other things that go to make up living conditions in a town.

Reporting on a community is called a survey, and one has recently been made in this country that bids fair to become the standard. The place was Springfield, Illinois, in many ways a typical American city.

* * * * *

It is impossible in so brief an article as this to tell the fascinating story of each of the nine lines of work studied—schools and recreation, housing and charities, public health, the administration of city and county, corrections and the care of mental defectives, industrial conditions—in its entirety a more complete community study than any previously attempted in America. But one story is more or less typical of the others, just as the time and money expended for one is an average for them all. So here only one of the reports is considered, the subject of greatest importance perhaps to the entire population of any city—its schools.

For education in Springfield is one of its big industries, though we seldom think of school and factory as being in the same class. But count all the children, the teachers, custodians, office forces, and board of education, and you have the amazing total of nearly twelve thousand persons, more than half the number engaged in all the industries of the city. One out of every five persons in Springfield is directly concerned in education, to say nothing of parents and employers.

Indeed, the survey was in part a result of the community's interest in school questions, suddenly aroused when the last census put Springfield into the class of cities electing their board of education, the electorate in Illinois including both men and women. Elections were lively affairs, widely discussed and argued, with sometimes as many as forty-seven candidates, to choose seven serving without pay!

There were the most conflicting beliefs about the schools, some insisting that Springfield had every right to be proud of them, and they wouldn't hear of any hint to the contrary. Yes, if they'll hold their own in comparison with other cities; but do they? was the reply. One group pointed with self-satisfaction to the new buildings, for which so much money was being expended, while the next questioned if they were fully up to the highest modern standard of construction and equipment. And still others asked if perhaps the work in the schools ought not to be readjusted to the changed and changing new generation.

But every one felt that spending forty-five cents of every dollar of taxes was none too much if forty-five cents was coming back in education; for Springfield is proud, and for its children the best is none too good. In fact, said some, we pay for the best; are we getting it? Let us have a survey.

So in 1914 Dr. Leonard P. Ayres, with his five assistants, spent ten weeks on Springfield's schools, studying, comparing, interpreting, recommending. And his report, containing both diagnosis and prescription, was eagerly awaited by the entire community.

For the board of education he suggested a simplification of work. Meeting for several hours almost every week, each member serving on at least three committees, a large part of their time was given to petty details that should be looked after by superintendent and principals. They, not the board, should discharge a janitor, decide about new geographies, transfer teachers, change ventilation and heating systems, buy supplies, make repairs, determine as to adjustable desks and how often to oil the floors, and all the thousand and one little things that are matters of school housekeeping or questions needing special professional knowledge.

More and more the board should act, says the report, like the directors of a great corporation, putting authority on their general managers. This change was made almost at once, and the result in these two years has been all that was anticipated and more. Principals and superintendent accepted the extra responsibilities, and the time of the board has been freed for big questions—bonds, new sites, building plans, extensions of the school system, needed legislation.

A change making little difference on the surface? Perhaps; but it has meant less work and worry, it has lessened the danger of petty politics and personal influence, it has greatly increased the efficiency of all concerned. And this is one instance in the survey where it takes an outsider to point out the underlying difficulty, suggest a remedy, and show how to carry it out.

As to the children, whether they were in school or not, there was nothing to judge by at the time of the survey. Springfield pays for a school census every two years, but it gets one that fails to answer fundamental questions though the city stands near the head of the list, in Illinois, for illiteracy. An efficient school census, says the report; and to insure attendance a trained truant officer with some social service experience.

The census has been replanned, and a trained woman is looking after the boys and girls who "play hooky." And not only are the working certificates for school children now given under a new system, as the survey recommended, but there was all last summer an employment bureau managed by a committee of teachers; and here Springfield has gone one step beyond the report, which pleases no one more than the surveyors.

A special study was made of the misfit children—those over age, those extremely retarded, those who drop out of school the minute they are thirteen years old. In a list of thirty cities Springfield ranks above the average in its low percentage of these "specials"; but there are nevertheless a thousand of them, and for their care two special classes are to be started this winter, lessons for the most part individual.

To prevent the leaving school, which occurs much more among the boys than the girls, the surveyors looked into the course of study to find its weak spots. Much of it was behind the times, artificial, unrelated to the needs of real life. And, as proof of this, a most amusing section of the report tells how the experts prepared from their 684 class room visits short examinations to see whether or not the upper grades were being taught what is actually used by able business men in Springfield. These tests in spelling, history, arithmetic, and geography were given to eleven of the most prominent and successful citizens. And the lamentable and laughable result of those examination papers has made over the course of study. For the marks showed between the work of the school and the work of the world little intimate relationship. This is changed now, and the course of study is being made—*being* made, not *was* made—not by the board of education but at conferences joined in by all the teachers of a grade, principals, and superintendent. And this is true for grammar schools and high schools.

High schools? you ask. Does a city of sixty thousand have more than one? Springfield does now, thanks to the survey. And so enthusiastic was the community in putting into effect the recommendation for the junior high schools, so enthusiastic has been the response of pupils and teachers and parents, that it has been said that these schools alone are justification for the survey.

It has always been true in Springfield that the high school cost more per pupil, and for many less children, than the grammar schools. Instead of having eight and four year systems, try the six-three-three plan, with intermediate groups called junior high schools, of seventh, eighth, and ninth grade children, said the report. This gives a special kind of schooling for the difficult adolescent period, with a fine chance for vocational training for both boys and girls. And it is especially wise for Springfield now, when the high school is overcrowded. Ninth grade children remain in school, in their own communities, and when the break does come, changing to the senior high, it is accompanied by no break in studies.

This worked like a charm in the three junior high schools organized in the city. One outlying district, generally sending one or two children to high school, graduated 19 on a Friday at the end of January, and on Monday the whole 19 turned up for high school work!

Regarding vocational training, Springfield's greatest need is for the boys, and this could be given in the junior and senior high schools, using for its material all the kinds of work involved in maintaining the school buildings—painting and carpentry and plumbing, electric wiring for lights and bells, steam-fitting, tin-work and masonry—vital and fascinating work because it is real, instead of formal and artificial exercises assigned in the school shops. It is an economical plan, using the $9,000 of manual training salaries and the $22,000 for building maintenance, this fund having just now an ample margin.

The plan fits in with manual training classes as at present organized, with part time and continuation classes in the senior high school. If work in the school buildings gives out, playgrounds and parks, hospitals, and children's institutions could furnish more. There are limitless possibilities!

But the plan has not been adopted. Perhaps it seemed too great a departure from the old system to let a boy help the plumber during school hours and count it as school work. But manual training and domestic arts teachers are more than doubled in number since the survey, and perhaps unconsciously they are doing this very thing.

Last year one group of boys made boxes and chests of drawers for the baby welfare station and nursery in their school. The girls made the curtains and kept them laundered. One class made steps for the auditorium platform, a ladder for the motion picture booth, and the framework for the curtains over the semicircular windows. This last item proved the survey correct as to economy, for the curtains cost ten dollars less than the lowest estimate from a downtown store!

Another school made most of the apparatus for a playground that is one of the indirect results of the survey and a good illustration of community action; for this summer of supervised play was financed by the Woman's Club and carried on in a school yard; the boys of the neighborhood did the work and received in return a recommendation in both school and recreation reports.

In any factory it is the little leaks that spell inefficiency; and one of the valuable parts of the report are the many suggestions for little things which in the past meant waste but may be easily corrected; such things as that the filing system in the main office is needlessly complex, that few towns spend so much for supplies, and recommending a businesslike way to remedy this and save money; that class rooms and corridors and coat rooms have waste space, with the result that Springfield's buildings are fifty per cent larger than those of other cities for the same number of children.

It is a little thing, perhaps, to point out that coat-room hooks and blackboards and seats should have some reference to the size of the children using them; that there should be no running in fire drills; that all outside doors should have "panic bolts"—preventions of tragedy; that the lighting in class rooms is below standard in amount; that just two rooms have windows at the left only, these same windows being washed twice a year in some schools, twenty times in others. But it is the little things that count in school housekeeping.

You ask, however, is there nothing found satisfactory in Springfield? Indeed, yes; scattered all through the report you will find emphatic indorsements and little pats of approval, on which parents and teachers and children and board may justly pride themselves; classes averaging only 36 and no part-timers; high promotion rates; friendly relations between pupils and teachers; discipline good; writing and spelling up to the average of other cities, though the arithmetic is done more rapidly and less accurately; efficient collection and accounting of funds; and board members unsparingly generous in the time and attention they give, "their altruistic interest and personal self-sacrifice" being "splendid and valuable assets to the city."

But the surveyors did not go to Springfield with any idea of bestowing only approving nods, enlarging on the good points or work already well begun. So these statements are briefly put, and almost every one is followed by some little recommendation for still better results in the future. The school nurse is entirely competent and devoted to her work, but has more to do than one person can do thoroughly. Springfield needs three nurses and a half-time doctor; why not have a competent physician for this and the municipal work, as suggested in the public health report? The city now has an extra nurse.

Bubbling drinking fountains are a credit to Springfield, but place them in the corridors, not in the toilet rooms as in some schools. The generous grounds are another score in Springfield's favor; but unless they are used after school hours, Saturdays, and in the summer they are a costly investment lying idle. The surveyors would have been delighted to see the supervised play carried on in five schools last vacation.

And the buildings themselves should be used more. Well, in these two years the branch libraries have increased to eleven, all in schools, and five hundred books circulating in a month is a frequent occurrence. In one week last spring there were no less than seventy-five meetings held in the schools, and in not one was there any disorder—meetings for debates on municipal questions to be submitted to the voters, pre-election talks by the city commissioners, mothers' clubs, even elections! Aside from the economy, polling places in school houses have helped the community.

"If you could know what this district was like before!" said one principal. "They used to drive right up to the door with their carriages of voters, half of them drunk. But last election there was nothing like that, and I heard one fellow advise the others, 'None of your rough stuff here—our kids are having school upstairs.' "

But how, people frequently ask, is the expense of carrying out the survey recommendations to be met? Increased taxation? Impossible for Springfield, already taxed to the limit. A survey is all wrong if it tells only how to spend money—anybody can do that.

Here the cogs do not fit exactly; they can be made to fit. Try this. There oil is needed; spend money for your oil but make sure you have the right kind for this particular machine. And there is not, in the whole survey, one wild guess, one chimerical recommendation. On the contrary, there is a list of ten cities that have tested this plan and found it good, and there is a list of states that have passed this law and tried it out.

Many of the school suggestions finance themselves, especially if you put two and two together. Springfield could balance the additional nurses against bookkeeper's and attorney's salaries, two offices to be abolished. You can secure a trained truant officer for no more wage than must be paid the policeman whose job it formerly was to round up truants. And one item could be met by adopting the suggestion that the county treasurer turn over each month the school funds collected, that the board may have the interest on these balances. The building suggestions are, for the most part, minor in cost but all-important in prevention and good housekeeping. Not increased funds, but increased diligence from building committee, architect, and parents' clubs, making impossible in the future waste space, badly drawn specifications, and the paying of Springfield's good money for what was never obtained.

The new buildings cannot be charged to the survey, as they were all under way or planned before. But the junior high schools can, legitimately, for the high school is still overcrowded and more teachers are employed. But just as two neighboring towns may have an enormous disparity in tax rates, where one gives remarkable parks and free lectures and music and clean streets and good water, and the other none of these, but a man locates in the former because he gets his money's worth from his tax, so in Springfield the people are getting something for the junior highs in that children go to high school who never went before, and children who dropped out are staying in school.

One of the things traceable to the survey but not suggested by it directly, is the establishment of bank accounts for school children. Begun by four banks at the request of the superintendent of schools, 1,314 children (17 per cent of them all) now have accounts which last June totaled the sum of $38,156. The Commercial Association became interested, and has offered two cups to be awarded twice each year to the schools with the largest percentage of children depositing and the greatest percentage of increase.

Does it pay the banks? No; in not one is the extra clerical expense met by the extra interest on deposits. But wait a decade or two until these youngsters now getting acquainted with the bank become investors and borrowers. "And this isn't wholly selfish," commented a bank president. "Children who failed to form the right habits at home, and the saving habit is one, used to be at a disadvantage all their lives. Now the community is trying to balance things up, to give the handicapped child a show. And in this savings habit the banks of Springfield are doing their share."

These are but a few of the tangible results that can be pointed out. But still more important are the intangible ones summed up in Springfield's new view of things. Not only is the taking of the next step made easier, but in those instances where the survey recommendations have been discussed and rejected or where to date nothing has been done the city finds it impossible to go back to the old standards, to have the old indifferent spirit about the community's work.

Perhaps Springfield hasn't a new conscience, for it must have been some vague stirrings of community conscience that made the survey wanted; but it has been aroused and stimulated. In the survey and its follow-up work Springfield has resolved that the community "shall have under God, a new birth of freedom." And this not for themselves alone but for the other Springfields, the 26 that share its name, and the 196 that share its problems and opportunities.

III

SPRINGFIELD SURVEY DEVELOPMENTS[1]

By Reverend G. C. Dunlop

Rector, Christ Episcopal Church, Springfield, Illinois.

Springfield has undergone a social awakening in the last eight years and has made more progress during that time than at any other period in the city's history, Rev. G. C. Dunlop, rector of Christ Episcopal church, declared last night in his farewell sermon. Rev. Dunlop will leave Springfield January 31 for Cincinnati, where he will take up new religious duties.

He referred to the survey of the Russell Sage Foundation as an event which roused and quickened the dormant life of the community to do things never before tried in Springfield. The speaker said in part:

[1] Farewell sermon as reported in the Illinois *State Register* of January 29, 1917.

THE SPRINGFIELD SURVEY

What Pastor Said

The progress of this community in the past eight years has been truly remarkable. I began with seeing the city in the depths—in the hands of rioters. I now see it scaling the heights. The city of Springfield in these years, I venture to say, has made more progress than in all the previous years of its existence. There is no other city of its class in the Middle West that can begin to show a corresponding awakening of the civic conscience and the realization of so many dreams of social betterment. The outstanding fact is the social survey of the Russell Sage Foundation, noteworthy not because of what has been accomplished but because it aroused and quickened the dormant life of a somewhat ultraconservative community.

Sees Better Springfield

It took us out of the flat existence of our prairie life and carried us up to the higher levels to give us the vision of a new and better Springfield. It stimulated our interest in constructive social work and encouraged us to believe that what has been done in so many cities could readily be brought about here. The value of the survey lies not so much in what has been done but in the spirit which it generated—in the social awakening which has taken place.

Forerunner to Survey

There is to my mind, however, danger of being puffed up when we talk about the net results of the survey. Like every great and good movement it had its forerunner which helped to make it possible. We had sanitary and housing surveys before the Sage survey was contemplated. Good work has been done, as, for example, the closing of the saloons on Sunday, the purification and increase of the city's water supply—work which had no relation to the survey whatever.

After all, our best asset has been our leaders, all Illinois and most of them Sangamon County men who saw visions, dreamed dreams, and had the audacity to work out what they saw and the courage to fight for the defense of that for which most of them had sweat blood. So seven years ago this city acquired the first real health officer; but to bring about milk inspection and all the other good things which he accomplished as the pioneer of a better Springfield he had to stand his ground against most offensive opposition.

Has Praise for Sheriff

Then comes a man who, as sheriff, wipes out the red light district. At once every abuse is heaped upon him. His very life has been threatened on more than one occasion. Again, one of the best servants of the people is forced to defend his progressive policies as superintendent of schools, and fight a group of reactionaries who want economy at the expense of efficiency.

It is manifest, therefore, that the city is blessed with leaders of no ordinary intelligence—men of courage and strength of character. What is to be done with them? Stifle their convictions, persecute them, block them at every turn? The thing is impossible. Springfield is not going to slap her prophets.

Wants Preachers To Act

And in my humble opinion it is the duty of the preacher, if he claims kinship with these modern prophets as he does those of Israel's day, to make their cause his cause and the cause of his church. We have read our Bible to little purpose if we cannot preach social righteousness and give strength to a group of men who would help to make our city one wherein dwelleth righteousness.

IV

SOME OUTCOMES OF THE SPRINGFIELD SURVEY[1]

By George Thomas Palmer, M.D.

President of the Illinois Tuberculosis Association; President of the Illinois Public Health and Welfare Association, Springfield, Illinois.

In the social and civic development which follows a general community survey it is very difficult to determine how much is to be attributed to the survey itself and how much is to be credited to the progressive spirit which, among other things, made the survey possible. The very fact that a community realizes the need for a survey indicates that that community has experienced a considerable degree of social and civic awakening and, whether the survey comes or not, that community will be very likely to go ahead progressively and more or less in the right direction.

And so, in enumerating the things which have occurred in Springfield during the past two or three years, and bearing in mind what has happened there during the past ten years, it is quite impossible to determine which of these things are directly due to the more recent Springfield survey and which of them would have occurred without the survey.

For a number of years there had been growing a spirit of civic unrest—a desire for better things—an interest in sounder methods for solving the community problems. The survey was one of the products of this unrest. The advent of the surveyors did not terminate this temper of the people. It

[1] Presented at the Second Annual Better Community Conference, Urbana, April 10, 11, and 12, 1917.

stimulated and increased it. We believe that the survey rendered its most useful service in directing the energies of an already awakened people along the soundest and sanest lines of action.

The benefits of the survey have proved greatest, of course, to those organizations which felt most keenly the need for the survey and whose officers and directors were instrumental in bringing it about. That these organizations felt the need for the survey does not imply that they needed reorganization and reform more than others. In fact, I think the contrary is generally true.

The Springfield survey and its influence upon the community cannot be fully appreciated without some knowledge of the things which went before it—the gradual awakening of the town to its civic needs.

Only a few years ago Springfield was stumbling along with the community equipment common to most mid-western, overgrown towns. Generally uninterested in social progress, most of the citizens went calmly on with the assumption that the local conditions were quite as good as they need be. The schools were better than some and worse than some. The sewer system, which had followed the natural gullies and ravines with the same foresight that was used when the streets of Boston followed the cow-paths, sent off sewers in all directions with a polluting outflow at seven different points near the border of the city. A cigarmaker held the job of health officer; saloons operated on Sunday in violation of the state law but with the sanction of the city officials; a red light district stretched along the streets traversed by the incoming passenger trains of four railway lines, the houses so boldly labeled that there could be no doubt as to their character. Shallow wells and privy vaults were unrestricted in spite of the fact that the city had expended almost five million dollars for sewer and water supply. Typhoid fever prevailed to an inexcusable extent and a shabby pest house opened its inhospitable doors to those sick with communicable diseases—a pest house perched on a hill with the open town branch sewer on one side and Oak Ridge cemetery on the other, with nearby slaughter houses and rendering works making their presence known to the afflicted.

A struggling associated charities was attempting to meet the needs of the people under the direction of a volunteer worker. There was no public hospital; no general dispensary; no tuberculosis dispensary; no visiting nurse service; no school nurses; no infant welfare work; no tuberculosis sanatorium, and no bed for the tuberculous except at the poorhouse. The poorhouse was worthy of its name. Thus, ten years ago, Springfield slumbered: prosperous, indifferent, corrupt, and contented.

The social development of Springfield since that time appears to me to be intensely interesting, its most interesting feature being the gradual but definite change in the attitude of the people toward community betterment.

Hard-headed business men, who once believed in relegating all relief and social work to women and yet who frowned upon giving women the legal authority to better local conditions, are now serving actively on the boards of the charity organization, the tuberculosis association, the day nursery, and similar organizations.

Perhaps Springfield's first step forward came with the creation of the park system which, with only a few pages of blackened political history, has always been the source of the utmost pride to the people. The wise expenditure of large sums of public money for playgrounds, parks, drives, golf courses, swimming pools, amusement halls, and flower beds was Springfield's first step in the line of social progress.

The upheaval in the Springfield health department through the employment for the first time of a medical health officer, who served with the pay but without the authority of a uniformed policeman, was perhaps the second step and the one which led directly to the survey which we are considering today.

Milk inspection was established; quarantine laws were enforced, at times through the prosecution of physicians; analyses of public and private water supplies, made at public expense, led to the discovery of the great soil pollution of the community and pointed out the need for a sanitary survey.

This sanitary survey, now referred to as the old sanitary survey of Springfield, soon attained nation-wide repute. In a way it set a pace in sanitary work of the smaller city, and it gave to the people of Springfield their first idea of studying their own living conditions. Incidentally, a report of the old sanitary survey appeared as an important part in one of the first publications issued by the Department of Surveys and Exhibits of the Russell Sage Foundation, which was later to have so much to do with the extensive surveying of Springfield.

The old sanitary survey awoke the people to the serious sanitary conditions of the city; impressed them that they had a real housing problem, real slums, and deplorable lodging houses. Further, it seemed to stimulate social activity in almost every direction. Following, or coincidental with the sanitary survey, as the case may be, a tuberculosis association was organized with general visiting nurse service and a dispensary. A detention home was established under the jurisdiction of the juvenile court. A trained worker was employed by the associated charities. Then, with increasing rapidity, came a day nursery, a probation officer, a general medical dispensary, a tuberculosis sanatorium, school nurses; the establishment of schools as community centers; the Sunday closing of saloons and the abolishment of the red light district; the improvement of conditions of the almshouse with provision of humane care for the destitute sick.

THE SPRINGFIELD SURVEY

As to what started this interesting procession of civic progress, what continues its force and gives promise to its future, it is entirely impossible to say. Whatever the part played by the first sanitary survey, whatever the part played by the larger and more recent Russell Sage survey, the important thing has been the rapidly developing spirit of the people, the rapidly growing army of citizens marching steadily onward and upward. It is this spirit, which has been in process of development for about ten years, which makes it exceedingly difficult to determine just what influence any single event has had in the social history of the town.

During that time certain fundamental changes have come in the community which have had much to do with shaping the course of events. The city has adopted the commission form of government with more centralized responsibility of public officials. More important, women are voting in all municipal elections and are serving on the board of education. The voting of women goes further in altering the social and civic complexion of a community than any other single thing.

Then, too, Springfield has been singularly favored by the presence of a few strong individuals who have done things far in advance of public demand or public sentiment. Conspicuous among these is Sheriff John A. Wheeler who, single-handed, wiped out the red light district and brought about the Sunday closing of saloons, and thereby brought upon himself the wrath of many godly but conservative business men and the full wrath of the ungodly. As a matter of good measure, Sheriff Wheeler has added the employment of the first, or one of the first, women deputy sheriffs in the state.

Conspicuous also is Willis J. Spaulding, who set out years ago to secure an abundant and pure water supply for the city and who has attained his purpose. Conspicuous also are a few others who fearlessly, enthusiastically, and alone have been piling up civic assets for Springfield, often in the face of public opposition.

And out of all these things, marking an era of social awakening, the Russell Sage survey came to Springfield—the most noteworthy of Springfield's community achievements—crystallizing the restless spirit of progress and directing it along the best and most promising lines.

A survey is not self-acting. It is a picture of the community—not a still picture, but a movie of a community living and at work. It shows imperfections and perfections with equal fidelity. It neither overcolors nor undercolors. It is neither yellow in its criticism nor all pink in its praise. And the Russell Sage people took the movie of Springfield as accurately as the well-focused lenses of men could get it—as well as the camera of their minds could interpret it, and they printed the picture as well as the pens of men could draw it.

SURVEY RESULTS

But after the motion picture is completed and the artists have pointed out the important parts of their picture and what it means to the experienced eye, the survey is finished. It is up to the community to get the value out of it—to act upon its teachings. And it is very likely that the community which has not been sufficiently interested in itself to actually want a survey will derive very little from it. The sleepy lad, forced to church by parental authority, does not absorb much from the sermon.

But Springfield, with its preceding years of awakening social conscience, had wanted a survey. Groups of people had gotten together to consider the matter. Finance had been discussed, and even a program had been outlined with the assistance of Sherman C. Kingsley and other social and medical experts. At this juncture it was found that we could secure the co-operation of the newly created Department of Surveys and Exhibits of the Russell Sage Foundation, under the direction of Shelby M. Harrison, whose interest in Springfield had been aroused by the pioneer sanitary survey.

The Springfield survey was financed by private subscriptions; by an appropriation by the board of education for the school survey; by an appropriation from the city council, and by a liberal grant by the Russell Sage Foundation. In all, the expenditure for the survey and the exhibit which followed it, exceeded fifteen thousand dollars.

The investigations were divided into nine general groups: Schools, by Leonard P. Ayres; Recreation, by Lee F. Hanmer and Clarence A. Perry; Housing, by John Ihlder; Care of the Mental Defectives, Insane, and Alcoholics, by Dr. W. M. Treadway; Public Health, by Franz Schneider, Jr.; Corrections, by Zenas L. Potter; Charities, by Francis H. McLean; Industrial Conditions, by Louise M. Odencrantz and Zenas L. Potter; and City and County Administration, by D. O. Decker and Shelby M. Harrison.

The work was done in the creditable manner to be expected of this notable group of workers, and the results have been published in nine pamphlets supplemented by a tenth volume: The Survey Summed Up, by Shelby M. Harrison. All are now published except the report on City and County Administration by Mr. Decker, and Mr. Harrison's summary.

Incidentally, the association of this group of experts with those engaged as professionals or volunteers in the various phases of social work in Springfield was of the utmost value to the community—a beneficial phase of the survey which is not appreciated as much as it should be. It must be borne in mind that each of these surveyors spent at least several weeks in Springfield, while some of them were in more or less direct contact with the community for over a year.

As I have intimated, those organizations whose officers and directors were most intimately associated with the inception and carrying out of the survey have been the ones most benefited, not because there was the slightest discrimination in favor of any lines of work, but because these particular organizations have utilized the survey recommendations more thoroughly ana more conscientiously.

The charities survey has produced most excellent results. Mr. McLean has kept in close contact with Springfield, and Miss Margaret Bergen, one of Mr. McLean's most valued assistants, has been in charge of the Springfield Associated Charities for the purpose of reorganization. This has resulted in great improvement in methods; in closer co-operation between the various private relief agencies and between public and private agencies; placing-out work initiated in the Home for the Friendless; the organization of a central council of social agencies and a cosmopolitan directory including all social, religious, and racial classes of the city.

Among the more recent achievements of the Associated Charities has been the taking over of the material relief formerly carried by the tuberculosis association and the employment of a visiting housekeeper. Miss Bergen is also responsible for the organization of a club of the professional social workers of the city for exchange of ideas and better mutual understanding.

Perhaps the most significant thing in the development of charity work in Springfield was the willingness of the community to pay the relatively high salary for expert service naturally required by a woman of Miss Bergen's reputation and the general opinion that this expenditure is a good community investment.

The schools of Springfield have been directly benefited perhaps more than any other civic agency through the survey. The superintendent of schools, who has been one of the most conspicuous figures in the social advancement of the city, together with members of the board of education, including women of broad viewpoint, had urged the appropriation of school funds for the school survey with the idea of deriving all possible practical benefits from it. The board has, consequently, made the best possible use of the recommendations. While some of the survey recommendations have not been accepted as practical, there is no question but that Mr. Ayres' investigations and advice have been of the utmost value. The school board committees have been reduced to a practical working basis; the junior high school plan has been adopted and four junior high schools have been established; a modern high school building is being erected to accommodate 1,500 pupils; lighting, ventilation, and general sanitation of schools have been improved; a special supervisor of buildings has been employed, and school buildings have been very generally employed for social centers, as meeting places for parents' clubs, and for political meetings and polling places.

The employment of dead time for public good in our expensive school property I regard as one of the big results of the survey. It is to be regretted that a similar use of the dead time of expensive church property for public good could not have come out of it.

But the Springfield schools have had other improvements since the survey. The number of teachers in manual training and household arts has been doubled; the school census has been revised to secure more valuable information; the standards for principals and teachers have been raised and a salary schedule has been adopted based upon efficiency; seven branch public libraries have been established in the schools and the general course of study has been modernized.

The citizen of any community will find much to interest him in the Springfield survey school report, and much benefit will come if he will take the findings and recommendations and apply them to his home town.

If the entire expenditure for the Springfield survey had been charged to schools and charities, the results would have proved the investment exceedingly profitable. Yet it must be borne in mind that the officers and directors of the associated charities and the members of the school board were among those who especially wanted the survey and who made the most out of their recommendations.

It is difficult to measure exactly the benefits derived from the survey on recreations. The park board was already extending its means of public amusement at the time the survey began, and it is possible that the survey has not caused the program of the park board to be advanced more rapidly than it otherwise would have been. On the other hand, the far-seeing recommendations of the survey may have justified, in the eyes of the board, more liberal expenditures and longer steps forward than they would otherwise have regarded advisable.

Following the recreation survey, however, one of the most notorious of the old-style burlesque theaters, purveying wine, woman, and song as it is seldom done in this generation, has modified its methods of operation until it is no longer an open scandal. Municipal dances, adequately chaperoned, have filled the great state armory building. A board of censors of moving pictures has been created by the city commissioners and has been given limited power.

A director of recreation, advised by the survey, was employed by the board of education, but the position has been abolished.

The housing survey has served to accent and give publicity to those glaringly bad conditions which were brought to light during the old sanitary survey, but which the people had apparently forgotten. It is not improbable that the housing survey report may be instrumental in aiding the passage of a state housing bill, similar to the excellent laws of Indiana and Minnesota, now pending in the General Assembly. It must be borne in mind that there is no organization especially interested in bettering the housing conditions of Springfield, and it must be recalled that a survey is not self-acting.

For the corrections survey to claim credit for the unusual personal accomplishments of a very exceptional sheriff is hardly fair. Whether one is for him or against him, it may be said by all that Sangamon County had never had a sheriff of this particular kind. He has voluntarily refunded to the county the profit on the dieting of prisoners which former sheriffs put in their own pockets. He has closed the red light district. He has appointed a woman deputy sheriff to deal with women and children. He enforced the state law closing saloons on Sunday. He has been active in attaining the wonder of wonders—the making of Springfield dry. And yet for all of these things I believe that we must credit the eccentricity of a man who determined to observe his pledge of office and who had the courage to carry out his determination in the face of powerful opposition.

But these things have occurred since the survey. How much inspiration Sheriff Wheeler received from the survey no one can tell. In addition, however, two more probation officers have been appointed, the detention home for children has been improved, and the city has established a farm for its prisoners.

I approach the subject of the health survey almost with reluctance. The survey itself was carried out by Franz Schneider, Jr., with the utmost skill, and his recommendations, if followed, would have placed Springfield far ahead of most Illinois cities in health administration. The presence in Springfield of Dixon Van Blarcom, who had charge of the tuberculosis survey, gave an opportunity for an interchange of ideas which did much toward bettering the methods of warfare against tuberculosis. It is a rather delicate matter for me to say, as I am compelled to state if I touch upon the matter at all, that health administration in Springfield has not improved since the survey.

The establishment of a free general dispensary, under the supervision of the city physician, illustrates as well as any single thing the change in sentiment of the people of Springfield. Ten or more years ago, when such a dispensary was suggested by Dr. Charles L. Patton, Dr. Don W. Deal, and myself, the storm of protest it aroused in the medical profession was insurmountable. A year ago or less this excellent dispensary was established, with an expenditure of $10,000 from St. John's Hospital without a word of protest.

This dispensary and the establishment of child welfare work with a nurse employed by the city, mark practically all of the progress Springfield has made in public health since the time of the survey. If anything, the health department has shown distinct retrogression.

In saying this of the administrations of my friends Dr. Griffith and Dr.

SURVEY RESULTS

Deichmann, I want to add that the failure of the Springfield health department points out one of the glaring defects of the commission form of government. This form of government places the health department under a commissioner of public health and safety who is likewise charged with the police and fire departments. Regardless of its actual paramount importance, the health department is almost invariably the third in consideration in this group. The competent health officer is placed on the plane with the fire chief and the chief of police and yet, because he can be slighted without protest from the hard-headed citizen, his appropriations are never comparable with fire and police appropriations.

I do not believe that there can ever be a really efficient health department operating under the present Illinois commission form of government law. I could not serve under it, Dr. Griffith could not serve under it, and I feel quite sure that Dr. Deichmann will not try to serve under it long. The idea of complete subordination of a competent medical officer under a superior officer without the slightest vestige of medical knowledge is intolerable. That is why the Springfield health department has failed—survey or no survey.

Evanston is the only Illinois city under commission form of government which has risen above this condition, and that was through a violation of the spirit of the law. The north branch of the Chicago Medical Society concluded that no member in good standing should serve under an unschooled commissioner of public health and safety, and through the guidance of Sherman C. Kingsley, then an alderman, an arrangement was made whereby the health of the city should be governed by the commissioner of public health and safety, the health officer who had equal authority in matters of health, and the mayor as the third person in the event of disagreement.

And now, to return to the survey. No one can measure the influence of the Springfield survey on the people of the community. That will be told in coming years. For those who were sufficiently awake to civic needs to actually want the survey, sufficient returns have already come. Springfield is ahead in dollars and cents and in better civic conditions. But I cannot resist the feeling that the survey performs its greatest good in outlining the course of communities that have already had their first civic awakening; by directing the course into safe channels of those communities so thoroughly aroused that "they don't know where they're going, but they're on their way."

V

A LETTER INQUIRING ABOUT RESULTS AND THE REPLY

Joliet, Illinois, March 10, 1916.

*Mr. Victor E. Bender, Sec'y,
  Commercial Association,
    Springfield, Illinois.

Dear Mr. Secretary:

Your city some time ago had a survey under the direction of the Russell Sage Foundation.

Joliet is interested and would like to have some information from you as to the value of the survey results.

As a commercial organization proposition, would you let me hear from you as soon as you can just how your business men regard this survey?

I am co-operating with the Ministerial Association in an effort to determine on a survey, and if such is to be handled here it will more than likely be under the auspices of the Joliet Association of Commerce.

I desire the fullest information and data on all angles of the survey so that our board of directors may act intelligently in the premises.

Yours very truly,
WILLIAM KENNEDY, Secretary,
Joliet Association of Commerce.

March 25, 1916.

Joliet Association of Commerce,
  Joliet, Illinois.
    Attention Mr. William Kennedy, Secy.

Dear Mr. Kennedy:

We received in due course, your letter of March 10th in reference to the survey made in our city two years ago by the Russell Sage Foundation of New York. I have been somewhat delayed in replying, as I wished to discuss this matter with some of the people who were particularly interested in the survey and instrumental in having it put through.

The idea of having a survey of the important facts of civic and social conditions in Springfield originated with two or three persons in this city about three years ago, as they realized some of our faults, as in school conditions, recreation facilities, health conditions, etc. As a result of this, some of those interested asked Mr. Shelby M. Harrison, Director of Department of Surveys and Exhibits of the Russell Sage Foundation, to come to Springfield and make a preliminary investigation, which he did two years ago in November. As a result of his suggestions, a committee of twenty-three persons, called "The General Survey Committee," was organized, and this committee raised a sum of something over $6,000 to defray the cost of the survey in the various lines as finally determined upon.

The field work of the survey was carried out during the spring and early summer of 1914 by investigators of the Russell Sage Foundation, including

SURVEY RESULTS

several of the best known experts in the United States in their various lines. The work of tabulating and publishing all the results of the survey has not yet been finally completed, but I may say that we have now received reports as noted on the enclosed slip, and expect to receive within the next month the final reports on industrial conditions in Springfield and on city and county administration.

As you will note from the attached slip, giving the list of reports, practically every phase of municipal activity has been covered except city planning, and this was omitted only on account of lack of funds.

The first report received was on the public schools, this having been issued in June, 1914, immediately following the field work. I think I can safely say that as a result of the school survey and the suggestions therein contained, more improvement has been made in our schools, including the introduction of special medical and dental examination of children, the junior high school system, etc., than we have had in many years before. Equally important improvements have already appeared and are now appearing as a result of the survey on recreation facilities, on public health, on the correctional system, and on charities.

I might add that aside from the money raised here, the Russell Sage Foundation contributed about an equal amount, realizing as they did that this was the first complete survey of a typical American city of average size and therefore laid the foundation for similar surveys in other cities.

Following the survey, we had an exhibition in the State Armory here, in November 1914, which showed in graphic form by means of charts, diagrams, models, and playlets, the important and vital facts brought out by the survey. This exhibition was attended by nearly fifteen thousand persons, and brought home the lessons of the survey in a vivid manner. The cost of the exhibition, aside from the survey proper, was about $3,500.

We now have available all the reports as listed on the slip herewith, except the two which are yet to appear, and would be glad to send you a complete set of the reports as issued up to date, if you so desire.

In conclusion, I would recommend, if your association decides to go further into this matter, that you get in communication with Mr. Shelby M. Harrison, care the Russell Sage Foundation, 130 E. 22nd Street, New York.

With best wishes, I am

Yours very truly,
Springfield Commercial Association,
WM. H. CONKLING,
Secretary.

APPENDIX B

SPRINGFIELD SURVEY BLANKS

A few of the blank forms used in the survey are reproduced below. In most cases the forms were drafted to meet the special case in Springfield, where a previous examination of records showed the kind of data available. The forms were thus not prepared as models for similar studies elsewhere.

PHYSICAL CONDITIONS OF CLASSROOMS—SPRINGFIELD, ILL. MARCH, 1914

Building................................Teacher......................Room No..................Grade............
Av. Attendance.......No. Sittings: Adjustable............Non-Adjustable............Total............
Length....ft. Width....ft. Height....ft. Floor Area....Sq. Ft. Cubic Contents....Cub. Ft.
Sq. Ft. of Floor Area per Sitting............Sq. Ft.
Cubic Ft. of Air Space per Sitting............Cub. Ft.
Total Window Area............Sq. Ft. Distance from Top of Window to Floor.........ft.
Sq. ft. of Floor Area for each Sq. Ft. of Window Area............Sq. Ft.
Windows at Left, Back, Right, or Front of Children..
Lineal Ft. of Blackboard............ft. Lineal Ft. per Sitting............ft.
Inches from Base of Blackboard to Floor................inches.
Do Seats Project under Front Edge of Desk............How Far?............Inches
How Many Pupils Cannot Easily Rest Feet on Floor..
Distance from Rear Seat to Rear Wall................ft.
Color of Walls.............Color of Ceilings.................Color of Window Shades.............
Do Shades Roll from Top or Bottom..................Has Room a Thermometer..................

CARD 4 BY 6 INCHES. USED IN SCHOOL SURVEY

SPRINGFIELD PUBLIC SCHOOLS
TEACHER'S RECORD

Name _____ School _____ Grade _____
     (Last)   (First)   (Middle)

Permanent Address _____ Age _____

Preparation:

High School, Place _____ No. Months _____ Graduate, Date _____

Normal or Training _____ "   "   _____ "   "   _____

College or Univ. _____ "   "   _____ "   "   _____

Other Special Work _____

Years taught, including current year, in Rural Schools _____ in Graded Schools _____ in High Schools _____ in other Schools _____

Years taught in Springfield Schools _____ In other Schools _____

Grade of Certificate held _____

Salary this year _____ Springfield, Illinois, Date _____ 191__

CARD 4 BY 6 INCHES. SCHOOL SURVEY

VOCATIONAL INQUIRY – 13-YEAR-OLD PUPILS – SPRINGFIELD, ILLINOIS, MARCH, 1914

NAME _____ SCHOOL _____ TEACHER _____ GRADE _____

WERE YOU BORN IN SPRINGFIELD? _____ IN ILLINOIS? _____ IN THE UNITED STATES? _____

DO YOU INTEND TO FINISH THE 8TH GRADE? _____ DO YOU INTEND TO GO TO HIGH SCHOOL? _____ TO COLLEGE? _____

DO YOU INTEND TO GO TO A BUSINESS SCHOOL? _____ WHAT DO YOU WANT TO DO FOR A LIVING WHEN YOU GROW UP? _____

WAS YOUR FATHER BORN IN SPRINGFIELD? _____ IN ILLINOIS? _____ IN THE UNITED STATES? _____

WHAT IS YOUR FATHER'S OCCUPATION? _____

HOW MANY BROTHERS LESS THAN 21 YEARS OLD HAVE YOU WHO ARE AT WORK? _____

TELL THE AGE OF EACH BROTHER AND THE KIND OF WORK HE DOES:

1. AGE _____ KIND OF WORK _____
2. AGE _____ KIND OF WORK _____
3. AGE _____ KIND OF WORK _____

HOW MANY SISTERS LESS THAN 21 YEARS OLD HAVE YOU WHO ARE AT WORK? _____

TELL THE AGE OF EACH SISTER AND THE KIND OF WORK SHE DOES:

1. AGE _____ KIND OF WORK _____
2. AGE _____ KIND OF WORK _____
3. AGE _____ KIND OF WORK _____

(IN GIVING OCCUPATION OR KIND OF WORK, STATE BUSINESS AS WELL AS OCCUPATION WITHIN THE BUSINESS, FOR EXAMPLE:)
(CONDUCTOR ON STREET RAILWAY, CLERK IN SHOE STORE, MACHINE OPERATOR IN BOX FACTORY)

CARD 4 BY 6 INCHES. SCHOOL SURVEY

PHYSICAL PLANT AND EQUIPMENT, BUILDINGS---SPRINGFIELD, ILL. MARCH 1914

Building_____Principal_____
Total number of sittings in classrooms_____Seating capacity of assembly room_____
Average attendance: boys_____girls_____Average enrollment: boys_____girls_____
Classrooms: First floor_____Second floor_____Third floor_____Total classrooms___
Has principal room for office?____Location of assembly room_____
Heating system: hot air furnace, direct steam, indirect steam_____
Thermostatic regulation_____Humidification_____
Ventilation: window, gravity, plenum fan, exhaust fan_____
Location of fresh air intake_____Location of cloakrooms_____
How ventilated_____Location of toilets_____
Toilets: Number seats for boys_____Number seats for girls_____Automatic flush____
Number of individual urinals for boys_____Do urinals have automatic flush?_____
Material of walls and divisions of urinals_____of toilet floors_____
Number feet of urinal trough_____Material of urinal trough_____
Number of wash basins_____Individual soap provided____Individual towels_____
Number of bubbling fountains_____How often are windows washed?_____
System of cleaning employed_____
How often are floors washed?_____Are floors oiled?_____
Stairways of fireproof material?_____Are stairways enclosed?_____
Material of enclosure_____Handrails both sides____Center handrail_____
Width of stairways: first floor_____second floor_____Width of steps_____
Height of risers_____Width of corridors_____Corridors unobstructed_____
Fire escapes: number and kind_____
Signal connection with fire department____Inside hose equipment_____
Chemical extinguishers_____Automatic sprinklers____Automatic fire alarm_____
Heating plant separated by fireproof walls, ceilings, and floors?_____
Is building of fireproof construction?_____of fire retarding construction?_____
Material of outside walls of building_____of floor beams_____
Gymnasium facilities_____Area of playground_____
Area of site_____Area of space occupied by building_____Date of construction____

SHEET 8½ BY 11 INCHES.   SCHOOL SURVEY

SURVEY BLANKS

NAME OF FIRM	ADDRESS	BUSINESS	FLOOR
		DEPARTMENT	

NAME OF WORKER _____ ADDRESS _____

PROCESSES OF WORK _____ DATE OF ENTERING; LEAVING _____ NATIONALITY _____ DATE OF BIRTH _____

TRAINING IN WORKROOM _____ POSTURE AT WORK _____

_____ BY WHOM GIVEN _____ KIND OF WORK _____ LENGTH OF TRAINING _____

WEEKLY WAGES _____ T. _____ P. _____ T. _____ P. _____ T. _____ P.
FIRST IN THIS ESTABLISHMENT; LAST _____ MAXIMUM WITHOUT OVERTIME _____ MAXIMUM WITH OVERTIME _____ IF STILL HERE, WAGE LAST WEEK _____

FINES _____ CHARGES FOR SUPPLIES _____ VACATION WITH PAY _____

RATE FOR LATENESS _____ SPOILED WORK _____ OTHER _____ NO. WEEKS _____

REGULARITY IN PAST _____ MO>_____
WEEKS LOST, IN THIS JOB, DUE TO SLACK SEASON _____ PART TIME _____ VACATION; HOLIDAYS (WITHOUT PAY) _____ ILLNESS (SELF) _____ OTHER CAUSES _____ TIME IN OTHER JOBS _____ TOTAL LOST _____

HOURS OF LABOR _____ A. M. _____ P. M. _____ P. M. _____ HR. _____ HRS. _____ HRS. REMARKS _____
NORMAL _____ BEGIN _____ END _____ SATURDAY _____ NOON _____ TOTAL DAILY _____ TOTAL WEEKLY _____ (NOTE VARIATIONS FROM NORMAL SCHEDULE)

OVERTIME _____ P. M. _____ P. M. _____ MIN. _____ HRS. _____ HRS. _____
NUMBER OF TIMES PER WEEK _____ CLOSING HR. _____ SATURDAY _____ SUPPER _____ TOTAL DAILY _____ TOTAL WEEKLY _____ SEASON OF OVERTIME IN YEAR _____ RATE OF PAY _____

HOME WORK _____ KIND _____ HOURS _____ EARNINGS _____

WORK ROOM _____ LUNCH ROOM PRIVILEGES _____ DRESSING ROOM _____ TOILETS (CONDITION) _____ LIGHTING _____ HOUSE LICENSED? _____ DRINKING WATER _____

ILLEGAL EMPLOYMENT OF WORKER _____

DATE _____ INVESTIGATOR _____ SOURCE OF INFORMATION _____

COMMITTEE ON WOMEN'S WORK. FORM 12; DEC. '11.—WORKER'S RECORD OF FACTORY

Card 5 by 8 Inches. Survey of Industrial Conditions

CARD 5 BY 8 INCHES. SURVEY OF INDUSTRIAL CONDITIONS

SURVEY BLANKS

CARD 5 BY 8 INCHES. SURVEY OF INDUSTRIAL CONDITIONS

CARD 5 BY 8 INCHES. CHARITIES SURVEY

INDEX

INDEX

ACCIDENTS: data on, 168-169; Employers' Liability Commission, 169; legislation to prevent, 170-174, 204-205. See also *Hazards*

ADMINISTRATION. See *City and County Administration*

ADULT OFFENDERS: cases of arrest, 256-259; court sentences, 258, 280-282; fines, 258-262; suspended sentences, 263; jail sentences, 263-274; state care of, 274-277; temporary detention, 278; indeterminate sentence, 278-279; parole, 279; probation, 280; minor courts, reorganization, 280-282; legislative inquiry, 282-283

AGENCIES: social service through private, 146-152; public agencies, 152-158; Central Conference, 148, 155, 158, 161, 162; confidential exchange, 159; for law enforcement, 200-203; and public health, 224

ALCOHOLICS: inadequate treatment of, 88-89; number of arrests, 88; care of, 141, 144. See also *Drunkenness*

ALMSHOUSES: and mental defectives, 140

AMUSEMENTS: public recreation, 90-112; municipal, 93; extension of, 95-99; schools as social centers, 98-102; parks, 102-103; associations, 94, 105; community art, 96; homes and resources, 96-97; high school survey, 100; parks, 102, 103, 109-110; institutions, 104-105; commercial, 106-107, 111; program of, 110-112. See also *Recreation*

ARRESTS: police records, 254-260; disposition of cases, 256-260. See also *Corrections*

ASSESSMENTS: real estate values, 336; officers, 336; Somers system, 337, 338; personal property, 339, 341; land value map, 340; special, 345

ASSOCIATED CHARITIES: families known to, 143; and Tuberculosis Association, 145; social service work and recommendations, 146-148; agency co-operation, 158-163

ATHLETICS: recreational activities, 94-99; use of school yards, 101-102; festivals and pageants, 109-110; program of, 110, 111. See also *Recreation*

ATTENDANCE AT EXHIBITION, 388-391; publicity methods, 391-392; volunteer work, 392-395

ATTENDANCE BUREAU: suggestions for schools, 157-158; at exhibition, 391

AYRES, DR. L. P., 7, 35

BEDFORD, CAROLINE, 8

BERGEN, MARGARET, 8, 416

BILLIARDS: and pool rooms, 91, 92, 93, 108-109; licenses, 108

BIRTH REGISTRATION: in 1913, 214, 215, 252, 253, 371

BLANK FORMS: for survey work, 422-428

BOARDS: city government, 308

BONDS: and sinking funds, 343-345

BOWEN, A. L., 16, 399

BOY SCOUTS: and recreation needs, 94, 111

BUDGET: defects, 309; classification, 310; county, 347-349

BUILDINGS, BUREAU OF, 321

"BULL PEN," 266, 378

CABOT, DR. R. C., 110

CAMP FIRE GIRLS: and recreation needs, 94, 105; program for, 111

CATHOLIC ORPHANAGE: at Alton, 124

431

INDEX

CEMETERIES: administration, 333-334

CHARITIES: directors of survey, 8; institutions for children, 124-137; outside aid for the sick, 137-141; family rehabilitation, 141-146; social service from private agencies, 146-152; public agencies providing social service, 152-158; recommendations, 158-162; exhibit, 381

CHILD LABOR: legislation for, 174-177, 199, 206; work certificates, 174-176, 206; State Factory Inspection Department, 176, 206; trade unions, 199; law enforcement for, 206

CHILDREN: institutions for dependent, 124-163; detention home, 128, 286; Department of Visitation, 125, 129, 160; placing out, 129, 134, 135, 136; community welfare, 134, 135, 160; infant mortality, 213-218, 252; contagious diseases, 218-222; juvenile offenders, 283-294; arrests and jail, 284-286. See also *Juvenile Delinquents*

CHILDREN'S HOME AND AID SOCIETY, 136, 160

CHILD WELFARE PROGRAM, 134-135, 136

CHURCHES: recreation and social service, 105-106; co-operation needed, 160, 209, 366; Federal Council of Churches, 165

CITY AND COUNTY ADMINISTRATION: directors of survey, 9; work of public agencies, 304-350; city government, 305-315, 335; budget, 309-310; community service, 315-335; current income of city government, 335-342; funds, handling of special, 342-346; Sangamon County, 346-350; exhibit, 382-384

CITY MANAGER FORM OF GOVERNMENT, 306

CITY PHYSICIAN, 138, 139, 269

CITY PLANNING, 119-120

CIVIL SERVICE, 307-308; county, 347

CLAIMS: payment of, against city, 313-314; county, 349

CLARK, EARLE, 9

COMMERCIAL ASSOCIATION OF SPRINGFIELD, 167

COMMITTEES: general survey, members, 2-3; local volunteers, 12, 14; exhibit work of, 366, 388-389, 392-395

COMMONS, JOHN R., 203

COMMUNITY ART: and recreation, 96

COMMUNITY BETTERMENT: and child welfare, 160-163; forces for improvement, 194-210; city government, 304-315; community service, 315-335; funds, handling of city, 342-346; need of accounting system, 348-350

COMPLAINT BUREAU, 314

CONFERENCE OF SOCIAL AGENCIES, 148, 155, 158, 161, 162

CONFIDENTIAL EXCHANGE: agencies recommended for, 159-160

CONTAGIOUS DISEASES: of children, 218-222; death rates, 219, 251

CO-OPERATION: national and state organizations, 5-6; Russell Sage Foundation, 6; in preparing exhibits, 12, 14; high school needed, 64-65; value of organized, 129-131, 136, 158-163; for safety, 205; health officers, 250; exhibit workers, 388-395

CORRECTIONAL METHODS: conclusions regarding present, 272-274; institutional standards, 275-277; police recommendations, 303

CORRECTIONS: directors of survey, 9; delinquency problem, 254-256; adult offenders, 256-283; juvenile delinquents, 283-294; police department, 294-303; exhibit on, 377-381

COSTS: of survey, 14; operation of institutions, 125; living, 145; survey conclusions on, 146; feeding prisoners, 269, 270

COURT SENTENCES, 257, 258, 282; minor court system, 280-282. See also *Corrections*

CROSSINGS: deaths at grade, 332

DANCING: and public recreation, 90-93, 107-108. See also *Amusements*

DEATH RECORDS: and public health, 211-253; pneumonia, 212; infant mortality, 216-218; contagious diseases, 219; tuberculosis, 222-223; 252; typhoid fever, 229; venereal diseases, 231, 252; panel at exhibition, 373

432

INDEX

DECKER, D. O., 9, 116, 304

DEFECTIVES: directors of survey on, 8; special school classes for, 62, 76–77; classification, 74–75; census report on, 75; in the schools, 76–77; community care of, 78; as law breakers, 261

DEFINITION OF SURVEY, 357–359

DELINQUENTS, See *Corrections; Juvenile Delinquents*

DEPARTMENT OF VISITATION: and child dependency, 125, 129, 160

DEPENDENTS: institutions for children, 124–162

DETENTION HOME: for delinquent children, 124, 128, 284, 286; recommendations, 287–289

DIPHTHERIA: ratio of deaths, 219, 221, 251

DISEASES: and preventable deaths, 211; pneumonia, 212; infant mortality, 213–218; contagious, among children, 218–222; tuberculosis, 222–229, 252; typhoid fever, 229–231; venereal, 231–233; impure water, 233–235; sewerage, 235–236; wells and privies, menace of, 236–242; unclean milk, 242–243; food inspection necessary, 244; smallpox, 248; contagion hospital, 249

DISPENSARIES: planning for, 138, 139; Tuberculosis Association, 139; free service, 227

DRAINAGE: Sangamon River map, 234

DRUGS: fines as a deterrent, 260; federal act, 301

DRUNKENNESS: police records, 254, 259, 260, 300; and reforms, 271. See *Alcoholics*

DUNLOP, REV. G. C., 409

EARL GIBSON SUNSHINE SOCIETY, 151

EDUCATION: vocational, 67–72; institutional workers, 132, 133; limitations, and future scope, 136–137; school attendance, bureaus to regulate, 157–158; and work certificates, 175; children leaving school, 193; open-air schools, 228. See also *Public Schools*

28

ELECTIONS: and polling districts, 334–335

ELECTRIC METER INSPECTION, 325

ELEVATOR MILLING COMPANY, 27

EMPLOYERS' LIABILITY COMMISSION, 169

EMPLOYMENT OFFICES: state agencies, 182–186; shortcomings of, 183, 184; comparative work, 184–185; recommendations, 185

EXHIBIT HALL: descriptive tour of, 354; floor plan, 355; in First Regiment Armory, 356

EXHIBITION: of survey findings, 11–12, 353–395; purpose, 12, 352; committee work, 12, 14, 353; exhibit hall, floor plan, 354, 355, 356; schools, 359–366; housing, 367, 368; milk, 369; mental hygiene, 370; health, 371–374; playhouse, 374–377; correctional system, 377–381; charities, 381; city government, 382–384; industries, 384–386; "last word" section, 386–388; attendance, 388–390; publicity, 391–392; volunteers, 392–395

FACTORIES AND WORKSHOPS, State Department of, 199

FACTORY INSPECTION DEPARTMENT, 176, 177, 206

FAMILY DISABILITY: outside care of sick, 137–141; charity work, extent of problem, 141–146; agencies for social service, 146–158; study of conditions in 100 families, 192–194

FEDERAL COUNCIL OF CHURCHES: principles of, 165

FEDERATIONS OF LABOR, 197–203

FEEDING PRISONERS: cost of, 269, 270

FINES: and law breaking, 257, 258–262; ineffectiveness of, 260, 272

FIRE DEPARTMENT: statistics, 315–316; organization and operation, 316; engines and equipment, 317–318; alarm system, 318; water supply, 318–319; instruction of members, 319–320; records, 320

FIRE HAZARD: in multiple dwellings, 115; regulatory powers, 122, 204–205

433

INDEX

FLAG, MUNICIPAL, 15
FLOOR PLAN OF EXHIBITION HALL, 355
FOLLOW-UP WORK: personnel of survey committees, 17; for employment offices, 183
FOOD SUPPLY: inspection of, 244
FOREIGN-BORN GROUPS, 21-22, 25, 213, 219, 222
FUNDS TO PARENTS LIST: juvenile court grants, 156

GARBAGE: collection system, 116, 333
GAS METER INSPECTION, 325
GEOGRAPHICAL CHARACTERISTICS, 28-29, 113, 213
GODDARD, H. M., 261
GOLDMARK, JOSEPHINE, 187
GOVERNMENT: survey reports, lines of, 304; organization, 305; city commissioners, 305; city manager form of, 306; short ballot, 307; civil service, 307-308; public boards, 308; budget, 309-310; municipal departments, 315-335; current income, 335; handling special funds, 342-346; Sangamon County, 346-350; efficiency exhibit, 382-384

HANMER, L. F., 8, 90, 299
HARRISON, S. M., 9, 116, 304
HART, DR. H. H., 9
HAY, LOGAN, 3
HAZARDS: industrial, 168-174; work accidents, 168-170; occupational disease, 170-171; fire, 172-173, 204; legislation, 199-210; grade crossings, 332
HEALTH: director of survey on, 8; school inspections, 60-62; special classes for children, 61; housing inspections, 120-123; in children's institutions, 133; outside aid for the sick, 137-141; city physician, 138, 139; hospital care, 139, 160; Tuberculosis Association, 138, 139, 141, 145, 148-149, 162; occupational diseases, 170-171; insurance, 204; preventable diseases, 211; pneumonia, 212; infant mortality, 213-218; nurses, 217, 227; contagious diseases of children,
218-222; tuberculosis, 222-229, 247, 252; typhoid fever, 229-231; smallpox, 248; exhibit, 371-374
HEALTH DEPARTMENT: housing recommendations, 120-123; and public health measures, 221-253; health officers, 246, 247
HIGH SCHOOL: recreations, 100; printing demonstration at exhibition, 369
HOME FOR THE FRIENDLESS, 124, 127, 128, 129, 132, 133, 134, 137, 160
HOSPITALS: care of mental defectives, 83-86; state, 85-88; city physician, 138; dispensaries needed, 138, 139, 227; free beds, 139; Springfield Hospital, 139; Open Air Colony, 139, 140; St. John's Hospital, 139, 140, 224; Jacksonville State Hospital, for insane, 140; provision of adequate, 226-229; for contagious diseases, 249
HOURS OF LABOR: standards for, 165, 187, 209; and social welfare, 186-191; manufactures, 187, 190, 209; mines, 188, 202; railroads, 188-189
HOUSING: director of survey on, 8; homes and tenements, 28, 113-119; multiple dwellings, 113-116; bad conditions, 114-119; city planning, 119-120; recommendations, 120-123; exhibit, 367-368
HUMANE SOCIETY, 124, 149, 159
HUMPHREY, GRACE, 402

IDE, F. P., 17
IHLDER, JOHN, 8, 113, 121
ILLINOIS JUVENILE COURT ACT, 293-294
ILLINOIS STATE CONFERENCE OF CHARITIES AND CORRECTION: survey activities of, 2, 6; on mental detectives, 140
ILLINOIS WATCH FACTORY, 5, 27
ILLITERACY: percentage among foreigners and natives, 22, 25, 213; and school attendance, 42; a health factor, 213, 222, 252
IMPROVEMENT LEAGUE, 152, 161
INCOME OF CITY GOVERNMENT, 335-342; assessments, 335-341; taxes, collection of, 341-342

INDEX

INDUSTRIAL BETTERMENT: forces for, 164-210

INDUSTRIAL COMMISSION, 202-203; Commons on, 203

INDUSTRIAL CONDITIONS: directors of survey on, 8; census of occupations, 26-28, 68-70; scope of survey, 164-174; child labor, 174-177, 206; wages, 178-182, 206-208; irregular employment, 178, 179-186, 206-208; employment bureaus, and recommendations for, 182-186; hours of labor, 186-191, 209; wage-earners' families, 192-194; forces for improvement, 194-210; labor unions, 197-199, 207, 210; exhibit on, 384-386

INDUSTRIAL INJURIES: compensation for, 173-174

INFANT MORTALITY: death ratio, 213, 215-218, 373; principal causes, 217; panel at exhibition, 373

INQUIRY: survey results, 420-421

INSANE: commitment laws, 81-88; in jail annex, 82-83, 267, 285; hospital treatment, 83-85; after-care, 86-88; at Sangamon County Poor Farm, 140, 152-154; cells illustrated, 153; Mental Hygiene Exhibit, 370

INSTITUTIONS: and recreational education, 104-105; churches and social service work, 105-106; Sangamon County Poor Farm, 84, 140, 152, 153, 154; Catholic Orphanage at Alton, 124; for dependent children, 124-137; Orphanage of the Holy Child, 124, 127, 132, 133, 136, 137; Lincoln Colored Home, 124, 126-127, 132, 137; Redemption Home, 124, 127, 130, 133, 136; record keeping, 125-126; as educational forces, 132; Home for the Friendless, 124, 127, 128, 129, 132, 133, 134, 137, 160; Detention Home, 124, 128; Rescue Home, 132; Children's Home and Aid Society, 136, 160; Open Air Colony, 139, 140; Springfield Hospital, 139; Jacksonville State Hospital, 8, 140; St. John's Hospital, 140; King's Daughters Home, 151; St. Joseph's Home, 151-152; standards for correctional, 275-277

INSURANCE: health, 204; unemployment, 208-209

IRREGULAR EMPLOYMENT: and wages, 178-181, 193, 206, 210; in mines, 178, 207; manufactures, 179, 208; mechanical industries, 179, 207; unemployment insurance, 208-209

JACKSONVILLE STATE HOSPITAL, 8, 140

JAIL ANNEX: insane patients in, 82, 141, 267, 284, 285; illustration, 285

JAILS: county jail and annex, 267-269, 274, 284-286, 287; men's ward, 286; women's, 268-269; feeding of prisoners, 269, 270. See also *Prisons*

JUVENILE COURT: widows' grants, 156; child offenders, 283, 284, 289-294; act and amendments, 293-294

JUVENILE COURT ACT, 293

JUVENILE DELINQUENTS: complaints against, 283-284; detention home, 284-288; county court, 289-292; publicity, 290; probation, 292-293; legislative needs, 293-294

KING'S DAUGHTERS HOME, 151

LABOR AND MINING, Department of, 201-202

LABOR UNIONS: miners, 28, 197, 207; growth of movement, 197-199; and wages, 207-210

LAND VALUE MAP, 337, 340

"LAST WORD" Section at exhibition, 386-388

LATTIMORE, FLORENCE L., 8, 124

LAW DEPARTMENT, 326

LEGISLATION: industrial, 170-172, 174-177, 187, 191, 199-203; compensation for injuries, 173; child labor, 174-177, 206; violations of hour law for children, 176-177; labor federations, 197; Department of Factories and Workshops, 199; Department of Labor and Mining, 201-202; industrial commission, 202-203; Municipal Court Act, 281; for correctional reform, 282-283; Juvenile Court Act, 293

LIBRARIES: Lincoln, 104

LIGHTING PLANT, 324; gas and electric meters, 325

435

INDEX

LINCOLN AN INSPIRATION, 18–20, 30
LINCOLN COLORED HOME, 124, 126–127, 132, 137
LINCOLN STATE SCHOOL AND COLONY: mental deficients in, 79
LINDSAY, VACHEL, 16, 395
LIVING COSTS: data on, 145
LONG BALLOT, 346–347

MCLEAN, F. H., 8, 124.
MANUFACTURES: Illinois Watch Factory, 5, 27; census reports, 26–27; physical safety, 168, 172, 204; occupational disease, 170–171, 204; hours of labor, 187–188, 190, 209; labor unions, 197, 198, 199, 206, 207; State Department of Factories and Workshops, 199
MEDICAL INSPECTION OF SCHOOLS, 60–61. See also *City Physician*
MILK SUPPLY: dairy inspections, 242–243; recommendations, 243; exhibit, 369–370
MINING: coal, 7, 27; housing at Ridgely, 119; income of coal miners, 178–179; unions, 188, 197, 207; irregular employment, 207; exhibit chart, 385–386
MINISTERIAL ASSOCIATION, 161
MOTION PICTURES: survey of theaters, 106; program for, 111; exhibition hall, 367
MULTIPLE DWELLINGS, 113–116
MUNICIPAL COURT ACT OF CHICAGO, 281
MURDERS: and suicides, 273
MUSEUM OF NATURAL HISTORY, 104

NATIONAL ORGANIZATIONS: co-operation of, 6
NEGROES: census of, 21, 22, 25, 213; housing conditions, 117–119; Lincoln Colored Home, 124, 126–127, 137; deaths from tuberculosis, 222; ward statistics, 253, 268; police records, 254

OCCUPATIONAL DISEASE COMMISSION, 170

ODENCRANTZ, LOUISE C., 8, 164
OPEN AIR COLONY: private sanatorium, 139, 140, 224; for tuberculosis, 224
OPINIONS: and testimony on survey results, 399–421
ORPHANAGE OF THE HOLY CHILD, 124, 127, 132, 136, 137
OVERSEER OF THE POOR: for Capital Township, 154, 162

PALMER, DR. G. T.: 2, 15, 16, 139, 236, 411
PARKS: area of, 102; facilities for recreation, 102, 103, 109; Washington Park, 103; program for, 110
PENSIONS: for police, 297, 298
PERRY, C. A., 8, 90, 299
PLACING OUT: and children's institutions, 129, 134, 135, 136
PLANNING THE SURVEY, 2–5; main lines of inquiry, 3; analysis and interpretation, 4; recommendations for improvement, 4; educational measures, 5
PLAYHOUSE: illustrations, 147, 375; at exhibition, 374–377
PNEUMONIA: deaths from, 212
POLICE DEPARTMENT: headquarters, 264; size of force, 294; control of, 295; efficiency methods, 295, 296, 297; pensions, 297–298; policy of on crime and vice, 299–302; recommendations, 303
POLLING DISTRICTS, 335
POPULATION: in 1910, 6, 21; distribution of, 23–25; health factors, 213, 222; percentage of arrests, 254
POTTER, ZENAS L., 8, 9, 164, 254, 292, 303
PRISONS: description of city prison, 264–266; "bull pen," illustrated, 266, 378; county jail and annex, 267, 284–286; exhibit booths, 378–381. See also *Jails*
PRIVIES: number of, 116, 236, 237, 239, 241; sanitary surveys of, 236, 237; pollution from, 240

436

INDEX

PROBATION: for first offenders, 263; juvenile work, 292-293

PUBLICITY: directors of survey, 9; publication of reports, 10-11; campaign of, 12; juvenile crime, 289, 290; attendance at exhibition, 388-390; newspaper and advertising, 391-392; testimony on survey results, 399-421

PUBLIC SCHOOLS: census of attendance, 35, 41, 50-53; administration, 35-41; board of education, 36, 38, 40; buildings, 37, 43; organization, 39, 65; purchase of supplies, 40; compulsory attendance, 41, 42; certificates, 41-42; lighting, 44; heat and ventilation, 45, 46; drinking water, 46; janitors, 46; furniture, 47; toilets, 48; fire protection, 48; auditoriums, 48-49; teaching force, 53-54; training schools, 54-55; class room work, 55-56; tests, 56, 57; courses of study, 56-57, 63; textbooks, 58; finances, 58-60; medical inspection, 60-61; special classes, 61-62; high school, 62-66; teachers and salaries, 63; study courses, 63-64; need of co-operation, 64-65; vocational education, 67-72; utilization of school plants, 72-73; mental defectives in, 75-80; as social centers, 98-102; yard areas, 100-101. See also *Education; Schools*

PURCHASING: recommendations for commissioner, 312-313; county, 349

PURPOSE AND METHODS: of survey, 1-20, 164-167

RAILWAYS: irregular employment, 181; hours of labor, 188-189; labor unions, 197-198

RECOMMENDATIONS: constructive, 4; educational, 5; recreation program, 110-112; housing, 120-123; charity institutions for children, 152-163; social agency co-operation, 158-163; industrial requirements, 165, 167, 171, 179, 185, 208; for state employment, 185-186; public health, 221, 222, 225-253; correctional standards, 275-277; for municipal court, 281-282; detention home, 287-289; on police department, 303

RECORD CARDS: for children's institutions, 125; survey blank forms, 422-428

RECORD KEEPING: child dependents, 125-126; and public health, 249; service and cost, 311

RECREATION: directors of survey, 8; needs and resources, 90-110; to overcome evils, 93, 108-109; organizations which promote, 94, 105; dancing and festivals, 96, 100, 107-110; schools as social centers, 98-102; parks, 102, 103; churches, 105; commercial amusements, 106-107; billiards and pool, 108-109; program and recommendations, 110-111; in children's institutions, 134; exhibit, 363-367. See also *Amusements*

REDEMPTION HOME, 124, 127, 130, 133, 136

RESCUE HOME, 132

RESULTS OF SURVEY: and opinions, 14-17, 399-421; welfare problems, 164-210; addresses on, 399-419; inquiry about, 420-421

RIDGELY: miners' houses in, 119

ROUTZAHN, E. G., 9

ROUTZAHN, MARY S., 9

RUSSELL SAGE FOUNDATION: preliminary study of Springfield, 2; Department of Surveys and Exhibits, 3, 5, 9, 11; departments co-operating in survey, 6, 7-9; publicity by, 11, 155, 187

ST. JOHN'S HOSPITAL, 139, 140, 265

ST. JOSEPH'S HOME: for aged, 151-152

ST. VINCENT DE PAUL SOCIETY, 150, 162

SALMON, Dr. T. D., 8

SALOONS: and public recreation, 91-92, 108-109, 254, 299; license investigations, 108-109, 299, 300; recommendation, 303. See also *Vice*

SALVATION ARMY, 151

SANGAMON COUNTY GOVERNMENT, 346-350; long ballot, 346-347; civil service, 347; budget, 347-348; accounting, 348-349; claims, 349-350; reports and publicity, 350

SANGAMON COUNTY MEDICAL SOCIETY, 138

INDEX

SANGAMON COUNTY POOR FARM: insane patients at, 84, 140, 152; description of, 152; changes recommended, 152–154, 161; cells in basement, illustrated, 153

SANGAMON RIVER, 29, 213, 233, 234; drainage map of, 234

SANITATION: and health survey, 8, 211; multiple dwellings, 114–115, 117; water mains and sewers, 116, 233–236; garbage, 116; Negro districts, 117–119, 223, 253; recommendations, 120–123, 225, 253; and typhoid, 229; drainage and sewers, 234–236; wells and privies, 236–242; dairies, 242–243; food supplies, 244; inspectors, 243, 244, 246; disposal of manure, 245; garbage, 246

SCHNEIDER, FRANZ, JR., 8, 116, 121, 211

SCHOOLS: for child dependents, 127; attendance bureau, 156–158; work certificates, 175–176; open-air, for tuberculous patients, 228. See also *Public Schools*

SCHOOL SURVEY: Department of Education, Russell Sage Foundation, 7; exhibit booths, 360–366

SEWERAGE: and sewage disposal, 116, 235–236, 237–241; recommendations, 252

SHERIFF: feeding prisoners, 269, 270

SHORT BALLOT, 307

SICKNESS: outside aid for families, 137–141; occupational diseases, 170–171. See also *Diseases; Health*

SMOKE NUISANCE, 166

SOCIAL CENTERS: recreation needs, 95–102; in other cities, 98; schools as, 98–102; organizations and churches, 104, 105; recreation program, 110–112; private agencies, 146–152; public agencies, 152–158; recreation at the exhibition, 365, 366

SOCIAL STANDARDS FOR INDUSTRY, 165

SPECIAL FUNDS: handling of, 342–346; bonds and sinking funds, 343–346

SPRINGFIELD FEDERATION OF LABOR, 197

SPRINGFIELD HOSPITAL: children's free ward, 139

STAFF: of survey, 7–9; administrative, 132

STATE CONTROL: over industries, 199–201; Department of Factories and Workshops, 199; Department of Labor and Mining, 201–202; Industrial Commission, 202–203

STATE ORGANIZATIONS: co-operation of, 6; State Board of Administration, 125, 129; industrial legislation, 199–210

STATISTICS: preparation of by Earle Clark, 9

STREET SYSTEM: and city planning, 119–120; roadway economy, 120, 328; public improvements, 326–333; pavements, 328–329; cleaning methods, 329–330; dirt roads, 330–331; grade crossings, 329, 332; sidewalks, 331, 333

STUART SCHOOL, 127

SUBJECTS OF INQUIRY, 3; on industrial conditions, 164–167

TAXES: collection, 341; transfer, 342

TEACHERS' TRAINING SCHOOL: yard space of, 101; play festivals, extension of, 110

THEATERS: and recreation survey, 106–107; motion pictures, 106, 107, 111

TRANSPORTATION: railroads and electric lines, 26, 28; Transportation Agreement, 155

TRANSPORTATION AGREEMENT: of National Conference of Charities and Corrections, 155

TREADWAY, DR. W. L., 8, 74

TUBERCULOSIS: deaths from, 211, 222–223, 251, 252; agencies for control of, 224–229, 252; Open Air Colony, 224; campaign suggestions, 225–228; free dispensary, 227; responsibility for control of, 229, 252–253; exhibit booth, 374

TUBERCULOSIS ASSOCIATION, 138, 139, 141, 145, 148–149, 162, 224, 228, 374

TYPHOID FEVER, 229–231, 240, 251

INDEX

VAN BLARCOM, D., 8

VAN KLEECK, MARY, 8

VEILLER, LAWRENCE, 120

VENEREAL DISEASES: measures against, 231–233, 272, 302; segregation of vice, 301, 302, 303

VICE: environment a factor, 90–93; billiards and pool, 91, 92; dance halls, 92, 93, 107–108; fines as a deterrent, 259–262; drugs, 260, 300; gambling, 260, 261; police attitude, 299, 301. See also *Corrections*

VIOLATIONS OF HOUR LAW: for children, 176–177, 206; and health, 186–187; in manufactures, 187–188; railroads, 188–189; women, 190–191, 209; unions would regulate, 209–210

VOCATIONAL EDUCATION, 67–72. See also *Public Schools*

VOLUNTEERS: co-operation of, 6, 9, 12; at exhibition, 372, 388, 392; valuable work of, 392–395

WAGES: miners, 178–179, 198, 207; and unemployment, 178, 193, 206–209; in various industries, 180–181; five-and-ten-cent stores, 181, 182; labor unions increase, 197, 198, 207, 208

WARDS: population and map, 24, 25, 213; health facts, 213, 219, 252, 253

WASHINGTON STREET MISSION: relief work of, 149–150

WATER SUPPLY: and sewerage, 116, 233–236, 240–241, 252; waterworks system, 233, 321; Sangamon River, map of drainage area, 234; wells, 236, 237, 238, 241; for fires, 318–319; department supervision, 321–322; consumption and rates, 322–324

WATERWORKS: description of plant, 233–234; cost, 321–322

WEIGHTS AND MEASURES BUREAU, 325–326

WELFARE: and children's institutions, 124–163; public agencies, 152–159; recommendations, 158–163; countywide organization needed, 160; purpose of survey of industry, 164–167; safety in industry, 168–174; industrial betterment, 194–210; labor legislation, 199–210.

WELLS: number of, 116, 236, 237–238, 241; pollution, 240

WIDOWS' GRANTS: Funds to Parents List, 156

WOMEN'S CLUB, 152, 161

WOMEN WORKERS: industrial standards for, 165, 199, 208; wages, 181, 182, 196, 208; employment agencies for, 182–183; hours of labor, 190–191, 209

WORK ACCIDENTS. See *Accidents*

WORK CERTIFICATES: and child labor, 175–176, 206

YOUNG MEN'S CHRISTIAN ASSOCIATION, 105

YOUNG WOMEN'S CHRISTIAN ASSOCIATION, 105

AMERICA IN TWO CENTURIES:
An Inventory

An Arno Press Collection

American Association of Museums. **A Statistical Survey of Museums in the United States and Canada.** 1965

Andrews, Israel D. **On the Trade and Commerce of the British North American Colonies, and Upon the Trade of the Great Lakes and Rivers.** 1853

Audit Bureau of Circulations. **Scientific Space Selection.** 1921

Austin, E. L. and Odell Hauser. **The Sesqui-Centennial International Exposition.** 1929

Barnett, James H. **The American Christmas.** 1954

Barton, L| eslie | M. **A Study of 81 Principal American Markets.** 1925

Bennitt, Mark, comp. **History of the Louisiana Purchase Exposition.** 1905

Bowen, Eli. **The United States Post-Office Guide.** 1851

Bureau of Applied Social Research, Columbia University. **The People Look at Radio.** 1946

Burlingame, Roger. **Engines of Democracy:** Inventions and Society in Mature America. 1940

Burlingame, Roger. **March of the Iron Men:** A Social History of Union Through Invention. 1938

Burnham, W. Dean. **Presidential Ballots, 1836-1892.** 1955

Cochrane, Rexmond C. **Measures for Progress:** A History of the National Bureau of Standards. 1966

Cohn, David L. **The Good Old Days.** 1940

Cozens, Frederick W. and Florence Scovil Stumpf. **Sports in American Life.** 1953

Day, Edmund E. and Woodlief Thomas. **The Growth of Manufactures, 1899 to 1923.** 1928

Edwards, Richard Henry. **Popular Amusements.** 1915

Evans, Charles H., comp. **Exports, Domestic and Foreign, From the American Colonies to Great Britain, From 1697 to 1789, Inclusive;** Exports, Domestic, From the U.S. to All Countries, From 1789 to 1883, Inclusive. 1884

Federal Reserve System, Board of Governors. **All-Bank Statistics, United States, 1896-1955.** 1959

Flexner, Abraham. **Funds and Foundations:** Their Policies, Past and Present. 1952

Flint, Henry M. **The Railroads of the United States.** 1868

Folger, John K. and Charles B. Nam. **Education of the American Population.** 1967

Handel, Leo A. **Hollywood Looks At Its Audience:** A Report of Film Audience Research. 1950

Harlow, Alvin F. **Old Waybills:** The Romance of the Express Companies. 1934

Harrison, Shelby M. **Social Conditions in an American City:** A Summary of the Findings of the Springfield Survey. 1920

Homans, J. Smith, comp. **An Historical and Statistical Account of the Foreign Commerce of the United States.** 1857

Ingram, J. S. **The Centennial Exposition.** 1876

Institute of American Meat Packers and the School of Commerce and Administration of the University of Chicago. **The Packing Industry:** A Series of Lectures. 1924

Leech, D[aniel] D. T[ompkins]. **The Post Office Department of the United States of America.** 1879

Leggett, M. D., comp. **Subject-Matter Index of Patents for Inventions Issued by the United States Patent Office From 1790 to 1873, Inclusive.** 1874. Three vols.

Magazine Marketing Service. **M.M.S. County Buying Power Index.** 1942

Martin, Robert F. **National Income in the United States, 1799-1938.** 1939

McCullough, Edo. **World's Fair Midways.** 1966

Melish, John. **Surveys for Travellers, Emigrants and Others.** 1976

National Advertising Company. **America's Advertisers.** 1893

Peters, Harry T. **America On Stone:** The Other Printmakers to the American People. 1931

Peters, Harry T. **California On Stone.** 1935

Peters, Harry T. **Currier & Ives:** Printmakers to the American People. 1929/1931. Two vols.

Pownall, T[homas]. **A Topographical Description of the Dominions of the United States of America.** Edited by Lois Mulkearn. 1949

Reed, Alfred Zantzinger. **Present-Day Law Schools in the United States and Canada.** 1928

Reed, Alfred Zantzinger. **Training for the Public Profession of the Law.** 1921

Rogers, Meyric R. **American Interior Design.** 1947

Romaine, Lawrence B. **A Guide to American Trade Catalogs, 1744-1900.** 1960

Scammon, Richard M., comp. **America at the Polls:** A Handbook of American Presidential Election Statistics, 1920-1964. 1965

Smillie, Wilson G. **Public Health:** Its Promise for the Future. 1955

Thompson, Warren S. **Population: The Growth of Metropolitan Districts in the United States, 1900-1940.** 1947

Thorndike, E[dward] L. **Your City.** 1939

Truman, Ben[jamin] C. **History of the World's Fair.** 1893

U.S. Bureau of the Census, Department of Commerce. **Housing Construction Statistics: 1889 to 1964.** 1966

U.S. Census Office (12th Census). **Street and Electric Railways.** 1903

Urban Statistical Surveys. 1976

Wayland, Sloan and Edmund de S. Brunner. **The Educational Characteristics of the American People.** 1958

Woytinsky, W. S. **Employment and Wages in the United States.** 1953

U.S. Census Office (1st Census, 1790). **Return of the Whole Number of Persons Within the Several Districts of the United States.** 1802

U.S. Census Office (2nd Census, 1800). **Return of the Whole Number of Persons Within the Several Districts of the United States.** 1802

U.S. Census Office (3rd Census, 1810). **Aggregate Amount of Each Description of Persons Within the United States of America.** 1811

U.S. Census Office (4th Census, 1820). **Census for 1820.** 1821

U.S. Census Office (5th Census, 1830). **Abstract of the Returns of the Fifth Census.** 1832

U.S. Census Office (6th Census, 1840). **Compendium of the Enumeration of the Inhabitants and Statistics of the United States.** 1841

U.S. Census Office (7th Census, 1850). **The Seventh Census of the United States.** 1853

U.S. Census Office (8th Census, 1860). **Statistics of the United States in 1860.** 1866

U.S. Census Office (9th Census, 1870). **A Compendium of the Ninth Census.** 1872

U.S. Census Office (10th Census, 1880). **Compendium of the Tenth Census.** Parts I and II. 1883. Two vols.

U.S. Census Office (11th Census, 1890). **Abstract of the Eleventh Census.** 1894

U.S. Bureau of the Census (12th Census, 1900). **Abstract of the Twelfth Census of the United States.** 1904

U.S. Bureau of the Census (13th Census, 1910). **Thirteenth Census of the United States: Abstract of the Census.** 1913

U.S. Bureau of the Census (14th Census, 1920). **Abstract of the Fourteenth Census of the United States.** 1923

U.S. Bureau of the Census (15th Census, 1930). **Fifteenth Census of the United States: Abstract of the Census.** 1933

U.S. Bureau of the Census (16th Census, 1940). **Sixteenth Census of the United States: United States Summary.** 1943

U.S. Bureau of the Census (17th Census, 1950). **A Report of the Seventeenth Decennial Census of the United States: United States Summary.** 1953

U.S. Bureau of the Census (18th Census, 1960). **The Eighteenth Decennial Census of the United States: United States Summary.** 1964

U.S. Bureau of the Census (19th Census, 1970). **1970 Census of Population: United States Summary.** 1973. Two vols.